The Tyranny of Pleasure

By the same author:

La Refondation du monde, Paris, Editions du Seuil, 1999.

La Trahison des lumières: enquête sur le désarroi contemporain, Paris, Editions du Seuil, 1995.

Return to Vietnam, photographs by Raymond Depardon, New York : Verso, 1994.

Sur la route des Croisades, Arléa, 1993.

Le Rendez-vous d'Irkoutsk, Paris, Arléa, 1990.

L'Accent du pays : mille jours en France, Paris, Editions du Seuil, 1990.

L'Ancienne comédie, Paris, Editions du Seuil, 1984.

Un Voyage vers l'Asie, Paris, Editions du Seuil, 1979.

Les Confettis de l'Empire : Martinique, Guadeloupe, Guyane française, Paris, Editions du Seuil, 1976.

with Pierre Veilletet:
Chaban-Delmas ou l'Art d'être heureux en politique, Paris, B. Grasset, 1969.

The Tyranny of Pleasure

Jean-Claude Guillebaud

Translated by Keith Torjoc

1999
Algora Publishing

Originally published as *La tyrannie du plaisir,* © Éditions du Seuil, 1998.

Library of Congress Cataloging-in-Publication Data 99-052299

Guillebaud, Jean Claude.
   [Tyrannie du plaisir. English]
   The Tyranny of Pleasure / Jean-Claude Guillebaud;
   translated by Keith Torjoc.
      p. cm.
   Includes bibliographical references.
   ISBN 1-892941-05-8 (alk. paper)
   1. Sexual ethics. I. Title
HQ31 .G954 1999
176—dc21   99-052298

Front cover: variation on a theme by Pierre Bonnard, *Man and Woman,* 1900

New York
www.algora.com

TABLE OF CONTENTS

Note of Author's Intent . . .

The aim of this book is to pose clearly and without ambiguity the question of sexual morals (i.e. place of the forbidden) and their definition in a modern society. For practically a generation, we have lived in the illusion that this question no longer matters. Today, that illusion is gone, as society struggles to regain the moral foundation it has lost. A desperate, painful search for the keystones that once supported mankind's moral framework is under way, and we offer this book as a contribution to that search.

Two intentions, rather simple in principle, govern the drafting of this work. I would like to escape as much as possible from Manicheism, which comes to bear today as soon any question of sexuality or, worse still, of sexual morals, crops up. Discussion of this subject is linked inevitably to a debate that, for my part, I refuse: unbridled permissiveness or nostalgic moralizing. This approach limits us to one choice or the other, black or white; moralistic rigidity or libertarian irresponsibility. This argument comes up often in books addressing sexuality, books that either rise in aggressive defense of a particular sexually emancipating mindset, or vigorously castigate the alleged immorality of the times. This division explains why discussion of the subject has been destined to an inconclusive outcome.

Though seemingly harmless ideals, these short-sighted theories are more powerful than they appear. After 30 years of unwise permissiveness, they paradoxically indicate a return in force of the prudish, as is the case in American society. History shows that this could have a reversed effect. Society instinctively recoils from anything that polices or threatens it, and is liable to lurch without transition from one excess to the other.

I would like, for my part, to try to look at this question objectively, to present (peacefully) the principal data, while rectifying the numerous untruths about sex that are allowed to circulate.

The second intention, more daring perhaps, deals with knowledge itself. Those who take an interest in this topic are amazed by the plethora of scholarship in this field. Sexuality is addressed from a vast number of perspectives and disciplines, among them: history, psychoanalysis, anthropology, theology, political philosophy, demography, economy, and criminology. But one perspective rarely acknowledges another. Between the abyssal ignorance that propels the contemporary polemic, and the singular application of knowledge, there is little true help in forming a confident understanding of the topic. I thus accepted the challenge of patiently reviewing vast elements of knowledge with the maximum of attention and an emphasis on producing supportive evidence. Specialists in the various fields that I address will undoubtedly agree that certain topics are in need of further development.

If I have kept only to the essentials, in each case, if I have taken a rather "panoramic" view, it is because only that approach allows us to put together the pieces of the puzzle of our different fields of knowledge on the subjects of sex and pleasure, and to answer this fundamental question: Where are we? As for the title of this book, it is borrowed from Plato. In The Laws, Plato speaks in praise of pleasure, but regards nevertheless as weak and shameful the man one who lets "the tyrant Eros" be established in his heart to control the movement of his life.

CHAPTER 1

BEYOND SMALL TALK

Human societies seldom understand the history that shapes them. They are inspired to action by obscure motives, and the resulting change sometimes cannot be measured in significance for years to come. Few realized, for example, in 1964, that a significant cultural break had just occurred in all the industrialized countries. No one appreciated, in 1971, the fundamental importance of the end of the Bretton Woods monetary system. Similarly, no contemporary of the 1740s was aware that a demographic cycle fraught with consequences was under way in the West.

The true interpretation of history is retrospective. It takes time, often generations, to identify the true significance of an historic event. Thus, let us not be too preoccupied, day to day, with idle theories that all too often fail to address what is essential.

An example is our relationship to pleasure and to sexuality, that "tyrant, Eros" which Plato said was capable of "insinuating itself into our hearts and controlling our every movement." However, it's not for lack of talking about it! Michel Foucault noted, twenty years ago, that a superfluity of speeches, narratives, testimonies, and all forms of rhetoric had made us, at least since the 19th century, "a society that is singularly up front about" sex. "Western man," he added, "has become a beast of consents." And Foucault invited us "to ponder a society that for more than a century has been noisily fustigating its hypocrisy, generating prolix discourses about its own silence, striving to enumerate all the

9

things that it does not say, denouncing the powers that it exerts and promising to release itself from the very laws that make it work."[2]

That verbiage has swelled still more since those lines were written. It has gone far beyond the "generalized discursive erethism" mentioned by Foucault. An extraordinary sexual din has infiltrated the last recesses of democratic modernity. Pleasures promised or exhibited, freedom displayed, preferences described, performances given and procedures taught to everyone who passes through: no society before ours devoted so much discursive eloquence to pleasure, none gave sexuality such a dominant place in its comments, its images and its creations. Whether we are delighted or astonished, it is clear: a thousand voluptuous convocations besiege us at every turn, without any respite in sight. It would not do much good to take offense. Sex has become the background noise of our daily life. Compared to earlier times, whether Greek or Roman, ours literally talks only about "it." But just what are we saying about it?

That is the only real question. The paradox lies in the extraordinary and pervasive contrast between the significance of the word and its own prolixity; the opposition between the basic meaning of the speech and its fevered tone. The substance proclaims freedom when the superabundance suggests distress; the message celebrates triumph but the excess of words betrays a concern.

Freedom? Or concern? For some thirty years, it has been acknowledged that we are living through a sort of "end of History" regarding sexuality. Such, in any case, is the somewhat optimistic contemporary *doxa*. Rumor has it that the centuries of obscurantism and repression are finally abolished. Our post-industrial societies have reached a radically new intelligence of pleasure and its innocent sovereignty. We hold it as a given that, before our era, men and women lived for millennia under the yoke of a constraint that which we, and only we, have broken. This tyranny that we have overcome, we think, was itself the grievous product of primitive anthropological ignorance, of religious "superstition," even of a plot perpetrated across every latitude and in every culture by the powerful, who were anxious to keep the people in a prison of interdicts. Our modern era just keeps mulling over the splendid magnitude of its liberation and its historic novelty. In all good logic, we have nothing left to do but the merry process of getting underway with the act itself.

Why, then, isn't it that simple?

By its very profusion, all this talk introduces a doubt, and the insistence seems to refute what is being said. If History is over (the history of constraints and interdicts), if this boundless pleasure is available now, why does it take up so much of our attention? If the problem no longer exists, why do we care about it so much? And why are we still on the defensive? Could it be that victory is threatened again by what the Calvinist puritans of the 16th century called "the cold clatter of morality"? Could the famous "return of the moral order" really be upon us? Would our freedom to enjoy carry, in its own bosom, a muffled concern that we need to expiate without abating? Are we afraid, like George Bataille and André Breton feared toward the end of their lives, of some attenuation of our desires, weakened by disillusionment, until day after day we have to reawaken ardor with a flood of words? And of images? If that were the case, then we will have merely exchanged one tyranny for another.

We have no real answer to all that. Not that these questions are irrelevant, but because we have expended so much effort to avoid them. Even though we talk about sex all the time, we don't say anything. It's as if we are afraid to calmly examine what the historian Peter Brown nicely calls "the seismograph of our subjectivities,"[3] i.e. sexuality. Thus we insist on an emblematic conquest of which we refuse to investigate the true significance, the conditions that apply and the possible limits. A "seismographic" conquest, indeed, since in our eyes it supposedly measures our contemporary individualism better than anything else. It is mainly in this field, we think, that the emancipation of the Western individual seems to be without historical equivalent: by this pleasure that we are permitted — this pleasure emancipated from social constraints, religious interdicts and the considerations of procreation — we present ourselves as mutants in the course of History. Western Man was indeed the first to break so daringly with what Max Weber called "the authority of the eternal yesterday, that of the habits sanctified by their immemorial validity and man's deep-rooted practice of respecting them."[4]

So there is no question of doubting. For some thirty years, we have been defending tooth and nail this fantastic nest egg (sexual freedom) with an ambiguous obstinacy. Not wanting to worry any more about what it all represents, we have ended up transforming this whole thing into a taboo question. That beats all!

An Unexpected Fear

No, societies definitely do not know the history they are living!
Are their reactions (or over-reactions) any more lucid? It's doubtful.

Look at the anxious shock that fills us when something crops up,
unexpectedly, that we were trying to forget. Who foresaw the tremors
that would run through the realm of sexuality at the beginning of the
Nineties?[5] An unexpected menace welled up in those years, which
soon evolved swelled into a panic. It was heralded by a "detail." Incest
and pedophilia suddenly seemed to be threatening the social body. We
were warned that danger was lurking. Children weren't safe at home,
in school, or anywhere else, from wretched appetites that we suddenly
had to re-stigmatize. Various incidents (including the exposure of the
pedophilic murderer Marc Dutroux during the summer 1996 in Belgium) worsened this collective anxiety.

Our societies, in a word, rediscovered unimaginable instances of
sexual abuse in their midst and hastily sought to eradicate the threat
(by police action). Incestuous fathers, obsessed teachers and priests,
murderers obeying their perverted impulses, suspicious wives, lubri-
cious bosses tyrannizing their employees: the same anguished denunciations, the same aura of repression invaded the media. Not a day went
by without a hidden story coming to light, or a drama, long buried in
silence, being plastered across the front page of every regional newspaper. An endless lugubrious litany. . . Everybody tried to outdo each
other, revealing secrets, spilling tales of past suffering, naming perpe-
trators to be castigated or removed from society. Bravo.

New times and a new *doxa*, indeed. Through the media, the innumerable televised debates, the testimonies exhumed years later, a new
inquisitorial glance was cast on the adult, the husband, the tourist and
the sports coach. Any questionable contact was described in inquisitorial tones, along with abusive caresses and the hideous trade in children's flesh. Everyone was invited to re-examine personal memories
and retrospectively assess the sufferings hidden there. Manipulation
and aggression, various cases of abuse, sexual tourism and exotic pornography preying on children, the baby sitter with ambiguous intentions, fifty-year-olds getting into action: fear took over.

What is the true significance of this emotional torrent? Was it
only a moment of panic? Mere media excess, following a series of re-

volting stories? Really? Legal statistics, in their dryness, testify to a much more significant and more concrete shift. A shift achieved over just a few years, and almost silently. Whereas in the space of nine years (1984-1993) the number of rape convictions (primarily on minors) increased by 82%, the number of indecent assaults made by people in authority tripled and, from 1990 to the present, family rapes went up by 70%. Convictions for indecent assault on minors increased by 65%.[6] At the beginning of 1997, so-called "morality" crimes accounted for up to 60%, even 80% of the legal activity in some jurisdictions. This penal crackdown was especially spectacular in France. Our country now imposes the most severe sentences in Europe for sexual abuse (81% of the sentences exceed five years in prison).[7] But the civil law was not far behind. Charging one's spouse with incest became common currency in divorce proceedings; such allegations testified to an unprecedented obsession.

The prevailing mood spontaneously became so repressive in these matters that, paradox of paradoxes, today it is the magistrates who are alarmed and denounce the excesses of a witch hunt that goes far beyond reason. "We are going backward in time," writes one of them, "We have gone from a time when nothing was said or done about incest, to a time where our punitive tendencies are carrying us away. Hasty removals of children to foster homes and incarceration of the father now reflect violence by the State, violence due to a lack of differentiation. All that may be inevitable, but why is it so sudden?"[8] "Broad areas of conduct that were considered trivial, until now, have been criminalized," observes another, "especially among the middle class which is becoming the true breeding ground of condemnable violence, like 'date rape.'"[9]

Obviously, no one would think of denying the gravity of these offences against children or the need to combat them. No one would go so far as to contradict the reality of certain crimes nor, especially, their welcome release from the tomb of silence. But nevertheless! No judge should accept at face value the assumption a real and striking increase in sexual offences. France, Europe, and America have not suddenly become delinquent, incestuous societies or pedophiles. What the breaking of the silence and the calls for justice express most of all is a profound shift in our point of view. Commenting on the figures above, published in July 1996, two statisticians from the [French] Ministry of Justice made it clear. "This sizable increase," they wrote, "does not necessarily mean that there have been more incidents. The increase reflects at least to some extent the growing repressiveness tied to the general evolution of sensitivities and conducts."

Indeed, it is not the facts that have changed so much as how they are judged. Now, a hidden truth is immediately revealed; now, a buried or vaguely tolerated secret is a horror, and what used to pass as trivial starts a scandal. Something has indeed *returned*, at the deepest foundations of our societies. A "something" which it would be useful to identify.

A Certain Idea of Evil?

Let us start with a modest effort of memory. Let's admit it: we could, without much trouble, let loose polemical effects by inviting everybody, quite simply, to remember. It would be enough to contrast today's indictments for incest and pedophilia with what was said yesterday (from the same media platforms and sometimes by the same people) on these same subjects. By naming names, recalling forgotten stupidities, shaking off the general amnesia, pointing out blatant transgressions here and poor judgment there, we could compile an overwhelming collection of misdeeds. But what good is it? Polemics are of little of use in this matter. Excesses on one side are quickly answered by strong counter-reactions on the other, as vainly as the easygoing "permissiveness" of the Left, in the 1970's, echoed the priggish pedantry of the Right.

But the phenomenon that we are trying to elucidate (without polemical intentions) is far more complex. What happened in just a few years is quite simply that we have had an unacknowledged transformation of what Emile Durkheim called our collective representations (the symbolic touchstones that a society uses and which it considers well outside the ostentatious pugilism of "opinions").

The fact is that, from about 1970 or 1975 until the last third of the Eighties a relatively neutral, if not benevolent, point of view had prevailed in our Western societies with regard to pedophilia and incest. They were even listed, sometimes, among the "taboos" that were considered as possibly obsolete. Not, obviously, that they had become so common that you could mention them in public without raising a debate or an argument. Things were at the same time subtler and more gradual. While these two subjects still sparked rage and protest in 1971, later a progressive indifference and benign neglect took over.

As one of a thousand possible examples, Malle's film, *Le Souffle au coeur*, is revealing. It evokes incest between mother and son, with great tenderness and a clear intention of taking away the drama; the film was selected in May 1971 for the Cannes Film Festival and was well-received by the critics. Invited to justify himself in *Le Monde*, after some of the readers had protested, Malle did so with humor but also with a libertarian mischievousness in keeping with the times. "Everything takes place [in my film] naturally, clearly, and, I believe, truly. If traditional morality is out of sync with that, too bad."[10] In the press, Malle was congratulated many times on having built this "war machine against middle-class ideology and culture" (*Pariscope*), on having dared "to tear the veils from our eyes and expose the false mysteries and ashamed silences" (*France Nouvelle*). "In one shot," a commentator added, "he gives us the notion of Evil as that which is basically repressive, and questions it as a 'metaphysical' category" (*Lettres françaises*).[11]

Fundamentally, and independently of the film's qualities (which were obvious), the interpretation of the event was clear. A taboo was thankfully transgressed. And so delicately that it became banal.

Only very indirectly did the film make a scandal. On May 11, 1971, the management of the ORTF (the former French broadcasting company) decided not to show a debate in Michel Polac's magazine, *Post Scriptum*, which was to comment on the question of incest and Malle's film. This brutal censure was denounced even in the columns of *Le Figaro*, in the name of freedom of expression. That was legitimate, but said nothing about the content. Note that less than twenty years later, this same television station did broadcast *Le Souffle au coeur* without any concern and that anyone who was still sensitive to its supposedly subversive tone, was considered atavistic. And at the end of the Eighties, even a proposal by certain lawyers to ease the penalty for incest did not raise any real furor.

Thus an average sensibility was expressed by the initial reactions, taken together with this later general indifference; a sensibility which clashes severely with the sudden vilification of this same question (incest) in the mid-Nineties. Suddenly, it was not a a matter of tender weakness but a crime; no one was talking anymore about "a punch in the nose for middle-class morals" but of pathological horror. More concretely, for acting more or less like the heroine of *Le Souffle au coeur*, hundreds of fathers were tracked down by the court systems, and publicly (and unanimously) designated as perverts without proof. The lackadaisical atmosphere was replaced overnight with the unamimous brutality of a lynching. And no one would go so far as to write today, in connection with incest, as *Le Monde*'s excellent chronicler of cinema Jean de Baroncelli offered in 1971, "There is nothing foul, ambiguous or vicious, in this embrace. And nothing tragic. A little waywardness, a natural misstep. A kind of exorcism."[12]

It is not often that public opinion changes so much, or so fast. The questions raised by such a reversal cannot be brushed off. And all the more so, given that the change of perception regarding incest was even more spectacular in connection with pedophilia.

The Era of the "Pedophile" Adventure

In the wake of the great liberalization of manners before and after 1968, as we know, a whole literature of permissiveness flourished in Europe as well as in the United States. A literature of protest, it was part of an irresistible trend toward liberalization and, in particular, it put an end to the ancestral reprobation of homosexuality and the old antifeminist ostracism. These are two exemplary struggles that we will return to later on,[13] and whose legitimacy is not, in hindsight, in any doubt. The same does not apply to pedophilia that, in just one stroke, became blameless, celebrated and the object of much theorizing. It was discussed in terms that today would be shocking, anywhere you might go. It is that shift, in just a few years' time, which invites reflection.

Among the homosexual militants, yesterday's complacently ambiguous reception for pedophilic professions of faith are now the subject of soul-searching. This complacency endured for some fifteen years and was used against homosexual liberation itself, to "compromise" it. "While the homosexuals were defending freedom of desire," wrote Frederic Martel, "the pedophiles wanted to play around with the age limits of minors and refused to be governed by any standard. An impasse was close at hand: soon, they would try to legitimate rape, thereby setting themselves up in total contradiction to the feminist movement, which was working to criminalize it. Consequently, legitimate fears about pedophilia fed irrational criticism of homosexuality. . . From the mid-Eighties onward, pedophiles and homosexuals went their separate ways."[14]

Upon reflection, this alleged blunder by the homosexual movement was not, originally, such a mistake. It was in phase with the sensibilities of those years; a sensibility that extended to all sorts of indulgence, pedophilia included. There was hardly any public comment when a recognized writer (Gabriel Matzneff) was invited to a televised literary show to present one of his books praising physical love with those "under the age of 15." No one would have dared go against the general admiration for Nabokov to object that the heroine of his famous novel *Lolita*, an appetizing young girl who yielded to the passions of a quinquagenarian, was not yet twelve years old. And more disconcerting still, nobody was offended (for long) that the major press expressed a sententious pedophile militancy.

The comments published in 1978 by philosopher Rene Schérer are vivid testimony. "We are speculating about the possibility of a love shared between a man and a child. If you try to impose on this strange couple the adult eroticism of compartmentalized individuals, it seems like a lie, an enigma, an impossibility or a crime; but pedophile love becomes, on the contrary, all lightness as soon as it is introduced to the field of puerile eroticism." The same text also goes on about "middle-class repressiveness," another sign of the times. "The pedophile adventure," wrote Schérer, "reveals the unbearable confiscation of being and of meaning, for the child, that results from the limited and inferior position to which children are ordinarily relegated."[15] If this pathos makes us bristle today, remember that yesterday it did not.

It is an understatement to say that between 1970 and the mid-80's, for fifteen years, public opinion was lenient toward the role of adult pedophiles; these adults whose misdeeds are now denounced in the major press while their arrests are hailed as a valorous victory. Fifteen years ago, one had to appear to be "understanding," or risk looking like a "reactionary." A sexologist who campaigned in the 1970's for the liberation of morality had some experience with this. His personal hostility toward pedophilia (later shifted) brought down upon him the active hatred of certain militants of the FHAR (Front homosexuel d'action révolutionnaire).[16] As for the organizations (especially the Swiss) that were already fighting against international pedophile tourism, they received hardly any support from the major press.

Good Sex (Badly) Illustrated

Another example, a real textbook case, makes it possible to measure still better how radical was this about-face of public opinion, and
even to roughly recall its chronology. This is the example Tony Duvert.
An excellent writer of the 70's, he not only was a relentless proselytizer
of pedophilia but made it the main topic of his writings. Literary criticism of his work evolved over time, modeling the shifting current of
public opinion.

In 1973, Tony Duvert made a name for himself when Editions
Minuit published his novel, *Paysage de fantaisie*, which was actually his
fifth work (the first four having been published semi-privately). Sexual
games between an adult and children, a fantasy representation of the
relationship between torturer and victims ("As children play Cowboys
and Indians, I play at being a torturer," announces the author), this
transparent text was highly enough regarded and, in spite of some reservations, was acclaimed as a healthy subversion, "a fundamentally voluptuous book." It was awarded the Medici prize!

The following year, Duvert wrote a libertine lampoon, *Bon Sexe
illustré* [Good Sex Illustrated], directly denouncing "the family ideology," lambasting the "saccharine Western and militarist Chinese" in-
doctrinations, meanwhile calling for full sexual freedom for children
and a rejection of "old repressive morals." Here and there, this
"generous lampoon" was welcomed for destroying "the repressive notions of vice and virtue."[17] In an interview about two new novels, *L'Île
atlantique* and *Journal d'un innocent*, published thereafter, the author defined his position by advising the reader that [for him] "pedophilia is a
culture." He would confess his special hatred of women and mothers in
particular, culprits who impose an authoritative and castrating matri-
archy. "If there was a Nuremberg Court for Peace Crimes, we would
have to turn in nine mothers out of ten." Duvert would add that protective mothers are an annoying obstacle for the pedophile. He suggests
that children should be taken away from them some day.[18]

In 1978, a new novel, a companion to the earlier one, *Quand mourut
Jonathan* [When Jonathan Died], tells of the (consummated) love between a painter of ripe age and an eight-year-old boy — a less provocative novel, but perpetuating the same campaign. New praise from the
literary press, not only for the literary form but for the meaning of the

18

text itself. "One learns [in this novel] that love dies when it tries to conform to society's laws, and thrives when it is plunged into animality;"[19] "The great passions are the forbidden passions," and "Tony Duvert is among the purest," etc..

In 1979, the year *L'Île atlantique* was published, the sulfurous but heroic personality of the "clandestine writer" was still critically acclaimed. Witness this exclamation by Madeleine Chapsal: "In this fantastic archipelago of ten books, Duvert, a keen and solitary writer, has quickly raised from the depths the liveliest of our literature: those which touch on the body and soul of childhood."[20] Likewise, this enthusiastic review by Annick Geille: "A eulogy to desertion, a denunciation of all our internal prisons, *L'Île atlantique* violates a taboo: that of maternity, the sacred cow of the exploiters."[21] In 1980, in *L'Enfant au masculin* [Boy Child], Duvert still rode the wave of an ambient "false permissiveness" which, in his eyes, hypocritically stops on this side of the limits of the Penal Code. "There is only one means of discovering someone's sexuality, small or large," he wrote, "and that is to make love with him." That is clear enough!

After 1986, however, the writer's image suddenly seemed to deteriorate. In 1989 he published, under the title *Abécédaire maleveillant* [A Malevolent ABC], a collection of provocative aphorisms, sayings and maxims which this time garnered some alarmed censure, especially from Jerome Garcin, who saw it as "the last bitter scribblings of a Sixties hippie drunk who stayed too long in the WC at the Turkish baths, where the decrepit walls still bear obscene graffiti and the choleric debris of a now obsolete revolution."[22]

Other critics showed the same irritation. The times had changed, and not only in the field of literature. It would be wrong, indeed, to interpret the recollections above as so many ephemeral episodes, passions and traditional quarrels of the Republic of Letters. The Duvert case is cited only as documentary evidence and not retroactively and wrongfully to transform this writer into a scapegoat. It illustrates the changing mood, not of the critics but of the times. The fact is that what "passed" in 1974 no longer did so in 1989.

What happened?

The Return of the Forbidden

It is always (much) too tempting to look for simple explanations. In the mid-80's, it is true, several spectacular incidents had moved French public opinion and put pedophiles on the defensive. There was the case known as the Corral affair, in 1986, which featuring handicapped children and unscrupulous "pedagogues." A scandalous situation, emblematic of an iniquitous power relationship (adult pedophiles/handicapped children), an event that was broadcast widely enough to set off a wave of protest and long polemics.[23] Those preceded, by ten years, the famous "moral insurrection" of Belgium after the Dutroux affair. The mass media took a greater interest in child prostitution in the southern countries, Asian especially; and in a tone that was not simple curiosity.

Previously, certain rumors had drifted across the Atlantic and made a great noise in Europe: the appearance of snuff movies on the pornography market (which was liberalized at the beginning of the 1970's), films where sexual murder is the object of high-priced voyeurism, films with pornographic scenes accompanied by murder, real or otherwise. The postface of a book published in France that year testifies to the emergence, in the most enlightened opinion, of what one might call a hesitation or a doubt which, little by little, would begin to seep in. This book of interviews, *Les Femmes, la pornography et l'erotisme*, was intended to lightheartedly poke fun at some taboos and to break women's silence on the question of pornography. In the conclusion, one of the co-authors, Marie-Francoise Hans, confessed nevertheless that this discovery of snuff movies raised some troubling points. "[This reality] raises a fundamental question: should the existence of snuff shows be considered a mishap, a misadventure in the field of sexual entertainment? Or is it not, rather, a stain on the entire notion of pornographic production? The road to death? . . . For the murder is ordered by men with money for the disgraceful pleasure of other men with money."[24]

Other concerns are expressed, as a subtext, elsewhere in the same book. The psychoanalyst Luce Irigaray was almost prophetic. "It is certain that we see signs of exhaustion of the power of discourse, so sexual, that is grinding us down. There are growing signs of degeneration. The question is whether we are heading for a new dawn, or toward a kind of collective suicide." Faint but indisputable signs, as though the times were imperceptibly moving away from the optimistic "liberation" of the 1970's. The incidents mentioned above certainly had something to do with it.

Moreover, it is a fact of life, in social history, that a collection of factors acts together to induce change. The crackdown on homosexuals at the end of 17th and the beginning of the 18th centuries, for example, was obviously linked to major crimes involving pedophiles.

Take the case of Jacques Chausson and Jacques Paumier (known as "Fabri"). They were convicted in the attempted rape of a seventeen-year-old boy (in 1661) and wound up admitting to procuring much younger boys. They were condemned to have their tongues cut out and to be burnt alive, which was done on December 29, 1661. In theory, the sentence called for their "customers" (a marquis and a baron) to be prosecuted, but they never were. The iniquity of this obvious injustice revolted the people, and many vengeful stories were written, such as the *Complainte de Chausson et Fabri*.

Sixty years later (in 1724-1726), the Benjamin Deschauffours affair even more closely resembles the Dutroux incident. Pedophile, assassin, pimp supplying little boys, Deschauffours was the head of a pedophile network supplying rich customers. He "tested" the boys beforehand or had them tested by his lackeys. He even had one young boy castrated on behalf of a wealthy Italian. Deschauffours was burned in the Place de Grève on May 24, 1726.[25] There was a social symbolism of "the rich" preying upon the children of "the poor," just six decades of before the Revolution.

But while various events like this can be the catalyst in changing public opinion, they are never the explanation. More essential ideological questions are involved. We will discuss later on how this hypersensitivity to the incidents of pedophilia and incest relate to the great contemporary debate over the status of children themselves, the status of families and, in the final analysis, to Western individualism.[26] More immediately, the question just posed has to do with the return of the *interdict* to a society that foolishly believed it had been freed from it. The interdict, that is, the very idea of limits, of consenting to be regulated, of minimal standards of behavior acceptable to the majority.

This thesis was especially favored by Jean-Pierre Rosenczweig, president of the Bobigny juvenile court during the Dutroux case — a case that had the merit, according to him, of "waking up all of Europe."[27] For this magistrate, who also defends very radical theses on the question of "children's rights," our Western societies were trapped by their internal contradictions. For some thirty years they had given up setting limits of permissible behavior, in sexual matters and others as well, thus losing sight of what Freud called the "structuring" and humanizing role of the *Law*. In a context of playful permissiveness and voluptuous Utopia, "tolerance" was dangerously confused with license.

However, it is hard to re-acclimate our societies to the fundamental principle of the interdict, including on sexual matters. That is the real explanation for these erratic tensions in public opinion, the panic and this abusively repressive demand from society. Not to mention the retrospective distress or "guilty conscience." We are not at peace with our pleasures. Or our desires.

An Misplaced Condescension

On this very awkward question of the interdict, some contradictions should be highlighted since they seem so untenable. The first has to do with the fact that we have imperceptibly slipped into an extraordinary schizophrenia. Obeying nothing but their own gravity, our societies now combine permissive *talk* unprecedented in the course of history with a *practice* that is more repressive in many ways than that of traditional societies — societies against which we continue to measure our alleged emancipation.

Researchers like Michel Foucault and Peter Brown, to cite just two, were ironical about this misplaced condescension for the past and the "smug, even malicious, familiarity with which modern man feels he can mock the sexual anxieties of the men and the women of a distant past."[28] In this "distant past," however, one would find a thousand examples of an art of compromised which we have lost. The anxious societies are not always the ones we think they are.

In the 17th century, no one saw anything wrong in the nannies' practice of masturbating little boys to help them sleep. As for the famous medieval repression of homosexuals, it was so seldom put in practice since the 14th century that historians have barely managed to come up with 38 cases of capital punishment actually applied between 1317 and 1789, i.e. in four and a half centuries! And most of those were instances of criminal pedophilia perpetrated on boys or girls of ten years or even younger[29] (acts which would be punished similarly in the post-modern America of today). Let us add that most of the penalties that the famous ecclesiastical courts of the Middle Ages imposed for sexual transgressions consisted of prolonged fasts or voluntary penitences — punishments well on this side of the sentences given today. Contrary to our own practices, in moral matters the traditional societies combined severity of principles with moderation in practice.

Our conduct is pretty much the opposite, today. We are dizzy with theoretical license, but cannot, in reality, indulge. A man from the Renaissance or the 18th century would be shocked by certain contemporary legal restrictions — restrictions which are very strictly followed. For example, in 1986 the U.S. Supreme Court upheld a law in the State of Georgia, by five votes against four, making crimes of sodomy and fellatio even between a married couple. Or another decision by the same Supreme Court, in Bowers vs. Hardwick, allowing the States to declare homosexuality between two consenting adults a crime.

Thus we find ourselves, without fully realizing it, in the bitterest contradiction between apparent permissiveness and a niggling repression. Our daily life is a constant conflict between solicitation and suspicion, a proselytizing pan-sexuality and a nosy vigilance, extraordinary "sexual invitation" and the maniacal threat of an inquisition (sexual harassment, etc.). We are caught in a double bind. That is undoubtedly one of the explanations for the flood of proclamations and noise we endure, the inexhaustible discourse about love. It betrays a strange existential discomfort, as if the presumptuous Western societies had lost the art of measure, the capacity for amicable "arrangements," the virtue of silence which still prevails, for example, in African cultures. It is as though we are orphans of an erotic, patient culture made up of internalized rules and consenting transgressions, devastating inclinations and accepted risks, license and the half-light of prudence, which yesterday perpetuated — more intelligently than is imagined — the unstable equilibrium of desire.

An African scholar describes it beautifully. "What Westerners take. . . for a lack of transparency, even duplicity, is only a modest reserve that surrounds human relations like a halo of mystery, a protective opacity and something impalpable connected with respect, especially self respect. *Damma rouss* ('I am ashamed'), the Wolofs say. We are shocked by the distance which traditional cultures place between men and women. But we should be aware that the terrible face-to-face discussion of the Western couple, stripped of decency and reserve, is profoundly destroying relations in love, desire and any closeness."[30]

The second remark relates to the paradoxical vulnerability of our societies vis-a-vis the returning flames of Puritanism. Floating in the atmosphere, in America as in Europe, is an insidious temptation to moralize, founded on nostalgia for a lost equilibrium; that is, on an illusion. Having been too carelessly discarded, the interdict is making a strong comeback in the form of disciplinary injunctions, religious fundamentalism and cults, under the guise of a frightening Catharism as a vehicle for who knows what pathological form of "purity." These reactions are the admission of weakness. After three decades of overblown permissiveness, our modernity is defenseless before a great moralizing reflux. A backward flow that tempts but terrorizes at the same time, as if an ontological rupture had taken place upstream and left us with no resources, either of morality or of moralism. We dreamed we were in the avant-garde of humanity, conquering pleasure; we find ourselves wandering in the open countryside, without food or water.

We had a vague presentiment of this vulnerability, and it does not come without consequences. It generates an inconsolable panic; it radicalizes people's views and scrambles their thoughts, as panic always does. Because we proudly believed we could do away with the prudence and the cautious compromises of the past, here we are empty-handed and dispirited. Because we had thought we were allowed quite simply to stop *thinking* about desire, now we are unable to desire *in fact*. Now everyone thinks he has to choose sides, between black and white, moral order and license, "anything goes" and the interdict. Thought itself is driven backward, to dogmatic quarrels, to imbecilic simplification and boasting. Should we take that as good news? Of course not. We would even blush in confusion if we re-read Plutarch's subtle *Dialogues sur l'Amour*.

There is a strange parallel between this dereliction of the discourse on love and the likewise troubling impoverishment of the discussion of economics and social thought. After the collapse of communism, the downfall of a Utopia that had transmuted into tyranny, we would appear to have no other recourse but a symmetrical Utopia of ultra-liberalism, the past mistake in reverse. The injustice of the jungle and "might makes right" are already plowing over the ruins of that leveling progressivism. Exactly as the discipline of Puritanism is little by little replacing the overly naive hedonism of yesterday. There doesn't seem to be much space between the two.

But this book rests on the conviction that that is the only space that is habitable. In these pages, we will try to regain some room for humanity and reason; to loosen as much as possible the vice grip of the double bind; to challenge every example of the blackmail that has become so widely accepted: the opposition of morality and immorality. Such is the objective. Only the method remains to be explained.

Resolutely Modern

We are not talking about archaism or nostalgia. We have no intention of starting a funereal renunciation of pleasure and its freedoms. Quite the opposite, in fact. We propose to take modernity at its word, to develop a new idea of progress. Equally resolute but better informed; more attentive to what is real; less amnesic. In a luminary work, the philosopher Bruno Latour very aptly defined the foundation for this approach.

"The old idea of progress," he wrote, "which we recently left behind, allowed us to stop paying attention, it released us from any prudence, any caution; the new concept appears rather as that which obliges prudence, selective choice, a meticulous triage of all the possibilities. . . .Whereas the old idea of progress made it possible to escape from the useless complications of the past, the new one keeps sending us deeper and deeper into the complexities of traditional anthropology. In becoming the same as other people, after three centuries during which Europeans believed themselves to be radically different from 'the others,' we are not losing our soul, we are finding our humanity. We will finally understand the meaning of the word 'civilization,' which will no longer mean sweeping away the past and modernizing in the European way, but will mean sorting through the possibilities and will make life unlivable for those who would simplify it."[31]

Mark those last words. This resolute attack against the "simplifiers" opens vast new perspectives. No domain of human activity has produced so much powerful thinking as that of love and pleasure; none since the world began has justified so many debates, reflections, generous Utopias and fears to be allayed; none has been so closely tied to the very idea of culture and humanity. And none has been more immune to "simplification." That the latter have wrongly triumphed for three decades is neither deniable, nor very pleasant; that they have invested that field with a brusqueness "liberated of any prudence, any caution," justifies, today, an attempted revision. Could any project be more stimulating than to relearn, deliberately, peacefully, and cheerfully, to "sort through the possibilities"?

We must reflect not only on the misadventures of the "sexual revolution" but on the fragile foundations upon which it was built, its naïve promises, is rudimentary postulates. Ultimately, that enterprise was founded on the idea of a clean slate. It flowed from an acknowledged ambition: to sweep away the past and to promote "a man of pleasure," like the New Man proclaimed in political revolutions. A man freed from rules and from prudence, dedicated only to infinite pleasure. OK! And where are we now, on this path to the shining future?

The failure of Utopias, as we know, is the main event of the late 20th century. But at least the collapse of the communist revolution has generated over the past several years some minimal reflection. It produced an immense body of contrite reflections, compassionate *mea culpas*, clarity in hindsight and all kinds of revisions. By now, mourning for that Utopia has become an obligatory part of any political reflection.

Not for the "sexual revolution" which was its contemporary. Did it succeed any better? Did it stumble over any fundamental contradictions? No one has risked answering these questions. A stubborn silence prevails. We continue to celebrate, mechanically, without arguing; we make claims without actually showing any evidence, we go on and on without humility or proof. We used to refuse "to give up on Billancourt." *Mutatis mutandis*, we prefer to entertain the illusion of a victory, the ambiguous charms of a "liberation" of principle, the fading light of an old star. That question, we are sure, will never be asked.
OK, let's ask!

CHAPTER 2

THIRTY YEARS LATER

"Make love, not war;" "Enjoy without inhibition;" "Prohibitions are prohibited;" "The more I make love, the more I want to make revolution." In hindsight, all utopias are funny. From a distance of two or three decades, the passions that drove us in the past seem silly, short-sighted and infantile. It is very hard not to treat them with irony. Every generation is cruel to the one that preceded it, cruel in the sense that they think of themselves as being endowed with clearer vision and they are condescending about the naive "commitments" taken on by their forebears. But that is a mistake. There is no glory in winning battles that have already been fought, and it is easy to see through illusions when time has already worn them away. This is an easy cruelty. It always comes up after the fact, and rarely goes far: triumphant posturing but lacking in new ideas.

In truth, we should never laugh at utopias whose days are over, nor too thoughtlessly make fun of the popular trends of the past — for at least two reasons. First, because in their day they embodied a hope, which should always be cherished. (Only those who are satisfied with the order of the day take pleasure in humiliating those who dream of a better future.) Second, because nothing is more perilous than self-satisfaction. It is always a mistake to think we are smart, especially in hindsight. Every era pursues its own utopias, without realizing it — the "invisible ideology" that it takes for reasonable plans. Every era be-

27

lieves in something. Every generation thinks that it knows "more" than the one before, and talks louder; but it is only obeying a system of beliefs and assumptions that is "falsifiable" (in the sense that Karl Popper used the term). Criticism of a utopia is thus generally founded, unconsciously, on a new utopia which tomorrow or the day after will be revealed for what it was. Since it is a false clarity, it will be debunked and, in turn, will be gauged against a new set of beliefs and will be judged with the same allegedly "enlightened" ferocity. And so on, a gloomy alternation of vanity and blindness. The history of ideas should incline us, rather, to be modest.

Down with the "Old Order"

Without being either condescending or too kind, it is to the chapter on utopias that we must consign the "sexual revolution" of the late Sixties. A mixture of hope and arrogance, bold initiatives and crazy ideas, playful exuberance and sententious ideologies: a great libertarian wave washed over all the industrialized societies from 1964[1] to 1973. From Japan to California, from old Europe to young America, an insurrection against authority, the forbidden, constraints and carnal pessimism mobilized a youth which suddenly could no longer put up with the "old order." In a few years, a whole edifice of collective representations and their legal implications was shaken from top to bottom. Thirty years after, the edifice is flat on the ground. But what does that mean? Sex was "liberated," but with what result?

So much has been written about this formidable historical turning point, so much has been published, so many arguments have been posited that a discouraging fog enshrouds the event. Looking back, it seems like a historical given, massive and fuzzy, impossible to analyze in detail; something so overwhelming that one can hardly conceive of looking at it more closely. It just happened. There was an earthquake. And it would be ridiculous to try to sort through everything that was being imagined and undertaken at the time. Does anyone consider "sorting through" the factors that for thirty years have determined a good measure of Western culture itself? This is our heritage, take it or leave it. Endless praise for the "sexual revolution," or the Grinch-like grumblings of the "puritan reaction" — those are our only choices, and the reason is well known.

However, obviously, it is not it.

28

The Western sexual revolution wiped away many forms of prejudice and ostracism that it would be insane to bring back; on the contrary, we must continue to fight relentlessly (against homophobia, machismo, inhibitions, guilt, etc.). The fact remains that it *also* gave birth to a thousand new illusions and suggested a thousand nonsensical ideas, and spread lies that were carelessly mixed in with the heritage. Those are the things we must patiently flush out. But how? By taking one strand of this impressive skein and persistently following it from one end to the other. A strand that would enable us to trace the path from the beginning. And this strand, if we might say so, has a name: Wilhelm Reich. This Austrian psychoanalyst, who died in 1957, had so much to do with causing the irruption of the great Western permissiveness that he has come to represent it, and to symbolize it in its entirety.

For the record, let us recall that at the very beginning of 1968, at the University of Nanterre, a conference on "Wilhelm Reich and Sexuality" led to the fight against the rules of procedure, the fight that gave rise to the Movement of March 22. "This conference," states a contemporary text, "led to a number of petitions, in particular a leaflet from the Resident Students' Association which denounced the university cities' sexual repression that separated the girls from the boys, with a whole series of examples illustrating this repression."[2]

That doesn't mean that everyone, at the time, was reading and re-reading all of Reich's works, from the *The Sexual Revolution* to *The Function of the Orgasm*. No one is maintaining that crowds of Westerners were learning and reciting *La Lutte sexuelle des jeunes*, or *Écoute, petit homme*, nor that whole generations were piously absorbing the teachings of *L'Analyse caractérielle* or *The Cosmic Superposition*. More likely, Reich was read very little, and superficially. But were the students of '68 who hung posters of Che Guevara on their walls very well informed about the Bolivian guerrilla's adventures or the *foco* strategy? Not likely. Che simply appeared, at this juncture in history, as an emblematic reference, a symbol and cultural code for a generation in revolt.

Wilhelm Reich, too, played a primarily mythological role. That becomes clear, looking back. For a decade, 1965 to 1975, he was above all "a face," the vague and blazing image of a revolution, the alibi for speechifying. His very name and the title of his books meant that there was an outrageous line of thought, lurking in the depths of knowledge, which it was not even necessary to know specifically. To a lesser extent, Herbert Marcuse — a rather tedious and difficult to read philosopher — fleetingly played the same role in the political field.[3] His work was neither closely studied nor, in truth, very important. He is one of those leading thinkers who become known without being read. Without even being opened, their books become Gospel. That's the way it is.

That was undoubtedly the case with Reich. The role that he played, and continues to play, in this great sexual business has as much to do with firing up the imagination as with any conceptual advances. It should be mentioned that the appearance of this "figure," in the Sixties, happened to match several diffuse requirements. It is even disturbing to analyze, after the fact, how historical chance managed to gather so many messages — and promises — around this one name. And with a biography that appears tailor-made.

Birth of a Cult

Born in 1897 in Austrian Galicia, Reich met Freud in Vienna in the Twenties; later he broke with him. Having settled in Berlin, he joined the Communist Party and participated in the ideological effervescence of the October Revolution. He created an Association for a Proletarian Sexual Policy (Sexpol), before being kicked out of the communist movement in 1933. A Jew, he had oddly enough toyed with the theses of the Nazi party, before later rejecting them. Exiled in the United States on the eve of the Second World War, he succumbed little by little to a scientistic delusion, to which we will return later. Starting in 1956, he was persecuted by the American FBI, which had his works, his "products" and his laboratories destroyed. Reich died in the penitentiary in Lewisburg, Pennsylvania, on November 3, 1957, which added the suggestion of being a political martyr to the symbolism of persecution.[4]

From start to finish, this was a life made to be mythologized.

Let's take a look at how, at every stage, this biography could resonate so immediately with the sensibility of the student revolts of the Sixties. The original link, and then the rupture, with Freud attested that Reich had taken psychoanalysis into account, but seemed also to imply that he had managed to *go beyond* it. All the ambiguity of the epoch was encompassed in his relations with Freudianism. Similarly, Reich's evolution indicated that he had "surpassed" Bolshevism and then had risen against the "fascist" drift of Stalinism.

Now, while European youth of May 1968 expressed a retrogressive desire to appropriate Bolshevik rhetoric, its symbols and memories, and its heroic epic (Kronstadt, Potemkin, etc.), fundamentally, in fact, it broke with Marxism completely. Nothing could have coincided so nicely with this contradiction as Reich's "case." Thanks to Reich, indeed, the Western "sexual revolution" was mythically and permanently connected to the great proletarian revolution, in its youthful and thundering phase, before it was corrupted and coöpted. It was grounded in sexuality, desire, the sublimation of pleasure, and the very idea of revolution (as was Western Maoism, in a way). As for the FBI's supposedly persecuting the Austrian immigrant to death in a Yankee prison, obviously it helped ignite the anti-Americanism of the late Sixties, and coincided beautifully with anger of European (and Californian) youth against "American imperialism" and their solidarity with Vietnam crushed by the B52 bombers.

Let us add that one of Reich's favorite topics, from the start, was the sexual liberation of children and teenagers who, according to him, were victims of the family, which he described as "a factory of authoritative ideologies and conservative mental structures." Let us remember, finally, that Reich intended to politicize daily life and in particular sexuality, as the social movement would do in the Seventies. Nothing could be more appropriate for student revolts than this "sexual youth" as fertile as it was radical. One of the first topical writings published at that time (*De la misère sexuelle en milieu étudiant* [*On sexual misery among students*]) was directly inspired by Reich.

Rebellious son of Freud, dissenting Marxist, Jewish anti-Nazi, supposed victim of American "repression," every detail of Reich's life came together almost miraculously into what Max Weber called "a specific pathos," the chaotic and romantic pathos of the Sixties.[5] Even the cosmic delusion of the end of his life, and what must be called his insanity, added a Rimbaudian or post-surrealist dimension to the seductive appeal of this thinker who was opportunely resuscitated. As for examining his theories a little more closely. . .

The quasi-religious devotion of his following is shown line by line, paragraph after paragraph, in the innumerable articles, files, glosses and commentaries devoted to Reich between 1968 and 1978. The way his works were republished and re-translated,[6] the way each of them was greeted and paraphrased in the name of a strict Reichian orthodoxy,

the nitpicking reverence expressed in the forewords and the press reviews: it all looks like part of a sacramental process. This was not just
an author, but a prophet. When Reich's work was rediscovered in
Europe (by German students on the extreme left),[7] it was designated at
once as an immense gnosis to which only certain recognized exegetes
had the key. There were quarrels over heritage and testamentary legitimacy, pirate editions, and editorial lawsuits, all of which made the
whole business seem more significant.

Which nicely supports the development of myths.

What stands out, above all, is the unflappable *seriousness* with
which Reich's theses — even the most extravagant — were brought
out and approved over a ten-year period in France; it is the aplomb of
the commentary, the bombastic servility with which he was celebrated.
It's enough to raise questions about Western intelligence. Actually, no
one really "discovered" a thought, rather it was celebrated instantane-
ously, without reservation nor perspicacity, and mainly because it came
at the right moment. From the invention of the Reich cult by a handful
of priest-intermediaries (they could be counted on the fingers of two
hands)[8] was soon born a rather rudimentary popular version which
was, indeed, truly publicized, promoted, and covered by the media. Our
societies once were Freudian or structuralist; now they have become
more or less "Reichian," without knowing it.

This popular version has survived up until today, even if it is hard
to identify. Roughly speaking, the four or five postulates, the basic ten-
ets proposed by Reich, continue to thrive, haunting even the most naïve — even most out of touch — a little like the epistles of a forgotten
prophet, that would be mechanically chanted by the survivors of an
apocalypse. Thus, the great proletarian revolution, absorbed by history,
passed through the crucible of historical reasoning and decreed to have
been a bloody totalitarian heresy, still lives on in this single chapter —
the "sexual" chapter, preserved in state and, of course, exempt from
criticism.

A Rousseauian Fantasy

Yes, exempt from criticism and judgment. Certain rather easily
identifiable proponents control how his thought is used today. Postulates which history has discarded but which live on, nonetheless: the
most deep-seated Rousseauianism, resolute anticapitalism, the rejec-

tion of psychoanalysis, hatred of religion, radical scientism and unrestrained vitalism. Let's take a closer look.

Needless to say, Reich's Rousseauian view seems terribly ingenuous today. Reich was convinced (he wrote about it constantly) that man's sexuality is naturally harmonious and peaceful. Only social alienation and repression by authoritarian society diverted this sexuality toward the pathological. "Anyone who is not dying of hunger," he said, "feels no impulse to rob and thus does not need morality to keep him from robbing. The same fundamental law applies to sexuality: anyone who is sexually satisfied will have no impulse to rape and does not need morality to counter the impulse. It is a matter of self-regulation according to sexual economy (*sexalökonomische regulierung*), as opposed to coercive moral regulation."

For Reich, perversion, the urge to rape, the possessive instinct, pedophilia, jealousy, voyeurism, and impotence do not exist in a natural state, any more than robbery, murder or treason. Human nature is naturally good; sexuality is naturally "healthy." This extraordinary ontological optimism is expressed throughout his work with a clear certainty and a kind of obstinate ingenuousness, both of which are unusual, coming from a psychoanalyst.

"The healthy individual has practically no morality in him," Reich wrote, "for he has no impulses requiring moral inhibition. Whatever remains of his antisocial impulses is easily controllable, as soon as the basic genital needs are satisfied. This all becomes clear in the attitude of the individual who has achieved orgastic power. . . . The ability to give oneself up to the flow of biological energy without any inhibition, the ability to completely release all sexual excitation by means of pleasant involuntary contractions of the body. Relations with a prostitute become impossible; sadistic fantasies disappear, expecting love as a right or even raping one's partner becomes inconceivable, as well as the idea of seducing children; anal perversions, exhibitionism and others disappear, and with them the social anxiety and the guilt feelings which accompany them; incestuous fixations among parents, brothers and sisters lose their interest, which releases the energy bound up in these fixations. In short, all these phenomena indicate the organism's aptitude for self-regulation."[9]

In sum, Reich was convinced that "genital needs" were elementary and natural. Repressing them, regulating them on moral or religious grounds, was the only thing that would lead the individual to neurosis, to any kind of vice, to social resentment and even to Fascism. Ensuring the free satisfaction of these needs is all it would take to render the very concept of morals completely useless. "The healthy individual, suited to full sexual satisfaction, is capable of self-regulation." In other words, the sexual well-being of the population is the best guarantee of the social unit's safety. And perhaps the only guarantee. It is the free satisfaction of "healthy" sexual pleasure, and not its domestication or its regulation within the family, which makes it possible to pacify life in society.[10] If these vital genital functions are still perverted in our middle-class societies, it is because of the social systems and institutions which intend to divert to other purposes this persecuted sexual energy.

According to Reich, the majority of psychic diseases originate in the repression, since childhood, of genital activity. This repression and this guilt produce what he calls the "emotional plague," contaminating most humans and pushing them "toward authoritarianism, partisan politics, moralism, mysticism, denunciations and slander, authoritative bureaucracy, warmongering and imperialist ideologies, and racial hatred."[11]

Convinced that humanity has not yet experienced true culture nor civilization, he assures us that, thanks to the imminent sexual revolution, "they are about to appear on the social scene." We must hasten its advent by fighting against the family, morals and all forms of sexual repression. But for Reich, "There can be no more doubt. The sexual revolution is under way, and no power in the world will stop it."[12]

Upon examination, and with the passing of time, this idea seems to us so ingenuous and superficial that it strikes us as ridiculous. Nice, and rather stupid. The most extraordinary thing is not that such a Rousseauian fantasy could be expressed so ingenuously in the 20th century. It is that it could find so many disciples, so many commentators, critics and advocates to take it literally — and over the course of several decades. At the time, it was quite rare for anyone, following the example of philosopher François George, to offer courteous irony about a pleasant but very rudimentary naturalism that failed "to understand that the *libido*, the capacity to love, works according to a social structure which provides a story, a subjectivity, a human world." The same François George pointed out that Reich's approach, in the name of nature, reduced "sexuality to its physiological, biological aspect, in order to ignore its role in the human drama, its relation to the overall significance of our experience of reality."[13]

A voice in the wilderness, a minimal clairvoyance that we should welcome, three decades later.

Is Sex Revolutionary?

Reich's anti-capitalism (at least before he went to the United States) was no less radical than his Rousseauianism. His thesis is simple: if middle-class society tries so hard to repress children's, and then adults', sexual energy, it is so that it can be channeled toward productive purposes. The worker is kept at his station and the proletariat is kept in "sexual misery," in order to confiscate the greatest share of the aforementioned energy in the form of profit. And it is because it aims to abolish this slavery and release men from the "emotional plague" that the "sexual revolution" is part and parcel of "Revolution" itself.

"Capitalist morality, class morality," Reich wrote in November 1935, "are *against* sexuality and thus generate a fundamental conflict. The revolutionary movement eliminates the conflict first of all by building an ideology favorable to sex and by giving it the practical form of a new legislation and a new mode of sexual life. In other words, the authoritative social order and social repression of sexuality go hand in hand, and revolutionary 'morality' and the satisfaction of sexual needs go together."

This idea of sexual repression inspired primarily by middle-class and capitalist values was omnipresent in the great movement of the Sixties and Seventies. Money and big capital were considered to be among the main natural oppressors of sex. The "evidence" was largely shared on the Left and the extreme Left. Hints of it are found in all the political literature of the time. In December 1972, for example, the weekly magazine of the (Trotskyite) Communist League, *Rouge*, published an editorial defending a teacher suspended for having allowed his students to organize a debate on Wilhelm Reich and Gabrielle Russier.[14] It concluded on this heavy doctrinal note: "If sexual repression is the centerpiece of our blasé society, still we should not overlook the social dimension of the practice of pleasure. Learning how to make love is not enough to release the bodies which capitalist society transforms into anaesthetized productive instruments."

The prevailing idea is that of a sort of permanent plot hatched by the ruling classes against the free access to pleasure of the working classes, lest they "waste" their force of labor. Behind the sexual paternalism of middle-class morality, we should expose the intentions of this "higher social stratum which, gaining control through its increased economic power, has a clear interest to repress the natural needs, which, nevertheless, in themselves, did not obstruct sociability"[15] in the least. This analysis results in throwing "suspicion" on any authoritative morality and on the mysticisms (especially the religious ones) on which they may be based. As though at the heart of all moral proselytising, since eternity, was a trick and a fundamental lie: defending class interests by passing them off as universal values.

Reich felt that the October Revolution, by releasing people from this oppression, made possible for the first time in history an extraordinary "sexual revolution" which was going to usher humanity "into an absolutely new phase of social upheavals." As a very young man (twenty years old in 1917) he was full of enthusiasm for the explosion of permissiveness which marked the first years of the Revolution. Alexandra Kollontaï was preaching and practicing free love since 1917.[16] Lenin's decrees of December, 1917, and then the first Soviet Code of 1918, recognized free unions, pure and simple divorce upon request by one of the spouses, and free access to abortion at no charge. In the revolutionary effervescence of the early days, swapping communities were formed in Moscow and all kinds of experiments were made in what was called at the time, "the new ways of life" (Novyi Byt).

This unstructured permissiveness, however, lasted only a few years. In particular it ran up against the question of juvenile delinquency and child prostitution. In 1923, Soviet political literature started to issue warnings. Weren't this unbridled sexuality and this destruction of the family going to end up legitimizing the "bourgeois vices" and diverting Communist youth from the necessary revolutionary virtue? Batkis, the director of the Institute of Social Hygiene in Moscow, published a booklet entitled *The Sexual Revolution in the Soviet Union*, in which he expressed this concern publicly: "We have reason to fear. . . that our youth, bored and disillusioned as in 1905, may turn to unrestrained eroticism. Free love in Soviet Union is not wild and unbridled libertinage, but the ideal relation of two free and independent people who love each other."

In fact, the family was soon rehabilitated. Homosexuality was dubbed "a manifestation of the cultural degeneration of the depraved bourgeoisie," and in 1934 it again became a "social crime" punishable by imprisonment. In 1936, a new Family Code was promulgated, prohibiting abortion. Better still, some of the old Bolsheviks began to promote, in the name of the Revolution, an ascetic ideal and a "desexualized" ideology which, indeed, left its imprint on all of Soviet culture from the end of the Thirties onward, right up until the end.

Hostile to what he regarded as "betrayal" of the Revolution, Reich was ejected from the Austrian Communist Party in 1930, and left Vienna. "Irresponsible politicians," he wrote, "who had promised the masses a paradise on earth, expelled us from their organization because we are defending children's and teenagers' right to natural love." As for his book, *The Sexual Revolution*, the first edition of which was published in Vienna, in 1930, by Munster Verlag, under the title *Geschlechtsreife, Enthaltsamkeit, Ehemoral* (*Sexual Maturity, Continence, Conjugal Morality*), his primary goal was to explain and denounce the failure of the USSR in this field. In 1944, he wrote, "Soviet Russia, which owes its existence to a proletarian revolution, is today reactionary in its sexual policies, while America, with its underpinnings of middle-class revolution, is at least progressive in its sexual policies. The social concepts of the 19th century, which are based purely on economic factors, thus no longer apply to the ideological stratification that obtains during conflicts in the 20th century."[17]

A clearer reversal could not be imagined. Curiously, however, Reich's early anti-capitalism, which took a beating from both the Soviet experience and the American "case," was confusedly picked up by his readers and disciples in the Sixties. Besides, it is the weakest link, the most contestable creed of what one might call "the ideology of permissiveness." The use of sexual morality by the dominant classes did, indeed, mark the first ages of capitalism and the writings of the first Calvinist puritans. In the ideological sense of the term, it is a problem of the 19th century which no longer has the least relevance today.[18]

A Voluptuous Christ

In more or less the same fashion, Reich's theses on religion, and especially on Judeo-Christianity, were caricatured by the same people who claimed to be building on his heritage. From the beginning, it is clear that Wilhelm Reich considered "religious mysticism" to be one of the principal factors promoting repressive sexual morals. However, unlike the very anti-religious Freud (*Die Zukunft einer Illusion* [*The Future of an Illusion*]), before his exile in America Reich spent very little time denouncing the Gospel; an allusion here or there, an indirect reference, nothing more.

In the Fifties, Reich, living in Maine, expressed a true fascination with Christianity — a fascination that was somewhat unanticipated for such a resolute scientist. In *The Murder of Christ*, published in 1953 (four years before his death), he outlines a carnal and eroticized Jesus embodying a kind of revolutionary sexual plenitude. Enrolling Christ in his combat, Reich makes of him a splendid embodiment of "the orgastic power" pushed to the extreme, and invites mankind to release its pent-up vital (i.e. sexual) energy. As for the murder of Christ, it heralded the (temporary) triumph of the social, economic and political forces aiming to maintain their domination.

At the eyes of his admirers, Reich merely takes Christ at his word, while denouncing the imposture of Catholicism which "relies on the mystification of Christ, his disincarnation, his complete [and false] spiritualization." This vision of Christ as a vagrant, nonviolent and voluptuous, faced with the virtuous hypocrisy of the mighty, obviously appealed to the American youth of the time, and *the Murder of Christ* paradoxically became one of the founding texts of the beat movement and then the hippie movement. In his later years, Reich thus became a precursor of the New Age spirituality that is still current today.

This was a vague and pansexual spirituality, which contrasts with the intemperate hatred of Christianity and the Nietzchean-inspired atheism of some of his European heirs on the extreme left, especially the proponents of situation ethics. For example Raoul Vaneigem, who claims to be a follower of Reich, attacked Christ and Christianity with extraordinary violence which set the tone for later commentary. In his *Traité de savoir-vivre à l'usage des jeunes générations* [*Treatise on good manners for the younger generations*] (published in 1967), Vaneigem rails against "the wretched stain of religions" (p. 57), "clerical vermin," "the disgusting effigy of the man on a cross," "the stupid aureole of the militant martyr" (p. 58), and the "shadow of that crucified toad from Nazareth."[19]

This livid denunciation of Catholicism in particular and religions in general, carrying "a fecal culpability," is nothing more than an exalted version of the anti-Judeo-Christian temper of the times. If sex had been oppressed for centuries, he repeats, it is mainly because of the religious bigotry; if the flesh is still a matter of sinfulness and shame, religions are to blame, etc.. This was an extremely reductive view, an eminently contestable postulate,[20] but for the most part it was accepted.

It's not surprising that Reich's followers misrepresent his thought on this point. The American Reich of the Fifties was, in fact, sinking into a protean delusion. His evangelical neo-mysticism coexisted with a scientistic obstinacy that even his most loyal followers, even his third wife,[21] judged extravagant. Comparing his theoretical work with that of Darwin, Nietzsche, Lenin and even Aristotle, he thought he had discovered once and for all the source of vital energy and the bio-electric nature of sexuality. In his view, the aurora borealis is a gigantic cosmic orgasm from which it should be possible to collect energy, "orgon."

Having baptized his estate in Maine "Orgonon," Reich devoted himself to all sorts of idiosyncratic experiments, from hunting flying saucers to manufacturing and marketing "orgon accumulators" supposed to cure frigidity and cancer, lyric descriptions of the "oceans of galactic orgon," celestial observations using wooden cylinders, etc.. Reich, who did not believe in psychoanalysis, was in fact inspired by a strictly scientistic and biological vision of life and the cosmos. "We are revolutionary in approaching the processes of life with the methods of *natural science*, instead of taking a mechanistic, political or mystical approach," he proclaimed in November, 1944. "The discovery of orgon, which serves in living beings as a biological energy, gives our social research a solid basis in natural science."[22]

Human nature is perfectly in tune — or should be, to the greatest possible extent — with external nature. In other words, it is of utmost importance that the life of the individual should be in harmony with the great machinery of the universe. Only the biological needs, health, hygiene, and the liberation of vital energy, count. For Reich, as François George observes, "Happiness can be reached not through obedience to the social order but through subservience to the cosmic order. Similarly, reality is not defined by the laws of society, but by the great universal effusion."[23]

The Ambiguities of "Vitalism"

This naturalist intoxication, this will to be as one with "the womb of nature," the dispenser of vital energy, is not unrelated to what would later be called "deep ecology," a theory that was proposed in the United States in the late Seventies by authors such as David Ehrenfeld and James Lovelock.[24] Challenging certain postulates of the "arrogant" humanism of the Enlightenment, deep ecology invites us to recognize, in addition to human rights and sometimes even against them, the true "legal rights" of nature, trees, and mountains; rights which would be binding on us. It preaches fusion with *Gaia*, the earth as a living creature and nurturing mother. This "deep ecology," in its most extreme forms, has led to a rejection of technology, modernity, Western humanism, etc.. This is a disastrous belief that has been denounced by authors including Luc Ferry.[25]

But the cult of "sexual energy" released from inhibitions, morality and sin, vitality liberated from the limitations that Reich calls the "psychic carapace" or "emotional plague," leads above all to a more virulent Nietzchean vitalism. The optimistic confidence in biological vitality ("genital" in particular), the will to completely release it from the yokes of moralism, asceticism and religious mysticism, is part of a romantic tradition that goes back to the French and German thinkers of the counter-revolution. The celebration of sensual energy and the worship of pantheist hedonism often go hand in hand with "might makes right" and the acceptance of the "natural" inequality of men.

An important detail: it is often forgotten that that sensibility was present, and very active, in the early years of the Russian Revolution (as it is at the beginning of most revolutions). Without realizing it, the young Austrian Reich, in his Vienna years, was distantly aligned with certain Russian writers, hallucinatory chroniclers of the great Muscovite maelstrom. One may cite, for example, the literature of Boris Andreevitch Vogau, known as "Pilniak," who died in the late Thirties. Tellingly, one of his characters exclaims: "I feel that the entire Revolution smells of sexual organs!" Professor George Nivat, a specialist in Russian literature, gives a significant description of this overlooked work.

> For Pilniak (he writes), the Bolshevik Revolution was a return to healthy cruelty, with the violence of the popular horde. A torrent of blood, sweat and brutality shakes the foundation of the country, while the crust, in other words the cities, cracks sinisterly.... Pilniak's universe is above all a biological universe. The unifying thread in his

work is the glorification of animal energy. The revolution liberates this energy, which is both sexual and
physiological. . . . It is return of the happy and muscular
animal, it comes from the steppes and the wandering
nomads, it smells the absinthe of the steppes. . . . The
anarchistic new Russia thus is symbolically built on top
of the old legendary Russia. Sorcery, rapes, orgies, peas-
ant rites of pagan origin are used to create the backdrop
for this intentionally disordered chronicle. At the end,
the desecrated monastery burns in the middle of the
night, the commune disappears, and only the impenetrable, indestructible pagan and country of Russia remains.[26]

The orgiastic and blasphemous neo-Christianity of Reichian
thought is astonishingly analogous to the work of another Russian
writer, Vassili Rozanov (1856-1919). A weird member of the Orthodox
church, avid fan of Slavonic songs and liturgy, Rozanov hated Christ
and hated the preaching of sexual abstinence and fasting, but venerated
the powerful harmony of the Russian Church. He regretted, however,
that the radical young priests no longer knocked up their wives, and he
proposed that in the future nuptial deflorations should take place inside the orthodox churches!

"More Christian than sacrilegious," Nivat notes, "Rozanov sows
all his writings with his hatred of Christ's 'sterility.' You never see him
take up a zither, he wrote in *Apocalypse de notre temps*, and sing and pray
like David. Christ condemns the flesh, and the world; the only real
prayer he came up with is 'cold' and unmusical. There is no 'terrestrial
seed,' he knows nothing of fecundity. Moreover, he is the Son, and the
son is an incomplete Father, the son is a refusal of fatherhood. . . . Rozanov was haunted by the *degeneration* that he felt Christianity had
caused. What is divine in man is his sexuality. Every religion had celebrated man's genitals. With Christ, it is the voluntary eunuch which is
proclaimed superior."[27]

Rozanov was an important influence on the Russian movement to
personalize Christianity, embodied by authors like Berdiaev and Boul-
gakov. His representation of sexuality is, indeed, a reference to God.
"Sexuality's connection with God," he wrote in *À l'écart*, is greater than
the connection of intelligence with God and even the moral conscience

with God."[28]

With the passing of time, the conscious or unconscious relation-ship of Wilhelm Reich's heirs of 1968 to this vitalistic sensitivity ap-pears more than disconcerting. One finds, for example, Situationists who readily proclaim themselves adherents of Reich (and Nietzsche), and who make unambiguous proclamations such as this, by Raoul Vaneigem:

> Taken over by the irrepressible passion to enjoy, there is no one who does not find in himself an equally violent urge to satisfy his pleasures and to break the reins that restrain him. With the revolution, the living will surge toward life. And there is no way that such a tidal wave will leave intact the stucco walls of the hierarchy, the State, commercial civilization.... This commercial society which has endured every form of terrorism and intellec-tual revolution — I submit that it will not resist the warriors of all-out pleasure, the creators of the new in-nocence, people who don't even want to know if there is a death against which they are not inoculated by the violence of life.[29]

Original Sin or "Strong Blood?"

It is on this vague and perilous border separating the austere Vi-ennese Freudo-Marxism of the Twenties and the torrential vitalism of the October Revolution that we find all of Wilhelm Reich's work and his heritage. After he broke off with Freud and rejected the idea of psy-choanalysis, which he considered to be "repressive," Reich located him-self at the bloody intersection of two great ideological and cultural cur-rents. Michel Foucault, without quoting Reich, frequently mentioned the cardinal importance, in psychoanalysis, of the reference to the *law* (which was precisely what Reich found objectionable) — an impor-tance based on the resistance this caused between fascistic psycho-analysis and vitalism.

"It is the political honor of psychoanalysis, or at least the part of it that makes the most sense," wrote Foucault, "to have suspected (since its inception, that is, since it split off from the neuropsychiatry of de-generation) that within these mechanisms there might be a power, proliferating irremediably, which aimed to control and manipulate the everyday aspects of sexuality. Hence the Freudian effort (no doubt in reaction to the growing racism which was its contemporary) to give sexuality the principle of the law — the law of alliance, of prohibited consanguinity, the Father-Sovereign, in short *to convoke around desire all of the old order of power*. With that, psychoanalysis had to be (with a few exceptions) theoretically and practically opposed to Fascism.[30]"

Reich challenged any "law" or interdict in relation to sexual matters. He rejected the very idea, present already in Plato's writings, of a necessary regulation of the force of desire, of that tyrannical *energeia*, a regulation that was necessary not because it was "bad" in itself but quite simply because it is carried to excess. Rejecting the *law*, Reich ventures to the brink of the territories occupied by the dubious apologists of pagan hedonism and vital space.

Let us be more precise. Admittedly, it would be absurd to show Reich sympathizing with Nazism. He even devoted one of his books, and not of the least of them,[31] to denouncing the close ties between Hitlerian Fascism and sexual repression, of which the Hitlerian Fascism was supposedly a sadistic expression. He insisted (without being really convincing) that racism and Nazi anti-Semitism are primarily the translation of fantasies caused by sexual inhibition. However, the fact remains that two passages (at least) of *The Sexual Revolution*, written in November 1935, two passages never analyzed by his exegetes, show a passing empathy for Nazi vitalism. Should they be considered merely anecdotal?

> The National-Socialist ideology (he writes), is built on a rational core, expressed in the slogan of 'fidelity to blood and the land,' which gives the reactionary movement exceptional momentum. In practice, on the other hand, National-Socialism continuously adheres to the social forces that oppose the principle of revolutionary action, to wit, the unification of society, nature and technology. It clings to the principle of class-based society, which has by no means been eliminated by the people's illusion of unity, and to the private ownership of the means of production, by no means eliminated by the idea of 'public property.' In its ideology national-socialism expresses, mystically, that which constitutes the rational

43

core of the revolutionary movement: the idea of a class-less society and a life in harmony with nature.

A little further, he states more clearly,

> Vegetative life irrupted again with the neo-paganism that is German national-socialism. The vegetative impulse was better absorbed by Fascistic ideology than by the Church, and was removed from the realm of the supernatural. In this respect, the National-Socialist mysticism of the 'strength of blood' and 'loyalty to the land' was progress, compared to the old Christian idea of original sin; however, it was stifled by a new wave of mysticism and reactionary policies. Here, too, the affirmation of life is turned into a negation of life, in the form of ascetic ideologies of self-sacrifice, allegiance and duty. Nonetheless, one cannot prefer the theory of original sin to that of the 'strength of blood,' which will have to be guided in the right direction.[32]

In other terms, in these lines from 1935 (but read again and approved by Reich in March, 1949), if in addition he reproaches Stalinism for its "sexual moralism," he reproaches Nazism only for its "practice of class politics." This extraordinary confusion of values is less illogical than one might think. Indeed, given the repressive policies toward sexual minorities of the later stages of the Hitlerian regime, its hatred for permissiveness and its lyrical pro-birth policies for the Aryan family, we tend to forget that it was not that way from the start. In the Twenties and Thirties, national-socialism still presented itself as a subversive force, opposed to petit-bourgeois morality, eager to fight the family in the name of the community of blood in search of vital space, to establish, under the aegis of the State, eugenics affiliations (the famous *lebensborn*), etc.. Moreover, it was the German left that was, at the time, denouncing amorality and in particular the homosexual sympathies which certain Nazis expressed. (A frequent Leftist comment, which Reich attributed to Gorky, was: "Get rid of all the homosexuals, and Fascism will disappear.")

In an astonishing testimony, published on November 24, 1934 in the Prague magazine *Europäische Hefte*, the writer Klaus Mann attacks the German Left, which he considers heinous and repressive toward homosexuals, in the name of antifascism.

"In the Soviet Union," he wrote, "recently promulgated legislation subjects homosexuality to heavy sentences. That is a surprise, and one wonders on what logic and what morals a socialist government can justify curtailing the rights and defaming a specific group of people whose 'guilt' rests on particular inclinations which were given to it by nature. [But among us, too, I note] an aversion towards anything that is homoerotic, an aversion which reaches an intense degree in most of the antifascist milieux and almost all the socialist milieux. We are not far from equating homosexuality with Fascism. Hence, in antifascist newspapers, we are starting to see the words 'assassins and pederasts' together as often as we see 'traitors to the people and Jews' in the Nazi papers."[33]

Coincidentally, at the beginning of the Thirties, after the Röhm affair and the Night of Long Knives in Germany, the Soviet press undertook an incredibly violent campaign against homosexuality, which seemed to them the sign of "degeneration of the fascist bourgeoisie." The Soviet journalist Koltsov, very influential at the time, wrote a series of articles in which he evoked "the cuties at Goebbels' Ministry for Propaganda" and "the sexual orgies in fascist countries." It was common in the USSR to make ironical comments about the homosexuality of certain personalities close to the Nazis, such as actor Gustaf Gründgens.

Of course, that does not negate the later persecution of homosexuals by the Nazis. A directive from the "central command station of the Reich" explained during the war years how to detect this "deviance" among the Wehrmacht soldiers. An exhibition organized in Berlin in June 1997, recalling a century of homosexual militancy in Germany, estimated that 100,000 homosexuals were persecuted during the twelve years of Nazism, of which approximately 50,000 were condemned to death, or deported.[34]

A Tragic Contradiction

This ambivalence toward "sexual liberation" and hedonism with Nietzchean overtones is truly the blind spot in Reichian thought, the one that that his exegetes have preferred not to see. It is far from being a simple matter of a difficulty of interpretation. We would have plenty of exegeses of Reich's writings if they did not appear, today still, to re-veal a tragic contradiction — contradiction which continues to haunt the era. To liberate desire, to reject the old order and its morality, to dismiss the interdicts, to enjoy without obstacles and law: yes, the uto-pia was beautiful.

The error was in believing it could be had for free.

CHAPTER 3

THE RUBBER WALL

Thirty years later, we are at the same ramparts, still heckling and raising our fists. Prompt to mobilize the people against any "reactionary" backsliding, we continue to denounce "the moral order" which still threatens to make a comeback. We condemn the censure of the State, public hypocrisy and outraged virtue as valiantly as ever. We continue to fight heroically against the famous "taboos" and injurious silences. We never tire of pointing a finger at the castrating priests, the Petainist family policies and the secret inquisitors. In magazines, television, radio and movies, on every front, we mechanically prolong the battle for the liberation of desire; we remain, in the face of all the opposition, the zealots of pleasure, satisfaction, radiant voluptuousness.

The battle is gratifying. But does it still make sense?

Before answering, we should broaden the framework. For thirty years, the sexual revolution was more or less identified with Revolution itself, of which it was supposed to be a part. Thirty years! Time has passed in Western societies and nothing is the same as it was before. Today, nothing is clear-cut when we have to agree on a definition of historical progress or even of social justice. Since the collapse of the Red messianism and the fall of the Berlin Wall, we are all engaged in pure "activity," less concerned with final outcomes and often indifferent to *meaning* itself. The concern for being productive, the liberal consensus, the paramount power of money, cautious hoarding and disillusioned *Weltanschaung*: such is, roughly speaking, the new landscape. As for the rest. . . Temporarily at least, ideas offering collective plans seem to have disappeared in the West. The vision of the future has been fractured, immediacy is the order of the day and the greater market triumphs. We have accepted this pleasant day-to-day cynicism that we call realism. To hell with illusions! Yesterday's utopias have left nothing but a little heap of ashes which we politely salute when we pass by. As for the Revolution, we are especially proud to have learned — once and for all — that it was only a purveyor of death. We will not be taken in with it again.

Come on. In this world, the rich are no longer afraid and the poor have gotten used to living without hope. We are not really thinking about plans for a better world. In truth, historical hope itself seems, for the moment, to be an obsolete concept. Hope and will: nothing could be more alien to the present path of history than these two old claims of the public spirit. Change? Reform? Transform? Obsolete terms that make us smile. Without really acknowledging it, we have accepted that the world is *essentially* run by forces over which we have little control: the financial markets, international trade, intangible networks. Everywhere we turn, ungovernable forces limit our ambitions and take the steam out of our "voluntarist" inclinations [*ed. note*: i.e., the belief that our will determines our life]. Think what this means; this is a fundamental change in our mental landscape.

These are no longer the days when we dream of changing the world, but of making concessions. An individual's or a group's value is no longer determined by its ability to stand up to circumstances, but *its greater or lesser ductility and willingness to compromise*. To accept the world as it is; to learn how to direct our energy within the given framework; to give preference to reasonable flexibilities and to modest reason: the new Western *doxa* is unambiguous. It says to be of good heart in the face of misfortune. . . If we still want to be happy with ourselves, we must realize that that comes from playing by the world's rules better than others have done. That is how merit is measured these days. In earlier times, we hoped to re-shape the world. Today, we are more proud of our capitulations — clear evidence of perspicacity — than we were of our revolts. Yes, time has been turned inside out. Nowadays it is the dismal virtue of adapting to "constraints" that is promoted. What attests to our keen perception is a constant, weak assent to things as they are. And that is not all.

We are not far from believing, in the final analysis, that the history of the world itself is determined more by obscure anthropological or commercial forces than by the ingenuous human will. We are a hair's breadth from recklessly giving up the option of political plans, active representation, making decisions. If we already see the idea of revolution as nothing more than an amusing cause for nostalgia, then simple and modest democracy (the ambition to collaborate in shaping one's own destiny) little by little declines, and without anyone taking much notice. This insidious transition will lead us irresistibly from democracy toward the strict market economy, while allowing us to delude ourselves that the two terms are synonymous. The funeral we are about to attend is, essentially, that of politics, the common good, the collective will.

Is Sex Leftist?

Thank God, in this desert of ashes we still have the sexual revolution, shining like a lantern.

It is in this context of democratic dereliction that we clutch at that exception. In the realm of sex (and only in the realm of sex) belief in the possibility of social progress still valiantly stands against the weight of history and the tyranny of community pressures. Here, individual combat goes on as it did in the past. In this matter, nothing has changed; nothing has been proven wrong, or distorted or corrupted in thirty years. Neither revolutionary rhetoric, the devastating force of Utopia, nor the ontological maleficence of the established order has changed over time when it comes to pleasure. This conviction, or this illusion, gives us enough energy to still confront the enemies of progress. They shall not pass! We are surely living in a dream world, but also in the most reassuring libertarian continuum. Here, at last, we think, is a rampart that there is no question of giving up, a trench we will never evacuate, even under the united pressure of all the puritans in the world. Pan-sexualism and its revolution look to be the ultimate refuge of utopia, the everlasting revival of a heroic combat that has ceased everywhere else. Everywhere else, you say, compromise and docility reign? Too bad, because here, at least, the spirit of rebellion can still triumph. "No!" to the moral order!

This disenchantment is what really gives the sexual movement its driving force. Since we have given in to the prevailing order everywhere else, this combative obstinacy seems all the more precious, as if sex were the last metaphor of the insurrection. At any rate, that is the sort of role we assign to it: the final refuge and last landmark, when all the other ideological "traces" have been lost.

Lost? Let's take a look. Capitalism, with apologies to economic liberalism, has become a modernistic plan; yesterday's egalitarian aspiration has become an "idiotic" anachronism, unaffordable due to lack of growth and even suspected of being a disguise for totalitarian intentions. The public spirit, let's say the sense of the common good, is considered out of date; and the welfare state is being phased out by the modernity of the large market. With the new classifications, it is harder and harder to see which side is which and whether a position belongs to the Left or the Right. Public or private? Equality or competition? Poverty or unemployment? Progress or conservatism? It would take a genius to distinguish clearly among all these subjects. We may not have arrived at "the end of History," but its way forward has certainly been blocked. Witness our new and rather comical practice: "governmental" cohabitation. It is not only a constitutional misadventure of the Fifth Republic, but the perfect symbol of compromising consensus which, by default, defines the end of the 20th century.

Have we lost our bearings? Have we run out of ideas? Yes, we usually answer, and then add that the "sexual revolution" is an exception that shines all the brighter for being unique. Sex, that will always belong to the Left! If social progressivism has been lost in the fogs of post-communism and the ambiguities of globalization, there still remains, on that front, "a moral left," that is to say legitimately antiracist, porno-libertarian and anarcho-permissive.

Let's not be more ironical than necessary. The theatrical swirl around sexual "victories" is generally comical, but it testifies all the same to a persistent attachment (vague, even confused, even distorted) to the concept of progress. It shows that we reject an across-the-board capitulation to the allegedly natural order which, as we know, always reverts to that of the jungle. It expresses our refusal to *completely* believe in the myth of the constant return of that which we see is always a sinister "reversion." (This is easily identifiable as reactionary rhetoric[1]: nothing in the world really changes; the best ones win; eternity takes its revenge sooner or later; whatever is meant to be, will be; that which was will return, patriarchy just like everything else, etc.) And then, it is true that certain victories are worth defending. And it's also true that we are surrounded by regressive temptations (puritan or chauvinist, homophobic or hypocritical, etc.), which encourage us not to let down our guard. Just as some ten or a hundred Bonapartists may survive somewhere in the republic, five hundred Cossacks in the Russian steppes or a few faithful Cathari five centuries after the Albigensian Crusade, we still have in our societies some residual prudishness and a few handfuls of imbeciles who denounce "masturbation, which make you deaf" or who are anxious to send women back to the kitchen. It's a constant of history: in every era and every location, people feel threatened enough to justify remaining on guard.

So they say.

Morality Jokes

But even so! The constant chanting about the "moral order" that supposedly threatens our freedom to enjoy, rattling sabers day after day at imaginary foes, the tirades, the calls for resistance, the cardboard barricades, it all adds up to a strange form of paranoia. The historian Maurice Agulhon was rightly astonished to think that we could still confuse "the moral order" proclaimed by Mac-Mahon in 1873 with today's prudish regression, without laughing.[2] First, because this oft-cited historical reference is a misinterpretation (Mac-Mahon used the adjective "moral" in opposition to "material;" it had nothing to do with a moralistic plan in the modern sense of the term). And above all because the true state of our societies makes such a concern risible.

Do we take such ostentation seriously? Take a look around. Is it really order that threatens us? Look at our dislocated societies, the ambient violence, pervasive cynicism, sex for sale everywhere, debased children, families in distress and carnage shown on prime time. Moral order? Really?

It is true that denouncing "the moral order" is not just a joke. It is also a winning strategy. With this, we may enjoy both the privileges of freedom and the merits of dissidence. We benefit from the permissive conveniences of the era without giving up the symbolic gratification of revolt. We may be beneficiaries, but we are still soldiers. We benefit from the tolerance, but are "persecuted" in power; honest citizens on the whole, but resistance fighters in our imagination. By condemning "the return of the moral order," one can, without too much effort or inconvenience, reap the rewards of the obedient consumer and the prestige of the outlaw as well.

And it gets better. In the always open competition to be certified as "modern," this is an investment that costs nothing but generates a handsome return. Condemn, castigate the moralizing imbeciles and take on the "critics;" that's all you have to do. It's a Leftist paradise. And it doesn't matter what positions you take — or don't take: vehement denunciations of morality is like gold in the bank. Then you can just as make ironical comments about the inevitability of wage injustice, merrily sacrifice oneself to cash, idolize corporations, hang around with the rich and powerful, deride solidarity, mock the common man, be comfortable with racism and all sorts of things. The combat against "the moral order" ensures your virtue, and praising orgies will prove you have the modern spirit.

Let us remember how, during the Eighties, the general enthusiasm for money, the increasing social injustices, the pathetic disenfranchisement of the unemployed, the shipwreck of public morals were dissimulated behind a façade of "social standards." Certainly, it is legitimate to protest — when essential — against the oppression of homosexuals, of libertine artists, and school girls forced to wear headscarves, or of one or another pornocrat having a spot of trouble with the tax department. But only on the condition of not using these protests of solidarity to justify a broader indifference to oppression in general. Oppression of the poor, for example. Which is ongoing. . .

The Delights of Pugilism

We should keep in mind one cardinal notion: that it is precisely because it presents all these conveniences that the over-dramatized resistance to "the moral order" is so meticulously staged, repeated and perpetuated, even when it has become meaningless. It's as though everyone was striving to create a spectacular confrontation between the camp of happiness and the camp of mortification, between the happy advocates of pleasure and the sorrowful folks who despise sex; between the joyful disorder of desire and the icy orderliness of morality. This creates a *pas de deux* as well choreographed as any ballet, with a very well-known book, going over the same steps, re-playing the same verses, harping on accepted themes. Each camp then appears accessory to a duel that has been rigged, but which, with the help of amnesia, is re-ignited at every expression of opinion.

If a film poster aims yet again to be sexo-blasphemous, if a movie adds yet again to the subject of fetishism, necrophilia[3] or incest, if a novelist goes so far that he seems to be out of bounds: inevitably, the same pugilism will crop up according to a well-rehearsed script. The moral and the immoral will play off each other; puritan excess and per-missive irresponsibility will match each other word for word; the slightly ridiculous solemnity of the wrath will be met with insults of exaggerated insolence. It is all predictable, tiresomely defined in ad-vance, mouths running on with no new thoughts to express. Above all, everything will be *standard*. It's been going on this way for years; we think we are debating, month after month, the great affair of morality, while in fact we are missing the real issues by a long shot.

"This is how not to discuss things in a democracy," is Albert O. Hirschman's ironical assessment. "Even in the most 'advanced' democ-racies, many debates are only (to borrow a page from Clausewitz) 'the continuation of civil war by other means.' Today's politics offers too many examples of 'democratic' debates whose true goal is only to find the argument that will shut up the other side."[4]

Let us add, to be fair, that comfort and mental laziness are present in each camp.

On the side of the moralizers: prudish nostalgia a "niche" where one can comfortably drowse while dreaming of the golden age of sub-missive women, pure love songs and virginal children. Calling for a re-turn to the holy principles and the decencies of yesteryear, with raised eyebrows, is a way of removing oneself from contradictions of this cen-tury, to forget the passage of time, contraceptives, pay-per-view porn shows, drag queens and the Internet. They get carried away with their own arguments, and try to forget that these are empty words.

In the other corner we have the libertines, whose comfortable posture is not so different. Here, they can scarcely stand to feel so gen-erous and so noble. And at so little cost! Point a finger at the "reaction" that's underway, drape yourself in principles, attack anything that threatens the fundamental truths of bodily joy, the innocence of pleas-ure, the thrill of bending the rules — it's all self-flattery, without giving up anything in exchange. And it's an easy win: the wrinkled old prude will be the bad guy compared to the defender of free desire. Fighting this way, ostentatiously, you don't have to deal with any of the underlying contradictions. (What about the family? Where does ethics begin? Is it necessary to challenge the principle of relationships? Does fidelity make sense? And so on). We insist on the fine disinterestedness of the pleas. No one is ever asked to analyze the precise consequences of his choices or the social and political implications of his preferences. People just paint a seductive picture of a lifestyle revolution, freedom of desire, enjoying one's body, and what all — but too vaguely to be questioned. In other words, it's nothing but beautiful images and compelling words.[5]

So, each camp finds what it was looking for in today's moral polemic. This objective complicity between the adherents of permissiveness and those favoring repression frees everyone from prosaic realities. When reality embarrasses us, let us escape into words! This timorous evasion is evoked very clearly in this reflection by a Jesuit professor of philosophy:

> Doesn't fascination with sexuality-genitalia ensnare the declared enemies of the 'moral disorder' of our time as much as the partisans of a heightened 'liberation' of images and manners? Paradoxically, sensibilities that are as foreign as possible to each other share the same problem: fear, an overwhelming terror, with regard to everything that sexuality implies. To refuse to see (to castrate reality) or to force to see (to exceed reality), is to recognize (consciously or unconsciously) that it is hard to manage this reality and what it implies as far as the responsibility of the subject and the group. Where reduction dominates, whether in the guise of denial (human beings are like angels) or provocation (human beings are like animals), the obsession takes over the entire field of consciousness, making discernment impossible.[6]

As we know, the absence of discernment can make life more comfortable! It is because they are so much at home with these convenient arguments that the protagonists of "the sexual debate," tired old actors who know every theatrical trick in the book, do not want to leave. In fact, it's been thirty years and they are standing there still!

A Hidden Knowledge?

This vain rehashing is done on purpose. It is not (always) through carelessness that we come to loggerheads on key questions. We do it voluntarily. Consider the art of ontological caution, that elegant dodging, that way of continually turning the questions away from the essential, the subtle penchant for the insignificant. Beyond the boastings of the sympathizers and the protestations of tolerance, these techniques prevent us from broaching any of the complicated problems which used to fire the Greeks with so much passion: a thousand ways of organizing common rules and of designating which actions would be prohibited; the best method to distinguish clearly (and then internalize) what was licit and what was illicit; how to come closer to the ideal balance between each individual's aspirations and the cohesion of all. In short, the concern of building this elaborate human-wrought "thing" that we call a civilization.

Would we blush to use that word?

Nonetheless, that is what this is all about. Every human society must face a certain number of biological constants, social constraints (procreation and raising children) and dangers that lurk on the outskirts of desire, violence first of all. Through its interdicts, every society expresses its "own culture," that is, a specific, random, and always subject to question and always under discussion, way of combining the contradictory requirements of pleasure and social discretion, a particular way handling individual violence or the risks of breakdown of the group. Beyond magical thoughts and symbolic configurations, interdicts inevitably carry a hidden knowledge about the group and its survival. We should take a look at what this represents.[7]

Nothing of these minimal requirements was retained in the great permissive tumult of the last three decades. On the contrary, if there was any question that no one wanted to talk about anymore, it was that of the interdict in itself. It was no longer a question of examining it, disputing it, redefining it or controlling it but simply to do away with it. The goal of the Reichian Utopia, examined in the preceding chapter, had indeed been "unsurpassable."[8] It was stated in few words: no more interdicts at all!

Can a society live for long, that way? The fact is that this question has been eluded with obstinacy and even brusqueness. However, it was not always easy. Reality is stubborn. What is striking, in retrospect, is the confused panic that was felt when in spite of everything there emerged such a problem that literally created a short-circuit between two antagonistic elements of modern individualism (the rejection of prohibitions and the protection of human rights). Consider, for example, the questions of feminism and rape, incest, AIDS, sexual harassment and pedophilia. Gems of Jesuitism were brought forth, then, to deal with these problems "locally," without — ever — implying they might be "global." An extraordinary conceptual exercise in compartmentalization which recalled the constancy with which, for some fifty years, various persecutions of "flaws" of Communism were denounced without anyone ever questioning the dogma itself.

Thus we learned to castigate the timid complacency of the legal apparatus with regard to rapists, and the ribald scorn that might be shown for sexually harassed women, but without ever worrying about the obsessional eroticization of society or the pollicitation[9] of pleasure that was making our collective life hysterical. We were trying to deny, beyond any probability, that the two could be related. To recognize this linkage would have been a concession to the "reactionaries."

Pedophilia: A Sacrificial Lamb

The paranoia of the public discourse came to a head with pedophilia, as we saw above. One will long remember the sudden and clamorous media campaigns — of the holders of images of pornography pedophile. We can hardly forget the image of the teachers, priests and pediatricians suddenly yanked out of obscurity, thrown before the news cameras and designated as "monsters" for having bought some videos through the mail. One will especially recall in report the suicide of several of these middle-aged alleged pedophiles who were thrown to the wolves of social vindication overnight.[10] Nor will we forget the excesses of a press bent on a lynching, obviously in a hurry to sell papers by citing the "horror," the "crime" and the "traffic in human flesh," so many sacrifices appeasing so many gods. First, we couldn't do enough to compensate for our past complacency; then we couldn't *blame* repression enough so that we could avoid thinking about the rest.

Obviously, rejection of pedophilia was not the problem at this moment, certainly not. Essentially, our societies used the furious exhibition of culprits, with all possible haste, to continue "beating about

56

the bush" with regard to morals. The problem was that our eyes were obstinately closed to the context of pedophile crimes, for fear of giving fuel to the "reactionaries." Pornography has become a domestic art in the commercial society, televised hard core takes little notice of legal limits, the past reflects our frightening laxity and the present shows our myopia. This great round-up, vociferous but strictly circumscribed as to the suspects, recalled a periodic ritual of the old communist regimens: the sacrifice of a few corrupt apparatchiks and unlucky individuals, a sacrifice which made it possible to save the system. This open hunt for pedophiles and the few tardy polemics that it caused similarly exposed a corner of the hidden terror that secretly justified the enterprise, and the temporary relief from these repressions that it was counting on.

Was the question of the interdict thus reduced to a question of age and marital status? Ha! Fifteen, sixteen or seventeen and a half years old: one was a case of legitimate hedonism, one was a contemptible crime. Just a few months apart. We set up such a neat arithmetical divide between good and evil. The great moral distress was turned into a question of the calendar. Finally! Let the festival continue! To shy away from an unpalatable question (what sexual morals are right for what kind of society?), we quickly perfected a new form of double talk and slippery speech. The language of nitpicking repression on one side (Haul in every possible suspect! Into the slammer with every teacher who touches a student!); Nietzchean nonsense and permissive dogma on the other (Long live televised porn! Three cheers for nightclubbing and wife swapping!). Sententious admonitions in the morning (Protect the purity of childhood! Shame on bestial desire!) and permissive protestations in the evening (Down with the moral order!). This pathological double language has only one true function: to elude. By this means our societies, which at the same time repress and tolerate everything, leave the police to handle the dilemmas that they can't deal with anymore, cowardly fleeing the very thing they think they are facing up to directly: sex and the questions that go with it. Pierre Manent notes the paradox of this contemporary cowardice:

> Our societies are perhaps the least erotic ever. Appearances can be misleading. But the very fact that we are so concerned to say everything, to show everything and to look at everything — without blushing in the least —

proves that instead of looking at Eros such as it is, rather we flee. We cannot simply look at Eros 'such as it is.' It is impossible to find this neutral place between desire and the law, and decency, from which we would contemplate the phenomenon objectively. What we do, is to cast out a net of abstractions — 'facts' and 'sexual rights' which women's magazines so enthusiastically promote every week — which gives us a fictitious sense of control and allows us to derive a satisfaction that has nothing to do with the carnal, but which is our greater pleasure: that of feeling superior to all the worlds that preceded ours, because our science, our 'realism about life' has triumphed over the prejudices which controlled our forebears. Every era is a slave to its conventions. And ours must be the worst in this respect, if only by its claim to have overcome all conventions.[11]

The Time of the Plagues

But it was concerning AIDS and the means of protecting oneself that the ambivalence of the public discourse reached the heights of nonsense. This time, it was a question of life or death. The shattering outbreak of AIDS, all the more terribly palpable since it bore the faces and names of sick friends had a profoundly upsetting effect on far more aspects of life than we originally realized. To assess our later misconceptions, let's start by remembering the particular cultural context of the emerging epidemic, that of the early Eighties. Initially ascribed only to homosexuals ("the gay cancer"), poorly understood, initially, in its pathology and its propagation and thus giving birth to fantastical fears of contagion (through sweat, saliva, etc.), the disease immediately fed a moralizing reaction that bordered on hysteria.

The televangelists of the American moral majority, as we know, saw the emergence of AIDS as a providential sign announcing the end of the general concupiscence. They interpreted it as a "divine" warning addressed to the guilty modern city, the new Sodom of lust, that was promised punishment. More precisely, they saw it as the means to justify *a posteriori* the anthropological and religious interdicts concerning sodomy, menstrual blood, infidelity in love, etc..

This wave of moralizing that washed over the United States and, to a lesser extent, Europe, was targeted mainly on the homosexual community that had only just been freed from opprobrium and was beginning to benefit from a social recognition that was as recent as it was fragile.[12] Homosexuals were again pointed out, made to feel guilty, and ostracized. The sociologist-historian Michael Pollack, author of many works on the question (and who died himself of AIDS at the age of 43, in 1991), described the apocalyptic atmosphere of 1982-1986 and homosexuals' subsequent fear. "Even in commentaries that try not to preach, AIDS seems to be the end of this time of freedom, and the end of a certain homosexual lifestyle."[13]

This repressive climate of denunciations was comparable to the collective responses recorded in history upon any sudden appearance of a similar health threat. At the time of the great plagues of the 14th century, for example, minority groups (Jews, witches, sodomites) were isolated and persecuted as supposedly being responsible for the plague.[14] This was even more pronounced in the case of diseases directly attributed to sexuality, for instance when syphilis spread to in France the beginning of the 16th century, under the name of "the disease of Naples," and fostered the moral clamping down that had been started by the Catholic counter-reformation. Likewise, when great epidemics of syphilis devastated old China, at the beginning of the 16th century and then toward 1630, causing a renewed prudishness for some and a frantic search for pleasure among others.[15] Thus also — in a far less famous episode — when, at the end of 18th century, the strange disease *crystalline* appeared in France as a scourge of homosexuals. It resulted in pustules, filled with a transparent fluid, in the areas of the foreskin or the anus, and seemed to be caused by contact with sperm or blood. The doctors were not allowed to treat it. *Crystalline* was used to justify, in particular, the puritan severity of late period of the Revolution.[16]

It was in this same climate of moral reaction or sexual counter-revolution that AIDS had made its debut in Western societies. Fear that it would be used as an alibi for the backlash set the tone of the public discourse, and for a long time. It encouraged homosexual organizations, and the Left as a whole, to deny the severity of the risk. Such a repressive fantasy should not be taken at face value, it was thought. This widespread but irresponsible attitude remained in place some ten or twelve years later, as evidenced by the violent reactions that Frederic Martel caused, in 1996, in militant homosexual circles when he wrote,

"In the Eighties, all the rallying points identified with homosexuals (associations, newspapers, institutions) and claiming to protect them against society paradoxically (perhaps I should say *tragically*) misled homosexuals as to the reality of the epidemic which threatened them."[17]

Threat of a puritanical backlash on one side, denial of the risk on the other: the challenge of AIDS, we now see, was not a matter of concern only in terms of medicine and health. It set in motion a whole symbolic apparatus. Some (sometimes in good faith and without dispensing excessive sermons) were almost pleased that "a warning" was given against the permissiveness of the Seventies. Others, by contrast, undertook with maniacal care to see to it that AIDS would change none of what one could call the "sexual gains" of recent years. On both sides, it was suspected that the appearance of AIDS and the urgency of organizing ways to prevent its proliferation were going to call into question the primacy of individualism and sexual freedom, i.e. the very heart of Western modernity.

This gave rise to fantastic circumlocutions that had to be observed even while working to reign in the disease.

"Medical Pornography"

For the spirit of the time, the symbolic challenge was no trivial matter. First there was the question of relearning (how outrageous!) to pair the idea of death with that of pleasure; of reinjecting the concept of fate, infection and morbidity into the heart of hedonistic love; of promoting a program of prevention based on prudence without, for all that, limiting erotic imagination and promiscuity (inseparable from the idea of the new permissiveness). AIDS, in a word, dramatized (while at the same time caricaturing) the pseudo-debate on sexuality. Death, now, was invoked as a principal witness. And by both sides.

Then a strange and morbid symmetry developed. To compensate for the unfairness of the Right's talk about "AIDS-as-punishment," the victims were (somewhat bizarrely) glorified. Those who asserted that freely chosen homosexual "deviance" was to blame for the disease (in short, "they were asking for it"), were opposed by the quasi-Christ-like figures of HIV-positive victims of collective indifference, medical denial and state failure. (Take, for example, the emblematic declaration of a member of Act Up cited by Michael Pollack: "I was contaminated two years ago, and the government is responsible for it."[18]) AIDS patients and those who were HIV-positive were sometimes ostracized with a hateful cruelty; sometimes transformed into emblematic — and heroic — victims, "oppressed" by it is not quite clear just whom.

On one side, against a background of anti-homosexual hatred and indifference for the victims, a medical tragedy was transformed into an alibi for regression. On the other, AIDS patients (and even those who contaminated them) were discharged from any individual responsibility, and even from any notion of mistaken imprudence, and were presented as pure victims of destiny. The erroneous repressiveness was mirrored by its inverse, that is, by the acceptance of individual irresponsibility. One was not even accountable for his own imprudence and the choices he had made. Given the immanence of the plague, the freedom of behavior in love and its corollary, personal responsibility, were both dissolved in the same vague innocence. This disease, unlike cancer, Hepatitis B or cardiovascular trouble, was charged with abstract meaning. It was no longer mainly a medical but an ideological issue.

The psychoanalyst Tony Anatrella (who is also a priest) correctly observed, "Thus a true social dramaturgy of AIDS was created little by little. There emerged a medical clergy, a militant movement and a propaganda system based on guilt and denunciation, a processional and media liturgy, and finally a doctrine that skillfully shifted the blame inherent in sexuality onto symbolic scapegoats."[19]

These quarrels bordered on the nutty when it came to mobilizing the prevention campaign. The use, acceptance, and promotion of the condom, its distribution to minors, and how it was marketed threw Western societies into a frenzy of quarrelsome eloquence that would make us laugh if it weren't a matter of life and death.

It is true that everything about this business was ambiguous. The need for the most effective possible prevention campaign justified, initially, a public discourse that was precise, concrete, instructive and directing as regards sexuality. Sexual practices were described more meticulously, more precisely and in more detail than any society had never known before. The extent of the threat and the need to produce results prohibited embarrassed decency, delicate metaphors or allusive images. Not only did one have to call a spade a spade and fellatio fellatio, but it was also necessary to let go of traditional discretion, related to the age or the supposed maturity of the interested parties. From the deliberate crudeness[20] of the advertising campaigns by the distributors of condoms in schools, to the lessons given in the media or in school, the fight against AIDS generated in a few years a new "sexual language," omnipresent, obsessive, cold, clinical, proselytizing, but constantly legitimated by a crushing subtext: that of possible death.

The campaign resulted in the invention and ubiquitous promotion (even for those who did not need it) to some extent publicly funded, of a "medical pornography" that was objectively shocking but nevertheless exempt from criticism. This "medical pornography" become the very symbol of prophylactic duty and, as such, was handled by the State and addressed to all, including children and pre-teenagers. That was, indeed, without precedent in history. This led to polemics that followed the same symmetry of positions. Those who were shocked by the audacious "indecency" of the campaigns were countered by arguments on the urgency of the medical need. Grandiloquent and stereotyped reproaches were exchanged in both camps.

As just one example among dozens, in July 1995, the gay and lesbian center of Paris accused the government of having blocked the image of a homosexual couple, "suggested for the first time" (two pairs of naked men's feet were replaced, in the final version, by two pairs of men's shoes). The government was also reproached for having withdrawn from the campaign certain photographs intended to promote the practice of protected fellatio. The Socialist party observed that this affair made "the return of the moral order" disconcertingly clear, and denounced "the current prudishness."

The comments in the press were no less loaded. They regretted, whether by principle or practice, "the typically French timidity to mention these questions, when the Scandinavians and the British have already long since stopped being offended by 'real' images intended to encourage individual and collective awareness of AIDS."[21]

If There Were No Pope

Still more concretely, society found itself in the position of promulgating risk-free practices: group masturbation, interrupted fellatio, prolonged caresses or "cybersex," etc.. Without realizing it, (but how could it have been otherwise?) a resolutely functional, solipsist and hygienic approach to sexuality was being promoted; an approach that was quite out of touch with, for example, the sensibility of teenagers, who were the principal recipients of this pedagogy. The urgency thus justified a lugubrious impoverishment of the representations of pleasure, which was relegated to the status of a *function*, a gesture or, worse still, an immunization strategy.

"Now youth is being treated like a group at risk!" observed the script writer Sophie Chauveau. "But what image of sexuality do we hope to foster in young people by talking to them about sexual intercourse only in the context of AIDS? Love and pleasure, sex as an opening to the sacred? They have never heard it spoken of in those terms. Oh! It sometimes happens that they dream of it, all alone, back in their adolescent beds. But they do not find anybody to answer their distress. They are hammered by the issues of the day: AIDS, AIDS, unemployment, unemployment . . . like the tick-tick-tick of a time bomb."[22]

All those who, in the name of philosophical or religious convictions, criticized the cultural poverty of this "medical pornography" were reproached for collusion with the risk, for being accomplices of illness, even of death. It's not easy to stand up to this type of intimidation based in the name of life. It has become politically correct to assimilate love and sexuality, and the latter with fluid mechanics. All the rest is more or less related to religious bigotry. Never before has a society reduced the question of love and pleasure to such rudimentary occurrences.

By now, the condom was no longer a tool but a formidable standard. It was our answer to crime, our talisman against death, the sign of our valorous obstinacy and the proof that we refused both fatal destiny and the injunctions of moralism. It all seemed to have become simple: the proponents of latex were expressing their confidence in human progress; the others, fussbudgets and quibblers of every kind, constituted the sad army of the puritan order, the proven accomplices of the epidemic crime. Everything was clear: from now on the battle was waged on both sides this rubber wall. Anyone who ventured to object that the question of the condom might not, in and of itself, exhaust all of human reflection on the subject of pleasure, was rejected out of hand: would you be an assassin?

Medical urgency served as a mechanism supporting simplification. Perhaps that was what was expected? Complexity is repugnant to societies in their initial reflexes, their collective passions, movements and sudden panics. It became reassuring to use the media to lynch anyone who refused the simple lyricism of the condom. This thin rubber wall not only distinguished two camps, it protected all of our achievements. To call into question, even *sotto voce*, its magical (and ludic) power to prevail, would be to risk losing ground.

And that is how this incredible polemic came to be linked, remotely, to Pope Jean-Paul II, who occupied a central position in the public arena for several years. Heir to Polish Catholic traditionalism, that pope was perceived (with some reason) as a conservative caricature in terms of conduct. (That was not the case in terms of economics and social issues, where his critiques of savage capitalism proceeded rather from Social Catholicism, closer to the Left.) In his writings and encyclicals devoted to morality, he seemed to align himself (especially with regard to questions of sex and contraception) with the rigorous and disciplinary positions held by the Church between the two wars, for example those expressed by Pius XI's encyclical, *Casti connubi*.

Dated December 31, 1930, this encyclical marked a crushing conservative argument in the doctrines governing marriage. With this text, Pius XI, it is true, had deliberately stifled an intellectual current that had started, in the years 1925-1930, to elaborate a moral theology less obsessed by contraceptive means and more attentive to the spouses' intentions. "It took thirty years," wrote a specialist on this period, "for this current to see the light of day once again, with a renewed vigor and to benefit from the council to challenge the entire Catholic world."[23]

On contraception, condoms and the priorities of the fight against AIDS, Jean-Paul II deliberately stood his ground in rejecting the "sexually correct" and in more or less explicitly refusing to proselytize in favor of condoms. He did it with an authoritative and obsolete stiffness that was disturbing even to practicing Catholics.

That said, it was clearly absurd to expect the Vatican to step outside its role, forget the doctrines, and give in to the spirit of the times, by "joining the hegemonic and sterile chorus of 'Put on a condom, and do whatever you want."[24] However, that is what the mainstream public discourse and the media kept calling for. Now there was only one question, that of the condom and the pope, both transformed into characters of an amusing comic strip in line with the taste of the time. The pope and his Church were called upon to decide, ever more explicitly, in favor of the "hood."[25] It was never enough. To continue to beat around the bush was becoming "criminal." The pope, by his silence, "became a murderer," etc. Disturbing reductionism but a providential trick. The condom embodied the merry simplicity of rubber held up to ward off death. As for the pope, he conveniently (i.e. in the form of an

easily mocked archaism) represented all the questions which we refused to address.

CHAPTER 4

TO THE TRUE HAPPINESS OF CAPITAL

Without our realizing it, during the 1990's, another change of direction about sexual liberation was accomplished; an inversion of values so great that, for the moment still, we have not truly thought it through. Using an unforeseeable trick, history has ended up transforming yesterday's fresh "subversion" into a component of the established order, and the freedoms once asserted have become pillars of the commercial machinery. Today, far from contravening the rests of the great liberal market and the commands of money, the ambient permissiveness indisputably serves one and the other. And in a thousand ways. Erotic hedonism, even unwillingly, has become part of a well-defined market. Echoing the famous advice of the July Monarchy articulated by Guizot, "Get rich!," there is a paradoxical injunction circulating in public opinion: Enjoy! It takes the claims of yesterday at their word, all the better to betray them.

No to the "Bourgeois Order!"

We have only to remember. For thirty years (and even more), an elementary conviction was more or less shared by those who disputed the moral order and fought for free access for everyone to the pleasures of the body. Any repression of sexuality, it was thought, serves mainly to perpetuate a form of domination, to consolidate power, by satisfying the imperatives of production, that is by putting the people to labor. Declined a thousand ways, this analysis amounted to a designation of sexual morality, whether lay or religious, as "a strategy" in service of the feudal, aristocratic or bourgeois order. The domination which it sought to perpetuate was, obviously, that of man over woman, of the rich over the poor, of the haves on the have-nots. Whatever its religious or mystical guise, morality, it was said, has only one outcome.

The collective memory admittedly remembered the long centuries during which libertinage had been a privilege of the aristocracy.[1] Similarly, it was remembered that at dawn of the industrial revolution, and throughout the 19th century, the obsession of bourgeois morality had consisted in holding at bay, disciplining or repressing workers' sexuality, allegedly effervescent and barbarian. A fantasy vision[2] of a plebeian amorality, constantly threatening the established moral order and, especially, the peaceful operation of the factories.

"The capitalist," wrote Marx, "constantly seeks to reduce wages to the physiological minimum, and to prolong the work day to its physiological maximum; the worker constantly applies pressure in the opposite direction."[3] Pleasure in love is a luxury and a waste which industry can ill afford. This is also the thesis expressed by Engels in a book that Lenin, it is said, recommended reading: *The Origin of the family, Private Property and the State*. Since the Protestant moralists of the 17th and 18th centuries, the founders of capitalism cited by Max Weber (to whom we will return), it goes without saying that "the puritan concept of existence" "presided over the cradle of the modern *homo aeconomicus*."[4]

For Freud himself, "the domestication of our love life by civilization" and the promotion of "a civilized sexual morality" built on "the repression of impulses" had already long expressed a kind of unequal contract signed with the established order. "Each individual gave up a piece of his property, of his sovereign power, aggressive and vindictive tendencies of his personality,"[5] he wrote at the beginning of the century. All the critical and permissive literature of the Sixties and Seventies is still steeped in this conviction: that traditional morality, founded on monogamist marriage, pro-birth ideology, continence and paternal authority, is first of all a weapon in the hands of the profiteers ruling the "bourgeois society."

Wilhelm Reich consistently affirmed that conservative sexual morality "is the adequate expression of economic interests." "Any reactionary social morality," he said, "is necessarily a negation of sexuality, whatever concessions it grants to the realities of sexual life, whatever the variation compared to the principles in the sexual life of the dominant classes."[6] It is true that a few years before him, at the beginning of the century, the first militants of the French anarchistic movement were Reichian before the term was invented. They proclaimed free love and contraception. They even counted among their numbers some talented pornographic writers.[7]

In the leaflets, slogans, and proclamations disseminated during and after May 1968, one may find this insistent denunciation of the "fascistic," "bourgeois" and "commercial" order, which prohibits the free sexuality of the masses in order to better exploiting their productive force. One finds, in parallel, the denunciation of the *principle of authority*, presented as the principal instrument of this oppression. "The bourgeoisie has no other pleasure than to degrade everyone," one graffito put it nicely in May, 1968.

The rather austere situationist writings of 1959-1969 contain few direct references to "sexual subversion" (except by allusion in the indirect illustrations). However, their surrealist heritage, rule-bending and libertine, is explicitly asserted from the very start. "The surrealist program affirming the sovereignty of desire and surprise," notes a paper by Guy Debord dating from 1957, "proposing a new approach to life, is far richer in constructive possibilities than is generally thought."[8] It is this sensibility that inspired, in 1968, the famous situationist pamphlet entitled, *De la misère en milieu étudiant* [*On misery in the student environment*].[9]

In the "mad" rhetoric of this period, the linkage is continuously established between the workers or anti-imperialist fights on the one hand, and the new claims concerning manners (the homosexual cause, contraception, feminism, etc.) on the other hand. "Your fight is ours," proclaims a flyer from the Movement of March 22 aimed at striking workers. "We occupy university departments, you occupy the factories." This affiliation asserted between the proletarian heritage and the new battlegrounds of daily life is founded on the denunciation (which appeared obvious to everyone) of the same "oppression." Moreover, the founders of organizations like the FHAR (Homosexual Front of Revolutionary Action), the Antipsychiatric Movement and the PrisonInformation Group, which would play a major role in the Seventies, came for the most part from the extreme political Left. The students of the time were reading the situationist texts as well as, for example, a work by philosopher Henri Lefèbvre with the evocative title, *The Proclamation of the Commune of Paris*.

From Politics to Culture

This initial link between the two types of revolution was rather broadly conceptualized by the theorists of the Frankfurt School. The former warrior of militant feminism, Évelyne Sullerot, shows a tinge of retrospective irony when she writes: "The whole Frankfurt School — Adorno, Horkheimer, Fromm and especially Marcuse — set to work reinterpreting the paternal figure as being not only the mediator of family authority, but also (which validates all the related suspicions and anathema) mediator of authority in the broad sense, including political authority. The legitimate authority of the father, in fact, reinforces the political power. That's it. That is the "68 thinking" that would incite young people against "oppression."[10]

Fighting to overthrow bourgeois morality not only prepared the advent of post-modern individualism, it also — and even more so — fought the alienating tyranny of money, the vulgarity of commercialism, the gravity of puritan economism. Later, much later, would come (in fact but not in word) the rupture "between the Promethean, political and communal individualism of May 68, and the narcissistic and apathetic individualism of the late Seventies," a disjunction between "the political Left and the cultural Left," [11] of which Gilles Lipovetsky became the theoretician.

Thus the postulate commonly shared in 1968 — and since the Revolution of 1789! — is unambiguous. If desire has been repressed for centuries, with the dedicated support of every type of clergy and folk superstition, it was for the benefit (especially economically) a minority. Introducing his long reflection on the history of sexuality, Foucault explicitly takes into account what everyone seems to take as an irrecusable truth, even though he himself is guarded. "Isn't all this attention and noise we have been kicking up around sexuality for the last two or three centuries concerned with one elementary goal?" he wonders, "to ensure population growth, to reproduce the labor force, to renew the form of social relations; in short to establish an approach to sexuality that is economically useful and politically conservative? I do not know yet whether that is the ultimate objective."[12]

Today, still, the same conviction floats in the atmosphere, if only in the form of hints, mental reflexes or political prejudices. In the expression "moral order," there is the word "*order*," which suggests the idea of a real disciplinary structure for *somebody's benefit*. It is opposed to the vague assumption of a "ludic" and permissive disorder, which would be, by contrast, advantageous to all. When we denounce moralistic nostalgia or neo-puritan intrigues, we instinctively think that these various plots are something more than a simple matter of convictions or religious faith: the notion, remote as it may be, even fuzzy, of a tangible "benefit," intended for a minority. What benefit? Stability of power, the maintenance of inequality, reinforced control, it doesn't matter. In our mind, it goes without saying that any "moral order" has its profiteers and, therefore, its strategists who want to conceal something from the people. That is the reason why any sexual morality is, in the strictest sense of the term, suspect. Mainstream public opinion it is still perceived mainly as a form of repression, and not as a set of internalized values.

However, that has all been turned on its head these days. The very nature of the system which controls the economy, the great market, deregulated and prolific, that is presented to us like a new destiny, this bourgeois order, new and hegemonic, no longer functions the way it did in the era of factories and heavy industry. What does that mean? Something quite simple: free sexual consumption, far from being prejudicial to the new established order, meets its needs and satisfies its interests.

Let's take a closer look.

The Revenge of Commoditization of Love

The first level and the first observation: pleasure irremediably has been merchandised, and priced out. This is old news, but needs to be discussed anyway. Commerce, monetary compensation, regulation by supply and demand alone, have colonized just about every territory of love. From pornography to professional or casual prostitution, from the timed satisfaction of fantasies (phone sex, peep shows, etc.), from "service businesses" (certain saunas, bars, clubs, etc.), and the specialized press to the so-called derivative industries, that type of sexuality has been glorified and is sold as soon as it is "produced"; so that now, these new markets are discussed in terms of statistics rather than morals. It is the most anecdotal and, need we say, the most trivial side of the question.

A rather pathetic everyday image symbolizes this change: that of a housewife peacefully pushing her shopping cart between the porn shelves in a supermarket. A video cassette, selected from among a series of thematic and specialized shows, will make its way to the cash register, slipped between a box of diapers and a bottle of juice. A little shopping habit, a Cellophane-wrapped transgression, pleasure on sale: a well-worn routine!

That is just one image. There are other realities that are more bleak. Sexual minorities, both American and European, have generally become specific lobbies with sufficient purchasing power to constitute target markets. Jerry Rubin, one of the outstanding figures of the Californian counter-culture of the Sixties and author of *Do It*, made a telling statement in the early Eighties in *The New York Times* (after having incorporated a Wall Street financial agency). "Politics and revolt marked the Sixties," he wrote. "The search of ego characterized the Seventies. Money and power will captivate the attention during the Eighties."[13] He hit the nail on the head.

The gay researcher Michael Pollack was more severe still, since he dates this outbreak of commercialism to the first years of sexual liberalization. "During the Sixties," he wrote, "liberalization caused an explosion of marketing of sex. In addition to the increasing numbers of bars, movie theaters and saunas, we see the development of the homosexual press, pornography, and an industry of gadgets and sexual accessories ranging from leather toys, penis rings and creams to Poppers (vasodilators used as aphrodisiacs). As the early militants of Gay Lib might ask, 'Did we make a revolution just to have the right to open 700 more leather bars?'"[14]

Today, the phenomenon is far more pronounced.

One telling symbol among so many others: the great provocative demonstrations like Gay Pride parades have taken on the qualities of show biz, thoroughly planned, sponsored and showing a profit. By now, this *homo trade* has become the main subject of the media coverage with, sometimes, a touch of melancholy. "Why claim to be promoting togetherness, tolerance and a cause, when Gay Pride is becoming a marketing extravaganza, when it is run by a company whose interests are more economic than militant and when you find merchandise instead of demands: tee-shirts, watches and bath towels with the colors of the rainbow, and even a *Gay Day* for visiting the châteaux of the Loire for 579 francs?"[15]

The same remark could apply to the gatherings, meetings, demonstrations, and individual actions which, as recently as yesterday, were matters of moral transgression or activism and now have been entirely taken over by commerce. The most radical of the former activists do not hide their sad rage at this vulgar commercialization of the sexual revolution. "The right to pleasure," wrote Vaneigem, "began to look like a conquest, but the pleasures had already been conquered by the market. . . . Democratic access to pleasure has coincided, as inauspiciously as possible, with the conquest of new markets where pleasure is called comfort and happiness is called appropriation. . . . In a sense, the religious and moral taboos and interdicts had protected orgasms against the risk of commercial exploitation."[16] Today what is prohibited in love and pleasure can be expressed in three words: free of charge. Only that which is not paid for is suspect. Misery!

It is true that this exploitation entails sizable financial stakes. No economist, no statistician has yet estimated the global turnover of all the industries and services directly or indirectly linked to the planet's sex market. But the few available data make it clear that it is gigantic. In the United States, pornography, which represents only a negligible part of the whole, is a huge industry on its own. In 1996, according to *US News and World Report*, Americans spent more than 8 billion dollars on videos, peep shows, floor shows, cable TV and accessories, that is, *more than Hollywood's total revenue from movies.* By way of comparison, twenty years ago the American government estimated this branch of industry at a puny ten million dollars.

In France, sex by Minitel [*ed. note*: a version of the Internet within France] brought in 700 million francs total in 1994, including 2250 million in royalties for France-Télécom.

For a Few Dollars More . . .

This new industry also has its emblematic figures, its *nouveau riches* pioneers, fabulous tycoons and victorious conquerors, who have taken their places in the great cast of characters in the world's economic chronicles. One is the American billionaire Larry Flint, king of porn, on whom Milos Forman made a film (*The People vs. Larry Flint*). This man, in whom *People* magazine called "the nightmare version of the American dream," transformed himself into a respectable porn businessman. He earned his first million dollars by publishing photographs of Jackie Onassis naked on a Greek island. The victim of an attack, he has lived since 1978 in a gold-plated wheelchair in Beverly Hills.

Likewise, the 76-year-old German, Beate Uhse, a Luftwaffe fighter pilot during the Second World War. He reigns over a mail order company, Beate Uhse International, which sells 400 million francs' worth of erotic and sexual articles every year. "Known to nearly 98% of the Germans, Uhse is a model of the economic miracle of the post-war period. He gained more than a million new customers with the fall of the Berlin Wall, and has about fifty franchise stores throughout Germany plus mail order subsidiaries in Great Britain, Switzerland, Austria and Slovenia."[17]

Every country (or almost) has its own champions of the sex industry, especially the former communist countries of Central Europe (notably Hungary) and the former USSR, which filled these niches with an unprecedented brutality and cynicism. Throughout the East, this industry (just like drugs and the weapons trade) founds the fortune of various maffias that crop up when States crumble. For some ten years, the same scene has been returning again and again to the front page: the former Communist societies, puritanical, deprived, and heavily policed, which now themselves swimming in new-found freedoms but also in insecurity, pornography and large-scale prostitution. The images are indicative: Polish women, Czechs, Hungarians and Russians transformed into human cattle for the brothels of Istanbul, Arabia and Europe; former Komsomol activists thrown on the sidewalk; girls from Ukraine and Lithuania seduced by the easy money and tracked down by johns come from the West.

Such is the reverse side of the new permissiveness, freed from totalitarian prudishness but already controlled by money. And more cruelly than envisaged! At the same time, the growth of inequalities and poverty in the East seems to be worse than at any other time in history.[18] It is accompanied by a loss of hope among the poorest, and by rising rates of infant mortality, etc.. The former communist countries are thus an extreme case of the "sexual revolution" carried out at an accelerated, not to say delirious, pace. This caricatural aspect reminds us of our own disappointments. And still, such a commercial use of new sexual freedoms is not its most disconcerting aspect.

The commercial *exploitation of the discourse for permissiveness* itself is more disturbing, for it affects the meaning and compromises the actual word. From the sex shop to mail-order catalogues, from the subculture of the porn-video to that of the Internet and the "pink" Minitel, no one offers services nor products without accompanying them with a "liberated" sermon that borrows its themes from the revolutionary theses of the past. The merchandising of sex broadcasts, every day, a cunning, propagandistic, not to say sordid version of the professions of faith that were current in the Seventies. It parodies them with great advertising talent. It never misses a chance to formulate a new denunciation of the "moral order;" it never misses an opportunity to publicly celebrate (with demagogic slogans) the noble sovereignty of pleasure. More and more often, it is money that will initiate and manipulate the demonstrations and disputes in favor of permissivity, relayed by the press.

Thus, closing a porn shop, dismantling a prostitution ring, or confiscating video cassettes is emphatically denounced as a return to Puritanism. The most naive will allow themselves to be misled by this advertising charade disguised as a progressivist protest. We won't even go into the fact, here, that the media, purely and simply, has been corrupted by money related to these trades.

That is the true obscenity of today. It is not a matter of deliberate provocation through an erotic "show," but of the appropriation of a revolt, of a utopia and a language by the profit-seekers who are resolutely indifferent to anything that is neither exploitable nor quantifiable. Long live sex, provided we can charge for it! "The bourgeoisie," Vaneigem wrote, "reveals the only sin which is. . . in its eyes inexcusable: that of not paying. Pleasure without financial compensation is the absolute economic crime."[19] This confiscation of the discourse of love by the money men leads to an ontological twist so bizarre that that cannot be derided enough. It pathetically drives back a revolt to its starting point. It takes a form of "demand" literally, and responds with "supply." An obscenity and the perfect crime of diverting a utopia! When Marx took on the lies of bourgeois moralism, it was with the intention of liberating love, not to condemn it to a new distortion. "If only marriage based on love is moral," he commented, "it is only so where that love persists." In the same way, when they wrote "Let go and have fun" or "Take your desires for realities" on the walls of the Latin Quarter, the students of May '68 did not suspect that they were inventing, in anticipation, advertising slogans for the porn business. But that is exactly what happened. Advertising for the Ford Fiesta proclaims, "Exigez tout tout de suite," ["Get it all, the first time"]

Having gone to war against money, we find ourselves here still serving its interests. The trip was fun but its end result leaves us feeling rather sad.

Don't Mess with My Market!

With these few episodes we are still just looking at anecdotes. But at a deeper level, this great reversal produces its more lasting effects. The market's power to prevail, the game of supply and demand's hegemony in the world economy proceeds, as we know, from global deregulation. Mainstream thinking has returned to the *laisser-faire, laisser-passer* of the original liberalism. Seen through this lens, any intervention intended to moderate the brutality of the market is considered to be obsolete. The new utopia under way is that of a chemically pure market, relieved of every non-economic constraint. Cultural identity, national particularisms, political will: one after the other, the old forms of regulation are erased in favor of the market, and only the market, which we are eager to see functioning in its ideal perfection. Psychoanalysis itself is shown to be dated, or to use Jacques-Alain Miller's expression, "an accessory to the time of the market, whose identity is also crumbling."[20]

This is the new context for our representations of sexuality. Earlier taboos or interdicts are seen as obsolete, superseded by history. If push comes to shove, the *residual morals, proscriptions or instances of self-discipline are no longer rejected in the name of liberation, per se, but of liberalism*, which is not quite the same thing. The warning reproach which is addressed to them is no longer founded on a philosophical but an econometric objection. The objection to traditional sexual morality is that it embodies a nitpicking code of conduct that is contradictory to the requirements of free trade.

This economistic paradox shows clearly through some of the polemics, for example those relating to the Internet. The wish to control the ever-so-slightly anarchistic global communications networks, in order to eliminate immoral propaganda from them, such as revisionism, pedophilia or soliciting, encounters not only technological but doctrinal difficulties. Any plan of codification, however modest and toothless, is scandalous. It flies in the face of the irreproachable principle of the market. Moral concern is thus invited to give in to the majesty of the stock exchange dogma.

Upon second thought, that's all crazy.

In the case of the Internet (as was seen in certain court cases in Germany in 1996), every attempt to regulate the machinery is discredited by not one but two objections. First, we keep hearing, any possible regulation could be established and applied only at the national level. It would thus be the product of an outdated nationalism, incompatible with the intent to develop free communication worldwide, across borders, of which the Internet is the vaunted symbol. Then, as we have seen, it would contravene the free-trade catechism, which is now as strong as the first amendment of the American Constitution.

A feeble line of thought and a radically new language are thus imperceptibly gaining ground in the arena of sexual morality. The new advocates of permissiveness copy the semantics of commercialism. They hold a vision of a world that is indeed libertarian, but in the economic sense of the term (that of the American "liberals/libertarians"). They express a neo-cynicism that could be taken as innocent. If they challenge any moralizing inclination, it is not out of an individual impulse to revolt, it's not out of a will to break taboos, or a penchant for amorality or provocation, it is simply to obey the objective destiny of commercial modernity. Moral regulation, in other words, seems to them to be on the same order as nationalized factories, the status of the civil servants or even the welfare state as grandpa knew it: a touching but somewhat kitsch hold-over from social voluntarism.

Let us recall on this subject that the (ultraliberal) American libertarians, whose leader is Robert Nozick, author of *Anarchy, State and Utopia*, are sometimes called anarcho-capitalists. Partisans of an integrated market economy, they are indeed hostile to any regulation of morals. Defenders of radical sexual liberation, they think that the market alone can control the allegedly "moral" contradictions of our societies.[21] The American Left and certain "communitarian" thinkers (like Amitai Etzioni, who was one of "the gurus" of the Labour leader — and British

Prime Minister — Tony Blair) reproach them for this nihilism. Etzioni was frank. "The orientation [of the libertarians]," he wrote, "is illustrated perfectly by those works that suggest that the duel is an excellent way of settling a dispute, that speculate as to whether it is financially justifiable to try to prevent hijacking, and that "prove" that it is more efficient to buy and sell babies on a free market than to try to regulate adoption and risk creating a black market."[22]

The "Relocation" of Desire

A simplified, caricatured version of liberal-libertarian cynicism has become prevalent, without being recognized for what it is. The reversal is spectacular, indeed. Sexual transgression used to be a rejection of bourgeois capitalism. Now it is authorized, justified, exploited — and protected — by this same capitalism, which has been renewed and renamed "liberalism." Extraordinarily enough, this inversion was suspected, foreseen and even announced, some thirty years ago, by certain perspicacious individuals who were not much heeded in their own era. Consider authors like Lars Ullerstam, and several socio-psychoanalists from the Sixties. They suggested, at the time, that "it is in the interest of the dominant classes to liberate sexuality according to a codified genital consumption, a sublimated and easy to handle sexuality" and they wondered whether "the sexual liberation that we are experiencing" did not actually ensure "social integration more solidly than the brutal repression of the beginning of the 20th century."[23]

We are obviously engaged in this scenario of integration. Today's liberalism-libertarianism now views freedom (including sexual freedom) as just a form of adaptation to the market. This new vision of the world is both relentless and ingenuous, and it is gaining ground all the more easily since erotic language itself has been contaminated by the lexicography of economics: performance, competition, consumption, comparative evaluation, short term results, etc..

The vocabulary of advertising and "communications" betrays this linguistic infiltration candidly. There you find the portrait of the ideal individual, man or woman, speaking about himself as if he were a company. "Such a confusion of terms," observes an advertising specialist, "even presents borders on the pathological. Cosmetics advertising, for example, has become a course in micro-economics. The individual 'manages' himself. He 'seeks to maximize' his energy, 'manages' his figure, 'checks' the evolution of his 'capital hydration,' optimizes his 'patrimony' of youthfulness and 'invests' in the management of his body. In short, he becomes his own contractor."[24]

One of the rare essayists to specialize in the decoding and the critique of advertising language, François Brown, points up the following paradox. "From this point of view, the censures of traditional morality represent an obstacle to the empire of publicity, almost to the point of safeguarding people's freedom. Thus we see TV ads an posters that contrive to make reference to moral boundaries in order to bypass them all the more handily. 'Winston is so good, it's almost a sin.' It's all in that 'almost': the old scenario of the temptation of the forbidden is invoked to support the promise of pleasure through transgression; but at the same time, the guilt is exorcised because it is discredited with a touch of humour."[25]

As for reality itself, there is a striking, and growing, equivalence between the contemporary approach to pleasure (or desire) and the actual operation of the world's economy. Demand is shown and supply responds by diversifying; competition becomes global and competitiveness is evaluated at length in magazines; amorous nomadism accelerates and the time use (of bodies) is shortened. Will we be seeing just-in-time distribution soon? Just as in industrial concerns, new markets are emerging and expressing new needs. Sexual tourism is directly analogous to the "relocation" of the production facilities serving desire, and overseas prostitution amounts to what must be called erotic dumping. As for the poverty in these remote areas, it makes it possible to re-calibrate to the West's advantage (by a reduction, of course) the traditions of morality and decency which cannot withstand the influx of wealthy clients. In the streets of Bogota, Manila and São Paulo, it's not really that outlandish since they are selling themselves in order to survive.

Obviously, this generalized deregulation is bad news for the poor and the weak. Now money to police desire infinitely more brutally and more unjustly than any morality on earth. It is hard to look at this aspect of the question, because it is so disturbing. But it's easy to grasp the essence. From the moment the market takes over, our inherited sense of discriminating between which pleasures to allow or forbid, which desires to satisfy and which to frustrate, which indulgences should be accessible and which unattainable, is no longer hampered by any sense of humanity or the slightest compassion. The triage is brutal, without nuance or compromise. Either you can pay, or you cannot. You have to sell your body, or you do not. You are at the top of the food chain, or you are worthless. There is no more room for negotiation, flexibility or play (in the mechanical sense of the term). In other words, there is no more culture of love. And it is not only the poor societies that are in danger. We, too, have a form of sexual poverty that stems from poverty plan and simple, even though it is rarely mentioned. Conversely, many transgressions express the pure arrogance of wealth, too sure of its impunity. In the matter of pedophilia, to cite only one example, the mercantile aspect has been underestimated for too long. Sociologist François deSingly is one of the rare specialists to insist on this point.

> One of excesses of this purely individualistic society," he observed, "stems from the fact that individualistic logic obscures the balance of power. However, that there is no more status does not mean that there are no one is weak or powerful anymore. Rather, the pedophile takes advantage of this fading of apparent status, and exploits to the maximum the possibilities opened up by the demise of authority and interdicts. He misuses personal identity to his own benefit. I have needs, and I use society, as it is, to satisfy them.   Children are located at the heart of the capitalist market. They represent a market for food and clothing. The budget devoted to a family's children is very important. The child can no longer be separated from this market logic. By pushing this logic to the extreme, the child can become an object of consumption like any other.[26]

Let us add that, in many cases, it is now the market which determines the gravity of the transgression, and sets the price. Questioned by the press in June 1997, an Interpol investigator who specialized in curbing pedophilia, Agnes Fournier recalled that when it comes to the marketing of underground videos, "The younger the child, the higher the degree of horror reached, and the more the tape costs."[27]

The Limits of "Moral Progressivism"

That is a matter that bears thorough examination, but which is studiously avoided, at least in Europe: the reality of sexual liberation as it relates to social inequality. It is a politically incorrect question, since it amounts to speculating whether ostentatious permissiveness might not correspond (sometimes) to a class struggle carried on by other means. First, as we know, by allowing the advocates of sex to show their "progressivism" while at the same time they participate in an unjust order. Then, by keeping quiet about certain unexpected consequences of "progressivism" that is exclusively applied to morals.

Denouncing (in moderate terms) the disadvantages of what he calls a society of seduction, a social leader observes that nobody really asked himself whether this upheaval of sexuality in the West was in the best interest of the poor. Doesn't the contemporary fragility of families, he adds, penalize children coming from the most modest backgrounds?[28] Conversely, the author reproaches the alleged defenders of "family values," generally classified on the right, for being totally unfamiliar with the life of underprivileged families. Is his a lone voice in the tumult that surrounds us? In France, perhaps. On the other hand, these new social inequalities, directly induced by the change in morals, are addressed much more frankly in the United States. And not only by those in the moral majority, even if the latter use them to bolster their position.

It is true that in the U.S. the figures speak for themselves, when it comes to the differential evolution of the family, according to social community. One of the perverse effects of hyper-individualism is that it has given birth to, or aggravated, specific inequalities. Broken families, single-parent families, unmarried mothers are more numerous in the lower classes. Drug use, delinquency, and dropping out of school are far more frequent at the bottom of society, while at the same time the middle-class families invest heavily in the education of their offspring, destined for the best schools and the great universities. In the United States, of course, this debate is related to the racial question.

> Admittedly, the 'single mother' households also multiplied among American whites; between 1940 and 1984, their proportion doubled, from 6% to 12%. But, in the same period, fatherless households in the black popula-

tion went from 16% to 49%! Moreover, these 'single mothers' are no longer predominantly divorced but never-married. They often have several children, by different fathers — and none of these fathers is present in the home.[29]

Democratic academics, like Robert Reich and Benjamin Barber, advisors to President Clinton, have also written extensively on this subject, and in a rather catastrophic tone.[30] From this angle, the spectacular increase in inequality over the last twenty years in America thus leads to the moral question. Let's not be ironical about that form of moralism that has made such a strong comeback in the form of invasive meddling or puritanism, which sometimes seems ridiculous to us in France (and even straightforwardly alarming when it comes to the pro-life movement against abortion). All in all, the moral concern is no longer the prerogative of the Right in America. It testifies to a new awareness of the failures, injustices, and dislocations which can be partially ascribed to the excessive permissiveness of the Seventies and Eighties.

And cultural progressivism can have another kind of perverse effect, more directly political. The American liberal Left is starting to understand the costs, in terms of political influence, of the fragmentation of identity and community that resulted from the "sexual revolution." By dividing the democrats, this disintegration and the excesses that accompanied it helped the Conservatives rise to power, starting in the early Eighties, which led to the great conservative regression (on the political and economic level) of the Reagan years.

"Contemplating their failures," writes an observer of American politics, "the Liberals may be able to come up with a viable alternative to the 'identity politics' inaugurated in the Sixties. The fragmentation of the Left into a multitude of identity groups (Blacks, women, homosexuals) . . . seems, in the eyes of several intellectuals,[31] to be the main obstacle to the constitution of a shared political plan, essential to the fight against exclusion and poverty. Furthermore, as things stand, the 'poor' cannot constitute themselves as autonomous groups on the 'identity market,' which has become the American public space (or rather the media space)."[32]

In Europe, a comparable contradiction cropped up in the mid-Nineties. At that time, it became the practice to contrast a "moral Left" and a "political Left," whose sensibilities, more and more often, seem to diverge. Such was the case, in Germany and France, in connection with ecology and AIDS. It was also the case, in February 1997, with the immigration issue (for undocumented aliens). If this contradiction were to be exacerbated, it would undoubtedly produce the same effects as in the United States.

One thing is already sure. For thirty years, the disintegration of sexuality, identity and community that has accompanied the revolution of morals hasn't caused the "capitalists" to lose any sleep and money to lose its dominion. Today, we are forced to conclude that the situation pleases the "big guys" more than it comforts the "afflicted."[33]

Femininity and Class Warfare

There are other, more subtle ways that the liberalization of morals has penalized the poor. We should no longer accept that these ideas must be kept quiet under the pretext that naming them "would lead to a backlash." This blackmail has gone on too long. To pose these questions openly does not mean that one calls into question all the accomplishments like women's liberation or the recognition of homosexuality. But the fact is that the manipulation of symbols corresponding to this type of change is never neutral.

François de Singly raises a big question when he analyzes certain effects induced by the feminization of our societies, the modification of the symbolic representations, the slow transformation of the dominant culture. Feminization, to cite just one aspect, was logically accompanied by the symmetrical obliteration of older social values like virility, physical strength, male authority, etc.. This obliteration was aided by the fact that the social groups most involved in questioning gender relations were the middle class or higher. For them, the "symbolic capital" represented by virility and physical strength had little importance, as the "domestic" qualities formerly expected of a woman had little real symbolic significance.

However, the same did not hold true in other social classes (laborers, clerical workers, farmers) who were infinitely more attached to these traditional distinctions, for cultural reasons that are easy to understand. What is seen as liberalization for some can be depreciation for others.

As de Singly wrote, "It all came about as if gender relations were renegotiated on the back of the popular classes. The physical value of workmen, their only asset, like the domestic value of the housewife, had served as foils for the men and women of the modernistic executive milieux. The moment the latter smiled at any mention of class struggle, they took part in it by engaging in the fight against the old ways, against the vestiges of male force, which they perceived as the manifestations of brute force (on the male side) or of the routine (on the female side).

"Gender neutral" is a concept that appeals, mainly, to the men and women of the executive level; it doesn't significantly throw off their own sexual identity. All and sundry are convinced that they have no need to affirm their virility or their femininity (except during the game of seduction); they consider that they have left these obsolete trappings behind. On the part of the men (of the executive class) this strategy, consciously or not, rests on the hierarchy of capital. The "pawn" of physical strength (and ostentatious virility) was sacrificed to save the other pawns, those which have a greater value, scientific capital in particular. Men apparently succeeded in limiting the risks of the gender war by transforming it into a derivative form of class warfare. The men best equipped in social capital and educational capital broke ranks with the poorer men."[34]

We must analyze in-depth these innumerable shifts in meaning, depreciation/appreciation, the permutations of values which, while advancing personal freedom, cast whole categories of the population into quiet humiliation and distress. On the grounds of morals, the popular classes confusedly found themselves "out of date" and sometimes rejected for their conservatism. That is the aspect that is least often discussed, because it is the most embarrassing aspect of the "sexual revolution." Unconsciously breaking with a very old line of thinking, which had it that the damned on earth were the avant-garde of human progress (the proletariat, staunchly bearing hope for the future), here it became customary to assimilate poverty with conservative beliefs. The heroic proletarian of yesterday, the combative and admirable worker of the Sixties, became Archie Bunker, and voted for Le Pen. That's how much our perception changed. The fact is that the majority of surveys relating to values (family, morality, children, etc.) show that the most underprivileged are also, in many cases, most traditionalist. Not to mention the prison population, at the nadir of the social scale, which, by the effect of a paradoxical moralism, turned out to be more clear-sighted — i.e. more severe — than the rest of society as regards criminal pedophilia.[35]

In the final analysis, the problem is political. No social rift, no divide between the elite and the people has been so formidable, in the long run, as this one. The ongoing debate over the growth (in France) of the extreme Right voting bloc is usually conducted in terms of the traditional socio-economic explanations (unemployment, inequality, immigration, insecurity, etc.). We do not really take into account these cultural factors.

We are wrong.

The Profitability of the Disorder

There is one more detail. But is it just a detail? In the traditional (let's call it Reichian) concept of bourgeois oppression, where sex was suppressed in favor of work effort, production and appreciation based on the effort of the laborers, the argument rested on the evidence: the bourgeoisie needed this labor force. Since the birth of the bourgeois society and the first steps of the industrial revolution, the inventive Anglo-Saxon puritans of capitalism drove this point home relentlessly. It was important to protect the labor of the poor, of the workmen and their wives and their children from being wasted. Sexual continence and asceticism fulfilled this function. One should remember that, in 17th century England, all sports had been prohibited to the workers for this same reason, and so brutally that King James I, and then Charles I, reacted against the excessive influence of the puritans by publishing a *Book of Sports* which allowed the practice of sports on Sundays.

Max Weber puts it this way. "The monarchical and feudal society protected 'those who wanted to have fun' against incipient bourgeois morality and the ascetic conventicles that were hostile to authority, in the same way that today the capitalist society takes care to protect 'those who wish to work' from class morality and the anti-authoritarian trade unions."[36]

This shows how obsessed were the first capitalists, how concerned they were with putting the laborers to work. This was, indeed, one of the bases of sexual puritanism. Free access to pleasure threatened profits, because it depended on the labor of the poorest members of society. No morality, no sufficiency of labor; no labor, no profit.

However, the more our economies have been modernized, the less true is this elementary equation (already contestable in Reich's time). The global economy today *hardly needs its workers*. More precisely, there is a surplus of labor, and it is totally liable to servitude, less and less valuable relative to capital, exiled, bumped from one location to another, weakened, deregulated, etc.. Mass labor is no longer a determinant factor in the creation of wealth. Pervasive unemployment is the sign. Don't we keep hearing about the end of work? The new capitalists have no more use for "the masses" than the *nouveaux riches* have for the poor. And the consequence is obvious. Let the people do what they want with their desires! To the capitalist, things are quite clear, even if they are extravagant. Today's permissive chaos is more profitable than moral order.

Chapter 5

Pleasure as Drudgery?

Acknowledged and accepted in ancient China, prostitution there did not always mean what we think. It so happens that it allowed adult men . . . to escape from sex! Polygamy and the minute coding of marital rules imposed such thoroughly regulated duties upon men that they ended up making pleasure a chore. Thus, while China perpetuated the tradition of the famous "sex manuals," illustrating refined techniques, the men were burdened with what one could call "an obligation of sex." *Coïtus reservatus*, i.e. intercourse without ejaculation, was the rule so that they would not lose face. But still!

For a man to fulfill his amorous obligations, especially if he was a noble or upper-middle-class man, did not allow for any domestic evasion. The sexual life of the Chinese emperor in the 6th century is a good example of this subjection. In the palace bustling with wives and concubines, the monarch's love life was ruled by an extraordinarily meticulous and constraining protocol. As the number of women in the seraglio continued to grow from one dynasty to the next, it became necessary to maintain an exact accounting of the imperial pleasures. It became the practice to note the date and the hour of any successful sexual union, each woman's menstruations, the first signs of pregnancy, etc.. Following this voluptuous ritual allowed hardly any respite!

The great sinologist who researched this tradition, Robert van Gulik, sees in it the paradox of an approach to physical pleasure that became more oppressive than the most severe abstinence. In the permissive China of the first centuries of our era, the men sought to escape these obligatory pleasures by going to find other company. "If the men [of the upper classes] conversed with courtesans," he wrote, "it was not only to conform to a well-established social custom, but very often also *to escape from carnal love*, to find a kind of relief far from the female apartments, their sometimes overpowering atmosphere and obligatory sexual relations. In other words, they were starved for spontaneous female friendship, without sexual obligation. With a courtesan, a man could reach a certain degree of intimacy without feeling compelled to cap it off with consummation."[1]

From Liberation to Requirement

A comminatory pleasure? Compulsory sexuality? Have we arrived at the same contradiction? Is it possible that we, too, have spoiled the appeal of pleasure by trying too hard to support it and magnify it? The philosopher Jean Guitton was probably not aware of this thirteen centuries old Chinese example when, in the early Seventies, he said he feared more than anything that Western life might become, under cover of a proclaimed permissiveness, "an immense drudgery of pleasure." Drudgery? At the time, such a concern seemed absurd; better still, it sounded like the drivel of an old Christian moralist. Could pleasure, which was said to have just been emancipated from the hypocritical pruderies, constrained morals and taboos of yesteryear, ever seem like a punishment? Of course not! The libertarian optimism of the Seventies found the question idiotic.

Thirty years after, we may have changed our minds. Jean Guitton's fear is not so ridiculous any more. Free access to pleasure is no longer just a simple *liberation*, it has become — also — an *injunction* that is characteristic of the era, a *summation* of modern propriety. Attentive analysis of any advertising rhetoric demonstrates this. "Pleasure is [no longer] displayed there as optional but as required. You can't stop pleasure anymore than you can stop progress. It is not only omnipresent, it is sovereign. To resist would be a mistake, nonsense, a failure to move ahead in step with the times. What advertising has instituted [from now on] is the obligation of pleasure. This duty is naturally hidden under the guise of liberation."[2]

The result (damn!) is not quite what we were counting on when we cast down the old world. The former situational theorist Raoul Vaneigem complains in a tone that is downright whiny: "[Today] obligatory pleasure replaces prohibited pleasure. Indulgence is like a test that you pass or fail. Eating, drinking, devoting yourself to love, these are now signs of a good reputation. To get the stamp of approval as a radical, please list here the average duration of your orgasms! We used to throw ourselves into pleasures like going into a hopeless war. Now, it is pleasure that is throwing itself on us."[3]

An astonishing symbolic collapse, accomplished in three short decades! From liberation to challenge, permissiveness achieved to compulsory indulgence, prohibition to obligation. Are we, ironically, coming back to square one, that is to a simple question of freedom? It's a valid question. And here's the proof: look at the strange rejection, the incredible protests against this new drudgery that is already felt in the background. That was unimaginable a few years ago; and this rejection is not at all related to religious or lay moralism, even if it does point in the opposite direction from the past demands for permissiveness. It is an imitation of those aggravated Chinese men of the 6th century: in the face of abusive insistence on sex, one withdraws; given an official campaign for hedonism, one becomes a dissident. And in acting this way, we are not doing so out of prudery but in the name of free will, i.e. by taking the word *permissiveness* at face value.

Hardly a week goes by without the media pounding on this postmodern theme: the return of the voluntary abstinence, a new penchant for chastity inspired more by weariness than by a moral response in the traditional sense of the term. The description of LSD (Low Sexual Desire), for example, has become a "chestnut" of Western journalism. In March 1995, Germany's *Stern* came up with another by announcing "the end of sex orgies" and conducting the inevitable survey: between the ages of 17 and 35, one out of three Germans feel they could do without sexual relations at all.

In the Anglo-Saxon countries, a campaign called "True Love Waits" follows the same trend. Originating in America, in 1997, it had more than 500,000 young volunteers. Recycling the feminist values and slogans of the Seventies, it invites girls to defend their "right to say no" and to dissociate themselves with the contemporary pansexualism. An interesting detail: this unexpected split, far from being presented as an acceptable return to the bosom of interdicts, is seen as the testimony of a fully assumed freedom. "I am a feminist," one of the members declared to the British *Guardian*, "and I feel that my abstinence is a much better proof of my emancipation." In fact, the most recent studies on the sexual behavior of the young Americans "show, for the first time since the very first investigations, a 5% drop in the number of young women having sexual intercourse before the marriage."[4] In the United States today, there are thriving centers that provide a new kind of care. Patients come to be looked after for sexual "preoccupation" that they consider to be excessive and catalogued as pathologies or addictions that are detrimental to free will.

This backing off from sex expresses a will to re-appropriate the concept of freedom (but in reverse). Are they simply flukes, the kind of marginal media events that come up in every era? That is not entirely clear. The testimonies describing these behaviors and predicting their extension are not all frivolous, not by a long shot. The psychoanalyst and ethologist Boris Cyrulnik has also noted the appearance in our societies of a strange reverse permissiveness (the permission to say 'No'!). "For some 20 years," he says, "we have been witnessing in the United States cases of people who regard themselves as 'dependent on sex' and who seek medical attention to help them to get rid of what they regard as a problem, even a kind of addiction. Their main idea is that suppressing the sexual desire would represent a gain in personal freedom."

"This phenomenon," he adds, "has started to show up in France. Male and female patients with strong libidos come to me, to have me prescribe a drug that will reduce their desire. Men have confided to me their joy at having become impotent: they can finally live in peace! Women tell me that they feel dependent when their partner satisfies them, and that they suffer from this dependence. These cases are increasingly frequent, even in Europe."[5]

Paradox of paradoxes: modern psychoanalysis, too, gives the impression that sexuality has been stripped of meaning, to the point that certain more orthodox experts accuse it of "betraying Freud." Such, at any rate, is the thesis advanced in certain recent works like that of André Green, a Lacanian psychoanalyst born in 1927. Green estimates that sexuality has almost — and annoyingly — disappeared from the theory and the practice of psychoanalysis. According to him, Melanie Klein's and even Jacques Lacan's criticism of the theory of human drives has contributed to devaluing the function of the sexual. In his eyes, however, that is not the only factor. Finally — and here, his explanation becomes more interesting, the sexual occupies a place in psychoanalytical practice that is inversely proportional to that which it holds in society (which is, indeed, freer than in Freud's day). In other words sex, through its omnipresence in social life, public discourse, and "shows," has succeeded, psychoanalytically speaking, in devaluing itself.[6] Only psychoanalytically?

For the Sake of Freedom

All these phenomena are rather disturbing for anyone who sets store by pleasure, bodily enjoyment or quite simply the pursuit of happiness. Rejection of sex, mistrust of desire, the will to affirm one's individual autonomy not through free sexuality but by opposing it, the aspiration to relative chastity, presented as a healing effect given the eroticized general climate: this priggishness is indeed the diametrical opposite of the radiant future promised by the popular Reichianism of the Seventies. That is why we find them so incredible. But are they as new — and as unique — as we think? Not a bit.

What makes these regressive impulses so enthralling to consider is not their radical strangeness, it is, quite to the contrary, the fact that over the centuries they are confusedly falling into alignment — unconsciously — with points of view and with behaviors that are perfectly well-known to historians. Take Plato's perspective, for example, when in *Laws* he evoked the ability to resist "the tyrant Eros" as proof of individual autonomy, and the conduct of the Jewish communities (the Essenes) and the Christian women of the first centuries of our era, who did not consider chastity a renouncement of freedom but a blatant assertion thereof.

A specialist in late Antiquity and a good friend of Foucault, Peter Brown magnificently described the Encratite (abstinent) assemblies of men and women "living so close together in the small churches of Syria and northern Iraq," and convinced that they had freely achieved "a permanent serenity and a kind of pure friendship between the sexes."[7] He also showed that by choosing chastity, some of those Roman women of the 4th century who converted to Christianity were not expressing subservience but rebelling against the lifestyle of the empire, rejecting paternalistic authority, and claiming a freedom which we would describe today as feminist.[8]

Even the extreme and blatantly pathological cases of renouncing pleasure are not as new as we imagine, nor a prerogative of a modernity gone mad. Consider the extravagant choices of the New Age cults from California, which, due to collective suicides (in particular in San Diego in March 1997), were found to have persuaded their followers to voluntary castration, so that they could escape the dominion of sexual instincts. However, the idea of self-castration practiced for this purpose does have its precedents in history. In some periods, it was even fairly common — not only during the first centuries of Christianity and Islam (Origen is the most famous example), but since Babylon and the dawning of history.

"Many pagan priests practiced voluntary castration in order not to be sullied by sexual contact and to be able to fulfill, in purity and holiness, their role of intermediary between mankind and the gods or goddesses. This religious emasculation existed in particular in Babylon, Lebanon, Phoenicia, Cyprus, and Syria, in the worship of Artemis of Ephesus, Osiris in Egypt and Attis and Cybele in Phrygia; the last of these cults was widespread in both the East and West."[9]

Thus, even in our most profound anguish and folly, we do not invent anything new but, without knowing it we go backwards; we feel our way back through the centuries. Toward what, and why? That is the question. The thousand and one ways of "freely" giving up sex to protect ourselves from pleasure probably betray the impalpable exhaustion of a utopia, the sense of reaching some hard to define limit, the insidious rise of a vague feeling of disgust, more instinctive than considered. So many things recall the famous disenchantment of the Roman poets, who greeted the decadence of the Roman Empire at the beginning of our era with rhymed *Satires*. The wrath of Juvenal and Martial,[10] to cite just two, the howling nausea inspired in them by what Juvenal tellingly called "a surfeit" of pleasures, money and games.

Are we weighed down now by the same satiety?

A Breakdown of Desire

Other signs also raise the question. Together with this rejection, cohabiting with it and shedding further light on it, is another form of anguish that runs through the modern subconscious. It may be even more revealing of our distress in love. It is the fear that desire itself is fading, the fear of impotence caused by progressive disinterest, the terror of an immense collective fiasco that will punish the excesses of what Foucault called "the sexual sermon."[11] Our so aggressively eroticized societies are actually tortured by an obsession with the lack of desire. And that obsession further feeds the eroticization, in a never-ending cycle. We talk about sex so insistently that we have to allay this vague terror, day after day. In any conversation or entertainment, our societies insist on spurring desire as though to prevent it from giving in, and to reassure ourselves.

The recent media popularity of certain words betrays this same anguish: the word "fantasy" for example. As recently as yesterday, giving in to fantasy was a serious fault, the admission of a delicious and dreamy turpitude, the upsetting projection of a forbidden and possibly cataclysmic desire. Today, fantasies are piously treated like so many needy orphans who deserve our solicitude, fragile treasures, neglected companions in danger of dying out altogether. The contemporary advice about fantasies is almost desperate: pamper your fantasies, develop them, cajole them for fear they might fade away. By now, that is practically the *only* thing the women's magazines are saying. They recommend every reader to cultivate her own fantasies as if they had become scarce commodities. Sometimes the gibberish of economics is used: "take care of your "fantasy-capital." As for the erotic reveries that each of us shelters in his heart of hearts, they are a new intimate treasure that we are entreated to look after with care, so threatened they are with evaporation.

This humanitarian rhetoric applied to desire is part and parcel of a new concern: that of a slow emasculation by default, an inexorable weakening of our impulses. The real challenge is no longer to fight against the repression of desire but rather to keep it from running dry.

And the same holds true for how we view transgression. Transgressions are no longer perceived as destructive risk-taking, as a subversion of taboos in the name of desire, but rather as an old convenience that unfortunately no longer works. Now we hear people hearkening back to the time of sin; now the past is being idealized as a time when there were still taboos to be transgressed. This nostalgia is generally expressed with a rationalizing — and ratiocinating — ingenuity specific to our time.

In 1990, a few months after the fall of the Berlin Wall and the re-unification of Germany, several Western newspapers published reports claiming that the women of the former GDR, just liberated from tyr-anny (i.e. still untouched by our sexual liberation-vulgarization), ex-perienced far more intense orgasms than the Germans of the West. The journalistic outcry spoke for itself. On another plane, advertising cam-paigns like those praising Winston cigarettes, Michaelmas wafers and Suchard chocolate, make our nostalgia for sin into appealing slogans. Collections of books ("Cardinal Sins," from Editions Textuel) candidly invite us to "dive into the sensual and jubilatory universe of sin." In 1995, a television series baptized "The Seven Deadly Sins" was broad-cast with great commercial success in France.

Exhibitions are even organized around the same topic, with a con-solatory backward glance. The George Pompidou Center, in Paris, held one in 1996-1997 devoted to capital sins. Its commissioner Didier Ot-tinger presented the show as follows: "Sins are the sign of playing with the mechanism of taboos, although there are no more taboos." Gilles Lipovetsky, cantor of contemporary individualism, puts it even more candidly. "Sin," he said, "is no longer something to dream of, but it does manage to perk up, to stimulate desire."[12]

Loving to Death

This nostalgic search for lost sin is intended to awaken the flag-ging desire. It is not always so nice. As we know, sometimes it leads people to push the limits of the taboo to the very end, to engage in a frightening and futile game of taking greater and greater risks, whose ultimate limit is obviously death. One could give a thousand examples of this desperate flirtation with the final interdict; one of them is the acknowledged fascination, in these times of AIDS, for unprotected rela-tions that young people call Russian roulette. "Suddenly," said a homo-sexual who was questioned on this subject, "I had to reflect on the rea-sons why I wanted unsafe sex, and I realized that the danger was part of the attraction."[13]

There is an ambient sense of lusting for risk, violence, and death. It is not unrelated to the breakdown of desire, which is in fact a break-down of life. The Canadian film *Kissed*, produced by a woman and presented in 1997 to the fifteen-odd directors of the Cannes Film Festival, raised the question directly. In fact, it tells the story of a young woman, Sandra Larson, who is sexually aroused by death and especially by corpses, which excite her to the extreme. A major newspaper wrote a telling headline about this film: "Loving to Death. *Kissed*: a stylized production making necrophilic sexuality presentable."

Dealing with death would be the ultimate aphrodisiac for our societies whose desires are extinct. As for Western modernity, so concerned with taking the drama out of sex in the Sixties, now it is rediscovering — with a puerile terror — that desire is linked to violence and death. Marvelous! Didn't most human cultures know that all along? Wasn't that precisely *the* problem with sex throughout the centuries?

*

* *

In a ludic and ritualized form, the sadomasochism so popular today is also an expression of the confused search for "true" transgression. An adherent of S/M clearly indicates what, for her part, she expects: "There is no doubt that in recent times the limits of transgression were pushed back by the sexual liberation and the new image of the body. Simple nudity, which was at one time enough to inspire sexual desire, has become banal. So you have to go farther, to approach the taboo. S/M has perhaps become the quintessential place arena of the taboo today."[14]

In spite of the subject, a somewhat comic contradiction crops up concerning S/M. Its aficionados, contaminated by the ambient permissiveness as much as the rest of us, regard themselves as a community apart, an honorable minority with, therefore, grounds for asserting its right to existence. On September 15, 1996, they paraded through the heart of London with a fake gladiator in the lead, wearing a latex skirt and pulling his friend along in a cart. It was the fifth S/M Pride parade. What started these processions was a police raid against S/M parties in Birmingham. Newspapers like *The Guardian* and *The Independent* wrote articles in favor of the new right to do what one wants with one's own body,[15] and that mobilized the activists and launched these joyous parades. But this leads to the insoluble — and even comical — contradiction between a respectable S/M filing along the pavement of Trafalgar

Square amidst mothers and children and debonnaire bobbies, and the search for sulfurous and dark taboos which was the original object of this cult.

A freedom asserted, an identity displayed, a vice made banal but, in spite of all, the self-conscious celebration of the interdict: now, that is a strange mixture! It is perfectly emblematic of our times which, when it comes to pleasure, tries to swim in a sea of innocence while burning in the fires of sin at the same time. And which of course it fails to do; but why, in fact?

The *irremediable* antagonism between desire and the excesses of permission seems to support those prophets like André Breton who, toward the end of his life, feared that by revealing and permitting all, we might end up depriving desire of its force. George Battaille shared the same fears.

"In my view," he said, "this sexual chaos is a curse. In this respect, in spite of appearances, I oppose the tendency which seems to be winning out today. I do not agree with those who see it as a goal to do away with sexual taboos. I even think that the promise of humanity *depends* on these interdicts."[16]

In numerous other texts, this leading apologist for transgression and pleasure spoke in praise of the interdict, repeating that abolishing it too radically would threaten desire itself and, in the final analysis, our humanity.

"It seems to me," he wrote again, "that the object of the interdict was initially indicated by the interdict of lust itself: if the interdict were primarily sexual in nature, then according to any probability, it emphasized the sexual value of its object (or rather, its erotic value). That is precisely what separates man from animal: the limit imposed on free sexual activity, which gave a new value to what was, for the animal, only an irresistible impulse, fleeting and meaningless."[17]

The fear that eroticism would lose all its force for want of any prohibitions runs through all of Bataille's work; just like the idea that the only solution is to symbolically invoke abjection, simulated violence, dirty language, a mime of degradation in order to *provoke* desire. In its own way (which is often trivial), that is what our era appears to be trying, more and more hopelessly, to do. Just look at the language being used in the pornographic email services. Since they can't take advantage of erotic taboos that don't get anybody excited any more, they use a constant verbal and descriptive violence which seems to be a substitute taboo. An infinity of linguistic stratagems are used to re-ignite the feeble flame: recorded or interactive scenarios, simulated violence, fantasies of sexual slavery and insults.

It is only play-acting that has people stirred up, which is consistent with this other remark by Battaille: "Rather than lose the meaning of the primary interdict, without which there can be no eroticism, [we] have resorted to the violence of those who deny all taboos, all shame, and who can maintain this denial only through violence."[18]

But we need to acknowledge that that violence is not satisfied, always, with simulation and play-acting.

The Age of the Sexologists

Given these misfirings, these fiascoes, and these anguishes, there is a strong temptation to go as far as the primary vice, if there is one. What went on before? What errors were made, what have we willingly forgotten, while conducting this great thirty-year revolution of manners in the Western countries? A revolution so radical that the historians ensure us that it was unprecedented in all of human history. Indeed, it is above all its scale that should be recorded in our memory. In a few lines, George Duby invited us to reflect on that. His words, which go back to 1984, are still impregnated with the lyricism of the time.; but they cover the essence.

"With an abruptness that left more than one of us speechless," wrote Duby, "the barriers drawn up over the centuries to regulate relations between the sexes were broken down before our very eyes. Taboos were removed. Bodies were stripped. We have gotten used to not blushing any more at certain suggestions. Conduct that was, at one time, carefully dissimulated, began to be displayed, while conjugality took on new forms. The revolution was more decisive — much greater than all the changes which have occurred over the generations in the economy or the culture; the other shocks, which we also call revolutions, are superficial and fleeting compared to this one — the revolution, I say, that overturned all the provisions established since the origins of mankind, and wrought havoc with the distribution of roles and powers between men and women."[19]

Outlining the extraordinary scope of the "sexual revolution" this way makes it possible to set into context the disappointments that attended it; taking the true measure of this historical shift helps us to pin down the original naivety, and the errors. Looking back, the latter seem so glaring that we find it hard to understand that they could have been made.

One of these original errors was undoubtedly in considering, from the outset, sexuality as a *function*, which had never in history been the case — never! The very idea of function introduced that of *dysfunction* and, therefore, a concept of sexual health that implies, by extension, quantitative evaluation and the concept of performance. With that as a point of departure, the idea is suggested of standards that are neither moral or cultural, but physiological and arithmetical (how much? how intense? with what result?). It wasn't really freedom that was substituted for the prohibitions of the past, but a concept of measurable flourishing or recovery, a utopia of perfect sexual health, a goal of voluptuous success approved by science, a therapeutic view endorsing all the hopes and justifying all the claims.

A few little new concepts were enough to upset the entire Western mental landscape, to change our idea of the relationship between pleasure and happiness, the will, and freedom, right down to how we depict our own desires. Extraordinary: this profound transmutation of values, was neither noticed at the time nor really understood. We quarreled over the persistence of such and such taboo, such and such reactionary prudishness, such and such obscene "scandal" in Paris, without understanding that the real game was playing out at another level, that of shared values. The true rifts are quite invisible.

When it comes to sexuality, for example, it is no longer a question of contrasting the normal and the abnormal, license and interdict, the moral and the immoral, but dysfunction and correct organic operation. The priests, moralists and confessors of yore have been replaced by men in white coats armed with measurement equipment, strange instruments and statistics. The glacial era of sexologists has arrived. The scientific power that the latter hold in their hands (and will continue to wield for a long time) rests entirely on a capacity — or a presumption: that they, together, define sexual health, a concept that would have seemed strange (not to say absurd) to a contemporary of Ovid or Brantôme. Hence the creation, in particular with the work of William H. Master and Virginia E. Johnson in the late 60's,[20] of new and sometimes revolutionary therapeutic definitions. Now we have the "ideal orgasm," for example, which has upset our perception of sexuality more surely than all the libertarian proclamations.

This utopia of perfect sexual health, to which everyone might now aspire, the perception of sexuality as almost a public health issue, naturally led our view of pleasure to slide from freedom to duty, from permission to obligation. And there you go! "The right to happiness," wrote a researcher from CNRS [the National Center for Scientific Research, in Paris], "That is, among others, the right to orgasms, has been transformed into 'the duty to have an orgasm;' since the proper tutelary authorities recognize that we have a right to sexual pleasure, it would be stupid not to use it as much as possible. As they say, 'It can always be taken away'; taken by death, taken by the State. So now we have been instructed to produce orgasms, and, generally, 'to explode,' that is, to be Stakhanovites of hedonism. But be careful! Don't be (too obviously) boorish! Respect your partners! Help them to function!"[21]

For Master and Johnson, it was clear that sexual ineptitude was a social plague, sometimes compared with "a new disease," and that it should be eradicated like variola and malaria. In the Fifties, they encouraged sexologists to form associations, to create new private orgasm clinics, which it was hoped would one day be taken over by the public administration. Pleasure came to be treated as a health care issue and plans were made to distribute it equitably. "Insufficient" pleasure became one affliction among others, to be treated medically.

That's not all. The very way in which we viewed our quest for pleasure was profoundly altered. Guilt, for example, was no longer seen in the same light. Guilt did not disappear (as so many candidly believe) but it changed. "Now we find it more acceptable, and sometimes grounds for vanity, to belong to a sexual minority. On the other hand, we feel guilty if we function poorly."[22]

Function poorly in regard to what? Certainly not a cultural or moral standard, since there is no more. No; it is the *average statistics* that each one will compare himself to, tempted to evaluate how normal is his sexuality. Our societies accept this insidious decline, a phenomenal cultural impoverishment, without reacting (immobilized as they are by the promises of the sexual revolution). "Now we give people standards, statistics, points of comparison," acknowledges sexologist Gilbert Tordjmann, "which make them question themselves. The media gave rise to an enormous demand in every domain, and especially on the sexual level. That is how the 'sexual complaint' was developed."[23]

This new kind of "sexual complaint," this claim of entitlement to pleasure, copied on wage and welfare benefit claims, soon became commonplace, part of the landscape. It expresses both a social demand and a concern, a demand for the pleasure that has been *promised* to everyone and has been made the responsibility of the welfare state. The concern is that we may not be able to measure up to the new role model of the era: neither a saint nor a hero, but an athlete of orgasms.

The seeds of all future ambiguities are found in this complaint.

First There Was Kinsey

How could anyone be so blind to the nature of sexuality? The true origin of this move to treating sexuality as a medical issue and the heavily statistical approach is, in truth, more than two decades old. In 1948, at the end of the war and at the beginning of the immense economic boom of the post-war era, a study was conducted in the United States and soon disseminated throughout the world; it was baptized the "Kinsey Report."[24] A liberal and Anglo-Saxon version of the utopia suggested by Wilhelm Reich, this report proposes the first objective description (i.e. stripped of any value judgement) of sex life in America. Based on questionnaires, surveys, statistical evaluations, it takes a cool look at the various forms of sexuality and attempts to measure the frequency, the rate of success, the socio-economic and geographical distribution, etc.. Kinsey, without worrying about the psychological, cultural or social effects of such and such sexual practice, uses only one criterion: statistical representativeness. So many who engage in sodomy, so much in cunnilingus, so many fetishists, etc..

It is important to comprehend what a publication of this kind would represent, in 1948. In the still puritan America of the post-war period, this suddenly shone a floodlight on the darkest secrets; it brought out into clear daylight the hidden face of the country. It was a splendid catalogue of silences finally broken, it pointed the finger at hypocrisies, it "standardized" and dedramatized various forms of turpitude. The publication of the Kinsey Report opened a new era for all the West.

The real interest of this report is obviously not its documentary richness, its quality as an inventory. More especially — and very effectively — it provides an individual and collective excuse. It seems to show that nothing is so serious, that no one need fear the flames of hell for a sexual preference or even for assiduously practicing masturbation. And most important, this excuse is not derived, as in the past, from a progressivist reinterpretation of morals and interdicts nor of the obligatory contrition. It is an excuse which one could call statistical and imitative. This time, it is the other people, my neighbor, my peer or my fantasy companion, which legitimates my own practice; it is the duly indexed crowd of everyone like me that dedramatizes my whims; it is the misery shared with such and such a percentage of adults that soothes my own frustration. ("Everybody else is doing it, should I still be worried?)" Based on numerical proof, associated with strict rationalism, measured like a perfectible function, sexuality is no longer the dark continent, alarming and fascinating at the same time, that it used to evoke. It becomes a simple matter of success/failure, majorities/minorities, innovation/habit, investment/return, etc..

For the rest, this report fits in with the liberal generosity (let your imagination run wild!) and confidence in the future that were both in tune with the times. It applies the Keynesian post-war optimism to the field of sexuality. The desire to consume, even if it means going into debt, as the principal engine of the economy; desire itself, and the hope of a perfect pleasure as the engine of life in society: they are complementary. The Kinsey Report in any case seems so daring in its approach, and so benevolent in its intention, that rare are those who reproached it for its incredible reductionism.

It would take time, a long time, to understand that with the best intentions in the world, pleasure had been torn out of its most intimate framework and its most essential joy. It took time to understand that sexuality is not a *function* but a *culture*, and that the wrong turn we took was in those terms. At the time, the translations of the Kinsey Report were welcomed everywhere as evidence of a liberation underway. No one looked any further. Only a few dissenting spirits expressed a premonitory circumspection. Bataille is one. In spite of the sympathy that Kinsey inspired in him, in principle, he objected that all these curves, graphs and statistics were unable to apprehend "the irreducible element of sexual activity," the "intimate element" which, according to him, "remains elusive, invisible to outsiders, to those who are looking at the frequency, the method, the age, the profession and the class."

"We should even ask, openly," adds Bataille, "whether these books really talk about sexual life? Would we talk about man by limiting ourselves to giving numbers, measurements, classifications according to age or eye color? What man means, in our eyes, undoubtedly goes beyond these concepts. They get our attention, but they add only inessential aspects to knowledge we already have."[25]

In a few lines, he said it all; but no one heard. Quite to the contrary. The Kinsey Report, soon followed by a quantity of others,[26] marked the debut of an era that is still going on: that of the sexologists, of functional pleasure and the obligatory orgasm; obligatory to achieve unless you are willing to be considered "dysfunctional."

"In fact," the American philosopher Allan Bloom wrote fifty years later, "Kinsey had a political, and very obvious, intention, even if it was by no means based on any perverse personal interest. He was one of those scientists who, faithful to a degraded version of the Enlightenment, believed that science would end up making men happy. He believed that the statistics would speak for themselves, showing to everyone that there is an extraordinary diversity of sexual practices, and that the official talk was wrong, that discourse that ensured us that the great majority of people were satisfied, for the most part and as they should, within monogamous marriage. This statistical approach would establish that the practices studied had the weight of real things, while the moral judgements which applied to them were only prejudices."[27]

The Logic of Performance

The recurrent anxiety over a pleasure that has become a chore, the obscure frustration that abides in us even while "anything goes," the indefinable distress in love, the reflex of refusal and the reinvented encratism, the possible suppression of our desires under the weight of contemporary injunctions: can all that be ascribed to this one single wrong turn? Have we really gone off in the wrong direction? It's hard to say. We don't challenge the achievements nor the main thrust of the "sexual revolution." Who could miss, for even one second, the simple-minded prudishness of the past? We cannot subscribe, without reflecting, to the definitively negative assessment suggested by Bloom when he wrote, "On the whole, if one puts on one side of the scale its contribution to the abolition of hard and blunt laws, and other the induced loss of a human perspective on love, one will conclude that scientific sexology has done us much more harm than good.[28]

One thing is sure, however: the perception of the sexual, inaugurated first by the Kinsey Report, then taken up again by all of sexology and, in the final analysis, by the contemporary popular culture, has entailed unforeseen "collateral" effects. Effects from which we have great difficulty today . . . to free ourselves.

The first is to have rather disconsolately locked up pleasure in the logic of performance. From now on we share the conviction that, according to the example of health in general, sexuality is — technically — infinitely improvable, and that our earthly happiness depends upon it. Pleasure is not really the benefit of freedom any more, but the goal of a sporting challenge which we should raise, day by day. We are obsessed these days not with moral judgement but with comparative evaluation. Alain Finkielkraut's optimistic co-author of *Nouveau Désor-der amoureux* [The New Love Disorder] published in 1979, Pascal Bruckner notes today a little bitterly, "X-rated films are the latest domestic art, besides cuisine and gardening. Sexual compatibility has become the couple's criterion of success. This has led to an outburst of prescriptions and counsels in a certain press, since the 'doing it right' has become the modern couple's code of conduct."[29]

The American feminists were the first to denounce, in the Seventies, the logic of performance that was omnipresent in pornographic products, and its disastrous psychological effect. Let us cite, among many others, this reflection by Helen Gary Bishop dating from 1978. "The dick has to be at least 12 inches long. Otherwise, it doesn't count. And that is a lie. And this lie traumatizes men. It brings on what I call performance anxiety. In other words, the guy who doesn't have an enormous dick, who cannot go at it for hours at a time, he feels like he's totally out of it. These films set standards. And these standards don't correspond to anything, neither for men, nor for women.[30]

Since 1978, popular assumptions have increased this interminable Olympic recommendation, comparing sexuality to "exercise" where know-how, persistence and drive might apply. Sex, thus dispossessed of any symbolic significance, becomes a pure muscular functionality. It is reduced to the level of a sport, and more an individual sport than a collective one. As for pleasure, a perfectible body function, that too must be managed, in accordance with various prescriptions, to meet only one requirement: measurable excellence.

"At a time when the female orgasm was being described everywhere in dithyrambs," Gilbert Tordjmann says, "women went to consult the sexologist to ask why they weren't enjoying it in the same way, or with the same intensity as what they had read in the magazines. These alleged standards of duration or intensity led to the creation of false pathologies.[31]

Naturally, the women's magazines are the preferred instrument of a new biotechnical sermon. "How long does it take for you to feel sexually comfortable with a man?" asks *Elle*. "Check the 'Guide to Sensual Moves,'" suggests *Marie-Claire*. "Have you walked into a sex shop yet? Had a ménage à trois? Offered the *Kama Sutra* to a guy? Made a skin flick? Made love with a girl?" asks *Cosmopolitan*, while *Biba* tested on behalf of its readers "hot plans that work," ranging from fluorescent body paint to "geisha balls." And *Répons à tout. Santé* offers "seventh heaven in six lessons."[32]

Television and, of course, the movies also offer, day after day, models of sexual behavior that strongly suggest standards and measurability. Not being able to conform often makes people feel ashamed, inferior, distraught. Sociologists interested in teen sexuality are sometimes surprised by their own discoveries. "In American movies," say two of them, "the orgasm goes hand in hand with crying out. So the girls make it a practice to moan, from the very beginning of their sexual life, even if they don't feel anything. To reproduce what they see, and to come across as 'normal,' they present themselves as super-pro's of pleasure. They concentrate on pretending throughout the act of sex. Their relations with their partner are thus fake."

This may make us smile. However, it only takes the tendency of considering sexuality as a medical problem (inaugurated over 50 years ago by Kinsey) to its logical conclusion. It clearly incorporates pleasure into the concept of perfect health, which Lucien Sfez showed is not only the great contemporary utopia but more especially an *ideology*,[33] an ideology that is all the more totalitarian since it has found a providential guarantor in the economy of the open market. Just consider the frank and direct declaration of a urologist from the Kremlin-Bicêtre hospital, who discovered a molecule supposed to encourage male erection: "The big pharmaceutical companies have clearly identified sexual dysfunction as a formidable field of research. For them, it becomes a very significant target market.[34]

Alone in Hell?

The second effect of the Kinsey logic is that it has precipitated us into a distressing labyrinth of imitation. What does this mean? Something fairly simple. If there are no longer sins to torment us, we should still be wary — of the new hell. The modern hell, without horned devils or bubbling cauldrons, but where a thousand new agonies are suffered. Poets being the best prophets, Rimbaud first gave a presentiment of their contours in 1873, when he exclaimed, "I believe myself in hell, therefore I am in hell." A hundred years later, René Girard was more specific when he corrected a famous sentence of Sartre's: "Each of us thinks we are alone in hell, and that is what hell is."[35] Girard's remark describes pretty well the paradox of permissive and nevertheless unhappy modernity.

Our desires, today, are not attacked any more, but, while we would like them to be autonomous, free and sovereign, here that they are corrupted at the root by a tropism of imitation that imperils our freedom. Our desires, including sexual, are now "connected." One cannot emphasize enough the extraordinary ingenuity of this expression, which fills the bill precisely. Connected to what? To the desires of others! Those of the crowd, the magazines, public rumors — the pressure of conformity, which, when we drive it out through the door, is coming back in through the window. And before this logic of imitation we are defenseless.

The above-mentioned magazines, and the innumerable surveys and research conducted on sexuality, have materialized in order to satisfy this new itch of our era. Everything tries to keep us informed about the pretended desires of the majority, the majority that some part of us anxiously feels we should conform. As for erotic literature, it no longer follows the recipe of a superb text for solitary consumption, but the mediocre confidences of some individual whose intimate secrets we feverishly scan. To tell the truth, we are obsessed by nothing so much as by measuring our desires against those of this "other," whose voluntary hostages we have become. That conformity is even more twisted and perhaps more exacting than the archaic moralizing constraints that we are so proud to have escaped.

Thus, free to do what we want but subject to these role models, we run pitifully one behind the other, feeling a little let down. And we are all trapped by the same illusion. Each one of us is persuaded that the other, that enviable person across the way, is perfectly autonomous in his desires. Of course, the game is circular. If we envy the other person, he is envying us. Thus everyone tries to imitate everyone, to copy behaviors feverishly, in a waltz of desires shaped by the media, air-brushed, retouched, and dependent on the same constraint dissimulated under the permissive slogans.

True freedom in love would be quite different: desire freely whomever you please (man or woman, it doesn't matter), but make sure that you are making your own choice. In other words, do not servilely desire the kind of partner that others suggest for you, and don't conform to others by obeying this tyranny of imitation. However, no one is actually looking to be freed from that constraint. And all of us, believing we have broken our chains, feels intoxicated by a false sense of freedom while we are, in fact, locked into a timid obedience to the model.

Roland Barthes flushed out, in the late Seventies, this fundamental contradiction of permissiveness. "The mass culture," he wrote, "is a machinery for directing our desire: here is what should interest you, it says, as if it had guessed that mankind is incapable of figuring out by itself whom to desire."[36]

The third negative effect consists of an extraordinary aggravation of *competition*. It's as if, to our detriment, the old traditions of discretion around sexuality have been verified: the immemorial fear of touching off, in one form or another, rivalry in love. The real basis of the interdicts and anthropological taboos (especially that of incest), this competition multiplies as freedom grows. We have entered a universe of unrelenting competition, a savage love competition which Vladimir Jankelevich saw as the sign of what he dubbed the contemporary drought.

This "overpowering, suffocating" eroticism, he said, "is neither a cause nor an effect of the contemporary drought; it is the drought itself. Where joy, sincerity, impassioned conviction, the spontaneity of the heart are missing, there is room for the industrialists of eroticism. Eroticism and violence are the two alibis of an age that is fundamentally deprived of love and which fans the sexual flames in search of some sort of compensation for his incurable drought."[37]

A drought, indeed, and one that causes a new type of fear. Aren't our societies already governed, in the other fields, by general competition and the requirement of excellence? What respite remains to us, when pleasure itself suffers the same fate? Will we never be able to win on every front at the same time? We are overcome by a pathetic distress. Rather flee than to fail! On this precise topic, Cyrulnik's report is particularly chilling. "Living in a society based on worship of the individual and effectiveness, those individuals who do not want to have any sexual activity figure that the more they desire a sexual partner, the more they risk reducing their individual performance; they thus believe that by managing to extinguish their desire they will become more powerful socially."[38]

*

* *

Ah no, this is not the free and merry pleasure we were dreaming of! Was this worth the trouble of clearing away the past? We can no longer be sure that the answer is positive. In the century just ended, we learned at least one lesson: any modernity starts with an attentive — and critical — sifting through of the contents of our memory.

PART 2

LOST MEMORY

"The notion that the beliefs of all of humanity are nothing but a vast mystification from which we are perhaps the only ones to have escaped is, at the very least, premature."

Rene Girard, 1972

CHAPTER 6

IMAGINARY ANTIQUITY

Why should we evoke Greco-Latin Antiquity and not Babylon or
the Hittites? Because when it comes to pleasure, there are few myths
more durable than that of a permissive Antiquity, few errors more solid
and fraught with implications. No matter what one writes and no matter what one does in the field of sexuality, our collective imagination
designates the nebulous concept of "the Greco-Latin world" a lost paradise. It is the pre-Christian centuries that we turn to, when we think of
innocent desire, pacified hedonism and infinite indulgence. Confusedly
mixing the love frescos from Pompei with the racy writings of
Petronius and Aristophanes, the supposed refinement of Greek homosexuality and the carnal poetries of Ovid, the priapic scenes from Hel-
lenic urns and the imperial orgies as related by Suetonius, we cherish
the idea of a Greco-Roman past that would be rich in happy pleasures,
the body glorified and Eros triumphant, on a background of harmony
worthy of Virgil.

This imaginary Antiquity embodies in our eyes "an earlier time"
before the invention of sin laid it all to waste; an original and sunny
happiness that the religions of the Book are supposed to have dramatically occluded with their shades of prudishness. In our mind, this lost
world is that of happy flesh and pleasure without sin. Even our language carries a trace of this nostalgic illusion: Roman orgies, Greek

111

statuary, bejeweled women astride curly-haired Adonis and sweet warriors, the intoxication of the poets. It is to this shameless and guilt-free
universe that the artists return to when they want to evoke the powerful joy of desire given full rein. Today still, there is scarcely any debate
on eroticism, sexuality and "religious prudery" which doGes not at one
time or another call on the precedent of Antiquity — as a witness for
the prosecution.

Irreplaceable Eden from which humanity was thrown out, the
Greco-Latin epoch occupies a position in "Western" time that is in
every point comparable to that held (in their respective geographic lo-
cations) the Cythera of the poets, and more precisely O' Tahiti and the
Polynesian archipelagoes populated with languid women and innocent
desires; women offered to our flame, as the count de Bougainville
(discoverer of Oceania) described them, in 1768. "The majority of these
nymphs were naked, for the men and the old women who accompanied
them had removed the loincloths that they usually wore. First, they
made provocative gestures, from their dugouts, etc."[1]

This imaginary Tahiti gave birth to the myth of a terrestrial paradise that modern man had lost through "serious" and constraining decency, and in the same way Antiquity was used to prove the existence
of a lost original harmony. To demonstrate how strongly today's man
rejects the ambient moralism and the religious "foolishness" relating to
pleasure, he will readily evoke the sweet freedom of these Greeks and
Romans who loved without modesty under the sky of *Mare Nostrum*. In
this way, he reaffirms his conviction that it is the religions and only
they — especially Christianity — that have kept Western men and
women dramatically chained to the burden of sin in connection with
sex. The essential function of this dream-world Antiquity is to embody
a time "before" Judeo-Christianity that was happier than the "after."

The Invention of the "Shameful Parts"

Is this a fanstasy Antiquity? It is it indeed — thoroughly. This vision of the Greco-Latin world is as fantastic as was the explorers' view
of Polynesia in the 18th century. All the serious historians of Athens
and Rome write with the same vexation, the same sad surprise, about
the numerous misrepresentations of ancient sexuality. "If there is any
part of Greco-Roman life which is distorted by legend," wrote Paul

Veyne, "it is that one [sexuality]; we are wrong to believe that Antiquity was an Eden of non-repression, before Christianity put the worm
of sin into the forbidden fruit. Paganism was actually paralyzed by interdicts."

"The legend of pagan sensuality originates in traditional misinterpretations: the famous account of the vices of the emperor Elagabalus
is only a hoax for well-read men, author of a late forgery, the history of
Augustus; it is tale whose humor is halfway between that of *Bouvard
and Pécuchet* [by Flaubert] and Alfred Jarry [author of the surrealist *King
Ubu*]. Let us not mistake Ubu for a true emperor. The legend also comes
from the awkwardness of the interdicts themselves; "The Latin dares
to be frank, in words," precisely: for these ingenuous hearts, it was
enough to pronounce a coarse word to give everyone a frisson of excitement and to make everyone burst into embarrassed laughter out ;
schoolboy escapades."[2]

In a number of other texts, Veyne reconsiders this recurrent mistake of the common view, a mistake which he denounces persistently.
"To think," he says, "that paganism is synonymous with absence of sin
is an error. The pagan time was repressive in its own way."[3]

The experts on this period, all those who in one form or another
have devoted books and work to the time period, share the same surprise. The chasm is immense between the Antiquity reconstituted by
our imagination and what it was really. Foucault mentions the question
on several occasions in his *History of Sexuality*, as did George Dumézil,
Jean-Pierre Vernant, Pierre Grimal, Jean-Christmas Robert, Peter
Brown and John Boswell. This reaction is corroborated by that of specialists in Western eroticism and its history. "It is an abiding preju-
dice," wrote, for example, Alexandrian in his *History of Eroticism*, "to believe that Christianity was the enemy of erotic literature, whereas paganism was the unconditional defender. Actually, it was not the fathers
of the Church but the stoical philosophers like Seneca who started to
call the genitals the "shameful parts" or *pudenda* (the Greeks say 'the
oïdia')."[4]

Curiously, these innumerable authoritative denials do not change
anything in our view nor do they diminish the belief. Such insistent and
persistent misinterpretation of the alleged carnal happiness of Antiquity obviously cannot be explained by mere ignorance, nor by some
kind of bad faith. It reveals a hidden agenda that we could describe as

ideological, if that word, applied to the past, did not seem so anachronistic. For two millennia, this false view of Antiquity was regularly evoked, but always with one intention. The past is seldom re-read without ulterior motive, and that applies to the Greco-Roman era has been ceaselessly re-examined, re-evaluated, idealized and — more seldom — impugned, according to the requirements of the times, and the great Greek and Latin authors have been retranslated and reinterpreted. This use of Antiquity affected our own perception of Christianity, to which Antiquity was the "before," in other words the negative. The idealization of ancient morality was above all — and remains to this day — a weapon in resisting Christianity. Or in the combat against it.

Like the epic of the crusades which kept historians and whole libraries busy for nine centuries, our perception of Antiquity thus has its own history, which one seldom takes the trouble to consider. A celebration, supported during the periods of criticism or emancipation with regard to religion, a systematic deprecation of "paganism" in every counter-reform or Christian restoration. However, our contemporary prejudices about Rome and Athens quite naturally fit into the context of this history of interpretations.

Readings of Gilles de Rais

It is a long history, indeed. Since the pre-Renaissance of the 12th century, as John Boswell, for example, wrote, "The contacts maintained with the Mediterranean world were both cause and effect of this cultural efflorescence: the crusades and the Spanish *reconquista* put the Christians in closer contact with Islam and, as Europeans became better informed about the treasure of traditional knowledge preserved by Islam, an increasing number of them went to Spain and Sicily to encounter the wisdom of Athens and Rome."[5]

Three or four centuries later, the Renaissance itself would bring Italy, then France, to rediscover and exalt neo-Platonism but also, in contrast to the rigors of Catholicism, the carnal permissiveness ascribed to the pre-Christian era. The intentional sensual provocation of Michel Angelo's painting, in the mid-16th century, is grand testimony of that. It ran so counter to the Church at that time that the Pope (Paul IV) required the characters be "dressed" by an indifferent painter,

Daniele da Volterra, who became known as Braghettone (loosely, "Mr. Panties").

The relative tolerance of the Renaissance for sodomy is recorded, that too being a rediscovered ancient memory, and is accompanied by a devotion to women and the feminine values which cannot avoid some eroticism, an exemplary devotion that literature expresses through Petrarch's love for Laura, Dante's for Beatrice, Maurice Scève's for his Delia (an anagram of "the idea").

A detail that is less well-known, though significant, is that in 1434, Gilles de Rais, accused of having raped and assassinated nearly two hundred children, declared in his trial that he was impelled toward these crimes by his discovery (in reading *Suetonius*) of the similar liberties ascribed to certain Roman emperors. "I read in this lovely history book," he explained to his judges, "that Tiberius, Caracalla and other Caesars played with children and took a singular pleasure in making them martyrs. So, I decided to imitate the aforementioned Caesars, and the same evening, I started to do so, following the images reproduced in the book."[6]

In the 17th and 18th centuries, the advantageous evocation of Antiquity was a powerful argument much prized by the libertines. Restiff de Breton was pleased, toward 1760, with the wise benevolence of Athens and Rome "where manners were much less exact on the article of marriages than they are today among us," and where "nothing equaled the cleanliness and the sensitivity of the Greek and Roman courtesans" so much so that "we are, on that score, lower than the Ancients had been."[7] The same holds true, in 1780-1784, for Mirabeau's libertine texts, in particular *Erotika biblion*,[8] teeming with favorable references to the supposed merry licenses of Antiquity. In *Erotika biblion*, Mirabeau tries to show that Moderns cannot be reproached for their libertinage, since the Ancients had morals far worse. In ten chapters with bizarre titles, drawn from the Greek or Hebrew (Anelytroïda, Ischa, Tropoïda, Thalaba, Anandryme, Akropodia, Behemah, Anoscopia), Mirabeau sketches a picture of Onanism, bestiality, pederasty, lesbianism and other sexual practices of Antiquity, with an explicit intention. The supposed license of Antiquity, particularly the Greco-Latin, comes at the right moment to justify contemporary libertine claims.

During the Revolution and throughout the 19th century, the "free spirits," the militant utopians, libertines and anticlericals continued to find in Antiquity apologetic examples of free morals and free dealings with the pleasures. We know how de Sade made use of these references. And, a certain Nietzsche, who demonstrated in one movement his admiration for Napoleon and his passion for pre-Christian Antiquity, tragedy, Homer, and Greece. "In the midst of this din [of the Revolution]," he wrote, "the most enormous thing occurred. . . and with a magnificence hitherto unknown; the ancient ideal itself was displayed in flesh and bone for all of humanity."[9]

Thus, for a long time, every attempt historians made to reestablish the truth regarding Greek or *Roman Eros*,[10] every proof brought to contradict the naivety that was in vogue, was met with a voluntary deafness. A myth sticks, when it serves a function. People are still incredulous today, when anyone claims that all the sexual interdicts ascribed to Judeo-Christianity and Islam were already in force in ancient times, and that consequently the critical examination of these interdicts, while no doubt useful, should in no case be confused with a critique of religions in general and Christianity in particular.[11] Even if the undeniable periods of obscurantism and stupid prudishness experienced by the Church could give the impression that they were founded on original dogmas.

Foucault has synthesized very clearly the four great objections that are articulated against monotheism in the current public opinion. The common view is that monotheism associated sex and "the flesh" with wickedness, subjugated woman and invented misogyny, exalted sexual continence and condemned homosexuality. Imposing these four interdicts, it is supposed to have broken with all the pagan traditions at once, and for centuries to have proscribed bodily happiness. Foucault, while recognizing something specifically Christian in the approach to the concept of "flesh," showed these four charges to be off-base.

Actually, all four categories of interdict, or wariness with regard to pleasure, were perfectly well-known and widely shared during the time of ancient paganism. Still, we should emphasize that each era showed considerable differences. It would be rather flippant to visualize a dozen centuries of Roman history, with all the fluctuations of the morals which one can imagine, as a consistent entity. Pleasures were not handled the same way under the virtuous Republic, before and after the Second Punic War, in the high Empire taken up with a pruritus of pleasure, or under the Antoninus family who were concerned for the security of the empire and the return to past virtues.

The fact remains that, overall, the concern over sexual morals — including severe and repressive concerns — were never absent from the ancient world.

The Tyrant Eros

They were wary of desire and pleasure? It is enough to read Plato. In *The Laws*, he invokes the (necessary) shame which, by decreasing the frequency of sexual activity, "will somewhat weaken the tyranny;" without their having to be prohibited, certain acts "should be cloaked in mystery," and the citizens should experience, upon their being discovered, "a dishonor," and that according to a duty created by custom, not the written law. It is because men and women have a certain role to play, for a goal common — as the progenitors of future citizens — that they are held exactly in the same way to the same laws, which impose the same restrictions on them.

In the same way, in *The Republic* (Book IX), Socrates ensures that the judicious man "will not give himself up to bestial and irrational pleasure." In *Gorgias*, Plato speaks of the body as a "prison for the soul." In *Nicomachean Ethics* (7,12), Aristotle stresses that sexual pleasure inhibits thinking. As the for stoic Seneca, he wrote in a famous letter to his mother Helvia: "If you consider that sexual desire was not given to the man for his pleasure, but for the perpetuation of his race, all the other forms of desire will slip by without affecting you, unless lust has already reached you with his poisoned breath. Reason does not overcome each vice separately but all the vices at the same time. The victory is total."

A good part of ancient philosophy is against sexual desire, not because it is "bad" in itself, but because it is the locus of an energy (*energeia*) carried to excess and thus possibly the purveyor of disorder and violence. "The two large and important philosophical cults," wrote Paul Veyne, "the School of Plato and the Stoics, whose influence spread everywhere at the same time, were themselves very repressive: pleasure is suspect, one should not indulge in it unless for a purpose, that is, for reproduction. As for the Epicureans, while they may be the apostles of pleasure, what they mean by pleasure is the peace which consists in not having passions. They preach calm, and condemn eroticism."[12]

For the Greeks as well as for the Romans, man should not obey his desires with servility, but command them like a master does his servants. The sexual impulse is necessary, but is so powerful that man must be able to keep it under the influence of his will. In the eyes of the Ancients, this vigilant control would be the very sign of virility, whereas intemperance or abandoning oneself to pleasure would more likely be an entirely feminine weakness. "One's relationship with the desires and pleasures is thus conceived as a combative relationship," wrote Foucault. "One should take an adversarial position to them, whether according to the model of the soldier at war, or the contestant in a competition. . . . The long [Christian] tradition of spiritual struggle, which was to take various forms, was already clearly articulated in classical Greek thought."[13]

Along the same lines, early Christianity is still considered to have been the first to magnify continence to the point of building its whole Church on the concept of chastity. This, too, is a false interpretation. The virtuous and abstemious hero is already celebrated in the writings of Philostratus, Xenophon, and Socrates. "The ideal of virginity was not invented by Christianity. According to his biographer (Philostratus), Apollonius of Tyana (first century BC), who achieved many miracles, had taken a vow of chastity which he respected until the end of his life."[14]

For most in the Ancient world (as for the 19th century bourgeoisie), this praise of continence, even of chastity, was just a part of a widespread obsession: the fear of weakening the man because of the loss of his seed. This obsession would bring certain philosophers or doctors of Antiquity, like Hippocrates and Galen, well before the Church fathers, wanted to keep sexual energy exclusively for procreation. "In the second century BC, Soranus of Ephesus, personal doctor of Emperor Hadrian, also regarded prolonged chastity as a factor of good health: in his eyes, only the concern of securing an heir justified sexual activity. He describeed the harmful consequences of all excesses that go beyond the simple will to procreate."[15]

In another example, we know that during the early Middle Ages the Catholic Church would endeavor to use the liturgical calendar to restrict the enjoyment of sex. The calendar listed a great number of days during which the husband was proscribed from carnal activity. Studying, decyphering and analyzing this calendar of continence has occupied theologians for centuries and still keeps specialized historians like Jean-Louis Flandrin busy.[16] However, the link between religious celebrations and provisional chastity was established by the Ancients, well before the birth of Christianity. In Greece, married women who celebrated Thesmophoria in honor of Demeter were required to keep away from men, and sexual abstinence was the rule for the three days of the festival. In Rome, when they honored Ceres, matrons were prohibited from carnal pleasure and any contact with their husbands until the end of the ninth night.[17]

More generally, the very rhythm of the Roman *feriae* turns out to be similar to that of the periodic Christian continences, tied to the famous religious calendar. There too, Christianity did not invent anything. "The *dies festi* are dedicated to the gods; as feastdays, they are characterized by *feriae*: rest, leisure in honor of the gods. Any profane activity during the *feriae* is a lack of respect towards the gods. It is *pollutio feriarum*, temporal pollution of the domain of the gods, a stain on the sacred repose. . . . A revealing example of the banishment of violence is that the marriage of young girls was prohibited: the defloration which it would constitute is associated with the idea of rape, whereas weddings with widows were permitted."[18]

Love in the Dark

In day-to-day life, the interdicts of the Greco-Roman era were sometimes contrary to the permissiveness one imagines. Thus an intrusive and modesty which hardly corresponds to the supposed nudity and exhibitionism, with which we credit the Greeks and Romans. Paul Veyne cites among the interdicts, which — sometimes — interrupt the Roman erotic elegy, the fact that making love without any clothing, during the day, and without establishing complete darkness, was regarded as reprehensible. It was a dubious privilege that only the libertine assumed. The libertine was, in fact, recognized as such on the basis that he knowingly violated three fundamental interdicts.

"He made love before the night had fallen (to make love during the day was supposed to remain the privilege of new husbands right after their weddings); he made love without darkening the room (the erotic poets used as a sign the lamp which shone on their pleasures); he made love with a partner whom he had stripped of all her clothing (only the most wanton women went without their bra and, in paintings of the brothels of Pompei, even the prostitutes preserved this ultimate veil). Libertinage even allows caresses that are more than fondling, but on the condition of doing it only with the left hand, and ignoring the right. The only chance to see a little nudity during love, for an honest man, was if the moon should pass in front of the window at the right moment. It was whispered that the libertine tyrants, Heliogabalus, Nero, Caligula and Domitian, had violated other interdicts; they had made the love with married ladies, virgins from good families, adolescents who were born out of wedlock, vestals, even their own sisters."[19]

If one wants to go into the details, consider that in Rome fellatio was considered such a horror that cases can be cited of ashamed fellateurs trying to dissimulate their alleged infamy, by passing themselves off as passive homosexuals. According to Paul Veyne, a second behavior was considered to be more infamous still: cunnilingus. "The height of infamy, was oral caresses made to women. Worse still, mentioned by a furious Seneca (in the first century), was the position where the woman is held above the man. The morals of the ancient city were chauvinist, virilist.[20] A barracks-like atmosphere reigned in Rome. To be much interested women was to be soft, effeminate." Seneca is indignant, in the *Letters to Lucilius*, to see Natalis offer his "impudent tongue" for the pleasure of women and, worse still, to see Mamercus Scaurus (a consul!) practice cunnilingus without being revolted by menstruation but presenting "his mouth opened to the menstrual flow of his maidservants."

There's no doubt that, contrary to what we imagine sometimes, the most libertine of the Romans would be shocked by our morals today.

Foucault suggests the following explanation for this ancient modesty, which only reinforces its significance. "It was readily agreed that lovemaking should only take place at night, " he wrote, "given the need for hiding from view; and the care given to avoid being seen in this kind of relations, was seen as a sign that the practice of *aphrodisia* was not something that honored what is noblest in man."[21]

As for the scenes given a thousand times as so much "evidence" of Ancient license, the interpretations given are usually absurd. Thus the gesture of Diogenes asturbating in public, a gesture in what one believed to see the sign of a freedom of Athenian manners. Actually, it is "a cynical provocation" going against all the customs of Athens, where decency reigned.

But it is the symbolic — and real — status of women where the most outrageous nonsense has been spread. Even today, they claim that misogyny was an invention of (depending on the case) Judaism, Christianity or Islam, at any rate, of monotheism. Nothing could be more absurd. The aforementioned misogyny is aggressively present among the majority of the Greek and Latin authors. Plato and Aristotle both considered that the female sex is naturally inferior. Woman is not made of the same matter as man. Plato regards them as a "second hand" being, and, for Aristotle, she is a man that didn't turn out. Ovid himself, in the *Art of Love*, does not hide his contempt for women and goes as far as to defend rape. "A woman taken by force, by a rape in love, is delighted by it; this insolence is, for her, a gift." The same Ovid recommends not to hesitate in misleading women, and he adds: "In most cases, this is a race without scruples. They lay traps: let them fall in."[22]

"Among the pagans," observed the theologian France Quéré, "the myth of Pandora recalls that man's misfortunes derive from the curiosity of a woman . . . For Plato, the female sex is imposed on a man who lived badly in a former existence . . . Aristotle thinks that woman is woman because of her shortcomings."[23]

In mythology, Pandora, which is a little like a Greek Eve, is born from the hatred that Zeus feels for mortals. In the texts of Hesiod, she is explicitly described as the essence of evil, and in terms of great violence. This can be judged by these few lines from *Works and Days*: "He created an evil intended for the humans, an evil well-suited to them, which they would surround by love.... The famous Boiteux takes earth and forms the semblance of a virgin inspiring respect....Then the herald of the gods gives it speech, and names this woman Pandora. This was, indeed, a gift from all the gods, who thus made misfortune a present to the men who eat bread."[24]

Ovid mentions the conviction that, on the sexual level, woman is more powerful than man, and therefore threatening and liable to specific constraints. The old notion of "a uterine fury," transmitted from century to century, in most of civilizations, and used as an alibi for the oppression of women; an idea that Rousseau would use abundantly in *Emile*. In *The Art of Love*, Ovid says, *Acrior est nostra libidine plusque furoris habet* ("women's desire is sharper than ours and more violent"). Vis-a-vis this presumedly insatiable female desire, virile energy is all the more celebrated since all of Antiquity — especially Roman — is haunted by fear of performance failure.

Crede mihi, non est mentula quod digitus (Believe me, this organ doesn't follow orders the way a finger does), Martial said in his *Epigrams* (VI, 23). The Romans were obsessed with the evil eye, the fate which prevents the *mentula* (the penis at rest) from becoming erect, from becoming the *fascinum* (the sex in erection). A man is a man (*vir*) only when he can sustain an erection. In the third book of *Loves*, Ovid reports in detail a failure and describes the superstitious terrors which surround it. "Thus we have the incredible arsenal that is never exhibited in museums," comments Pascal Quignard, "of amulets, obscene pendants, belts, collars, burlesque gnomes, all priapic in form, made of gold, ivory, stone, and bronze, which make up the bulk of spoils of archaeological excavations."[25]

Equally revelatory of this obsession with virility is the very obscure and very ancient Roman worship of the phallic stone, called exactly the *fascinus*, a talisman which was fixed under the chariot of the victorious warrior and which was honored during the festivals dedicated to the god Liber (whose favor, according to Augustinus, "helps males in sexual union to release the seed that they emit").

In fact, in this primarily virile Antique morality, the women seem to be objects of pleasure or partners of lower status whom men must educate and keep an eye on. Among Greeks, the concept of reciprocal fidelity does not exist. Only adultery by the woman is prohibited. As for misogyny, it is often expressed with an extraordinary virulence. Thus these lines of Pline the Elder, about women's menstrual blood: "A woman who is having her period makes sweet wine sour when she approaches; she makes cereals sterile if she touches them, and grafted plants die, she burns the plants of the garden; the fruit fall out of the tree against which she sits; her glance tarnishes the polish of mirrors and steel, and takes the shine off ivory; the bees die in their hives; rust immediately seizes bronze and iron and a stinking odor is exhaled; dogs that taste of this blood become mad, and their bite injects a poison that nothing can cure."[26]

Even Plutarch, the cool and soft Plutarch, while skillful in discussing the pleasures of love with women or boys, actually testifies to a resolute machismo quite in conflict with our modern sensitivity.

"Never, as far as I have heard," he wrote in his *Precepts for Marriage*, "did a woman bring forth into the world a child without the participation of a man; the shapeless fetuses which form by themselves give the aspect of masses of flesh. . . .Ah well, care should be taken that that does not occur in the heart of the woman. Indeed, if they do not receive the seeds of noble doctrines and do not take part in men's culture, reduced to themselves, they give birth to all kinds of strange products, plans and perverse passions."

Should we even mention, finally, that Greek democracy regarded it as self-evident that women should be isolated from public and political life, like the slaves who are not citizens?

The Matrimonial Order

Another example of the contradiction in our perception of Antiquity is everything that has to do with the family. The praise and the absolute primacy of family logic in Antiquity takes both a heavy and a tyrannical turn. Authors like Plato are neither the first nor the last to explain, to quote Foucault, that "the concern for reproducing requires that vigilance be exercised in enjoying one's pleasures." That is a matter of concern to the whole city. In the *Laws*, Plato is very clear on this subject. "The human race," he writes, "has a natural affinity with the entire sweep of time, which it accompanies and will accompany through the course of existence; it is by this means that it is immortal, by leaving its children's children and thus, thanks to the permanence of its always identical unit, by taking part through the generations in immortality" (Laws, IV 721).

Among the Greeks, it was Xenophon who wrote, in his *Economics*, the first treatise on matrimonial life. One idea haunts this text: that of shelter (*stegos*), which ensures a human being and his descendants a protected place and allows them "not to live outside like cattle." Within this shelter, under this roof, the roles are shared between the man and the woman exactly in accordance with what the anthropologists call "sexual differentiation." Outdoors, the husband cultivates the ground, while indoors the wife takes care of things, regulates the expenses and looks after the offspring. The house is already seen as the woman's domain.[27]

Pliny the Elder, in his *Natural History*, praises the elephant which not only remains faithful to its mate and never commits adultery, but reveals itself more virtuous than any other animal. "Out of modesty," observes Pliny, "elephants never couple in public...They do it only every two years and, so they say, never more than five days. They have no concept of adultery." Pliny's edifying remark would be used by several Christian theologians to justify the insolubility of marriage, particularly by François de Salles, in his *Philotée* in 1609.

For the great Lucretius, author of *On the Nature of Things*, the concern for procreating, and not pleasure-seeking, must guide the wife's behavior. Marriage has nothing to do with love. For Lucretius, in any case, the wife has no need to devote herself to that "voluptuous movement" which "excites the man and makes floods of liquor spout from his body" but, alas, at the risk of preventing conception by diverting the seminal liquid from the place for which it was intended. "They are whores," he adds, "who wiggle their hips, for they have an interest there, both to avoid being too often made pregnant — since pregnancy renders them inoperative — and for better accompanying the pleasure of men: a science of which our women, I would like to believe, have no need."[28]

For the Ancients, the *domus* is not the place for love nor pleasure. To associate marriage with the idea of sensual pleasure strikes them as the height of vice or shamelessness. Moreover, marriage or not, the woman's pleasure is hardly taken into account by this chauvinist society. It is even seen as misguided to attach the least importance to this "detail." Ovid paid the price for this. In the *Art of Love*, indeed, he called for reciprocity of pleasure. ("I hate those embraces where both parties do not give themselves.") But, to the Romans, this type of feeling shows a certain shamelessness. Ovid was exiled — we never fully understood why — by Augustus, and then by Tiberius.

Among Romans, beside the obsessional concern not to waste the virile sap, another obsession is to establish and ensure what one could call "the family order," i.e. social regulation by the house (*domus*) and matron (*domina*). In this order, what counts above all is the spermatic line, the perfect coincidence between effective filiation and legitimacy. Nothing terrorized a Roman more than the prospect of having a bastard child. Marital morality is used to prevent this with unimaginable brutality — and cynicism.

Fidelity is required of a married woman not due to some unspecified feeling but purely as a matter of procreation. An adulteress is exonerated when it is proven that she was sterile or was already pregnant at the moment of the act. Similarly, a free citizen can do whatever he likes with a woman, *so long as she is not married and is not a slave.* On the other hand, as soon as there is any risk of confusing the lineage, morality becomes imperative. A married woman (*domina*) who is violated must take it upon herself to commit suicide at once. That is what Lucretia would do, when violated by Tarquinius Sextus, six centuries before our era. According to Titus Livius, she stabbed herself in the heart after declaring, "While I might exonerate myself from blame, I cannot free myself from the punishment. Let no dishonored woman call upon the example of Lucretia to preserve her life." Hundreds of Romans did the same, at the very beginning of the fifth century (410), when they were raped by the Visigoth invaders. These Romans died in heeding their pagan morals.[29]

Certainly, the extreme severity of marital morality varied according to the social classes and especially according to the times. At the advent of Christianity, let us say between the last century before our era and the first century after, the Roman aristocracy considered itself quite free from these constraints. If we believe Veyne, "the conduct of the ladies (or their misconduct) was no less than that of the men." In the aristocracy, the situation varied as well from one family to another, so that it is dangerous, as always, to generalize. The fact remains that, essentially, rigor was increased during the first three or the four centuries of our era, the period called Late Antiquity.

At certain times, matrimonial laws were adopted to regulate marriage, to encourage morality in the city, to increase the birthrate and to punish adultery as well as celibacy. There were laws of an unimaginable rigor. Thus the *Lex Julia de maritandis ordinibus* and *Lex Julia de adulteriis* (18 BC) or *Lex Papia Poppaea* (9 AD) which obliged the citizens — including widowers, widows and those who had divorced — to marry and have children forthwith, under penalty of sanctions.

"The Roman ideal of marital harmony had taken on a very crystalline hardness under the effect of the colossal weight of the Empire: the spouses were less a couple of equal lovers than a reassuring microcosm of the social order. . . . Pagans as well as Christians, the higher classes all yielded to the codes of sexual reserve and public propriety, in which they liked to think they were continuing the virile austerity of Ancient

Rome. Sexual tolerance had no place in the public domain.[30]

Starting around the year 200, and well before the Roman Empire converted to Christianity, a very repressive moral order was established, as described by Veyne. Under the authoritative and populist State, the influence of the aristocracy was no longer admissible. The emperor was anxious to strengthen his power. Homosexuality was prohibited for the first time, and criminal law seriously punished adultery and rape. Literature was censored, and the last vestiges of free morality disappeared. Repressive sexual morality is thus not Christian in origin. In its toughest version, it dates from the end of the pagan era and had to do with the political motivations of an authoritative regime.

A Secondary Preference

In this fuzzy and happy Antiquity of our imagination, the most obvious misinterpretations are those having to do with homosexuality. Contrary to what we have read or heard a thousand times, "It is not true that the pagans took an indulgent view with regard to homosexuality. The truth is that they did not see it as a separate problem."[31] Sexuality was not judged by the Greeks or the Romans according to the partner's gender. That was a rather marginal consideration. The matter of tastes, preferences, circumstances. One finds with certain authors — Plutarch for example — patient debates whose object is to weigh the respective advantages of love with a boy or a woman. Let us say that that criterion was only very incidentally taken into account. (The term "homosexuality" was coined in 1869.) For Plutarch, "He who loves human beauty [will be] favorably and equitably disposed towards the two sexes, instead of supposing that men and women differ under conditions of love as they do under clothing."[32]

Boswell notes that "Xenophon expressed the opinion of the majority of the Greeks of his time when he said that homosexuality was an aspect of 'human nature.' All the Platonic debates on love are founded on the postulate of the universality of homosexual attraction, and heterosexuality, in certain cases, figures as a somewhat secondary preference."[33] Admittedly, Plato in the *Laws* and Xenophon in the *Memorable Ones* explicitly criticize homosexuality ("It is not permissible," wrote Plato, "to use men and young boys as women"), but, in so doing, they are primarily agitating against weakness and misplacing passion. The gender of the partners is only an side argument for them. In a word, the homosexual question interested neither the Greeks nor the Romans, because, for them, it did not come up.

This (relative) indifference with regard to the gender of love partners does not mean that the Ancients were liberal or permissive, however. They simply exercised their judgement according to *criteria that were different from ours*. Four categories of measure seemed to them fundamental in sexual matters, four parameters that could be debated: the ability or failure to control one's desires, freedom in love vs. marital fidelity, an active or passive role in love, the partner's status as a free man or slave.

Indifferent or indulgent with regard to what we call homosexuality, they were not so in the least when it came to "passivity." For a free man to have homosexual relations as a passive partner was regarded as an unpardonable offense. Weakness, effeminacy, the ways of a man imitating a woman's behavior were objects of universal mockery in the very chauvinist Greek — and especially the Roman — world. Of the many possible examples, let us quote this text from the father of Seneca (Seneca the Rhetorician) who would be regarded as an activist, today. "An unhealthy passion for singing and dancing fills the heart of our effeminate youth; tossing their hair, making their voices tender enough to equal the caress of female voices, competing with women in weakness of attitudes, studying at highly obscene research, here is the ideal of our adolescents. . . . Softened and enervated since birth, they willingly remain so, always ready to attack the modesty of others and not looking to their own."[34]

This condemnation of "shamelessness" (passivity) in love, whether homosexual or not, was more rigorous still if it related to a public figure. Human weakness in passion and desire became dangerous for the State when it concerned an elected official, and for the army when it concerned a citizen-soldier. Therefore it was savagely denounced. In Athens, for example, male prostitution entailed the loss of civic rights. A passive homosexual, if he had a mind to enter politics, was punished with death. He was regarded as even more infamous than the adulteress, who could also be condemned to death.

"He who is effeminate, the *pathicus*, who, although a citizen, submits to another's law, free or slave, offers the very image of dishonor and forfeiture. Nothing is more shameful than to see a slave burrowing inside his master, to quote Juvenal."[35]

As we know, the great paradox of the Greco-Roman world is that pedophilia was more acceptable than homosexuality between adults. "These acknowledged and exalted pederastic relations," wrote Maurice Sartre, "refer to couples formed of one young man (*pais*), of twelve, thirteen to seventeen or eighteen years, and a still young adult (hardly more than forty years). The initiatory character of the relation requires such an age difference."[36] Pedophilia was an initiation in every sense of the term, and not only sexual.

However, it was not always as pleasant and trivial as one imagines. First, it can be transformed into prostitution and is, in that case, condemned. (In Aristophanes' play, *The Clouds*, the author condemns the general degradation of morals and the metamorphosis of the young erotomane into a male prostitute.) But above all, the least inclination toward pedophilia (or active homosexuality) is immediately liable to the death penalty if it has to do with a slave. The radical contrast between free man and slave was, fundamentally, the great question hanging over the Greco-Roman society. When we refer to their morality, the supposed licenses and pleasures, we usually forget to take into account the overwhelming fact that this was a slave society, where sexual morals varied hugely according to one's social status. (The claim of equality would be "a subversion," of stoical origin, then Christian.)

A Slave Society

To evoke this socially unequal aspect of Roman morals, it is useful to quote Seneca the Elder, again. In his *Controversies* (IV, 10), he has the consul Quintus Haterius pronounce this sentence, which has become famous: "Passivity is a crime for a man who is free from birth; for a slave, it is an absolute duty; for one who has been freed, it is a service which he has the duty to render to his owner." In slave-keeping Rome, the master always has a right of cuissage over his slaves, whatever their sex, so that the slaves made a virtue of the necessity with a proverb that was widespread at the time: "There is no shame in doing what the master bids."

That means that one may agree to be sodomized by the master without shame. For him, full freedom consists in having the power to sodomize — and even kill — his slave. "Sodomizing one's slave," remarks the same Veyne, "was innocent, and even the most severe critics hardly bothered with such a trivial question. On the other hand, it was monstrous for a citizen to engage in passive indulgences."[37]

No, the society of Antiquity was not truly "soft!" It was still less so, if one takes the trouble to establish the link between this crushing reality of slavery and Ancient prostitution, including that of children. Thanks to Suetonius, we know the fairly revolting case of the emperor Tiberius, pedophile absolute, who called encouraged children of the tenderest age (whom he called "little fish" [*pisciculus*] to play between his thighs while he swam, to excite him with their tongues and little bites. He gave his penis to suckle children who were not yet weaned, so that they might discharge its milk. It is less well-known, on the other hand, that in late Rome, the wealthy bought themselves young African, Egyptian and Nubian slaves for sexual enjoyment. Merchants made a special trade of it on the edges of the Nile and as far as Ethiopia.

The Latin historian Stace, author of *Silves* and *Thébaïde*, described "the display of these human goods on a platform, among other products from the barbarian countries, and the attitude of these poor children who were obliged to look nice, to repeat words they had learned by heart, to make jokes that were prepared in advance, and to use lascivious provocations to try to get themselves purchased by some debauched old man whose libido might be excited by this disturbing comedy." He paints a picture of kids bought for the pleasure of adults and who were dubbed with charming nicknames: *delicati pueri*, *deliciae domini*, *deliciolum*, etc.

This traffic in slave children recalls — but far more brutally — our contemporary pedophile tourism. Except that, in ancient Rome, it was done in broad daylight. Boswell gave an even harsher description of this Roman tradition.

> The slave merchants, (he wrote) practiced on a large scale the castration of young boys, to the disgust of certain Romans; that seems to have been prohibited by the provisions of a law dating from the reign of Domitian. Petronius has one of his characters in the *Satiricon* give a burlesque harangue against this custom, but Seneca and others are sincerely indignant.... The association of homosexuality with ill treatment of children, noticeable since the 4th century, partly resulted from

the extreme diffusion of an ancient habit that modern industrial civilization rejects absolutely: the abandonment of the unwanted children, who were sold into slavery. A very great number of them became objects of sexual pleasure, at least between their adolescence and the moment when they were capable of servile labor. Testimonies of pagan authors (Justin the Martyr) and of Christian apologists (Clement of Alexandria) leave no doubt as to the omnipresence of this practice.[38]

This sexual exploitation of children was widespread and long enduring. "It took until the end of the first century AD for an edict by Domitian to prohibit the prostitution of young children."[39] It is true that, in general, "not until 374, under the Christian influence, was the elimination of new-born babies legally described as murder. Seneca explained that it was common in Rome to drown deformed or weak newborns. He himself considered this attitude reasonable (*De Ira*, 1,15). Suetonius (born in 70) says that it was up to the parents to decide whether to abandon infants (*Caïus Caligula*, 5). Plutarch wrote, in his biography of Lycurgus, that the city of Sparta subjected new-born babies to examination by old; babies considered to be deformed or runts were thrown from a cliff on Taygetos in order to keep them from becoming a burden to the State. He also relates that mothers bathed their new-born babies in wine and not water, for morbid children and epileptics did not withstand this treatment and died."[40]

These few examples remind us of the effective *cruelty* of the Greco-Latin world, at least from the standpoint of today's sensibilities. They render quite ridiculous the evocations of Ancient "hedonism" that the advent of our era supposedly destroyed. The Greek world, and especially the Roman world, were structured around certain forms of discrimination (slaves/free men, free-born/liberated, matrons/girls, patricians/plebeians), the rigidity and inequality of which would revolt the modern beings that we are. As would the fairly common practice of gang rapes, rapes which "Roman morality allowed for free adolescents, deflowered at fourteen or fifteen years, who chased hookers in the red light districts, beat up middle-class men that they met at night, for a laugh, or, still as a gang, forced the door of a woman of ill repute to rape her collectively."[41]

For the Roman citizen, admittedly, sexuality is above all a form of domination. "It was for him to break in the superb ones," wrote Virgil in the *Aeneid*. He is "absolute master in his house, has the right of life and death over his wife, her children, his slaves."[42] This mentality of the dominator is exercised in the same way in his sexual life, as myth testifies with the abduction of the Sabines.

In the same way, we would without any doubt be revolted by the incredible venality which reigned in the Rome of the low Empire and which largely influenced the alleged hedonism. Veyne wrote a gripping description: "Roman society was so charged with self-interest that an anti-Semite would have been able to take Rome rather than the Jews as an obsessional topic; by which I mean to say, simply, that economic activities were neither the specialization of certain professionals nor characteristic of a given social class. In Rome, every rich person made everything into a deal, every senator lent at usurious rates, and money-making mixed with politics was even more widespread than at the end of the *Ancien Régime*, except that it was not hidden. This multifarious omnipresence of profit made up for the absent middle class. The ladies, avid for gifts, made deals too; they ran after presents because the men ran after dowries."[43]

The omnipotence of money, the cruelty of slavery and circus, the instability of marriage and the fact that wives could be repudiated at will (especially since the third century BC), the harshness of pagan morals for adulterous or raped matrons, sexual abuse of children and slaves: this was the landscape in which Christianity emerged.

CHAPTER 7

JEWS AND CHRISTIANS CONFRONTING THE FLESH

On this subject, a cool head and a calm spirit are needed. This great question of Judeo-Christian religion and sexuality must be examined deliberately, without haste and without taking sides,. Nothing is more difficult today. In this domain, the condemnatory rages are exactly symmetrical to the favor that is still (in spite of everything) shown for the imaginary Antiquity evoked above. It is true that the moral rigidity of Pope Jean-Paul II, capping off long decades of clerical tension, does not help. Finding in the recent past some good reasons for it, the permissive discourse is still calling Christianity the inventor of sin, of "sexual pessimism," of the exalted continence, if not of misogyny itself.

"Nowadays in the West," says Évelyne Sullerot, "it is always the Judeo-Christian tradition that is attacked. It has been blamed systematically, without the least analysis, for everything that appears unfavorable to women. This unreflective haste is probably due to the fact that we no longer reason along any category but one: sexuality! Freedom, equality, rights, etc., are judged only according to material goods or sexual freedom. The monotheist religions take on the appearance of great systems for enslaving women."[1]

Hasty Remonstrations

This anti-religious fixation is part of a contemporary reflex which, on this topic at least, is extravagant. Have people lived for two millennia in neurosis, misfortune, frustration?! Has the West as a whole been trudging along for two thousand years under the cane of repressed desires and restricted freedom?! And, only today we, the emancipated individuals of the industrial society, have grounds for designating our ancestors as so many children persecuted by the priest and the theologian; as captives chained in the hold, rowing toward a world of freedom finally reached: ours.

Authors as free of religious bigotry as Foucault, Boswell and Brown have been as ironical toward this naivety of modern thought about Judeo-Christianity as they are about the hedonistic idealization of the ancient world. "We must guard against over-simplifying," wrote Foucault, "and reducing the Christian doctrines on marital relations to the procreative purpose and the exclusion of the pleasures. In fact, the doctrines are complex, they require discussion, and there are many alternatives."[2] As for John Boswell, militant homosexual and founder of *queer theory* (to which we will return later), he opened his long study on homosexuality in medieval history with these words: "The present volume expressly aims, in many pages, to refute the idea that intolerance towards homosexuals originated in Christian — or other — religious beliefs."[3]

When we say extravagant, we do so advisedly. Isn't it extravagant, indeed, to talk about Paul's contemporaries — Clement of Alexandria, the Jewish thinkers Philo of Alexandria and Flavius Josephus, Augustine and, more generally, our distant ancestors — as if they were poor little illiterates or eccentric conspirators? Significantly, this retrospective self-satisfaction is a fact among some contemporary commentators who are in the most hurry to put down their predecessors, even while claiming, despite everything, to be grounded in theology.

Let's take just one example, a caricature. In a book translated into French, a German "theologian" introduces Pope Siricus as a "a sexual neurotic," suspects Augustine of "a psychic disorder" and "pathological behavior," evokes "the apartheid practiced by the heads of the Church with regard to women [which is] as serious as political apartheid" (p. 156), talks about "straying sexual morality which, after almost two thousand years of proud dictatorship over conjugal bedrooms, has still not decided to give up its role" (p. 201). She finishes by quite simply denouncing "this unbearable Catholic heresy according to which the true misdeeds of humanity are made in conjugal bedrooms and not the war scenes and the mass graves."[4]

Beyond their unintended comic appeal, one will note that such extreme language reflects, in a falsely erudite way, an offhandedness that, alas, is too widespread. They testify especially to the contemporary habit of making approximations, disastrous for real thinking. This can become a little bit irritating to anyone who takes the trouble to revisit the texts, the debates of era or the work of real specialists. These hasty remonstrations ultimately consist in intervening retrospectively *against* one camp in favor of another, against a "repressive" tendency in favor of a poorly identified "liberal" tendency. They amount to questioning the past *as a whole* according to today's standards, without hesitating for a second over the anachronism of their approach: to take the conceptual framework of today's court ten or fifteen centuries back, to judge the actors of that time. They pretend to impose on the era under consideration an achievement that was actually very recent, a very new "point of view" with regard to history: individualism. Individualism was quite unthinkable in the holistic societies of yesteryear. It is intoxicatingly — and gratifyingly — convenient to denounce "religious oppression" from fifteen centuries away.

Three Million Lines

That's not all. Certain new exegetes are upset that the Bible may have been misinterpreted for two thousand years; that the Church of Rome has been embarrassingly captive of an error of exegesis, of translation even, like a political party encumbered by a badly written motion. When they hear all that, those spirits less inclined toward religiosity rebel in the name of simple reason.

But this seems too simple a thesis, too retrospective, indeed too condescending, to assume that one such as Thomas Aquinas, through some form of obtuseness, could have made an error in interpreting Matthew (19,12: *[There are some...] eunuchs, which have made themselves eunuchs for the kingdom of heaven's sake. He that is able to receive it, let him receive it*), or that Augustine, bishop of Hippo, should have inflected his reading of the

Gospel under the weight of his past fornications. Instinctively, we challenge the idea that purely "technical" matters of transmission could have influenced the destiny of the entire West for fifteen or sixteen centuries. Similarly, we reject the abrupt assertion that today we should have finally arrived at a moment of exegetic perspicacity, of a modern higher intelligence, which would make it possible to rectify, in short, these calamitous misinterpretations, like a clerk correcting a copy. It is the arrogance and the naivety of the approach that leaves us perplexed. What? Does our era have such a great record for perspicacity that we should claim to set straight the likes of, say, Pascal or John Chrysostom, Maimonides, Bossuet, St. John of the Cross (de la Cruz), Master Eckhart or Ignatius of Loyola?

We are asked to accept unquestioningly (it would be so simple, so comforting, so reassuring) the idea that for two thousand years the Church obstinately refused to understand the mysteries of sexuality and the requirements of happiness. Such a proposition causes a purely intellectual impatience. Let's not forget what kind of ethical debates were launched, in the first centuries of Judeo-Christianity and then of Christianity, with Roman ladies set on Latin stoicism, with Greek Platonism meeting Hebraic wisdom, those erudite talkers and "quibblers" who crossed the path of Origen and Clement of Alexandria, the finicky patricians and attentive jurists who unceasingly evaluated and re-evaluated the relevance of the Christian Epistles and the teachings of the Jewish sects. Were these innumerable assemblies of obscurantists? Were they so backward and ignorant, these attentive readers of Plutarch and Epictetus, that a superficial commentator from 1997 could, from a distance of seventeen centuries, challenge them and scornfully correct them?

Is it well-known that "Melanie — a friend of Jerome — had read three million lines of Origen and two and half million lines of more recent authors, the Cappadocians included? That means that she was familiar with a corpus of Christian literature three hundred times more extensive than Homer's *Iliad* (Jerome's *Letters*)." And shall we overlook the fact that in Rome, at the same time, "Marcella, a widow, disciple of Jerome, and her peers, aided the Christian men and women to understand a world where, come from the Greek orient, letters, manuscripts and doctrinal declarations were flooding Italy"?[5]

Ignorant, these people? Naïve, these remote ancestors? Actually, by remonstrating with the past, and with texts that, quite simply, we no longer know how to read, our era tells more about itself, as it feels its way through confusion and amnesia. Contemporary interpretations of the religious writings actually reflects a moment in history, expressing a quest, sometimes, is unconscious aware of itself. Today's eagerness to denounce the past is above all a sign of uncertainty. Nothing moreover, nothing less.

*

*   *

For all that, the current distress of Christianity about sexuality and the resulting disciplinary inflexibility *are not in doubt*. It is, indeed, an immense subject of reflection, to which Alphonse Dupront, the recent philosopher and Christian historian, called our attention. These few lines penned y him in 1993 are worth quoting, because they cover the essentials without arrogance or naivety:

"A Christian pessimism that has long been anxious about any attempt to exalt the gifts of God, including the body, a view of time as a continuous decline since the era of the lost paradise, the gnawing anguish of eternal salvation still present at the threshold of present times, still underlies man's belief in disincarnation. Something extra, more angelic and less beastly. Today this has taken its liberation with a furious insolence and joy, and the Church, faced with the exaltation and the intoxication of the bodies, finds itself empty-handed. Its precepts remain moral; they are not rules for acceptance or for self-maintenance. However, they become essential to a humanity that is now unrestrained in its flesh. Otherwise monism will triumph over the flesh, leading naturally to violence. That is a worrisome sign for the Church: the more the body anarchically takes up all the room, without any other end than itself, the more Catholicism retracts into religion, "the spirit of truth," reducing or even neglecting in the liturgies and the services that which had been a sacral collective therapy: ceremony."[6]

Something truly outrageous happened during the first three or four centuries of our era, at the moment when Greek thought met with Judaism and Christianity: something which formed us as Westerners and which we are now forced to relearn if we want to understand ourselves.

137

The Source of the Forbidden

In sexual morality more than in any other field, it is the (magnificent) idea of *confluence* that one must keep in mind. The Christian message as it was developed during these first centuries borrows directly from Greco-Roman thought and from Judaism. It is in precisely this arena that this extraordinary *encounter*, the founding of the West, most clearly took place. However, at the moment when Christianity was emerging, these two great currents (Greco-Roman and Jewish) had both just undergone what one could call a puritanical hardening. On the pagan side, in the preceding chapter we have already seen that stoicism, and later neo-Platonism, defied passion in love, desire and pleasure. Rejecting disorder and unruliness, it brought new sexual interdicts and moral precepts that would have a considerable influence on the first fathers of the Church. And not the reverse.

Foucault has shown that one of the first major Christian texts devoted to sexual practice, Clement of Alexandria's *Paidagogos* (*The Instructor*), was founded "on an ensemble of principles and precepts directly borrowed from pagan philosophy. Already a certain association is seen between sexual activity and evil, procreative monogamy as a rule, condemnation of relations with the same sex, and the exaltation of continence."[7]

But it is less well-known that the same held true for the Judaism of the time, that of the rabbis, who were themselves influenced by various pagan currents and marked by an overall tightening up. The rejection of the sexual deviance and the vices displayed in the Greco-Roman world played a part in this evolution. The practice of institutionalized prostitution and homosexuality — condemned in the Old Testament — scandalized the rabbis, whose reaction, to quote Josy Eisenberg, "transformed the modesty of biblical times into true Puritanism." But there were other factors too. The same Eisenberg recalls that the Jewish society of Paul's era was already changed, especially in relation to women. The biblical religion had already evolved to become rabbinical Judaism. "The majority of Jews," she writes, "no longer lived in Judea, but in the Diaspora. The nature of the religiosity changed. It was no longer centered around the cult of the Temple but around the Law; and the spiritual Masters were no longer prophets nor even priests but a new category of sages: the rabbis. . . . Thus knowledge became the true source of power: knowledge, that is, the knowledge of the Torah and its commentaries. However this knowledge was the prerogative of men; and thus, for the first time, a real imbalance was created between the status of men and that of women."[8]

In the last centuries prior to Christianity, the sexual interdicts and proscriptions already present in the Old Testament and the message of the prophets were reinforced. Which ones? In the original Judaism, the rules of periodic continence, for example, which carry within them the notion of sexual impurity, were founded on three passages from the Old Testament. "To prepare the Hebrews for the divine revelation of Mount Sinai, Moses required that they keep away from their wives for two days (*Ex.* 19:15). The priest Ahimelech gave hallowed bread to the famished David only after having been assured that the David had not had relations with a woman for several days (*I Sam.* 21:1-6). Finally, according to *Leviticus* (15:18), both spouses were impure until the evening after having been together maritally."[9]

Judaism and the Family

In practice, the various sexual interdicts were punished severely. "The death penalty," notes Josy Eisenberg, "was generally the penalty for transgressing those sexual interdicts considered most serious: in addition to adultery, various forms of incest in the first degree, homosexuality and zoophilia." To sanction adultery, *Leviticus* (20:10) is very clear: "If a man commits adultery with [another man's] wife, both he and the woman shall be put to death."[10] *Leviticus* is quite as severe on the question of homosexuality. "No man is to have sexual relations with another man; God hates that" (18:22); and "No man or woman is to have sexual relations with an animal; that perversion makes you ritually unclean" (20:13).

Women, unlike the many priestesses, vestals and pythias of the pagan religions, were isolated from worship and sacerdotal functions. The principle of impurity related to menstruation was a difficulty, but there was also a mistrust whose sexual origin is beyond doubt. "Jewish popular wisdom," wrote Peter Brown, "like that of the pagans, made much of the alluring tricks used by women and the disorder that was created when women asserted rights under pretext that they carried the men's children and shared their beds. "Simplicity of heart," let us not forget, was a deeply male quality: upstanding men were strongly inclined to see women as the cause of "duplicity of heart." Women had the reputation of encouraging the lubricity and jealousy that set men against one another."[11]

The *Talmud* is no gentler towards the seductive powers of women, whose "light spirit" it denounces and whom it compares on several occasions to witches. "The best of women, it suggests, is a witch. Sorcery is more widespread among the women."[12]

As for lust in general, the prophets denounce it repeatedly. The prophet Hosea, for example, stigmatized the moral corruption of Israel: "Listen to the word of the Eternal, children of Israel, for the inhabitants of the country are on trial before the Eternal: there is neither sincerity, nor love, nor knowledge of God in the country, but perjury and lies, assassination and theft, adultery and violence." Jeremiah, in a famous passage (*Jeremiah*, 5:8), uses a still more severe formula to condemn his contemporaries' lust. "They were like well-fed stallions wild with desire, each lusting for his neighbor's wife."

In spite of the omnipresence of sexual interdicts, the Old Testament supercedes everything with what one might call a super-appreciation of the value of the family and procreation, which reorients and softens the rigor of the same interdicts. Everything in Judaism favors — highly — the family, maternity, the attention given to childraising. This primary requirement makes it hard to conceive of a celebration of celibacy or chastity. A woman who becomes mother is said to be "built." The word "son" (*ben*) is derived from the verb *bnh*, "to build." "*Genesis* is crisscrossed almost obsessively with the topics of sterility and maternity. . . . The wives of the three patriarchs are struck with sterility. The book of *Genesis* is written on the background of the pitched battle that they had to carry out in order to give life, to the point, we might say, of making sterility and fruitfulness the great obsession of the first era of the Bible."[13]

In the *Book of Proverbs*, we find a long elegy endorsing the housewife: "She rises while it is still night, distributing food to her household and orders to the maidservants. . . . Grace is misleading, and beauty useless! The wise woman, now that is the one who should be praised." "In Judaism," summarizes Peter Brown, "the women were kept away from the central activity of the rabbis. Except for rare outstanding exceptions, the women did not participate in transmitting tradition through the intensive study of the *Torah*. On the other hand, the married woman ensured the biological continuity of Israel. She maintained the house from which the scholars and the sons of scholars came."[14]

The absolute power of procreation and the family to prevail is so powerful that it leads the Old Testament to tolerate sometimes the transgression of certain sexual interdicts, including the most serious, any time maternity and the survival of the species are concerned. The episode of Lot's daughters is most revealing. It takes place after the destruction of Sodom by divine fire. Lot and his daughters flee in an apocalyptic atmosphere. At this point in time, the girls decide to engage in incest with their father *in order to be able to procreate*. "The older daughter said to her sister, 'Our father is getting old, and there are no men in the whole world to marry us, so that we can have children. Come on! Let's get our father drunk, so that we can sleep with him and have children by him" (*Genesis*, 19:31-32). And the gravest transgression of Biblical interdict (incest!) is by no means condemned in the text.

As for the significance of the story of Onan, which occurs three generations later in the family of Abraham, it is similar. Tamar married Er, the elder son of Judah (great-grandson of Abraham), but he died without child. According to the law of the levirate, Tamar is given in marriage to her brother-in-law, Onan. But he, instead of impregnating his wife, spills his seed on the ground. It is the refusal to procreate and not his taste for solitary pleasure that makes him liable to severe condemnation and even death. "Er's conduct was evil, and it displeased the Lord, so the Lord killed him" (*Genesis*, 38: 7)."[15]

The Rabbinical Crackdown

During the last centuries before Jesus Christ, Judaism underwent an internal evolution, which took the form of a puritan crackdown. The evolution was already perceptible between the ancient texts of the narrative called *yahvist* (8th century BC) and the more particular and more clerical monotheism of the, Sacerdotal Document three centuries later.[16] It continued to be accentuated. In what are called the deutero-canonical books, the reprobation of adultery is intensified. A new concept appears, *Yetser Hara*, or "the bad proclivity," the impulse, the libido, that Jean Daniélou interprets as the evil spirit but also the sexual instinct. "Sexuality," he wrote, "seemed to be strongly linked to a wicked principle in man. This enables us to understand certain other aspects of Judeo-Christian asceticism. The use of purification baths, in addition to baptism, that one finds with the Ebionites and the Elcesaites but elsewhere as well, are related to the same principle."[17]

Another sign giving evidence of this harder attitude is that certain Jewish texts dating from the very first centuries of the Christian era contain passages that are far more virulently antifeminist than any in the Old Testament. Eisenberg cites two examples. In the *Talmud of Jerusalem* ("Treatise on the Shabbat," II, 6), these lines refer to women: "They lose their blood because Eve poured out the blood of Adam and introduced death into the world; they must make bread, because Adam was the bread of the world; finally, they should light the shabbat candles because they extinguished the light of the world." In the *Rabbah Genesis* (17, 88), is a passage more violent still: "Why do women need to perfume themselves, and not men? It is because Adam was created out of the earth, and the earth does not stink, whereas Eve was created out of a bone. And when you leave meat for three days without salting it, it stinks."

This evolution of Judaism took place under the noticeable influence of a pessimistic current which came directly from Persia and probably from India, called *gnosis*[18] (knowledge). It proclaims the vain character of all existence, rejects marriage and the consumption of wine and meat. Among other ways, its influence on Judaism is shown by the proliferation of cults professing a radical sexual rigor. The discovery of the Dead Sea Scrolls in 1947, then their deciphering, has made it possible to know more about these groups whose influence on early Christianity was decisive. The Essenes and the cult of Qumrân (from the name of the wadi running through the vicinity), which Daniélou regards as "an offshoot of Judaism," were among the most radical. Regarding themselves as warriors of Israel, as an army in order of battle, they required the male members of the cult to take vows of chastity and even celibacy. In their eyes, to quote Brown, "one should not allow to disperse in the disordered state of simple civilians, whose seed ran freely while they pleasantly shared their wives' beds." Contrary to the pagan traditions, they cultivated an absolute disgust for promiscuity, nudity and running homosexual love practiced among young people in the ancient cities. They expressed a great vigilance with regard to ritual purification governing the woman's menstrual cycle and the emission of seed from man.

Pliny the Elder left his assessment of this puritan cult (in his *Natural History*). It is rather revealing of what the pagans of the time were thinking. "A unique tribe, and more astonishing than any other in the world, without a single woman, all pleasures of love rejected. . . thus, for thousands of centuries (how incredible), a race continues to exist where nobody is ever born." Rather similar to the description of the Essenes penned by the Jewish historian Flavius Josephus (who died around the year 100 AD and who authored *Bellum Judaicum (History of the Jewish War)*. He writes, "The Essenes turn away from life like something evil and embrace continence as a virtue. They have an unfavorable opinion on marriage. . . . They are wary of the inconstancy of women, convinced that none of them is capable of fidelity to her husband."

Thus, in terms of sexual morality, the birth of Christianity and the four centuries which followed were conditioned by this threefold influence of pagan stoicism, the new rabbinical rigor, and Jewish cults inspired by Eastern gnosticism. Most of the sexual interdicts that are blamed on the fathers of the Church actually can be traced to this decisive confluence.[19]

One emblematic figure summarizes it completely. A contemporary of Jesus, Philo of Alexandria, an extraordinarily cultivated representative of Hellenized Judaism, fiercely determined to wed the Jewish faith with Greek philosophy of stoical inspiration. The sexual morality that he professed, even before the birth of an autonomous Christianity, is very severe. Philo praises procreation as the sole objective in marriage (as against the quest for pleasure). He goes further than the Greeks in condemning relations with a woman that one knows to be sterile, relations which are thus inspired only by the thirst for enjoyment. He stigmatizes contraception and condemns homosexuality in incredibly severe terms, recommending "to kill without hesitation. . . the effeminate man who disfigures the work of nature and. . . helps to depopulate the cities and turn them into a desert by letting his seed be lost."

"Encratite" Subversion

So the New Testament did not come up with anything new? That is not completely true. With Christianity, a perception of the "flesh" emerged in the effervescent East of the first century, that marked not a rupture with the Judeo-stoical rigorism (there is, indeed, continuity) but a marked shift. In the centuries to follow, this inflection, far from triumphing as a dogma, continued to be *debated*. Actually, this debate from the early days never ended, and still goes on today.

To describe this major twist, introduced by Christianity, Veyne uses a beautiful metaphor: "The age of the flesh and sin having succeeded that of controlled pleasures, man is no longer an administrator who rationally governs each detail of his affairs, or a motorist who manages as well as possible, yard by yard, the trajectory of his vehicle: he becomes a voyager, a pioneer through a wild region; this explorer must be vigilant against the wild beasts that may, at any moment, attack the improviser; these beasts are called the temptation to sin. One of them is *la lonza leggiera e presta molto*, that is, lust, which nearly devoured the traveler Dante in the first canto of hell."[20]

Our minds today have difficulty conceiving how this plan of "renunciation of the flesh," beyond any teaching, suddenly set ablaze whole groups of men and women, from Syria to Palestine. It was neither the theologians nor the priests who, initially, conveyed this idea of resolute chastity from province to province, but a mixed community, led by wandering preachers. They were poor; they walked along the shores of the Mediterranean, singing, drunk on absolute continence and waiting for the Kingdom. Under the incredulous gaze of the pagans, they offered an image that was amazing at the time, "of a lasting serenity and a kind of chaste friendship between the sexes. [In their eyes,] the presence of the Holy Spirit had seen to it that the formidable current that used to run through their bodies had been cut off. No spark could flare up, treacherously, between formerly charged male and female poles." [21]

Is this a kind of mystical madness? Is it a strange state of mind like the cult phenomena of the end of the 20th century? This movement, which was directly derived from the Essene cults and the Eastern gnostics, would soon be theorized and organized. From the end of the first century, it would have its theologians and its proselytes among the fathers of the Church, who would be opposed by all those who, on the contrary, remained in favor of marriage and procreation. Thus would be constituted, either within the Christian Church of the first centuries, or outside of it (as it was the case with the Manichean heresy), an extremist antipode regarding sexuality, comparable to the Jewish cults of the last centuries BC in relation to Judaism. This movement was baptized "encratism," from the Greek enkrateia, which means continence. The Cathares of the 12th century would be Encratism's distant heirs.

What motivated these first Encratites? First, the conviction that they were living in apocalyptic times, that is, close to the coming of the Kingdom. In other words, these men and women were convinced — like Paul himself — that they would see *in their own lifetime* the end of this world. No attempt to interpret Encratism makes sense if it does not start from this apocalyptic prospect. Then, by choosing continence, these first Christians were (clearly) not acting out of a concern to found a "morality" or some kind of lasting "civilization" as is usually believed. (Without procreation, that would be nonsense anyway.) On the contrary, they wished, they even considered it their duty, to hasten the collapse of "this world," a world that would soon be "swept away by the Messiah's tidal wave."[22]

To the pagan world, committed to the dull perpetuation of the terrestrial order (the *perpetuum mobile*), their approach was thus subversive in the strongest sense of the word. As Marcion, Tatian and Valentinus (three of the first Encratite Masters) expressed it, their intention was to stop "the firestorm raging in the universe" and the "formidable fire" (sexuality) which "helps the world." To abstain is to flip the switch, to stop "the cascading flood of mankind" and to precipitate the extinction of "the kingdom here below" in favor of the other one.

This subversion was not solely directed, in a very abstract way, against the world here below. It was also aimed at the ancient city itself and, of course, the Roman Empire. The Encratite Christians not only rejected procreation, they refused violence, and consequently military service. It is was this double refusal of family and army which would cause, the return of anti-Christian persecutions at the very beginning of the Third century, after those of Nero. The very first legal act directly targeted against the Christians was an edict by the emperor Severus, promulgated in 202. "While Severus was reforming the marriage laws, seeking to strengthen the family, these Christians were condemning marriage and calling on all their brothers to practice continence. While the borders of the Empire were being threatened by Parthians in the east and by Scots in the north, and when it was necessary to mobilize all forces, the Christians suggested refusing military service.[23]

"The Cause of All That"

But other motivations figured, at least in the beginning, in the birth of this Encratite movement. Among them, one must mention (for it would be a constant in history) the desire to escape the accusations of vice levied against the Christians of the first centuries. The fact of living in mixed communities, i.e. in promiscuity, of mixing men and women with the celebration with their worship made them liable to be suspected of license, even of lust. Many pagan authors, including Tacitus and Pliny the Elder, paradoxically reproached Christianity for supporting sexual laxness, including homosexuality. The apologia and the effective practice of continence would constitute effective responses to these charges.

For the same reason, the pagan tradition of voluntary castration (actually very ancient) saw a return to favor during the first centuries of Christianity. Several evangelists refer to it. Luke mentions married men, disciples of Jesus, who "left house, wife, brothers, relatives and children for the Kingdom of God" (18:28). Matthew adds that certain young men "have made themselves eunuchs for the Kingdom of Heaven's sake" (19:12), the intensity of their mission making them unsuitable to marriage (19:12). Monastic sources from the time of primitive Christianity report several attempts, failed and bloody, at self-castration by despairing monks. John's *Apocryphal Acts* (53-54, 2, 241) cite the case of a young man who castrated himself, spectacularly, using a sickle, declaring: "Here is the model and the cause of all that."

In the time of Justin, a young man from Alexandria had asked the prefect for permission to be castrated, for he hoped to persuade the pagans that Christian men were not looking for sexual favors from their "sisters." As for Origen, he had gone discreetly, around the year 206, to a doctor to be castrated in order to quiet the libelous rumors (according to its partisans) on the intimacy which he enjoyed among Christian women.

These intentional emasculations were not isolated cases. They became so widespread that two emperors at least took repressive measures to prohibit them: Domitian (d. 96 AD) and Hadrian (d. 138 AD) decided to punish them by death, a sentence extended as well to the doctor who had performed them.

But this choice of continence on the part of the Encratites (which did not always imply that one went to such extremes) had another

146

goal, more doctrinal: to dissociate themselves from Judaism by clearly affirming what one would nowadays call an "identity." To survive as a group, at the end of the First century, while Judaism and Christianity were still very much interrelated, the Encratites wanted to establish rules that were as clearly identifiable as the Jewish Law. Justin thus stated that Jesus had brought them "a law. . . against another law [that] countermands that which preceded it" (*Dialogue with Tryphon*, 11,2).

However the thorough codification and punishment of sexual interdicts hitherto constituted the main difference between the Jews and the gentiles. The Encratites felt they had to go farther. In their view, sexuality should no longer only be controlled, but purely and simply rejected, as a symptom of the fall of humanity into servitude. Starting in the second century, for example, Justin (who would be executed) presented Christianity as a religion that was distinguished from all the others by the rigor of the sexual rules observed by its faithful married followers.

"In concentrating unilaterally on abstention and sexual heroism," Brown notes, "the Christians of the age of Justin had found the means besides of displaying themselves out of carriers of an egalitarian and truly universal religion: by emphasizing how vulnerable all human beings are to sexual desire, they discovered or invented a human condition which underlies. . . the complexity. . . [And in so doing,] derived simplicity from confusion."[24]

From the first century of Christianity (better to call it Judeo-Christianity in this era), the Encratite movement was thus more powerful for being seen as having a specific prestige. Its followers were perceived as spiritual athletes, virtuosos of continence, able to face with equanimity the temptation of the flesh just as easily as violence and torture. But they were not, for all that, all of Christendom. It is on this point that the most serious misinterpretations are made. Paul's *Epistles* show to what extent there persisted in the Christian communities a plurality of attitudes about sexuality, marriage and procreation.

St. Paul's Compromise

A Jewish pharisee from the diaspora, converted to Christianity (on "the road to Damascus"), Paul of Tarsus is often shown (with Augustine) as the true founder of Christianity and, in any case, as the first leader of an alleged Catholic asceticism. It is true that certain of his exegetes, in the very center of the Church, were partially responsible for what we would have to call a false interpretation of Paulism. For example, Jerome, the 4th-5th century translator of the Bible and leader of a rigorous and inaccurate analysis of Paul. It is undeniable that many of Paul's texts were distorted and especially manipulated after the death of their author. On the question of women, for example, a female Christian commentator, Laure Aynard, suggests today that "one may suppose that St. Paul would have been quite astonished (and, let us hope, unhappy) to know that the instructions for good behavior which he gave one day in response to the indiscretion of some Corinthian ladies could be used, nineteen centuries later, as theological justification for putting half of humanity in all the Western world in an inferior position."[25]

Actually, from Paul's conversion until his martyrdom in a Roman jail, in about 67 AD, his whole life seems, on this question of sexuality, rather to be an interminable *bargaining*, or, if you prefer, a tireless search for a *compromise* between the extremism of the Encratites and the moderation of the pagan communities and families of Western Asia Minor (currently the territories of Turkey and Greece) in the process of converting to Christianity.

As a Jew, Paul was very familiar with the interdicts of *Leviticus* and those professed by the Essenes. As an evangelist of the gentiles, charged with bringing the pagans into the Kingdom, he was no less conscious of the specific requirements of the new Christians of Corinthia, Ephesus and Thessalonika, anxious to continue their family life during the indefinite period that would precede "the arrival by Our Lord Jesus with all his saints." In many Epistles a preoccupation with conciliation shows through, which later commentators would hasten to forget. Similarly, it became customary to forget that Paul, in particular when he tackles the question of continence, consistently expressed an apocalyptic point of view. Paul was convinced that decisive events were imminent, that is, the arrival of the Kingdom, which he expected to see *in his lifetime.*

This conviction is explicitly confirmed many times in his *Epistles.* "Everyone should remain as he was when he accepted God's call" (*I Corinthians* 7:20). "Then we who are living at that time will be gathered up along with them in the clouds to meet the Lord in the air" (*I Thessaloni-*

ans, 4:17). "Considering the present distress" (*I Corinthians*, 7:26). "There is not much time left" (*I Corinthians*, 7:29) and "for this world, as it is now, will not last much longer" (7:29).

For the rest, contemporary specialists have made a merry game of denouncing the thousand and one generalizations, even manipulations, that have made it possible to show Paul as the lugubrious inventor of Puritanism. Let us give just a few examples. Paul's phrases, selected on this subject, are drawn from Chapter 7 of the First Epistle to the Corinthians. "To the unmarried and to the widows I say that it would be better for you to continue to live alone" (7:8). "But if you cannot restrain your desires, go ahead and marry — it is better to marry than to burn with passion" (7:9). "But because there is so much immorality, every man should have his own wife and every woman should have her own husband" (7:2). "Do not deny yourselves to each other, unless you first agree to do so for awhile in order to spend your time in prayer; but then resume normal marital relations" (7:5).

When these sentences are quoted, it is not specified that one of them is in answer to a question that was posed to him in writing by the Encratites. (The famous sentence "It is good for a man not to touch his wife" is thus not his but his interlocutor's, as opposed to what Jerome would claim.) Moreover, he is addressing a group of young Corinthians, some of whom speak in praise of prostitution and others of whom express tolerance for incest. Still others are Encratites. His answer condemns Encratism, while acknowledging that it does hold some validity. He basically answers his interlocutors: he who sets out to make angels creates beasts.

"He simply uses common sense," summarizes Xavier Leon-Dufour, "supporting the side of truth of which Encratism is the deformation. 'It is good not to touch your wife,' did you say? Watch out! It should be by mutual agreement, "symphonically," (to apply the Greek term that was used), and only for a time. Lastly, especially, this is not a question of pure asceticism, of a sexual gymnastics that caricatures reality: this abstinence is given meaning only by prayer."

Moreover, it is generally not mentioned that, in the same Epistle, those sentences are followed by these, whose meaning is quite different: "A man should fulfill his duty as a husband, and a woman should fulfill her duty as a wife, and each should satisfy the other's needs. A wife is not the master of her own body, but her husband is; in the same way a husband is not the master of his own body, but his wife is. Do not deny yourselves to each other. . ." (7:3-5). Similarly, "a married man . . . wants to please his wife, . . . [and] a married woman . . . wants to please her husband" (7:33-34).[26]

It is difficult to do more in a few lines to explore the case of Paul; he has fed whole libraries. We will add just one more comment, modest but necessary, to aid in comprehending the whole. The interminable the exegesis, century after century, of the same hundred or hundred and fifty words drawn from the Epistles of Paul, has had as a threefold result. It has obscured their real meaning by depriving them of their spiritual sense, by removing any real basis, and by giving the aura of dogma to what was — sometimes — only simple, deliberately concilia-tory conjecture. Not to mention that Paul's message was sometimes, over the centuries, voluntarily distorted with a, let us say, moralistic intent.

The three centuries and half which followed — up to Augustine — showed, however, that the debate was not closed.

Confronting Pagan Turbulence

During these decisive centuries of late Antiquity, those whom it is customary to call the fathers of the Church were not all favorable to the rigor of Encratite inspiration. If it did not seem unacceptably simplistic, one would even be tempted to classify these Christian Masters of the first centuries into two big groups. Puritan radicals along the lines of Tertullian (author of an *Exhortation to Chastity*) — Tatian, Jerome, Ori-gen, Gregory of Nyssa, would be opposed by those who defended mari-tal love, the family and even legitimate pleasure.

For example, in the third century, a great Christian theologian set himself against Encratite rigorism, claiming the indisputable legitimacy of a well-regulated conjugal sexuality. Clement of Alexandria (150-215) tackled the sexual question at length in two essential texts — *Paida-gogos* ("The Instructor"), and the *Stromateis* ("Miscellanies"), the third book of which is a vehement defense of marriage. For Clement, the body is not the adversary but "the soul's natural ally and travelling companion." Inspired by stoicism and Platonic metaphysics, his thought ideally aims for a life relieved of any passion and attaining the apathéia (internal serenity) of the stoics. The fact remains that he challenges the idea of any mortification of the body.

John Chrysostom, the eloquent Christian speaker (John the "golden-mouthed")" of Antioch, a city still dominated by paganism, teeming with beggars and dedicated to orgiastic games, is a similar case. He was constantly praising the family and especially of the Christian home, which he described as a citadel protected from the disorders of the pagan city. In his eyes, the marriage of young people is itself a subversive act. It should not be regarded any more as a simple means of putting the energy of couple at the service of the city (which was the case in the pagan concept) but, quite to the contrary, as an alliance mutually helping them to take charge of their own bodies. It is paradoxically the awareness of the sexual dangers lurking in a young body which linked the Christian couple in a durable solidarity.

In practice, the bishops, who were in daily contact with the nascent Christian society, were more readily inclined toward moderation than toward the blazing and proud rigorism of the ascetics. "Among the bishops one finds a greater concern for the health of the greatest number, the solicitude of a pastor for his people, the quest for a realistic Christianity, the desire for an accord with the powers that be."[27]

Opposing this moderation, the disciples of Mani (the Manicheans) profess a sexual rigorism, inherited from the old gnostic tradition and Persian Encratism. Born on the shores of the Tiger in 216 (and executed in 276 by the Persian king), he was raised among the disciples of Elkesai (a Judeo-Christian Encratite, Mani saw sexuality as an impulse responsible for the propagation of "the kingdom of darkness." He expresses his loathing for the body in terms that recall passages from Jean-Paul Sartre's *Nausée*: "The blood, the bile, the flatulence, the shameful excrements, the dirty humus . . ." The Manicheans would be condemned by the Church (and by the Roman Empire) and would separate themselves from Christianity. But they constituted an autonomous quasi-religion, a popular and very widespread heresy (including in Africa) whose influence would last several centuries. Augustine himself was not unsympathetic, in his youth.

The Myth of the Desert

But the extraordinarily complex theological confrontations of these early centuries (during which other major heresies would crop up, like Donatism and Aryanism) are conditioned by a very specific reality: the anti-Christian persecution emanating from a decrepit Roman power, soon to be besieged by barbarians and increasingly "totalitarian." The concern of being able to face death, pain, and torture is present in all the Christian texts of the time. And the link between the courage expressed in regard to death and the capacity to dominate one's own desires was constantly evoked. The pagans were not insensitive to this Christian version of the *virtues*. The famous Galen, Marcus Aurelius' pagan doctor, would congratulate the Christians on being able "to behave sometimes exactly like those who are guided by philosophy. Their contempt for death and its effects is shown every day, just as their sexual continence."

We too often forget what incredible courage was required of these first Christians, a courage that made questions related to sexuality relatively less urgent. "The fear of death and physical pain was, rather than the subtle pivot of sexual temptation, the most pressing enemy that the Christian had to learn to dominate. Control of sexuality was only one example — and not a very important one — of the Christian's need to control a body subject to the immense pain of the world. For Cyprian of Carthage (248), "following Christ" was nothing less than an everyday martyrdom."[28]

However, there is obviously a direct link between the reality of these persecutions, the apocalyptic climate which they generated, and the variations in what is called patristics (that is, the teaching of the fathers of the Church) in particular about "the flesh." Henri-Irénée Marrou wrote some enlightening pages on this precise question.[29] The anti-Christian persecutions, after those of Nero in 67, came back during the third century in successive waves, interrupted by lulls during which relations between Christians and pagan become peaceful again and in fact closer than is imagined. The last great persecution was officially launched by four edicts of the Emperor Diocletian, in 303-304. It was implacably violent: the churches were destroyed, members of the clergy were arrested, Christians were excluded from public office, there were police raids, executions, torture, mass deportation to the mines, etc..

A good measure of the Christian sensibility would be affected, for centuries, by the cruelty of "this world." Veneration of the martyrs was inaugurated by Christian women and prefigured that of saints and relics, the worship of heroic virgins and of virginity ("Weddings populate the earth; virginity populates paradise," Jerome would write), a horror for the tumult and disorders of the pagan, keeping a distance from all the compromises of the flesh and the degradation of society, etc.. The teaching of certain among most ascetic Church fathers, and of Origen (himself tortured and executed at Cesarea), is inseparable from this repressive climate.

And that is not all. The immense movement to escape the world of the 4th century, which would found Christian monasticism, partially originated in these persecutions. "The desert fathers" (Antony, Hermas, John Cassian, etc.), in facing hunger, cold, loneliness *and* sexual desire, gave rise to a true founding myth: that of the desert. By the year 400, nearly five thousand monks, it was said, were established in Nitria alone, and several thousand others were dispersed over the entire length of the Nile and even in the mountains at the edge of the Red Sea, naked and without water.[30]

> The way of life adopted by these hermits (wrote Marrou), is not in itself an innovation: the *anachoresis*, literally, 'going up to the desert,' in modern terms going into the wilds, was a common recourse in Egypt of this era, for all those who had good reason to flee society: criminals, bandits, insolvent debtors, citizens pursued by the tax department, and the asocial of all sorts; under persecution, the faithful had recourse to this, and the monks chose it for reasons of a spiritual nature.[31]

But if these anchorites went into the loneliness of the desert, this time it was not only to flee, it was "there to face the forces of evil, and very precisely the Devil, his temptations, his attacks; thus the place that these deviltries occupy in the *Life of St. Antony* which, after having amused the imagination of Breughel, very often scandalized modern readers, but the great theological significance of which must be discovered." In the eyes of an unquestionable pagan (such as Julian the Apostate), these men are insane, while at the same time it was from among their ranks that some of the great bishops of the time would be recruited.

An Extraordinary "Friction"

As for the rest, the depth and the quality of the great theological, metaphysical and of course moral debates of late Antiquity are easily understood. For several centuries, paganism, Judaism and Christianity would remain closely interwoven in society, including within families where one of the members may have converted while the others continued to practice libations and pagan sacrifices. That was the case of Augustine, whose mother, Monica, was a fervent Christian, whereas the father was pagan. In general, it was the women who introduced Christianity into their families, the sons continuing to follow — at least in public — their father's pagan religion. In Rome, there was even talk of an alliance between the women of the nobility and the Christian clergy. This daily confrontation, this extraordinary "friction" is also found, of course, on the terrain of ideas, thus feeding the profusion of every kind of controversy which enriched the patristic texts.

Then, the irresistible progress of Christianity within the Roman Empire, going as far as the conversion of Emperor Constantine in 324, little by little attracted the social elites and especially what we would call today the "intellectuals." Already in the early third century, Christianity was no longer a religion of the poor and the pariahs of the Roman Empire as it had been at its beginning (and which made it the but of sarcastic remarks by certain pagan authors like Celsus). It gained ground among the elite milieux, the provincial governors, the magistrates, certain dignitaries at the court, even the imperial family itself.

"With paganism impoverished by the wear of time," Marrou wrote, "it is Christianity that represents the active sector, the ascending element, the directing principle of the cultural atmosphere of the 4th century. . . . Statistically speaking, Christianity had won; why be astonished that the new ideal of the Christian culture attracted most of the best minds of this time?"[33]

However, when it came to questions of sexual conduct or morality in general, the Christians of that era were not always the most moralistic. In the surroundings of the 4th century, it was often the pagans who expressed most the vehemently the need for re-establishing order, the concern for moderating the upheavals of Roman society. When, in 320, Constantine promulgated a very severe law regarding adultery and young girls who run away, he invoked the time of Augustus, the robust moral rigor of yore, and said he was giving Rome "new laws. . . established to reform morality and to repress the vices. . . Chastity will be preserved, marriage protected, wealth made secure." It was a pagan speaker, Nazar, who applauded it with the most ardor.

Conversely, the Christians — and Augustine himself — point to the sober rigor of ancient morality as the foundation for their point of view on the matter, and to show that they do not ask the impossible. For example, hostility toward abortion and divorce, which had become too easy, as Seneca had already expressed. "The Church fathers of the 4th and the early 5th centuries," (Marrou again), "represent a very special moment of balance between an ancient heritage still only slightly tainted by decadence and perfectly assimilated, and a Christian inspiration that had itself arrived at full maturity."[34] On the question of morality, there is really no more opposition.

Admittedly, the first council of Elvira (Grenada), in the south of Spain in 303, seems to have been largely devoted to morality, since the convened bishops devoted 34 of their 81 decisions — which were rather moderate — to questions concerning marriage and sexual misconduct; one quarter of their decisions implied a greater than ever control over the women of the Christian community. Moreover, (for the first time) the council imposed on clerics not celibacy again, but the renunciation of procreation. Indeed, it decreed: "All bishops, priests, deacons and all clerics who have liturgical functions must abstain from their wives and not generate children." The marital prohibition for priests would wait — for eight more centuries and the various Lateran councils.

But still! After the emperor converted to Christianity, in that slow process of christianizing Roman life that would go on over the centuries, questions touching on sexuality no longer set the pagan definitively apart from the Christian and, indeed, these questions were far less significant than is imagined today. Christianity confronted the pagan culture mainly on other grounds: eliminating sacrificial polytheism in the rural areas and prohibiting pagan sacrifices (decreed by Theodosius in 391); fighting against torture and the cruelty of the prisons; protesting against the massive reprisals carried out on the populations by the Roman armies;[34] condemning infanticide and gladiatorial combats (first proscribed in 325); attempts to ease the conditions of slavery, and so on.

Roman Christianity's progressive assumption of responsibility for the laws of the city implies what today we would call "compromises," for example on the military question. When they were an oppressed minority, the conscientious objectors (as we would now say) were adamantly hostile to war in the time of Tertullian, but the Christians became "more realistic" when they found themselves leaders of an empire threatened on all sides by the barbarians. "We see the appearance," wrote Marrou, "of opposing requirements of the terrestrial city and the city of God."[35] It was Augustine, terrified contemporary of the Visigoths' capture of Rome, August 24, 410, who invented the theory of the just war.

Saint Augustine, "Father of the West"

It was with Augustine that the question of "the flesh" returns to the foreground. Converted to Christianity in August 386 (during the famous scene of the Garden of Milan!), after a youth of relative debauchery, haunted by the fire of his own temperament, this Roman Berber from Africa (he was born in Tagaste (Souk-Ahras), in Algeria) is considered today as "the inventor" of original sin, the intransigent doctor of predestination and the promoter of an ascetic sexual morality. His phrases that are most often quoted support this interpretation, especially this one: "I decided that there was nothing so necessary to avoid as relations with a woman. I believe that there is nothing that debase the spirit of man more than the caresses of a woman, that bodily contact without which one cannot have a wife," (*Soliloquies*, I, 9).

Actually, Augustine's thought was often — and is still — oversimplified, more caricatured even than Paul's. It is true that, author of an immense volume of work (several hundred titles, pamphlets and bodies of correspondence!), of a spirited and combative temperament, Augustine lent a hand to such manipulations. His admiring biographer, Henri-Irénée Marrou, observes, "If, as the history of his influence shows, grievous misinterpretations of Augustine's true thought were so often made, he is himself, to a great extent, chiefly responsible." [36]

Clearly, it would be absurd to try to summarize his teaching on sexual morality here. One can only recall, through a few examples, how squarely the work of "the father of the West" is located at the crossroads of an immense debate which truly has not yet ended.

Initially nourished on Virgil, Cicero and neo-Platonist philosophy, Augustine (well before his conversion) was an adherent of the Manichean sexual rigor against which he later turned his eloquence. In a famous pamphlet, he denounced the ascetic heresy of Mani, in the same way that Paul had attacked the Encratites. However, having become bishop of Hippo, he turned against the other extreme, Pelagius and his supposed laxity, in particular in another pamphlet. A monk from Great Britain, Pelagius professed that man's salvation does not depend exclusively on divine grace but especially on his free will. Challenging the idea of original sin and the scandal of the cross, on practical grounds, he came up with an optimistic and will-centered vision of salvation. Augustine passionately attacked Pelagianism, just as he was the sworn enemy of the many Christian heresies recorded at the time (88 in all!).

Fighting on several fronts, Augustine, whom Marrou presents as "the spokesman of most constant and authentic Christian tradition," is in the absolute center, the precise intersection of two main "tendencies" which, in spite of polemics and excommunications, would cohabit inside Christianity for over two thousand years. The ascetic side, indeed, the austere Encratite and Manichean current would reappear constantly throughout centuries, in various forms, through Albigensian Catharism, Puritanism, even Jansenism. In fact it was a very rigorist interpretation of Augustine that the Belgian bishop Jansen, author of *Augustineus*, drew upon in the early 17th century. His concern was to counter "the very remarkable advocates of pleasure" (the Jesuits). Jansen would blame "the new theology," which in his opinion was moving away from Augustine and the fathers of the Church, for the low moral level of his time, which he called the *saeculum corruptissimum* (most corrupt century), devoted entirely to *delectatio carnalis* (carnal pleasure). Logically enough, the Jansenists of Port-Royal and Pascal himself would rely on this Augustinian interpretation.

As for the Pelagian sensibility, in subtle ways it was related to the humanism of the Renaissance and the accommodating morality of certain Jesuits, in particular Thomas Sanchez, who was, in the 17th century, the most famous of theologian on marriage and the sexuality. He published a treatise as enormous as it was famous, *Disputationes de Matrimonii Sacramento*, of which more than twelve complete editions and many condensed versions were published between 1602 and 1669. In this book, Sanchez even recognizes the legitimacy of caresses, since the couple "can touch each other to alleviate the concupiscence of the flesh or to provide testimonies of mutual love."[37]

This is What Makes Us Ashamed

Let's look at a second example: the cardinal importance attached by Augustine to the concept of will, which would make it into nothing less than one of the Christian founders of modern individualism. For

Augustine, the sexual desire is a force as explosive as it is troubling, because by definition it escapes the will. Thus one finds in his work many astonishing passages concerning erection or, on the contrary, its failure. Man is definitely not master of that organ. "Sometimes," he writes in *The City of God*, this ardor arises importunely, without being called; sometimes, it betrays desire; the heart is on fire but the body is ice. How strange! As for the organs of generation, they become so dependent on concupiscence that, if that should fail, if it does not rise, spontaneously or through excitement, they remain motionless. This is what makes us ashamed, this is what we hide, blushing."[38]

This utter failure of human will, this aspect of animality which, in us, remains outside the control of our minds, constitutes for Augustine the very definition of the fall. The physiological autonomy of sexuality that thus ridicules our will suggests an original dislocation, a *discordium malum*, "a constant principle of discord placed within the person since the fall" and as a matter of fact, in the final analysis, "a miniature shadow of death."[39]

The idea of "the fall" is fundamental. For Augustine, the sexual pleasure related to orgasm and associated with procreation may not have been absent from terrestrial paradise. But *at that time it coincided entirely with the will*. This dramatic dissociation is the consequence of original sin, of the fall (which was not sexual in nature), was the dramatic dis-association: now, the will cannot completely "control the body," man is crippled; and concupiscence, become a negative, now acts like a foreign power besieging him. To resist the flesh is thus to reinstate — with the assistance of grace — the human will in its original majesty, for "what shames the spirit is the body that resists it, the body, the lower nature, that is subject to the spirit."

By giving precedence to the individual will, Augustine was able to denounce, in *The City of God*, one of pagan morality's particularly barbarian requirements with regard to women. When Rome was sacked by the Visigoths, thousands of Roman women were raped by the invaders. Pagan morality held that it was the imperative duty of married women to commit suicide. Augustine entreated them not to do it, precisely in posing this question of the will versus the misadventures of the body. "First, let us accept as a certainty," he wrote, "that virtue, the essential principle of a good life, controls from its throne at the apex of the soul, the members of the body, and that the body is sanctified when it is used

158

by a holy will. As long as this will remains firm and constant, no matter what happens to or with the body, if one cannot flee without sin, one is innocent of that which one suffers. . . . Thus, as to these unfortunate [women] who killed themselves in order not to suffer such insults, what heart would refuse them forgiveness? And those who did not wish to commit suicide out of fear of preventing another's crime by committing a crime of their own, who could censure them without being accused of madness?"[40]

This defense is not only contrary to pagan logic, but it carries within itself a historically decisive "preference": that granted to the individual will *against* the tyrannical requirements of a holistic society. Louis Dumont sees this, well beyond the matter of sexuality, as the beginning of an immense cultural rupture which is still making its way through Western society: individualism. "With Augustine," he writes, "one can detect in the details a subtle advance of individualism."[41]

Hitherto, various "wisdoms" (from Indian thought to stoicism) did not allow for the emancipation of the individual except at the price of a temporal "renunciation," of a withdrawal from the world. Like the Indian "world renouncer," indeed, "the stoic must remain detached, he must remain indifferent, even to the pain which he tries to relieve."[42] One of our greatest contemporary sociologists, Norbert Elias, underlined this incapacity of ancient philosophy to conceive of the individual in the sense that gave Western modernity to the term. "The idea of an individual, outside of any group, a being, man or woman, just as it is and without any reference to 'us,' of the individual as something apart, to whom one grants so much value that all references to a collective entity, be it the clan, the tribe or the State, seem comparatively less important, was still completely unimaginable in the social practice of the ancient world."[43]

Only Christianity — and in particular Augustine — envisioned this incredible notion of a time when, according Louis Dumont, "holism would have disappeared from representation, life in the world would be conceived as entirely coinciding with the supreme value, and the individual-apart-from-the-world will have become the modern individual within the world. It is the historical proof of the extraordinary initial disposition."[44] The Christian is an individual who is capable of voluntary renunciation but, this time, *within the world*.

This became a formidable goal for the centuries to come, nothing less than the invention of the individual. "It would be said that, with Augustine, the eschatological view of the empire under which the first fathers of the Church worked, and whose mission is still far from being completed, started to change into something like the modern belief in progress."[45] We should keep in mind the reasons why Arendt, too, was so passionately interested in Augustine and especially *The City of God*, a text that she quotes on several occasions. For Arendt, Augustine was "the only great thinker who lived in a time that resembles our own, in many regards, and whose writings give a feeling of an end-of-the-world climate, which is perhaps not very different from that which we know."[46]

CHAPTER 8

THE TRUE INVENTION OF PURITANISM

We are happy to imagine that in the last fifteen centuries our so-cieties have gradually and painfully freed themselves from sexual mor-alism. From the obscurantism of the early Middle Ages to the Renais-sance, then the Enlightenment and, finally, the Industrial Revolution, Western man has little by little gained his autonomy and his "right to pleasure" as the religious influence receded. Such is, roughly speaking, the common view. However, that is an inaccurate but obdurate preju-dice, so firmly anchored that the denials of the historians are heeded no more than they were about Antiquity.

Actually, it would not be wrong to suggest that the evolution was, on many points, *exactly the opposite*. The Medieval era, highly religious as it was, does not seem to have been exaggeratedly repressive in regard to sex. "The reprobation of pleasure is not . . . specific to Christian thought," observes a medievalist. "It seems to me that it merely picks up the anguish regarding the flesh that is a far more general disposition of the human spirit.. . .The Middle Ages, because they had their taboos, their rhetoric and their social conventions, did not feel this anguish much more than did other times."[1]

As for Puritan tendencies, moralizing sometimes to the point of obsession (in particular about masturbation), their appearance coin-cided paradoxically with the emergence of the Enlightenment, in the 17th century and, especially, with the triumph of the bourgeois society

161

in the 19th. And that is not all. During the long centuries leading up to the Enlightenment, religion — and particularly of Christianity — did not always carry the weight that one imagines. In many cases, agnostic thinkers showed themselves infinitely more severe than the men of the Church as regards sexuality.

Jean-Louis Flandrin cites, among many others, the case of the "libertine" Brantôme who, in his famous *Gallant Ladies*, takes umbrage at certain love positions that were perfectly allowed by the Catholic theologians of the time. He also cites the case of certain deputies of the third state of Agenois who, in 1614, in article 54 of their register of crimes, claims — against the opinion of the clergy — that adultery be more severely punished. "Let adulterers," he wrote, "sufficiently judged and convicted, be punished with death, without the judges being able to moderate the penalty for any cause or consideration whatsoever."[2] And John Boswell has this to say about homosexuality: "Almost without exception, the rare laws aiming at the homosexual behaviors promulgated before the 13th century are due to the civil authorities acting without the opinion or the support of the Church. Sometimes, ecclesiastical councils or authorities ratified these legislative texts, in effect yielding to strong pressure, but the ecclesiastical documents stipulate a very light sanction or even do not stipulate any sanction."[3]

The accepted view of sexuality in the *Ancien Regime* as being long oppressed by the priests, but released by the Enlightenment and modern rationalism, bears no relation to reality.

A Time to Embrace

The facts speak for themselves. During the first centuries of the early Middle Ages, the Church little by little extended its influence in Europe, then frankly substituted itself for the temporal power after the collapse of the Carolingian Empire in the 9th century. The episcopate posed itself as heir to the imperial power. However, the societies that the Church thus took in hand were still largely pagan. The sexual codes in force among the "barbarian" people, especially the Germanic, were often more repressive than those of Augustinian Christianity. These were the codes and traditions that the Church would have to conform to or fight against. The pagan concept of the body often imposed a repressive sense. A historian specializing in the Middle Ages, Michel Rouche, takes the example of the law of the Salian Francs (7th century), which prohibited anyone other than her husband from touching the body of a woman.

"If a free man," he writes, "touched the hand of a woman, he was to pay 15 pennies; the arm below the elbow, 30 pennies; above the elbow, 35 pennies; and when finally he reached the bosom, 45 pennies. The female body was thus taboo. Why? The texts of certain penitentials reveal to us that during pagan ceremonies the girls and women completely disrobed, in order to encourage the fruitfulness of the fields, to cause the rain, etc.. To touch a woman was thus to undermine the process of life. Men and women could be naked only in one place, that where one procreated: in bed. Consequently, the naked one was holy."[4]

However, this apprehensive sacralization of the nude female contrasted with the Christian representation of nudity as a cheerful assertion of a creature that is "good but dependent on God, with or without sin." Until the 8th century, men and women were thus baptized on holy Saturdays entirely naked, like Adam and Eve at the time of Creation, in the octagonal pool that was part of every cathedral. Nudity did not have any sexual connotation then. It was *under the influence of pagan symbolism* that it took on such coloring, so much and so thoroughly that it would become necessary (since the 6th century) to get rid of certain crucifixes where Christ was depicted naked.[5]

Let's give another example. Among the Burgundians, while incest was relatively tolerated, adultery was regarded as an unpardonable crime. The "stench of adultery" was cited and the guilty wife was repudiated, then strangled and thrown into a muddy swamp. Among the Francs, "the custom was even more strict, for not only the husband but also his family and that of the adulteress regarded this act as a stain on all their lineage, and it had to result in the death of the culprit."[6] More generally, in the barbarian world still marked by its tribal origins, certain cruel traditions for the women, like repudiation or abduction, were still allowed. Charlemagne himself had several concubines and repudiated his first wife of Lombard origin. It took a major effort from the Church to end these practices.

The great medievalist Jacques Le Goff has shown that the famous ecclesiastical penitentials of the Middle Ages, i.e. the codes of sexual behavior, enumerating for the faithful the various transgressions (with their associated penalties), were *inspired to a great extent by the barbarians' codes*.

In these still pagan societies, admittedly, the Christian faith would remain superficial for a long time. Belief in astrology, magic and sorcery were widespread. The daily life retained its rhythms based on an ancestral calendar, only gradually substituted by the Church calendar. "A favorable day is chosen for travel, for spinning wool; some wait to marry on Friday, the day of Venus; astrology was in vogue; the new moon was a crucial moment awaited for the building of houses and to contract marriages."[7]

The appropriation of these very ancient temporal rhythms, inherited from a long anthropological memory, and the establishment of a specifically Christian liturgical calendar with public holidays, fasts and penitential periods, would be the great preoccupation of these centuries of the early Middle Ages. It is by this means — and in competition with the pagan and Jewish calendars — that the medieval Church set up, under the Carolingians, from the early 9th century, a whole social and moral organization for the Christian people. It is also through the instrument of the liturgical calendar that it endeavored to limit, for example, the violence of private wars and also to codify marital sexuality.

Most of the period's sexual interdicts thus relate to the meticulous arrangement of time, as Flandrin has studied and masterfully analyzed.[8] Periodic continence occupies a major place in medieval Christianity. Sexual relations are prohibited during certain periods, bound either to liturgical seasons (Lent, Easter, etc.), or to the woman's cycles (menses, pregnancies). . . . The rules, of course, fall under the general quotation of Ecclesiastes: "There is a time . . . for every purpose under heaven./A time to love and a time to hate, /A time to embrace and a time to refrain from embracing."

The full significance of this temporal coding of sexuality, and of daily life in general, is seen when we realize the cultural and symbolic goal represented, since the Christianization of the Roman Empire, *by the appropriation of social time by the intermediary of a calendar*. "To eradicate the last traces of paganism," wrote Fleming, "a Christian calendar had to be substituted for the pagan calendars — for that used by the State and elites as well as for those, less well-known to us, followed by the peasants in various areas of the Empire. For there were no neutral calendars: all were charged with religious connotations, so that the observation of a calendar always announced to a certain extent that one observed the religion from which it emanated."

In addition to the temporal interdicts and the periodic continences, we should not overlook the fact that Christianity's strength (like that of other religions) lay for a long time in this capacity to perpetuate an immense symbolic rhythm, often according to the pulsations of nature and the human species, internalizing and giving meaning to the constraints and governing the totality of the social life. Alphonse Dupront has shown, in contrast, how the quasi-dilution of these social rhythms in the immediate indetermination of modernity has weakened contemporary Christianity.

"Just think," he writes, "of the luminous correspondence (hardly recalled today) between the astral cycle and the annual liturgical cycle, the ritual teaching of the benedictions of Easter Saturday, the rites of sprinkling holy water (protective or exorcistic), the cool mornings processions of the Rogations, or even the various forms of fire-worship, disciplined by the Church."[9]

Established Morals

The formulation of the sexual interdicts was, itself, both very solemn and very meticulous in the Middle Ages. The Catholic theologians distinguish ten types of lust (including three that are against nature: masturbation, sodomy and zoophilia), of varying degrees of harmfulness. For example, fornication (traffic with prostitutes) appears less reprehensible to them than debauchery (defloration of a virgin, seduction without intent to marry) and adultery (comparable to theft, since it entails stealing another's honor). Certain councils, like that of Naplouse, in 1120, were principally devoted to the detailed codification of the sins of the flesh.

But these judgments, formally dramatized, are far from corresponding to an applied program of repression. Historians like Jacques Rossiaud insist that we need to establish a difference between this theological rigor of principle and "more nuanced realities of a social morality, a product of this Christian teaching and the resistance to it posed by the socio-economic complexities, the customs, the established mores."[10]

In terms of sexuality, the Middle Ages were rather dominated by a striking directness, with no complexes. The sermons themselves were obliged to reflect this, and would surprise our modern sensitivities by their crudeness, like the *fabliaux* [*Ed. note*: a comic and earthy literary genre] of the time. The very vocabulary of the penitents reflects this earthiness, with a sometimes comical anatomical precision. Upon due consideration, they are especially striking in the pragmatism and the moderation of the penances that sanction the various sins of lust. They generally consist of various types of fast or doing penance (see inset).

Have you fornicated?

Here are some of the best-known extracts from the penitentials, as composed by Burchard, the German canonist and Bishop of Worms in the 11th century. It constitutes book 19 of a vast table in twenty-five books of Church law, a table known as the Decree. In certain cases, the relative moderation of the sanctions should be noted.

"120. Have you fornicated as the sodomites do, by putting your rod in the posterior of a man? If you are married and if you did it once or twice: 10 years of penitence on the official days, one of them with bread and water. If it has been habitual: 12 years. If it is with your brother by blood: 15 years."

"122. Have you fornicated by taking another's member in your hand, and he taking yours, to agitate each other' member in turn and thus, by this pleasure, spread your seed? If yes: 30 days of penitence on bread and water."

"123. Have you fornicated alone, i.e. by taking your male member in your hand and, pulling on the foreskin, agitated it so as to spread by this pleasure your seed? So yes: 10 days."

"124. Have you fornicated by placing your member in a perforated wooden board, or in something similar, so that by movement and pleasure you spread your seed? So yes: 20 days."

"126. Have you committed sodomy or bestiality with men or animals, in other words with a cow, a she-ass or any other animal? If you did it one or twice, and if you did not have a wife to appease your lubricity, you will fast 40 days on bread and water – a Lent – and you will always make penitence. If you were married at the time, you will fast 10 years on the fixed days. If you were in the habit of committing this crime, you will fast 15 years. If you performed the act in question during your youth, you will fast 100 days on bread and water."

"166. Have you drunk your husband's sperm, so that he loves you more thanks to your diabolic intrigues? If yes: 7 years of penitence on bread and water, on the fixed days."

"172. Have you done as certain women do: they take a live fish, introduce it into their sex and keep it there until it has died and, after having cooked it or having roasted it, they give it to their husband to eat so that he becomes more impassioned for them? If yes: 2 years of fasting."

Quoted and translated by Jacques Berlioz,
Le Pécheur et la Pénitence au Moyen Age, Éd. du Cerf, 1969.

It should it be recalled that, until the first Lateran council, in 1123, marriage or common-law marriages was very widespread among priests (Nicolaïsm). Not only did it go on long after its effective prohibition, but the priests sometimes had "weaknesses" that it was common to joke about without excessive severity. In those days, a drunken priest was judged more harshly than one with a lover. It is significant, observes Jean-Louis Flandrin, "back then, they spoke of 'priests' girls' the way we later would talk about 'soldiers' girls." In 1536, one named Jean Maillet, who refuses to marry his fiancée, made it known in court that 'he will not marry Nicole because she is of bad conduct and has relations with the priests.'" Asked four or five times whether he wants to prove that she has carnal relations with anyone other than him, he answers consistently that she goes with priests."[11]

It should also be recalled that the Church was relatively lenient with regard to prostitution, which it regarded as an inevitable evil, and that the king Saint Louis tried in vain to prohibit it. Le Goff relates an anecdote that reveals the climate of the time: "When toward 1170 the Parisian prostitutes proposed to the chapter house of Notre-Dame to finance a stained glass in honor of the Virgin, the clerics wondered whether this money that they offered had been earned honestly, i.e. without intention to mislead the customer (by the use of make-up, etc.). It was concluded that it had been earned honestly, but that prostitution was in itself a morally reprehensible activity; however it was tolerated."[12] Tolerance of prostitution went as far as being codified, with the aim of excluding children, married women and nuns.

Of course, the Church's relative leniency in applying the sexual interdicts — which contrasts with its severity with regard to usury, for example — varied according to times. It was especially remarkable during the pre-Renaissance of 11th and 12th centuries, a period of openness and tolerance in most European societies. This liberalism sometimes came from the pope himself, to counter the overblown moralism of certain excessively pious people. The most famous example is that of Pierre Damiens who, in 1049, addressed a report to Pope Leon IX, the *Liber Gomorrhianus (the Book of Gomorra)*, denouncing the immorality of the era and asking for greater severity, in particular with regard to the "sodomites." The pope gave this request a rather chilly response and abjured its author to be more moderate. This was, in any case, a far cry from a prudish Christian society obsessed by sexual sins, as it later became.

If the Middle Ages had any sexual obsession, it was on the basis of repression, as is usually believed, but in connection with the risk of impotence or sterility, which was generally imputed to the intrigues of witches. "There are innumerable synods which, after the beginning of the 13th century, protested against the witches who 'cast a spell on the husbands to prevent them from achieving the marital act': Salisbury in 1217, Rouen in 1235, Fritzlar in 1243, Valence in 1255, Clermont in 1268, Grado in 1296, Bayeux in 1300, Würzburg in 1329, Ferrare in 1332, Basle in 1434, etc.."[13]

In connection with "the queers" and buggery, one probably cannot accept at face value all the analyses that American historian John Boswell devoted to the Christianity of the Middle Ages. A gay militant, he admits that his approach is biased. His goal is to rehabilitate homosexuality, including in the eyes of believers, by showing that at the time the Church tolerated it far more than is imagined, even accepted it. Hence his enthusiasm in holding up such and such example. Some of his observations are, in fact, not easily refutable.

When homosexuality was legally repressed, in 533, by Emperor Justinian, it was by no means at the request of the Church. "No text," Boswell writes, "indicates to us that the ecclesiastical dignitaries suggested or supported the imperial measures taken against homosexuals. On the contrary, the only people named as having been punished for homosexual acts are eminent bishops."[14] Similarly, in 650, the sovereign of the Visigoths of Spain adopted a legislation that was, theoretically, very severe with regard to homosexuals. It called for the culprits to be castrated. But, notes Boswell, it was a purely civil law. The Church had nothing to do with its adoption.

"[In the 11th and 12th centuries,] the Church refused categorically and on several occasions," Boswell adds, "to impose sanctions for homosexuality or to even apply the existing sanctions; and the majority of the clergy simply refused to lend an ear to the rare complaints from anti-homosexual Christians."[15] Homosexuality was not ignored but was treated as a minor flaw.

Homosexual acts became punishable indeed in the legal anthologies dating from the 13th century. But there was quite a gap between the texts and reality. We have very little information about actual instances when these measures were applied. Which leads one to think, says Boswell, that they were extremely rare. "The published sources

give us a negligible number of examples of application of capital punishment, just for the crime of 'sodomy.'"[16]

Marriage, Freedom and Female Pleasure

It was in the 12th century, after the Gregorian reform, that the
Church managed to impose its view of marriage as a sacrament, declared insoluble. In about 1150, Pierre Lombard definitively inscribed
marriage in the number of the seven sacraments. The modern spirit
readily accepts the obligatory nature of this reform. Actually, it was not
like that at the time. Considering the pagan traditions still in force, it
came rather as a spectacular conquest of individualism.

This concept corresponds to the will to make the *consensus facit
nuptias* inherited from Roman law prevail. Hugues de Saint-Victor (d.
1141) gave the first great theological discourse on marriage, which he
interpreted as "the spontaneous and legitimate assent by which man
and woman become each other's debtor." Lombard, for his part, evoked
the double bond of the spouses "according to the assent of the hearts
and the combining of the bodies."

Thus the Church was interfering directly in the prevailing social
practice, that of the arranged marriage. In those days, men and women
did no choose their spouses. Among nobles as among the peasants, and
since time immemorial, it was the parents who decided. By putting individual assent first, the Church took a subversive approach. "The assent which it validated was no longer, in theory, that of two families
but of two persons; it was a radical innovation and dangerous for the
social order. Christian marriage was opposed to the traditional [and
pagan] concept of the family."[17]

Christianity's resolute stand on the side of the individual against
social holism would lead sometimes to open conflicts with the temporal
power. The royalty frequently sought to defend the rights of the family
against this freedom of personal assent. "In France," writes Flandrin,
"from the 16th to the 18th century, the Church doctrines were in strong
tension with those of the State. The State constantly sought to reinforce
parental power to the detriment of the children's freedom and the sacral-
ity of the marital bond by circumventing the laws of the Church while, at
the same time, affecting to hold them in the deepest respect. . . .The most
famous of these laws reinforcing the paternal authority is Henri II's edict
of 1566 on the marriage of the family's children."[18]

And, don't forget that this sanctification of marriage gave the Church the means of sanctioning royal practices, like repudiation or imposed adultery, of which wives were the victims. "By accepting the Church's hold over the couple and the family, the kings had also accepted that their own intimate dealings would be unearthed and governed."[19] This fueled the innumerable quarrels that would arise henceforth between the Catholic popes and the French sovereigns on questions of adultery: Philippe I and Urban II in 1094, Philippe Auguste and Innocent III in 1200, Philippe the Beautiful and Boniface VIII in 1595, Louis XIV and Clement X, among others.

The Christian concept of marriage appears all the more subversive when we see that on certain questions, like adultery, it was less misogynist that Roman law or the Germanic practices. The Church indeed treats the spouses on an equal footing, and judges the husband's adultery to be as reprehensible as that of the woman. "In the lay view, on the contrary (and thus in the civil legislation), only the married woman's infidelity mattered: it is seen as a threat to the equilibrium of the family, through the possible intrusion of children foreign to the blood of the husband. This concept was the same as that in Roman law, which generally penalized only the woman's adultery, and that of Germanic law, according to which the erring husband did not incur any penalty, except the loss of some pecuniary advantages."[20]

Contemporaries of the troubadours and courtly love, certain theologians showed themselves still more lenient with regard to love, even while defending the "well-being of the families and of the community." The most famous case is again Pierre Lombard, whose *Sentences* would be analyzed by students until the 16th century.

But it is in regard to female pleasure, the orgasm, that the reality of medieval Christianity is diametrically opposed to what, in the 19th century, became the bourgeois and clerical prudishness. Christian theology actually found itself defending tooth and nail the married woman's "right to pleasure." This rather extraordinary matter deserves to be told, since it is so little known to any but the most specialized historians.

First, we should note that, until the 12th century, medical knowledge hearkened back to Galen, one of the eminent doctors of Antiquity. Born in Pergamum in around 131 AD, Claudius Galenus (Klaudios Galenos in Greek) was considered, with Hippocrates, the principal authority on medical matters. Abundantly translated, even in Arabic, he was a deist and non-Christian, but the Church followed his teachings. For fifteen centuries, the doctors and also the theologians would base their reflections on Galen's work, to such an extent that it was said that "to oppose his theories is to oppose the Church."[21] However Galen — just like Hippocrates — was in formal disagreement with Aristotle on one specific point that was fraught with consequences.

In his main work (*De Semine*, Book II, Chap. I and IV), he explains that procreation requires that two seeds come together, that of the man and that of the woman. However, he thinks that for the woman to emit her seed, it is necessary that she experience "complete venereal delight" and that she can attain the *voluptas plena mulieris* (female orgasm). A sex act that is accomplished for the "benefit" of the husband alone cannot, according to Galen, lead to procreation; it will be necessarily sterile. This point of view, adopted by the theologians, is contrary to Aristotle's, who suggests in his Treatise *On the Generation of Animals*, that procreation is connected to the phenomenon of the menses and is not related to pleasure.

The preference given, until the Renaissance (and even afterwards) to Galen's theses implies that *the Church became an advocate of the female orgasm*. Indeed, theology recognizes the legitimacy of the sex act when it is directed toward procreation, and only in this case. However, in all theological rigor, an awkward husband who neglects his wife's pleasure is acting against procreation. He is thus at fault.

Don't think that this question is anecdotal. Jean-Louis Fleming says that theologians held many debates on this subject, and on another question as well: the wife who was a little behind could excite herself manually "to catch up" with her spouse. Of the seventeen theologians listed by Fleming as having studied the question, fourteen allow it and only three were against it. "In a society which subordinated the woman to the man in all things," Flandrin wrote, "the theologians consistently proclaimed that the wife had rights to her husband's body that were equal to her husband's rights to hers."[22] Most of them even found legitimate that the faster of the two spouses should excite the slower one by kisses and caresses. Taking into account "the natural modesty of women," they even make it an obligation of the husband to understand his wife's unspoken requests for love.

In the support of their thesis, the theologians not only point to the medicine of Galen, they quote St. Paul himself. The first Epistle to the

Corinthians, already mentioned, but worth citing again, basically says, "Let the husband render unto his wife that which he owes her and let the wife do the same with her husband. The woman does not have authority over her own body, the husband does; and similarly, the husband does not have authority over his own body, the wife does." Besides, one might add, like Peter Brown, that this idea of a "eugenic" sexuality, which views the woman's pleasure as a sign of successful procreation, was already present in Jewish sources. But, on the other hand, "the concept of a eugenic sexuality subjected the man and the woman to codes which continued, in bed, the propriety adhered to in public."[23]

At all events, one could actually say that, contrary to popular opinion, *there was an actual medieval Christian eroticism.* Paradoxically, it is the lay or pagan authors who show themselves the least generous with regard to female pleasure. Some of them believe that excessive pleasure ("too ardent" a love) can stand in the way of procreation. "It appears," wrote Flandrin, "that the discrepancy between pleasure and procreation was prevalent largely *outside of the ecclesiastical environment* [my emphasis]." The attention granted by theology to the *necessary* pleasure of the woman for successful procreation would survive for centuries in the collective memory. The historian Alain Corbin stresses that it was not rare to find, at the end of the 19th century, testimonies of women "who still tried not to enjoy themselves, in order to avoid any risk of conception. Many would be the wives flabbergasted by the announcement of a pregnancy that was not preceded by any voluptuous experience."[24]

This "Christian eroticism" of the Middle Ages contrasts in any case with the extraordinary *egoism* which would prevail during the prudish and bourgeois 19th century, after the mechanisms of ovulation were discovered by Pouchet and Négrier (under the July Monarchy) and the absence of any direct correlation between the orgasm and procreation. Certain doctors, like Moreau de La Sarthe, obsessed with Puritanism, would declare that a frigid woman conceives more easily than a sexually fulfilled woman, for "she retains the seed better." "Men," adds Corbin, "could thus, with equanimity, forget about their partner's reactions. This was a dark time for women, during which the need for pleasure was officially denied to her. Many decades would pass before the majority of doctors would again enjoin husbands to help their partners to enjoy. That would have to await the post-war period and the advent of the new sexology."[25]

No doubt it would surprise certain militant contemporary feminists, disciples of Simone de Beauvoir, to show them that, in asserting their "right to pleasure," they unwittingly joined a very old theological preoccupation in line with the teachings of St. Paul. It is true that when they went about it (and this is a cardinal difference) they radically dissociated the concern for pleasure from the concern for procreation.

The Return of the Idea of Nature

The relative sexual liberalism of the Middle Ages was even more pronounced, as we have said, starting in the 12th century. This evolution, which involves theology as a whole (and in particular Thomas Aquinas), is inseparable from what one might call the rediscovery of the idea of nature by the Church and by Christendom. Several factors contributed to this evolution. The influence of Islam, which reintroduced Greek thought to the West and contributed to the foundation of courtly love, had a hand in it. But equally (or more?) important, will of the Church to oppose the growing influence of cults which were preaching renunciation of procreation and withdrawal from the world.

The Cathares ("the pure ones"), for example, like the Encratites of the first centuries (whose distances heirs they were), rejected the idea of perpetuating the species. For them, marriage is a state of permanent sin. They rejected procreation more than pleasure itself. That is why they were accused of homosexual practices during the Inquisition. Moreover, the word "bugger," which in the Middle Ages indicated homosexual sodomites, is derived from the word "Bulgarian" or "bogumil," the latter being the Cathares of Bulgaria.

The theology of those centuries, and especially of the 13th, was founded largely on the fight, and then the crusade, against the Albigensian Cathares. As a side-effect, the Church and the University, which was under its influence, ended up exalting the benefits of nature. "The great theologians of the 13th century, including Thomas Aquinas, are theologians of nature, and poets like Jean de Meun exalt Lady Nature, the Franciscans address themselves to Brother Sun or Sister Moon, and vegetation invades Gothic architecture."[26]

It is from this same point of view of rediscovery and exaltation of nature that it is necessary to evoke the fashion of the bestiaries, which became, as of the 12th century, the most popular works in Western Europe. Richly illustrated, accessible to the ordinary men as well as to the ecclesiastical, widespread, they carry a specific perception of nature as a benevolent guardian force. Aristotle's great zoological texts were rediscovered. This praise of "Mother Nature" inevitably induced a more physical concept of sexuality, less fraught with complexes. "It is true," suggests Le Goff, "that in the 13th century the idea of nature, born in the 12th century, was spreading. St. Thomas theorized it, and with it the idea of a nature of man, which implied a kind of right to pleasure. It is also true that marriage was rehabilitated in the 13th century; and that made it possible to make room for a kind of licit sexuality. Thus one sees a kind of legitimization, within limits, of the carnal."[27]

On the other hand, some prohibitions would be re-legitimized for supposedly infringing the "natural order." The idea, unfortunately promised with a beautiful future, that there exists defects "against nature" is the price paid for this reunion with reality. Thomas Aquinas would define sin as a kind of anarchism that does not respect the supposed laws of nature. "Covering masturbation, bestiality, homosexuality and sodomy, the *vicium contra naturam* is first of all the failure to observe a specific order, that of identity and difference."[28]

In an early 13th century treatise on love, *De Amores*, written by André the Chaplain, was a critical success and was translated into Italian and German. It is divided into three books: I) How to find love; II) How to preserve love, once it has been attained; III) How to cure oneself of it. He was condemned in 1227 by the Bishop of Paris, Étienne Tempier, mainly because he maintained that there are two truths, one answering to reason and philosophy, the other to faith and the Holy Scriptures.

From the 13th century on, certain theologians like Richard Middleton and Pierre de La Palud, are quite bold in authorizing, in certain cases (when the wife is pregnant, for example), sexual relations not intended to be procreative. Two centuries later, other theologians like Paul Gerson and Martin the Master, would go further, in accepting the idea of sexual pleasure completely free of the concern for procreation.

"As if someone had waved a magic wand, love invaded the landscapes, the cities and the monasteries of Europe during 11th and 12th centuries. . . . It transformed the ascetic spirituality of the desert fathers into an impassioned mysticism illustrated by St. Bernard.. . . The purely functional concept of sexual intercourse, inherited from the patristic theology, was forgotten, and Christian novels appeared that seemed to sweep away all that had preceded them."[29]

For Le Goff, King Louis IX (St. Louis) constitutes *the* emblematic character of this (measured) exaltation of nature and sexuality. He seems to have had, as we say today, "temperament." When he left on a crusade in 1248, he took along his wife so as not to be deprived of carnal relations. Queen Marguerite would have four children in the Holy Land. Even so, Louis was extraordinarily respectful of the interdicts related to the liturgical calendar. For Le Goff, "He embodies the other fundamental idea of the 13th century as well as possible, that is, all things in measure. He succeeded in living a measured sexuality. He endorsed the ideal which places the Christian at equal distance between angel and animal. In this sense also, Louis IX was a model for the men of his time."[30]

Enlightenment, and A Lot of Darkness

The hearty medieval directness, the 12th century liberalism in love of and the Renaissance appetite for life would be obscured in the following centuries. The Puritanism of the Protestant Reform would be succeeded in the 17th century by the Catholic Counter-Reformation, which would attack ecclesiastical moral laxity, blasphemous libertinage and the "vice" of certain monks and of the court. This Counter-Reformation began under the regency of Catherine de Medici, then under Louis XIII (this would come to be called "the century of the saints);" with vengeance, it went after the libertines who flouted Christian dogmas. History retains the case of the writer Theophilus de Viau, author of the 25 erotic plays of *Parnasse satyrique*, who was sent to prison on July 1, 1625. A rather extraordinary detail should be noted, however — his principal accuser, André Voisin, the Jesuit of the College de La Flèche, was also condemned to banishment. *They wanted to punish libertine blasphemy and at the same time to prevent the excesses of a too rigid Puritanism.*

At the court, a great repression was launched against vice, after the affair of the poisons, by Louis XIV and his "room of passion." With Mme. de Maintenon, from 1684, the pious party triumphed. That does not mean that libertine behavior among the aristocrats would disappear. Let us say simply that it would be displayed with less arrogance.

Paradoxically, Puritanism would get a real start only at the beginning of the Enlightenment, early in the 18th century. The philosophers of the Enlightenment and the *Encyclopédie* were much less permissive about sexuality than is imagined. As an example, Voltaire was vehement in expressing his aversion to homosexuality. In article XIX (*"On sodomy"*), he is pitiless toward what he calls "infamy," "turpitude," "a vice unworthy of man," and he avows, finally, the horror inspired in him by "that filth that would be done more to be hidden in the darkness of a lapse of memory rather than to be lit up by the flames of the butchers before the eyes of the multitude."[31] In *L'Esprit des lois* [*Spirit of Laws*] (Book VII, Chap. VI), Montesquieu likewise sees it as "a crime against nature." And Rousseau would express his disgust of "sodomy" in similar terms.

Faith in nature (and thus the aversion for anything that is against nature), and the desire to denounce the aristocratic privilege of libertine conduct, was joined by the anticlericalism of certain encyclopedists, who stigmatized vice among the monks. Most of the libertine authors of the time (and of course de Sade!), spontaneously associated lust with the clergy, whose "hypocrisy" is thus shown. "The most original was Jean-Charles Gervaise de Latouche who, before being an advocate to the Parliament in Paris, published in 1741 the *Histoire de Dom B. portier des Chartreux* [*The Story of Dom B., Porter to the Carthusian Monks*], a pornographic novel seized at once by the police. Constantly kept in print throughout the century, the book had such a success that Mme. de Pompadour had a copy of the 1748 edition, and the marquis de Paulmy had his decorated with 28 racy miniatures painted on vellum."[32]

The Enlightenment and the Revolution itself are thus quite ambiguous in terms of sexuality. On one side, human freedom was exalted, and the transgression of dogmas, emancipation, even libertinage (under the Directoire, for example, after the end of the Terror). On the other side, aristocratic turpitude and clerical vice were denounced in exceedingly prudish terms. We might recall that, in the years leading up to the [French] Revolution, innumerable lampoons had attacked Louis XVI, the court, and especially Queen Marie-Antoinette, in moralistic tones. Her levity and her pride were denounced, but also her alleged tolerance for lesbians. These calumnies became more terrible as the Revolution advanced. A two-volume *Scandalous and Libertine Private Life of Marie-Antoinette, from the Loss of Her Virginity until May 1, 1791,* was published in

1792 and reprinted in 1793, to prepare the public for the queen's execution. The most infamous charge levied against the queen, especially by the "witness" Jacques-Rene Hébert, evokes imaginary incest in connection with her son.

This "purifying" and moralistic tone continued under the Revolution and had concrete effects. In his indictment of Mme. Du Barry, Fouquier-Tinville even compares libertine women to prostitutes and sees sexual laxity as a weapon in the hands of tyrants (an argument that promised to have considerable success in the 20th century). "Despotism," he exclaimed, "has always been the enemy of public morals; prostitution is one of the means it employs to maintain its empire and to perpetuate the slavery of the citizens using the bait of libertine behavior and vice. There is no doubt any more that the dens of prostitution are just ordinary asylums for counter-revolutionaries who pay for their infamous pleasures with ill-gotten money." [33]

As for misogyny, some of the Revolution's lay speakers exceeded any measurement in calling upon the aforementioned "natural laws." Pierre Chaumette, a rabid anticlerical who had all the churches of Paris shut down and who was a participant in the introduction of the Terror, was one. At the Tribune of the Convention, speaking about women, he evoked "those degraded beings who want to defy and violate the natural laws. . . . Since when are they allowed," he asked, "to abjure their sex and to make themselves men?" [34]

An unrivaled specialist in the history of women, Michelle Perrot points out that the French Revolution, by excluding women from public life, paradoxically was *retrogressing* in comparison to certain customs and traditions of the *Ancien regime*. It was in the name of "nature," of "social utility" and the requirements of procreation, that women (considered to be dreamy, unstable, fragile and emotive) were relegated to domestic tasks by the French revolutionaries. [35]

While moral offenses were not grounds for legal prosecution, when it came to homosexuals, they were pursued, under the Terror, by the Surveillance Committee of Paris. This same authority would challenge "manufacturers of 'obscene mechanisms,' adult toys, and it is known that raids were organized, in March 1794, in the gardens of the Palais Royal. And it was common to find prostitutes in the cart heading to the guillotine.   The execution of Mlle. Leroy, a more or less unemployed young actress from the Louvois theater, was picked up without papers at night and executed during the messidor and thermidor [*ed. note:* two months, in the new calendar instituted by the Revolution] prison conspiracies; her tale illustrates the fundamentalist wind that blew during the bloody hours of Terror."[36]

But it is the very concept of carnal pleasure and sexuality that the Puritan bent attacked most spectacularly. And with most catastrophic long term effects.

Scientistic Onanism and Delusions

Simply put, three major factors came together at this time to support the gradual triumph of prudishness, which the Church took up at the Vatican II council. They were medical scientism, the influence of the Anglo-Saxon Puritans, and the birth of the industrial society and the bourgeois mentality.

In the medical field, it was not in the 19th century but actually in the 18th that supposedly a scientific approach began to invade the domain of morals and sexuality as a stratagem in moral reasoning. The most striking example has to do with masturbation. Admittedly, that was already denounced — under the term of "weakness" — by the confessors of the Middle Ages, and later by certain 17th century preachers. In 1640, for example, Richard Capel, a preacher from Magdalen College in London (a prime site for Protestant Puritanism), declared, in his work *On Temptations, Their Nature, Their Danger, Their Treatment*, that masturbation was the gravest sin against nature, and that it led to physical weakness and to incapacity in marriage and shortened life by leading to suicide. But, among the doctors of the Enlightenment, the assessment soon radically changed in nature. Masturbation was no longer a "failing," it became a "disease."

It is apparently in 1710 that an English moralist by name of Bekker for the first time mixed medical arguments with the traditional and — relatively moderate — denunciation of "weakness." His book, entitled *Onania, or the Heinous Sin of Self Pollution, and all its frightful Consequences in both sexes considered with Spiritual and Physical Advice to those who have already injur' d themselves by this abominable Practice,* was a considerable success and continued to be republished until . . .now.

Jean-Louis Flandrin has shown that "Onanism, as a serious illness leading ineluctably to madness or death, is a medical invention of the

18th century." The case of the famous Swiss doctor Tissot, of Lausanne, may be cited. In 1760, he too published a treatise that was continually republished: *Onanism, a dissertation on the maladies produced by masturbation.*[37] But it is not generally known that such treatises condemning solitary pleasure were countless in the 18th and 19th centuries. Fleming, by studying the catalogue of the medical works of the national Library, established a graph by which to visually grasp how rapidly these essays multiplied between 1750 and 1850, and, more precisely, during two well defined periods: 1760 to 1785 (with a peak of ten treatises published in 1175) and 1805-1850 (with a peak of twelve treaties in 1830).[38]

In the 19th century, this medical obsession with Onanism was confined to delusions. It was used to justify all kinds of recommendations, admonitions, and threats addressed to young people. Applied to women, it even led certain doctors to recommend excision (i.e. an ablation of the clitoris) similar to that practiced today in certain Arab and African countries. "The clitoridectomy was recommended in Europe, in the 19th century, to cure what one did not hesitate to term 'the too great lubricity of women.' The highest medical authorities practiced it without question. The Istanbul doctor Démétrius Zambaco consulted some of them. He had read the observations of Professor J - B Fonsabrives, a famous hygienist and declared enemy of 'vicious practices,' and in London he met with Doctor Jules Guerin of the Academy of Medicine. Guerin affirmed having cured several girls affected by Onanism by burning their clitoris with red-hot iron."[39]

This absurd terrorism, which had no basis in religion, was internalized by whole generations of Europeans up to the middle of the 20th century. And internalized with an unbelievable force, since even the great minds were influenced by the alleged harmfulness masturbation would have on hearing or sight. (Masturbation makes you blind, etc..) Here are two unexpected and rather tantalizing examples. In his *Journal*, Benjamin Constant reveals that he would groan "my poor eyes!" every time he masturbated. As for Nietzsche, Doctor Eiser of Frankfurt, who received him for consultation in 1877 (and to whom to Nietzsche admitted that he masturbated frequently), would write to Wagner that, "taking into account the tenacity of this vice," there was little hope that Nietzsche would ever find a happy optical balance.[40]

Aside from the anecdotal aspect, what should be remembered is the concept of sexuality that fed this obsession: a scientistic pretension (in fact very naive) of "telling the truth about sex," to have a *scientia sexualis* win out against the *ars erotica* of the Ancients; and especially a view that was completely dominated by the idea of economy, of vital investment, that Alain Corbin analyzed well.

What prevailed, then, was the obsession with loss by the means of "spilling" sperm. "The French scientists," writes Corbin, "defined the requirements of spermatic economy which the British doctors of the Victorian era were also much concerned. The emission of this seminal liquid, 'life in the liquid state,' according to Dr. Réveillé-Parise, and 'the purest extract of the blood,' according to Doctor Alexandre Mayer, requires an intense effort. They calculated that the loss of thirty grams this substance, as [a certain] Doctor Garnier noted, 'is equivalent to two hundred grams of blood.' Therefore it was essential above all to avoid wasting it, through ill-considered emission."[41]

Triumph over Bourgeois Discourse

Actually, this medical discourse reflected the fantasies of the bourgeoisie that was on the way to becoming the new dominant class. It imposes an economic vision, a management, an arithmetic of sexuality which we find all the way up to the 20th century. It also justifies the repressive frame of mind against that William Reich would attack in the 1920's. "Thus it became essential, above all," writes Corbin, "to avoid waste. Knowing how to save this force would prolong life and can lead to genius." There, the bourgeoisie, soon to replace the aristocracy, expressed its will to accumulate, not only materially (wealth, capital, etc.) but also symbolically and culturally. Controlling sex, they believed, would encourage creativity. Arithmetically making sexuality into a "thing" (which the Kinsey Report did again in 1948) originated there, as well as the obsession with *quantity*. "That also holds true," adds Corbin, "for the entire social body. While brothel managers made sure that the customers 'did not bend over,' Victor Hugo recorded in his notebooks his various performances, and Michelet recapitulates his annual coital events in his journal."

Once again, it was the doctors who consolidated these new bourgeois obsessions with "scientific" arguments. A certain Doctor A. Lutaud, a sworn opponent of the Church, would write for example, "The wise man should never repeat coitus without allowing, between each sex act, an interval varying from one to several days according to his age and his constitution."

This is a far cry, a very far cry, from the medieval theological regulations on the *necessary* female pleasure. "This series of injunctions is in accordance with what one can know of the brevity of the marital relations in the 19th century. In 1906, in a work that was widely-read in cultivated circles (Auguste Forel, *La Question sexuelle exposée aux adultes cultivatés*, Paris, G. Steinheil Publishers, 1906), the author arrives at the conclusion that, for his bourgeois clientele, the average duration of coitus was three minutes; and Kinsey, a few decades later, would arrive at very similar results."[42]

This bourgeois view is also — and perhaps especially — consubstantial with the industrial revolution and the emergence of capitalism. From that perspective, its link with Anglo-Saxon Protestant Puritanism is undeniable. Max Weber's analyses make it possible size this up. Weber emphasizes the determining influence, within the Protestant Puritanism that was a founding aspect of capitalism, of Richard Baxter's thinking (18th century) and in particular of his main work, *A Christian Directory or a Summ of Practical Theology and Cases of Conscience* (London, 1677).

"Baxter's principal work is permeated with endless preaching, almost impassioned sometimes, in favor of hard and continuous work, be it manual or intellectual. Two topics are combined here. First, labor had long been proven reliable as *an ascetic means*, and the Western [Protestant] Church had always favored it — in marked opposition not only to the East, but to almost all the monastic rules of the entire world. In particular, work is the specific remedy to employ preventively against all those *temptations* that Puritanism lumped together under the term of *unclean living* and whose its role is not insignificant. . . . Against all sexual temptations as well as against religious doubts or the feeling of moral unworthiness, in addition to frugal vegetarian food and cold baths, they lived by the precept, 'Work hard at your task.'"[43]

For Weber, the Puritan *wanted* to be a pure and hard-working man. In a certain way, he felt obliged to be so. "For, when asceticism was transferred from the monk's cell to the professional life and began to dominate secular morality, it was in order to take part in constructing the new religious cosmos based on the modern economic order. And that order was tied to the technical and economic conditions of me-chanical and machinist production which determines, with an irresisti-ble force, the lifestyle of all the individuals born within this mechanism (and not only that which relates directly to economic gain)."

Capital, Weber continues, is formed thanks to these forced and ascetic savings. At the same time, a model of "reasonable" management of life was being worked out, which was at the heart of our modernity until the mid-Sixties and which, in some circles, still is today. "One could say that as far as the influence of the Puritan concept of existence was extended (and this is important in ways other than the simple en-couragement of the accumulation of capital) this concept encouraged the inclination to a bourgeois life, economically more rational; it was the most important factor and, in fact, the only one that mattered."

In passing, the author of *Protestant Ethics and the Spirit of capitalism* underscores the opposition between this Puritan bourgeois morality and the Catholic tradition relating to the poor. Since the 12th century, old medieval Catholicism had exalted "gratuities," the mendicant or-ders and vows of poverty. For the Protestant Puritans, on the contrary, "wishing to be poor is like wishing to be sick, which is condemnable in terms of sanctification by one's works, and is detrimental to the glory of God. And in particular begging, on the part of an individual who could work, is condemnable idleness but is also, according to the word of the Apostle, a violation of the duty to love one's neighbor. Calvin had al-ready strictly prohibited begging, and the Dutch synods waged cam-paigns against beggars' licenses."[44]

The Syndrome of the Bourgeois Gentleman

But it would not be possible to understand the gradual hegemony of the bourgeois approach without referring to the complex relations that the bourgeoisie entertained, throughout the 19th century, with the aristocratic model it was itching to replace, which it detested and ad-mired at the same time. There is an imitative and vaguely delirious nervous tension in such behaviors. The bourgeois temperament first of all tried to differentiate itself from the nobility. For most historians, "the anti-masturbation hysteria, born in the century of Enlightenment, was a new 'value' invented by the bourgeoisie, jealous of all the powers. The bourgeoisie had to set itself apart from the nobility, a degenerate class exemplified by such wretched characters as the Marquis de Sade and Choderlos de Laclos, odious adversaries of the 'decency' that the bourgeois family had been exalting s the supreme virtue since the Middle Ages. Its fight against any form of sexuality not tied to procreation combined with its commercial spirit, another obsessive value which it would compare, throughout the 19th century, with 'the improvidence of the working class."[45]

Foucault used a still more telling metaphor when he said that, while the aristocracy had perpetuated its identity for centuries on the theme of "blue blood," that is, by focusing on ancestry and the value of alliances, the incipient bourgeoisie would be obsessed, on the contrary, by his own descent, procreation, the "healthy" and productive management of his sexuality. "The 'blood' of the bourgeoisie was its sex. During the 18th century, the bourgeoisie . . . converted the blue blood of nobles into an organism bearing organization and a healthy sexuality; it is understood why the bourgeoisie took so long and raised so many oppositions to the acknowledgement that the other classes had bodies and sex — precisely those classes which it exploited."[46]

But this mimicry of the old aristocratic model is vaguely infused by envy. The notion of the mistress and the specter of bourgeois adultery, which dominates the literature of the time, is the best example of this desire to imitate the nobility. Since the end of the second Empire, "the aristocratic model exerted a very particular fascination on the solid and even the minor bourgeoisie. These categories were concerned with legitimating their positions. To show themselves in the company of a mistress who was a fashionable woman, to be seen with a great courtesan (or even, in the provinces, with a cabaret singer), became part of that strategy of accumulating symbolic assets, which meant that it became fashionable to collect the Dutch Masters or to frequent major restaurants."[47]

Clandestine adultery as symptom of Victorian hypocrisy in the 19th century was related to a detestation of "scandal" ("sooner fault, than scandal)," to a preoccupation with dissimulation and a sense of modesty that was as dated and as it was bourgeois. Marx himself was, one might say, "contaminated" by this hypocrisy since he had a child by his maid, as a good bourgeois man of the 19th century, but refused to acknowledge it so as not to upset his disciples. This bourgeois dissimulation was in contrast to the impudent aristocratic ostentation. That is why, in the 19th century, bordellos were invented. "If we really must make room for illegitimate sexual relations, let them make their din

elsewhere: where they can be incorporated in the circuits if not of production, at least of profit. The bordello and the private hospital became
these places of tolerance."[48]

Sexual puritanism thus triumphed all across Europe. It took over
all of society since it made it possible to "put the people to work." It
was petty, prudish, stingy and hard on those who were faulty, a hardness which, in truth, is no longer remembered. Around 1830, a historian
wrote that "morals are so pure, in the surroundings of Chateaubriant,
that when girl has the misfortune to succumb — which is quite rare in
this country — the memory of the failure is carried from generation to
generation. One is astonished to hear it said of a girl: 'She is quite well-
behaved, but what a shame that her grandmother erred!' Often, nobody
even knew this dishonored grandmother."[49]

In the context of poverty and social precariousness of the 19th
century, the popular classes granted a particular value to the family and
its concerns. The family became a refuge "closed to the outside world,"
to use Philippe Ariès' expression. Between 1801 and 1846, the population of Paris doubled, going from 550,000 inhabitants to more than one
million. In Lille, in 1875, the poor accounted for approximately 20% of
the population. Authors like Le Play (*Les Ouvriers européens* [*European
Workers*], 1855) and Villermé (*Tableau de l'état physicque et moral des ouvriers
employés dans les manufactures de soie, coton et laine* [*A Portrait of the Physical
and Moral State of the Workmen Employed in Silk, Cotton and Wool Factories*)
revealed to their contemporaries the extreme misery of this segment of
the population. "This 19th century society was in full transformation,
conquering, enterprising, but hard on the poor and the weak; couples,
therefore, seeking a little happiness, attached great importance to the
family."[50] Paradoxically, the industrial revolution contributed to the
breakdown of the family while placing great importance on that which
it represented.

In hindsight, one phenomenon stands out: the haste with which
the Church joined forces with this bourgeois model, even upping the
ante in terms of puritanism. The Church, traumatized by the Revolution, then reassured by the Restoration that turned back the revolutionary reforms and restored the Church's prerogatives, became reactionary in the strict sense of the term. The Church would espouse that
moralism to the extent of allowing Christianity to be bound up in it for
ages. We will see below that, as of the middle of the 19th century and

during the first half of the 20th, the Church would help to propagate it and to defend it, through its priests, its confessionals, its sermons and its catechisms. Thus the contemporary puritanism would take on a clerical overtone that it did not have in the beginning.

The Church, in detaching itself from its own traditions, whose wealth was underestimated, acted as if it had also lost its memory.

CHAPTER 9

SINCE THE WORLD WAS FOUNDED

Imagine the surprise of Hernán Cortez and his companions as they disembarked, July 7, 1519, in the Aztec empire of the New World. They would soon be welcomed there (in November) by the sovereign Moctezuma II, who took these metal-helmeted white men for messengers from the gods. Surprised? These *conquistadores* discovered, at the ends of the earth, a powerful civilization that built cities and monumental palaces, and observed alarming sacrificial rites in honor of its own gods: Quetzalcoatl in the East and Huitzilopochtli in the South. Actually, it would have been a superficial surprise: the roughneck soldiers of Cortez were more concerned with conquest and plundering than ethnology. It is doubtful that they had the leisure — or even the desire — to discover among the Aztecs, beyond the strangeness of the languages and the magnificence of the ceremonies, astonishing points in common. Resemblances that would have disturbed them for sure. The surprise would have given way to shock.

Among these common points that archaeologists, much later, would bring to light, some concern the universal and at the same time intimate "mystery" of sexuality. For these soldiers and sailors, coming from the very Catholic Spain, familiar with bishops' homilies and priests' sermons, the interdicts were related above all to the very holy liturgical calendar, the great regulator of the rhythm of the days, the months and the years. For a 16th century Spanish Christian, it was the date, the hour, the period which rendered the flashes of desire [of a husband for his wife] licit or illicit according to each case. That, one is tempted to say, was a custom — a mania? — specific if not to Christianity at least to the people of the West.

However, strangely, the Aztecs, on the eve of the Spanish conquest, followed rules, interdicts, and regulations regarding sex that were not much different. They had their own liturgical calendar and similarly subjected their desires to it. During fasting periods, men and women were not entitled to sexual intercourse. Xochipilli, the god of youth, music and flowers, punished those who violated the interdict by striking them with venereal diseases, hemorrhoids or eczema.

"It was believed that the man or woman who gave in to illicit love would be spreading, by a permanent evil spell, what was called *tlazolmiquiztli* (death caused by love) and that the children or the parents would be struck with melancholy and consumption. It was both a moral and physical stain that one could only cure through steam baths and the rite of purification, and by calling upon the *tlazolteteo*, goddesses of love and desire."[1]

A Total Social Phenomenon

The bizarreness of the names should not make mislead us. On many points, the interdicts and the rituals of purification observed by the Aztecs exactly match those of the Christians, who were themselves inspired by the Jewish and Greco-Roman traditions. In mankind's memory, no exchange, no communication had ever been established between this New World and the Old one. Could there be, across the cultures and the differences, a universality of sexual interdicts? The historians cite many other examples that justify the question.

Along with pharaonic Egypt, the oldest civilization that left us written texts is Mesopotamia. Nearly a half-million cuneiform tablets going back to 3000 years BC inform us about the daily life of these Sumerian cities and empires along the Tiger and the Euphrates. Some of them consist of splendid poems exalting love and sexuality in crude terms. "Excite yourself! Excite yourself! Get it up! Get it up! Excite yourself like a stag! Get erect like a wild bull! . . . Love to me six times like a ram! Seven times like a stag! Twelve times like a partridge! Make love to me, for I am young!" The practice of love and eroticism clearly did not pose, for them, any problem of guilt.

Other tablets reveal, nevertheless, a whole system of constraints and severe interdicts. Celibacy is proscribed and scorned, strictly monogamous marriage is the rule, and preoccupation with conserving one's procreative faculties was omnipresent while holy prostitution was thoroughly codified. "In Mesopotamia as among us, the impulses and capacities in love traditionally had been channeled by collective constraint in order to ensure that everything was directed to the individual cell of the social body: the family, and thus to provide for its continuity. The fundamental vocation of each man and woman, their 'destiny,' as it was called, deferring to the radical will of the gods, was thus marriage."[2]

The medical texts list sexual relations that are qualified as sacrilege, and thus prohibited. These include sex with women "reserved for the gods," and incest with close relations, mothers or sisters. A periodic continence is imposed, although the archaeologists have not been able to determine the reasons. It is only known that on certain days of the year (the 6th of the month of tashrît, for example), it is forbidden to make love. Not everything is not allowed, not by a long shot, even in remote Mesopotamia.

However far the curiosity of the researchers goes, everything leads to the thought that human societies have always taken care to codify and to manage sexuality, that force that fascinates them and worries them. Better still, civilizations seem to have made the domestication of desire both the basis and the product of their cultures. "Human sexuality," says Georges Ballandier, "is a complete social phenomenon. . . . Obviously, it is a natural given. . . . But it is equally obvious that this aspect of man's nature is the one that has, earliest and most completely, been conditioned by the effects of life in society."[3]

All the evidence shows that the innumerable human groups that have inhabited the earth and populated history have been constrained to reconcile, each in its own way, a set number of opposing parameters: the individual's spontaneous inclination for pleasure and its refinement, the need to perpetuate the species, the explosive and thus subversive character of desire, the need to contain the violence generated by rival desires, etc.. To underscore this historical constant, Flandrin takes a look at passion, the sublimated manifestation of desire: "Because it impels us to couple with anyone, anyhow, anywhere, at any time, passion is dangerous for man and society. It causes social disorder and makes trouble for the individual. This is what the moralists of pagan Antiquity all emphasized — and not only the stoics. They condemned all wild, irrational behavior. . . . This is to some extent a universal feature of morality, since every society — except perhaps for our post-romantic society — more or less sensed the danger of love's passion."[4]

These commonsense reflections reveal the pleasant provincialism of most of our polemic on sexual morality, the severity of our interdictions and the supposed cunning of European morality. In fact, these repeated volleys on sexuality are as ethnocentric as can be. They act as though the question was strictly a Western conflict between puritans and libertines, the lay and the religious, Right and Left, etc.; while even modest attention to anthropology would show that the is far broader and would soften the edges of the debate.

Man Delivered from Rut

In Book V of his *Emile or Education*, Jean-Jacques Rousseau evokes — two centuries ahead of time — a key point of the reflection on sexuality. Comparing human behavior with that of animals, in reference to female modesty and the necessary reserve of the woman on this matter, he wrote, "While female animals do not have the same shame, what does happen? Do they, like women, have unlimited desires which this shame is used to curb? They experience desire only with need; the need being satisfied, the desire ceases. They no longer repel the male in play, but for real. They do the opposite of what Auguste's daughter did: they do not accept any more passengers once the ship is loaded."

Rousseau notes the strange singularity of women compared to the females of the animal kingdom: their constant availability for love, the fact that their desire (no more than men's) is never *naturally* controlled by the impulse that governs animals, which we call *rut*. Rut is a period of intense desire, characterized by competition and male violence, but narrowly circumscribed in time. And that is not all. In humans, female desire is not only present from one end of the year to the other but, in theory, it has no physiological limits — such as erection — which are piteously imposed on men. Before Rousseau, many racy authors had fun embroidering on this male infirmity which, in the matter of love, makes woman truly the stronger sex. And that has justified a good share of the fear that female sexuality inspires.

In *Facéties* [*Jokes*], by Poggio, the prominent concupiscent author of the Italian pre-Renaissance, a conversation is reported in which a man asks a woman: "Why, if man and woman have equal pleasure in making love, is it always the men who solicit the women?" The woman answers, "We others, we are always ready and willing to make love, while you are not; we would be wasting our time to solicit you when you would not be ready."[5] In the Middle Ages, men's apprehensive obsession with woman's sexual insatiability is a recurring topic of erotic stories. "The popular Middle Ages sees women's sexuality as extreme and worrisome. Another means of propitiating it is to call it evil. The woman is treated as a whore, she is a 'lecheress,' a bitch or a she-wolf. So it is with Mme. Hersant, wife of the wolf Ysengrin, who runs to get laid by Renart as soon as the wolf leaves. But fundamentally, despite all the magic, the legends and the 'tales' intended to reassure, the men of the Middle Ages remain distressed."

However, anthropologists consider this difference between woman and female animals, this constant sexual availability, to be one of the principal results of becoming human. Woman, they say, "escaped from estrus;" they also say that she has "lost estrus." The expression comes from the Greek *oistros*, which means fury. It refers to the phase of the estrous cycle which, in animals, produces ovulation and rut. It is this repetitive and constraining cycle which, in animals, takes the place of sexual morality. In a group of animals, the peace that is threatened animal by the outburst of rut is restored at the end of the estrous cycle. Among animals, the males only desire, and the females are desirable, on fixed dates.

Since humans escaped this involuntary regulation, which itself subject to the overall biological clock, it became necessary that *culture* should replace *nature* in codifying and managing sexuality. This has led certain anthropologists to say, "It is sex which makes the society."[7]   In reference to these same elementary facts that we must constantly bear in mind, even if it is little understood today, that sex is not a function but a culture. Or, more precisely, that it is at the nexus between biology and culture, at the very heart of the famous opposition between the innate and the acquired, between that which is *provided* by nature and that which is *achieved* by culture.

However, this immense debate over the innate one and the acquired, launched in the 19th century by Sir Francis Galton, cropped up again in the Sixties, first in the United States and then in Europe. Why? Because that had to do with the basis of certain questions like racial segregation (in the United States) and, most of all, *women's emancipation*. The fact that what is prohibited from one society to another seems almost universal and highly similar suggests that any cultural codification of sexuality rests on what Françoise Héritier calls "an accepted view of the difference" between the feminine and the masculine. That means a sexual differentiation of functions and tasks between the man and the woman. This allegedly irreducible biological differentiation usually leads to a devalued view, subordinate, of the feminine role. It is understood that feminism and, more generally, the Western movement of sexual liberation, undertook to mitigate this differentiation.

A Misogynist Buddha

This "view of the difference," and also the fear caused by a female sexuality perceived to be insatiable and without specific physiological limits, contributed to the persistence of misogyny in human cultures. The examples are countless. We'll look at only one of them, all the more revealing since it is one of most unexpected: that of Buddhism. Yes, even the soft and calm Buddhism, which regards the difference between the sexes as "illusory and impermanent," is marked, in its fundamental texts, by a very clear hostility towards women. In Buddha's dialogues with Ananda, his preferred disciple, and in other old texts as well, there are many passages as violent as this one. "A woman should look on her body as being full of offense ...This body is a receptacle of impurities, filled with nauseous rubbish. It is like a cesspool ...like a basin with nine holes from which all kinds of filth flow. This is the body that stupid and petty men get attached to! ...This body is food for vultures, wolves and dogs; that is why it is thrown into a cemetery. This body is a compound of pain and suffering."[8]

Even though Indian women in earlier periods (the Vedic era) enjoyed a relatively positive status, Brahmanism introduced the traditional anti-feminine suspicion. In later Indian tradition, this suspicion was embodied in the myth of Parvati, one of Shiva's wives, presented as a temptress, libidinous and impure. The commentators emphasize Buddha's reluctance to admit women in the ranks of his disciples. "And yet, at the same time as woman is feared for her powers as a temptress, she is exalted in her role of mother and wife.[9]

There is no doubt that sexual differentiation is the most widely shared "view" in the world. While she has certain reservations, Françoise Héritier suggests that "there is a strong statistical probability that men are universally considered the superior, in this question." Even so, this historically and anthropologically verified supremacy cannot be accepted as immutable and we do not have to accept it, giving up on any "progress." It is the honor and merit of the Western feminist movement to have rejected this ancestral subservience. But what are the real chances of a viable and lasting change of this established fact? That, ultimately, is the immense question going on behind the superficial quarrels. In other words, can what has been achieved be freed completely from what is innate, or must they be combined together?

With a scientist as scrupulous as Héritier, it is striking to note how, in all probity, the militant of hope of a feminist cohabits with the skepticism of the anthropologist. "I doubt," she writes, "that we will ever arrive at an idyllic equality in all fields, insofar as any society can only be built on that ensemble of reinforcements that are tightly welded together — the prohibition of incest, task distribution according to gender, a legal or recognized form of stable union, and, I might add, the valence differential of the sexes. If this construction is accepted (although it is not demonstrable but only equipped with a strong probability since this conceptual framework is based in immutable data that man has observed for eternity, i. e., his body and his environment), then yes, the main difficulty on the way to equality is to find the lever which would make it possible to make uncouple these associations.[10]

To uncouple these associations? By its slightly provocative radicalness, the formula itself shows the importance of the above-mentioned debate on the opposition of nature/culture. A debate which would have benefited from being more widely and pedagogically popularized. It makes it possible to put certain topical quarrels in their true perspective, such as, for example, the idea of quotas ("positive discrimination") to support women in politics. Anthropologist Michel Panoff describes the conundrum. "If we manage to establish that, originally, the sexes were fundamentally equal, then we can reasonably hope to return to that state by modifying the social relations which currently support male domination. If, on the contrary, it is shown that men have always dominated women, and for good biological reasons, then any attempt at redressing the balance in favor of the female sex would be going against 'nature' and would require very considerable efforts in the transformation of the society.[11]

Man the Hunter, Woman the Gatherer

Of course, no one is claiming to report any more than very briefly the scientific data on which this discussion is founded. But we'd like to understand why and how the disagreements expressed by the anthropologists are, still today, directly connected with the properly political aspect of the question.

If one follows Panoff's analyses, the prevailing trend from the 1920's to the 1960's placed the "social" explanation ahead of the "biological" one. This reflects the constructivist and progressivist optimism of the time; the conviction that the human will could change the world and *disobey* the alleged constraints of biology. It was also a question of fighting against the radical "innate-ists," who thought that it was naive to try to free oneself from reality. Besides, in the United States, anthropo-biologists and socio-biologists seemed to be defenders of the WASP establishment and the propagandists of racist ideas.

The anthropologist Margaret Mead, author of the famous *Male and Female* (1949), was one of the most ferocious adversaries of the partisans of the "biological whole." Following her, and fueled by ideological optimism, might we have gone too far toward the "social whole?" "all?" Might we have mistakenly played down the importance of the biological, in order not to give our adversaries any ground, as Mead herself said? What is certain is that innate-ism returned to center stage in America in the mid-Sixties,[12] just when — by reaction? — the civil rights movement and feminism were being affirmed. According to Panoff, the biological determination of female characteristics gained favor in scientific opinion, after four decades of being out of favor. Hence the scientific quarrel in the 1960's-1970's in connection with the origin of sexual differentiation.

Two texts from that period summarize both the contents and the virulence of the debate. The first is the collective work by R. Lee and I.

De Vore, *Man the Hunter* (Chicago, 1968). The authors, militant innate-ists, use the argument called *cynegetics* [*ed. note:* basically, Greek for "hunting"] to explain that hunting was the driving force in human pro-gress. Hunting, in effect — a domain reserved to men, for obvious bio-logical reasons — supposedly made him the inventor of the culture and therefore would have made women dependent on them.

This book was answered, in 1971, by a resounding feminist article by S. Slocum, *Woman the Gatherer*. The author intends to explain the fun-damental role played by women (while the men were out hunting) in the techniques of gathering, collecting, manufacturing the first contain-ers including baskets to transport babies, all things that are by defini-tion at the origin of culture. "Thus reducing their handicap compared to the men, the women are [here portrayed playing] the role which his-tory assigned to them and which the authors of *Man the Hunter* denied them. Quite simply, the invention of civilization."[13]

The question of feminism has pervaded anthropology and many other disciplines. In addition, one will see in connection with the ho-mosexuals' claim that this rather stimulating second reading or revisi-tation of our assumptions is one of the objectives of *queer theory*.[14] The question is, what are the limits of militant voluntarism. Today, certain ethnologists and anthropologists like Panoff and Ducros judge rather severely this will to deny the biological, beyond any reasonable ex-tent — a will that has been the rule for a long time the rule.

"For however well-justified it was in principle," writes Panoff, "the feminist dispute in our disciplines seems today to have had the perverse effect of diverting attention from the biological constraints and incompatibilities and instead giving primacy to the social aspect of sexual differentiation. The negative consequences of this orientation are still being felt. To give just one example: the state of scientific un-preparedness in which it left ethnologists, who had to confront ideo-logical campaigns launched in sociobiology works."[15]

Critics like Panoff recall that Margaret Mead herself had had to back-pedal and recognize that sexual differentiation proceeded neither from the social nor the biological but from a dialectic of the two. Let's stop for a moment on this idea of reciprocal interaction.

From Impudicity to Depravity

Judging from some of the concrete examples concerning sexuality noted by Héritier in the African societies that she studied, it seems clear that the biological is not seen as a single and irresistible given. The influence of social and cultural constructions (i.e. voluntary choices) on subjects as fundamental as filiation seems to be as important as the biological data. The Samo communities of Burkina Faso are among the most significant examples.

In a legitimate marriage, a little girl is assigned at birth to a husband belonging to an authorized group, according to certain prohibitions or parental preferences. Before being given to her husband, this girl, having arrived at puberty, must also take a lover selected from one of the authorized groups, but not the group from which her spouse was selected. She will join her legitimate husband at the end of a certain time: three years maximum if she does not have a child, or upon the birth of her first child (whose parent is thus the lover). This child is regarded as the first child of the legitimate husband, whatever the biological reality. At no time is it regarded as the child of its true parent. *Filiation is thus entirely social.*[16]

Even more surprising, among the Samo, legitimate wives sometimes run away and have extra-marital adventures which lead to illegitimate births. If the husband manages to bring back this fugitive wife, the children that she brings with her will be regarded as those of the husband just like the others. *A filiation will have been invented* that has no relationship to the biological truth.

These Samo societies are, however, not exaggeratedly permissive, nor indifferent to the idea of sexual interdicts. Quite to the contrary, the interdicts are as strict there as in many societies that we consider to be puritan. They can be categorized according to a precise gradation in four main groupings: *tia yè la* (impropriety) includes, for example, for a grandmother to bring children into the world when her grandchildren have already started to procreate; *gagabra* (impurity or shamelessness) indicates copulation in the bush, which is said to cause the rain to stop; *dyilibra* (perversion) refers to incest or adultery with one's brother's wife, which would bring on disease and sterility; finally being *zama* (a necrophile) represents the absolute abomination in the scale of horror.

Among the Mossi of Yatenga, zoophilia, especially a man copulating with a she-ass, takes the place of necrophilia as the worst horror. For the Bwa of Burkina-Faso, it is incest. The Navaho believe that a woman who masturbates will give birth to horrifying monsters. Lastly, the Ojibwa blame past homosexual relations between two married women, an aunt and a niece, for hydrocephalia in the children whom they will later bring into the world.

In these traditional societies, the rigidity of the interdicts does not preclude the possible intervention of free will in regard to filiation or relationship. In other words, the social is not strictly dependent on the biological. Anthropologists also have examples —admittedly very few, but undeniable — that illustrate the significant leeway that is accorded to what man has "achieved." These are matriarchal societies where the women exert the real power. Margaret Mead and Bronislaw Malinowski contributed to the renown of the Trobriand Islands, in the Pacific, in announcing that here, sexual initiative apparently remained the privilege of women.

As another example, the six Iroquois nations of Canada are more traditional still. They were studied since 1724 by the Jesuit, Lafitau, then by Judith Brown in 1970. In these Indian nations, the women enjoyed rights and powers without much equivalent in the world. For example, they set the rules of filiation and decided on the dwelling place. The great house gathering women, men and children of the same lineage was directed by a "matron," who also governed the agricultural labor (women's territory), which was carried out jointly on the shared land that belonged to them. The matron herself redistributed the food cooked at the various hearths of the lineage.

"These matrons were represented, if not at the Great Council of the Six Iroquois Nations, at least at the Council of Elders of each nation, by a male representative who spoke on their behalf and made their voices heard. This voice was not, in fact, negligible, since the matrons had a right of veto over war, if the war plan did not meet their approval."[17] In any event, they could keep such a plan from being fulfilled simply by forbidding the women to provide the necessary war provisions like dried or concentrated food.

For Héritier, the lesson is clear: differentiation based on gender — that famous view of the difference — does not lead *inevitably* to a hierarchy of powers in favor of men. The statistical frequency of that assumption is not the last word. The alleged rule does allow for exceptions.

Concurrent to these arguments, we should mention the idea of evolution, borrowed from Durkheim. In a famous book published in 1893 (*On the Division of Social Labor*), Durkheim suggested that humanity might not, originally, have divided activity and behavior between women and men. The course of evolution might have imposed a division of the labor between the sexes for greater effectiveness. This evolutionary argument is inherently *reversible*. What one stage in evolution has provided, another must be able to abolish, given a different concept of social effectiveness. The entire question would depend on the definition of the aforementioned effectiveness, in terms of certain requirements such as, for example, raising the children. The question, in any case, remains open.

When it comes to sexuality, the evolutionary character of interdicts is what stands out the most, when one takes a long view. No civilization has solidified its sexual morality once and for all. This matter is never static; it is dynamic, evolutionary, changing over the centuries and always dependent on specific historical circumstances. Two outstanding examples will serve to prove this: China and Islam.

Chinese Sex Manuals

No culture allows us to look at the long term better than China. Chinese society covers such a swath of history that it takes our breath away. Stretching across the millennia, divided into long reigns and dynasties extending over centuries, Chinese history is a constant lesson in eternity. What we know of it (even if that remains fragmentary for the most remote periods) allows the mind to span temporal expanses unimaginable elsewhere. However, the history of sexual morality in China is one of the least well-established. Two great events, at least, upset it profoundly, in the sense of restrictions and decency: the advent of Confucianism in the 6th century BC, then its Renaissance in the 12th century AD; and the brutal Manchu invasion, which put an end to the T'sing dynasty in the 17th Century.

If we take a sinologist like Robert van Gulik at his word, the principles which found Chinese sexuality succeed, in theory, in *supporting both pleasure and procreation*. In the Chinese vision of the difference between the sexes, as we know, two great principles are opposed and are complementary: the negative and female *yin* and the positive male *yang*.

(Sometimes the negative *yin* energy is considered to be higher than the positive *yang*). The sex act enables the man to reinforce his vitality by absorbing a little of the woman's *yin* essence, including by sodomizing her, which is allowed. The woman, for her part, derives a physical benefit in shaking up her "dormant," i.e. *yin*, nature through coitus.

According to old Chinese tradition, in any case, a refined sexuality is a sign of happiness and physical health. The ancient Chinese view on sex, Gulik writes, was clear: "...to accept with joy and without restrictions the most varied aspects of human procreation, from minute biological details of carnal embraces to the most elevated spiritual love, the sincerity of which the embrace attests and seals. Because it is the human analogue of the process of cosmic procreation, sexual intercourse was revered without ever associating it with moral culpability, without seeing the least sin in it. . . . They saw no difference between the rain that waters the fields and the seed that fertilizes the entrails; nor between the earth, rich, wet, ready for sowing, and the vagina whose moistness makes it ready for penetration."[18]

Being very much attached to the idea of sexual "success," the inhabitants of ancient China had the habit of recording their observations in "sex manuals," supposed to educate the head of the household on the best manner of governing his relations with his wife. These tutelary treatises of eroticism circulated, by the thousands, for over two thousand years; they were still studied in China in the 13th century.

Let us not conclude, however, that sexual interdicts were absent from this society that was ever so attentive to pleasure. Their prohibitions arose mainly from the absolute and primary imperative governing Chinese sexuality: the need to engender a line of descent that would be able to ensure the worship of the ancestors. Every man was charged with this sacred duty towards his parents once they were gone, since only those descendants still living could make the periodic sacrifices that would guarantee the happiness of the beings in the great beyond. Procreation — especially producing a son — was an ontological need. Plus, that was what justified polygamy. If a wife turned out to be unable to conceive a son, others would have to take up the task.

For this reason, continence was scorned as well as celibate women, who were suspected of the worst intentions and who were persecuted. Male masturbation was also scorned, and forbidden, since it entailed a loss of vital essence. "The medical books excuse a man for

Onanism only when particular circumstances deprive him of female company, and where the 'devitalized seed,' *pai-king* (i.e. seed activated inside the body for a prolonged period), could clog his organization. Involuntary emissions occurring during sleep are also a cause of concern; not only are they complete losses of vital essence, but they may be caused by evil spirits."[19]

In relations not intending to lead to procreation, the man is bound by strict discipline: that of *coitus reservatus*, i.e. without ejaculation. A difficult exercise and not very satisfactory, but justified not only by the consideration of giving the female pleasure, as in medieval Christianity, but by the inevitable dialectic of the *yin* and the *yang*. "According to this principle, the man was to learn how to prolong coitus as long as possible without leading to orgasm; for the longer the member would remain inside, the more the man would absorb the *yin* essence, thereby increasing and reinforcing his vital power."[20]

Fellatio, too, is allowed only if it is stopped before the "wasteful" ejaculation of *yang*. Female Onanism, on the other hand, does not pose any problem for the woman is considered to have an unlimited quantity of *yin* in reserve. For the same reason, Saphism is tolerated because it does not create any ill consequence. For the Chinese, on the other hand, extreme modesty pertained to kissing on the mouth, which was regarded as an integral part of the sex act and thus was unthinkable in public.[21] Homosexuality, which was pretty rare, was more or less tolerated in some periods, except when it constituted a means of emotional blackmail, which was often the case at the court.

Moralism, Anticlericalism and Pornography

With the arrival of Confucianism, there was a shift in favor of infusing society with a more solid family system. It is true that Confucius' teachings — like those of the stoics and the first fathers of the Christian Church — can be interpreted partly as a protest against the moral depravity marking his era. "Struck by the amoral inclinations of his contemporaries, he stressed the *jen*, 'humanity' as a moral force. . . . The sacred bonds of the family had become weak; Confucius became the defender of the *hsiao*, 'filial piety,'[22] and taught that a strictly organized and well-run family is the basis of the State."[23]

Women did not exactly benefit from this triumph of Confucianism. Certain very ancient texts, like the famous *Tsuo-chuan* appended to the *Ch'un-ch'iu* (*Spring and Autumn Annals*), an impressive degree of explicit misogyny is expressed. For example, "The *tö* [virtue, magical power] of a girl is unbounded; the resentment of a married woman is boundless;" and, "Woman is a sinister creature, able to pervert the heart of man." Words ascribed to Confucius himself mark an aggravation of this misogyny. In Book XVII of *Lun-yü* or *Analects* (*Interviews*), Confucius affirms for example: "It is not pleasant to associate with women and people of low condition. If one shows them too much friendship, they become turbulent, and if one keeps them remote, they are full of resentment."

The regulations pertaining to women that devolved from this are similar to those that were current in the West. The ideal woman was considered to be "inside," i.e. occupied with the domestic tasks, rather than public matters. Virginity at the time of marriage was essential, if the girl wanted to claim the title of principal wife. Moreover, toward the beginning of our era, an enactment was adopted that prohibited women from taking part in family rites during menstruation. (She was to indicate her impure condition by marking her face with a red spot.)

Preaching a rigorous separation of the sexes in daily life (including husband and wife), Confucianism inspired many moralistic treatises aimed at women. The oldest seems to be that of the Lady Pan (second century) who wrote the *Nu-kie* (*Precepts for Women*), a book that preaches reverence and subservience to the husband. During the Ming period, in 1405, there was Empress Jen-hsiao's *Nei-hsun* (*Instructions for the Domestic Apartments*), then Empress Kiang's, the *Nu-hsun* (*Instructions for Women*) which also gives councils for prenatal care. These two treatises, widely read throughout all of Asia, were studied in Japan until the 19th century.

Chinese society reacted to this sometimes stifling Confucian moralism be developing certain forms of elaborate transgressions, such as pornographic literature, painting and poetry. China developed a rich and more or less clandestine erotic culture very early on. They made fun of the rules and prohibitions that the Confucianism claimed to impose on sexual matters; they debated with the moralistic disciples of Confucius. As with the erotic *fabliaux* of the medieval West, pornographic novels and poems of the Ming era (1368-1644) portrayed the supposed turpitude of the Buddhist monks and nuns. In China too, the monasteries were depicted as dens of iniquity.

However, it was the Mongol invasion in 1279, then that of the Juchen tribes of Eastern Mongolia (who would take the name of Manchu, and would destroy the Ming empire in 1644), that caused the Chinese to close in on themselves and on puritan morality. Along with the Ming dynasty, a certain hedonistic lack of concern disappeared. Confronted once again with a long-lasting foreign occupation, Chinese society turned inward with a strict Confucian prudishness, which had the virtue of sheltering the private life — and the women! — from the invaders. The more or less liberal application of the interdicts gave way to a moralism that shrouded all sexual matters — private matters — in meticulous discretion. The Chinese reacted similarly in modern times, when the Westerners arrived. They met all the foreign enterprises and curiosities with an impenetrable wall of reserve and secrecy surrounding everything having to do with sex. "Thus a phobia formed," says van Gulik, "blocking any disclosure of what touches on sex, a phobia that would remain characteristic of Chinese behavior for the next four centuries."[24]

China illustrates an anthropological principle that has been confirmed many times in human history: any besieged society, threatened externally (or internally) tends to tighten up in the area of sexual morality. The holism that Louis Dumont favors then wins out over individualism. The other great example, of course, is that of Islam.

An Infinite Orgasm

Few paradoxes are as pathetic as this one: Islamic fundamentalism embodies, especially since the beginning of the Seventies, a caricatural Puritanism that veils the wives and proscribes sex, while no religion sang of physical love and bodily happiness with as much lyricism — and insistence — as that of the Prophet. That is not based on formal grounds. "All of life, according to Islamic teachings," writes a specialist, "is bathed in a sexual ambiance, to a sometimes obsessive extent. You must marry. You must have sexual intercourse. The parents must see their children married, and it is a part of the duties of filial piety to remarry your widowed father or mother. To make love is an imperative duty that takes precedence over everything else, even devotion to God."[25] This passage is drawn from one of the Prophet's hadiths: "It was given to me to love, of your world, women and perfume."

A striking detail: sexual activity which, in Islam, testifies to "being serious about life" is not, however, directed exclusively toward procreation as it is in many other religions or traditions of wisdom. Sexual play (*mula' aba*) is warmly recommended by the Koran. From the *Thousand and One Nights* to Omar Khayam's *Quatrains* (1050-1123) and the 16th century *Jawami' al ladhdha* (*Encyclopedia of Pleasure*) and the *Arrawdh al âtir fi nuzhatil khâtir*, more commonly known as *The Perfumed Garden*,[26] the pleasures are celebrated in poetic terms, with a *joy* seldom equaled in all the world. Islamic literature and poetry devoted to pleasure are incomparably rich. "When a man looks at his wife," says the Prophet, "and she looks at him, God looks on them with mercy. When the husband takes his wife's hand and she takes his, their sins depart by the interstices between their fingers. When he cohabits with her, the angels surround them from the earth to the heavens. Pleasure and desire have the beauty of the mountains."

This rich erotic culture bears the traces of an Indian influence. It is known, for example, that the *Thousand and One Nights* is derived directly from Indian legends, as was the work of several great authors, like Maçoudi's *Golden Meadows*.

Innumerable metaphors and striking images are used in Islam to refer to pleasure, desire and sensual joy. In the hadiths, Mohammed evokes fusion in love by saying that it consists of "tasting someone's little honey." The carnal act is comparable to virtue and even almsgiving (*sadaka*). Aïcha, the Prophet's favorite wife, affirms that coitus "rests the heart, strengthens the will, clarifies the spirit, improves the sight, removes diseases, prevents madness and softens the body."[27]

These precepts and this optimism were applied in real life. In his *Canon of Medicine* (*Qânoun fit-tîb*), Ibn Sinâ, known in West as Avicenna (the eminent 10th century Arab doctor) recommended sensual pleasure as a remedy for psychic and physical torments. "Allow young people to have sexual relations, for by that means, they will avoid pernicious maladies."[28] We also know that the Arabs were particularly taken with aphrodisiacs, and the importance in Islamic civilization of certain highly eroticized traditions, like that of the *hammam*. (In many Arab countries, to go to the *hammam* metaphorically means to make love. In fact, that is where one goes to perform his "great ablution," after making love.) "Baghdad boasted of having 27,000 *hammams* or even, according to certainly exaggerated claims, 60,000 in the 10th century. Cordoue had 5,000 — 6,000 of them. Whereas the Roman thermal baths were for the most part found only in the large cities, the *hammams* were more universal. There is no small village or town that does not have its own *hammam*."[29]

But most revealing is, without any doubt, the strongly erotic view Islam offers of the afterlife and paradise. It is populated with fabulous creatures — the *houris* — whose bodies are made of saffron, musk, amber and camphor; sensual creatures "tempting to sex" which are at the free disposal of the elect. In the writings of the famous Suyûti (Sheikh Jalal Addin al-Suyûti, *Kitâb al durar al h' isân fil ba' thi wa na' â imil-jinân*, 12th-13th century), one finds the most gripping descriptions this "paradise of the eighty year erection and the infinite orgasm." "[In paradise], one becomes more beautiful every day," Suyûti wrote. "The appetite is increased one hundred-fold. One eats and drinks at will. A man's generative power is also multiplied. One makes love just as on earth, but each time the pleasure is prolonged, prolonged, and lasts eighty years. . . . Every time one lies down with a *houri*, " adds Suyûti, "it is a virgin. Moreover, the elect's staff never bends; erection is eternal. Every coitus is accompanied by a pleasure, a delicious feeling, so outrageous in this lowly world that if it there were experienced one would faint dead away."[30]

Compare this explicitly voluptuous vision of eternal life, proposed by Islam, to that disembodied and strictly spiritual view of the Christian paradise, or with this austere description of world beyond given in the Talmud. "In the future world there is nothing to eat nor drink, neither procreation nor trade, neither jealousy, hatred, nor competition, but the righteous sit, diadems on their heads, and revel in the brilliance of the divine presence. . . . Something is promised, but this something is hidden."[31]

Respecting the Order of the World

The interdicts enacted by the Koran have been addressed in a thousand and one discussions and disputes, especially since the fundamentalist movement brought to the fore the most conservative interpretation of the sacred text, particularly that of the 13th century Syrian traditionalist, Ibn Taymiyya. The fact remains that the principal inspiration on which the interdicts are founded, and which formally proscribes lust (*mujûn*) — is not disputed. One of the great priorities of Islam consists in respecting the separation of the sexes, the bipolarity of the world between female and male. The unity of the world be made (will be remade?) in the harmony of the sexes, realized with full knowledge of the facts. "The best means of reaching the agreement wanted by God is for the man to assume his masculinity and for a woman to take charge of her own femininity. The Islamic vision of the world removes guilt from the sexes, but that is in order to make them available to each other."[32]

This bipolarity that God wants gives rise to Islam's theoretical hostility to any form of sexuality that violates this "antithetic harmony of the sexes:" effeminate men, masculine women, masturbation, zoophilia. "God, known as the Prophet, has cursed those who change the boundaries of the earth." Male homosexuality (*liwât*) and, to a lesser extent, female (*musâh' àqua*) are thus condemned in 35 verses, distributed across seven sourates. The malékite rite even calls for, in theory, stoning homosexuals, while the hermaphrodite (*ghoulâm*) is scorned. In practice, however, Arab societies have shown themselves to be tolerant toward what Malek Chebel calls "homosensuality," which consists of, "in the absence of partners of the other sex, conferring on a peer [of the same sex] the excess of sensuality."[33] This tradition makes it possible for men to hold hands or put their arms around each other's shoulders, even to bathe together, and, in the case of boys, to masturbate together.

In the course of history, the Moslems were accused by the Christians of practicing rape and sodomy. Anyone who has studied the time of the crusades is aware of the pseudo-letter addressed by Alexius Comnenus, the Byzantine emperor, to Robert of Flanders, beseeching his assistance against the Turks. In this document, one finds graphic allusions to sexual violence that the Moslems committed against the Christians.[34] "They degrade men of every age and rank by sodomizing them," the text of the 11th century ensures, "children, teenagers, young men, old men, nobles, domestics and, worse still and more criminal, clerics and monks, even, O shame! which has never been said or heard of since the first bishops. They even killed a bishop while perpetrating this abominable sin."

False charges? It is hard to say but that is probably the case, so politically "intentional" is this apocryphal letter that was delivered prior to the First Crusade in 1096. One thing is certain about homosexuality: the rigor of the interdict is directed especially against what we today call pedophilia, i.e. commerce with people who are too young. In Islam, it is facial hair that makes the difference. "Looking at a beardless male face (*amrad*) is illicit even if the look is not accompanied by concupiscence, and if one is safe from all *fitna* (seduction-revolt against God)." Mass'oud Al-Quanâwi wrote, "The beardless are like women. Worse still, looking at them is criminal in a different way than looking at an unknown woman."

This same obligation to respect the order of the world means that incest constitutes one of the most severe taboos, violently denounced in the famous Sourate IV entitled "Women." "Prohibited to you are (*'alaïkoum hourrimât*): your mothers, your daughters, your sisters, your paternal aunts, your maternal aunts, your brothers' daughters, your sisters' daughters, your nurse-mothers, girls who were nursed by the same woman, your wives' mothers, daughters-in-law placed under your care and born to women with whom you have consummated marriage."

In another sourate (II, 228), the holy text prohibits abortion. "Women are not permitted to hide (*yaktoumounna*) what God created in their entrails." The theologians, in fact, attenuated the rigor of this interdict by assigning it a temporal limit, comparable to the conditions provided by our own Western legislations. According to the *Fatawa Hindyya*, abortion may be stimulated as long as the foetus's form has not yet differentiated itself with the appearance of superficial body growths (hair, nails) or internal organs which, according to Moslem theologians, occurs only after 120 days.

As for the periodic interdicts, they are fundamentally not very different in principle from those enacted by Judaism and Christianity. Some are related to retiring to the mosque (whereas relations are permitted during fasts) and others to female menstruation. Sourate II, known as "Cows" (verses 222-223), commands, "Do not approach women while they are menstruating. Approach them only after they have been purified. When they are purified, go to them as God has decreed. God loves those who repent. He loves those who purify themselves. Your wives are like a fertile field for you. Go to your field however you like."

In One Hand, the Koran

The most astonishing aspect of the intolerance promoted by the Islamic fundamentalists is that neither the Koran nor the hadiths contain explicitly misogynistic passages. On the contrary, in its day, the sacred text imposed reforms to the cruel practices of pre-Islamic societies. It codified polygamy, for example, making it almost impossible for a good Moslem; it lessened his ability to repudiate a wife or abuse the rights of heritage; and it put an end to certain widespread crimes like infanticide directed against little girls. The texts of the Koran contain certain passages very favorable to women, like this splendid hadith: "Paradise lies beneath mothers' feet." And Sourate IV, "Women," affirms without the least ambiguity that men and women *are part of the same essence.*

However, Denise Masson (a translator of the Koran) recommends that we avoid taking too rosy a view. "Still we should specify," she writes, "that the man enjoys far more freedom than the woman. He has a prerogative that allows him to live for three or four days with a woman, without marrying her. But under two conditions: that he pays her and that she is not a member of his family. Toward the end of his life, it seems that the Prophet had some doubts regarding the validity of this practice; and yet it has persisted until our day. Tradition grants the man greater sexual freedom, provided that the two codes which govern Moslem life are secure: that of honor, and that of the family."[35]

The fact remains that the Koran's general tone about women contrasts with the misogynists outbursts of some of the holy texts (Buddhist, Hindu, etc.) cited earlier. Thus, the reality of social practices in the Islamic world are all the more shocking. All the specialists agree a huge gulf separates the Koranic texts from how they have been applied historically. In Islam, sensual lyricism has deteriorated into prudishness and — especially — an aggravated misogyny prevails. Admittedly, the same shift took place in Judaism and Christianity, but that is no explanation. "The beautiful principles of equality and democracy in the original Islam," writes Bouhdiba, "have sometimes remained at the level of pious intentions, and Arab-Moslem society has known inequality, aristocracy, and feudalism. Thus it is perfectly conceivable *a priori* that the lyrical concept of life devolved in Islam into a modest and prudish society."

What made that happen? Several explanations have been proposed. They relate, for the most part, to the vicissitudes of the history. Several elements have played against the Moslem woman and in favor of and exaggeratedly prudish approach to sexuality. For one, the Arab practice of keeping concubines, with the concubine (a slave, originally) ending up becoming an anti-wife dedicated to sensual pleasure, and the conflict between the influences of Bedouin culture and lifestyle and the more liberal traditions of the towns. Germaine Tillion evokes "the economic basis of endogamy systematized the practice of the cousinat, consequently limiting women's circulation and the expansion and the expression of any love that would not be in the group's interest."[36]

We should also bear in mind that there was some give and take of reciprocal influences took place between the old Bedouin culture and the advent of Sufi wisdom, which was as hostile to pleasure as the desert fathers in the early centuries of Christianity. Sufism borrowed from the austere culture Bedouin — and the 'udhrit (courtly love) — a rejection of the flesh and the sublimation of the sexual in the spiritual. Just like the Encratites of early Christianity, the Sufis practiced voluntary castration, despite the fact that certain hadiths had prohibited it. "In their insane speculations," says Malek Chebel, "some sufis went so far as to not only deny any inclination of desire and to drive out any possible concupiscence from their beings, but also to deprive themselves of the most visible member of their subservience to passion: the penis."

The concept and the practice of love in Islamic societies thus varied in the course of history, according to which influences were ascendant. Restrictive during the time of the mystics, the dervishes and divine love, they flourished under certain enlightened dynasties of the 10th to 12th centuries, and in several of the areas of the great "Islamic arc" that swept from Grenada to Ispahan. "Since then," adds Chebel, "art, manners, the culture of the bedroom, and romantic poetry have gone steadily downhill. In that, they follow all the other components of Arab-Islamic civilization."[37]

As was the case with China, finally, external aggressions including colonial occupation largely contributed to this puritanical tension in Islam. The Arab world turned inward most dramatically after the occupation, an intrusion that struck it like a rape. "Arab society girded itself and set up structures of passive defense around the zones rightly considered to be essential: the family, the woman, the home. To limit the colonial impact to the external, but to savagely preserve the domestic and the intimate aspects of life, that was the strategy. . . . Fanatic or not, 'savage' and 'intolerant' or not, the Islamic faith raised an effective barrier between itself and the new Masters, and checked any inclination to assimilate. Consequently, the Arab woman was promoted to the historical and unexpected role of guardian of tradition and maintainer of the collective identity."

These lines by Abdelwahab Bouhdiba go back to 1975, a few years before the Shi'ite revolution in Iran when part of the Moslem world plunged into intolerance. These days, they feel threatened by the Western standardization of cultures, which the fundamentalists interpret as a second colonization. The violence in Algeria, committed in the name of God, women in hiding, veiled or assassinated, the Puritanical delusions of Afghanistan and elsewhere, all this over-reaction illustrates that an extreme point has been reached in the distressing retreat, already begun long since, of a humiliated Islam, prey to the throes of doubt, and furiously repudiating its own wealth.

*
* *

But contrary to all that, in spite of the worst massacres that would be alien to any religion and, of course, to Islam, a stubborn will persists. The drive for transgressions in love and carnal happiness continues to bore through, here and there. And this, too, conforms with tradition. From the (Algerian) Oranian *Raï* to the licentious folklore of the (Berber) Tuareg singers, from the Izli kabyl to the Berber couplets sung by Mririda Aït Attik, from the voluptuous *cantilenas* chanted in the *hammam* to the orgiastic music of the Sidi-Bel-Abbès swampland to the salacious murmuring of the chikkates (courtesans) of Morocco, pleasure and desire are bearing up against all pressures. Pleasure and desire, persist, obstinate, and resolutely faithful to this stunning Quatrain by Omar Khayam, which dates from the 11th century:

"We take the Koran in one hand; with the other, we raise a glass. You think we are sometimes heading toward what is licit, sometimes toward what is forbidden. And so we are, under this azure vault — neither completely infidel, nor absolutely Moslem."[38]

209

CHAPTER 10

UTOPIA AND TRANSGRESSION

Anthropology, history, literature and of course poetry are thus the vehicles of a lovely lesson. This one: that in every era, under every heaven, a stubborn resistance to *the norm* is always found around the edges. Standard behavior is there, but transgression is too; a holistic coherence is preserved but there is also some *play*, in the mechanical sense of the term, some leeway at the edges of what is forbidden, even beyond. The memory of societies and their imaginings attest to the ubiquity of a sexual counter-culture, of a libertine underground, a kind of accommodation with the rules, including the most consensual. To invoke the lost memory about sexuality would be useless if we did not include this shadowy and joyous face of the human adventure.

Thus, from one century to the next, in every society, love has led a parallel history. And there are two common misperceptions about that — we should be neither woefully indifferent nor exaggeratedly reverent. These libertines margins, indeed, embody neither a heroic *truth* (of freedom) opposing a *lie* (the interdict), a hedonistic Good confronting the Evil of puritanism, nor a kind of clandestine *samizdat* denouncing the tyrant's rhetoric and the stupidity of censure. Rather, we should think of it as a clever trick of history, a dialectic that is unceasingly reinvented between the interdict and the transgression. Both suggest the idea of an indefinable point of social equilibrium that must constantly would be sought and constantly broken; the Omega that the societies are always striving to reach, yet always questioning, as if they had a presentiment that it would be impossible to achieve *stability*, be that in repressive holism (for the entire group!), or in anarchistic lawlessness (for the individual!). It is because they are the poles of this never-ending oscillation that sexuality and the regulation of sexuality fascinate us.

Together they summarize, compellingly, the humanity of our destiny.

This is where we should start: with the impossibility of the sexual utopia that we always long for but which can never be maintained in the long run. "The flesh in us is an excess that is opposed to the law decency," Bataille wrote. " If, as I believe, a vague and all-encompassing interdict exists, opposing sexual freedom in forms that depend on the time and the place, then the flesh is the expression of this threatening freedom's return."[1] The permissiveness that we have been experiencing for the last thirty-odd years in the West is threatened by confused repressive fears and unforeseeable breakdowns. We should realize that we are neither the first nor the last to experience both the attraction of the permissive utopia and the fatality of its limits.

Aristophanes to the Aid of Ugly Men

Sexual utopias have haunted every societies' imagination. From the beginning, men and women have dreamed of an ideal city where nothing would stand in the way of their desires, where the pleasure of bodies and their innocence would prevail. In the *Assembly of Women*, Aristophanes imagined this type of community, governed (and that is a sign, already) by the women. Praxagora, the heroine who incites the Athenians to take over, pronounces a decree founding the communality of goods and of sex. There should no longer be rich people nor poor, and the women will go to bed with whomever they like. But Aristophanes cares too much for the idea of justice not to understand that such an assembly would be impose a worse injustice. It would inevitably punish the ugly men and homely women, who would be disqualified by the crudeness of the liberated desires, while the beautiful and the strong would accrue for their benefit alone all the good consequences of the new freedom. (It is true that the sense of equality, which Aristophanes felt very sharply, is ironically underscored in his theater by the fact that the buttocks is called *O Aristodémos ["aristo-people"]* — since both plebeians and patricians have them in common.)

In the interests of justice, the leader of the Assembly of Women thus has a complementary law adopted, which expressly provides what we would call "affirmative discrimination" in favor of the unattractive, and those who have bad luck in love. Women will be allowed to give themselves freely to the beautiful and the great, *but only after having granted their favors to the small and the ugly.* Similarly, the men will have to serve the older and uglier women first. This is admirable Greek intuition, which highlights again some our contemporary obtuseness. By this simple theatrical codicil, Aristophanes recalls that in the matter of love, as elsewhere, too much freedom merely increases the iniquity by removing the inhibitions from the selfishness of the most well-endowed.

In 17th-century Europe, the heavier the moralism grew, the more literary and philosophical sexual utopias seemed to multiply. In a libertine book by Tomaso Campanella, *The City of the Sun*, we see pantheist ideas together with a plan to reorganize romantic customs. The author was a Dominican who fomented a conspiracy to liberate Calabria from the Spanish yoke; he spent 27 years in prison, was tortured seven times, and finished his life in France, where he was finally welcomed in St. Germain by Louis XIII, who granted to him a pension of three thousand pounds. In 1725, in his *History of the Galligènes*, Tiphaigne de La Roche prescribed a similar vision: "Everyone will have no personal possessions; everything will belong to the Republic, everything will belong to everyone. No one will say, 'this woman is mine,' because every woman will be the wife of all the citizens." The city which he imagines proscribes any idea of possession or of compulsory fidelity in matters of love.[2]

In the 18th century, the most interesting character on this matter seems to be Charles Fourier, political utopian and ardent propagandist for a plan of sexual liberation. A kind of early Professor Nimbus, born in 1772 in Besançon, he was overly impressed with his own inventiveness, walking the streets and talking to himself, an insomniac, distracted to the point of farce, a confirmed bachelor, a child-hater, measuring the monuments of Paris with a metric cane, and holing up in Montmartre in a tiny apartment crammed with flower pots. This great fan of geography is convinced he has invented the principle of a society freed from the constraints of any repressive morality. As for women and their emancipation, including sexual, he professes ideas that win our sympathy today. "Man's happiness in love," he says, "is proportionate to the freedom that the women enjoy." In the same way, he defends "the happiness of young widows, especially when they know how to preserve their freedom, and not to fall from Charybdis to Scylla, not to go from the yoke of a husband to that of a sentimental braggart, but to preserve independence in love and the right to change lovers."

The complicated structure of his *New World of Love* (the title of one of his books) envisages sexual orders and castes, and thoughtfully provides a "code" of polygamy. In this perfect city, the orgies themselves must be regulated as a social dance (an "omnigamous" dance) so that under every circumstance, a minimum of civility is safeguarded. For Fourier, this planned polygamy could be corrected by what he calls "a pivotal affection," i.e. a lasting preference in love. With a striking audacity for the time, he praises what was then called pederasty and saphism. Convinced of the values of Scientistism, he proposes to precisely evaluate the intensity of pleasure in its various occurrences, as a century later Wilhelm Reich (discoverer of "orgon") would do. On several points, in fact (for example, in connection with certain cosmic delusions), Fourier is Reich's direct predecessor. Doesn't he evoke "the androgynous planets" and does he not say that they follow the example of plants in copulating with themselves to generate life?

In Search of the Female Messiah

Claude-Henri de Rouvroy, Count de Saint-Simon (1760-1825), was a French economist and philosopher, whose work became influential in the 19th century. He offered refinements to the Fourierist utopias. In essence, he promoted a a mystical religion of love and seduction, organized around "the priestly couple" — a natural, though heretical, extension of Christianity. One of Saint-Simon's principal works, published in the year of his death, is entitled *New Christianity*. After the disappearance of Saint-Simon, the message was echoed by some enterprising disciples who, having met in school, wanted to put these theories into practice. Their leader was Prosper Barthélemy Enfantin (1796-1864), a kind of inspired guru, the son of banker and a former pupil of the École Polytechnique. "Father" Enfantin and his "apostles" tirelessly pursued this vision of a post-Christianity, with the principal objective of rehabilitating matter in general and the flesh in particular.

An advocate of beauty, softness and charm, "the priestly couple," according to the religion of the Saint-Simonians, is supposed to reconcile socially (and to regulate, in the precise sense of the term) "constant" love and "inconstant" love (which strangely call to mind that which Jean-Paul Sartre and Simone de Beauvoir called "contingent loves"). "Sometimes," wrote Prosper Enfantin, "the sacerdotal couple will calm the immoderate ardor of the intellect or will moderate the uncontrolled appetites of the senses; sometimes, on the contrary, they will spark the apathetic intelligence or will inflame the sluggish senses; for they know all the charm of decency and modesty, but also all the grace of abandonment and voluptuous pleasure." The priest, for his part, will be allowed to have sexual intercourse with the faithful.

The religious connotation of this utopia is obvious. "The rapture into which we throw the appreciation of physical beauty and all the pleasures that one tastes with the senses," Alexandrian wrote in connection with Enfantin, "should no longer be looked upon as obstacles to moral development, but as authentically religious inspirations. Religion should be organized so that one goes to church to see beautiful men, beautiful women there, and to derive a sensual exaltation — which one can usually do only by going to the theatres and ballrooms. Moreover, this would not be in order to exalt, contrary to Christian precepts, the flesh to the detriment of the spirit, but rather to find their perfect conciliation.[3]

Commenting on this future society, an advertiser enthused in the *Globe*: "One will see men and women united by an unparalleled love, that knows neither cooling, nor jealousy; men and women who would give themselves to several others without ceasing to be for each other, and whose love would be, on the contrary, like a divine banquet that increases in magnificence with the number and the selection of the guests..."

The Saint-Simonian utopia began, in 1832, to be fulfilled. Enfantin moved into his house with some of his disciples. They formed an intellectual community where the manual tasks were piously are accepted and distributed between everyone. The apostles wore beards and a singular costume (white trousers, violet tunics and red waistcoats buttoned in the back) which would elicit gibes from passers by. In the prudish and middle-class Paris of the 19th century, these precursors of the hippies made a scandal. Enfantin was brought before the magistrate in August 1832. In front of the judges, he denounced the hypocrisy of bourgeois adultery and the shame of prostitution, but was condemned to a year in prison.

The Saint-Simonians then organized a series of voyages to the East to seek the "woman-Messiah" who should fulfill the prophecy. In Istanbul, they were seen sauntering in the streets and the souks, dressed up in their costumes, singing canticles and prostrating themselves here and there to every woman they met. In France, other companions covered the roads of the South while proclaiming: "The reign of the woman is near, the Mother of all men and women will appear." They were greeted with unsympathetic scuffles and stones. But the Saint-Simonians settled in even more in Egypt, especially along the immense building site of the Suez Canal, where certain "young ladies of the dam," generous with their charms, have left longlasting memories.[4]

With the passage of time, it is easy to smile at these peregrinations and this grandiloquent sexual mysticism. However, both are very significantly *dated*. The love utopias seem to have been all the more inventive and lively in that era inclined to Puritanism. Obviously, that was the case of the 19th century. But that bourgeois and positivist century was also characterized by a formidable optimism, a resilient faith in progress and the power of the human will. The Saint-Simonian love utopia expressed a revolt against the new puritan hypocrisy as much as an unshakeable belief in the future. In that, it was exemplary.

Sex as Subversion

The sexual utopias that have followed one after the other in the course of history by no means were always so mystical or ethereal in form. Periodically, every human society is agitated by revolutionary turbulence, be it political, ideological or religious, and it (almost always) bears consequences for sexual morality. Periods when the prevailing rules are overturned, of eruptions of hedonistic license — a kind of festive parentheses — alternate with phases when matters are taken in hand again and law and order are re-established. This is not the time or place to go over this long succession of festivals and periods of penitence to examine the mechanisms at work. Still, by looking at a few examples, we can inquire into the nature of the obstacle the utopias encountered and the reality of the disorder they generated. In almost every case, these experiments tripped up on a *violence that became uncontrollable.*

One word on this topic. Georges Bataille perceived with great acuity this murky connection between desire and violence. Paradoxically, he still insists that the function of the interdict is primarily *pacificatory.* "By its activity," he writes, "man built the rational world, but he always retains a background of violence. Nature itself is violent and, however reasonable we may have become, violence can again dominate us; and that is no longer natural violence, but the violence a rational being, who tried to obey, but succumbs to an impulse that he cannot reduce to reason. . . . The fundamental object of the interdicts is violence."[5]

Without our realizing it, contemporary conversation — even the most trivial — is haunted by this dormant energy of desire-violence, this brutish force, always ready to break the limits and the interdicts, ready to subvert the order of the city at any moment. The famous fantasies that are so prized today are testimony to that. Just consider these few sentences, gleaned from a collection of female interviews on pornography. A certain Sylvie, 22 years old, murmurs: "The thought of the Revolution excites me, it is the most erotic historical time: there's fear, and fighting; there's violence. I don't support Nazism and yet it arouses me enormously. . . . It is the gratuitous violence that excites me the most. Scenes where they hurt a child, a woman. When they torture innocent people." A 33-year-old journalist, named Sophie, waxes lyrical on the same topic: "Impalement," she says, "is the torture scene that excites me the most. It's horrible and exciting... I would like to specify that only the scenes of sexual torture turn me on."[6]

These criminal desires, obviously, are fantasies. They are articulated "without thinking any evil" and without imagining even for a second to actually act upon them. They express, however, in their very ingenuity, an immemorial menace that must be kept in mind when we look toward the past. Indeed, it is that menace that history constantly has to deal with; and it is that menace most permissive utopias have foundered on.

For centuries, sexual license has turned up either in the form of a protest against the established order, or as revenge taken after a political collapse. Ancient China experienced clandestine movements with sexual connotations that made vice a political weapon. Toward the end of the Han dynasty, in the third century of our era, several Taoist revolts were announced, inspired by a sexual mysticism (in particular that of "the Yellow Turbans" [*hoang-kin*], which was drowned in blood but precipitated the fall of the dynasty). These "mystics" based their approach on a treatise, the Yellow Book (Huang-Chou), where vice was regarded as "the true art to obtaining the vital essence." In the following centuries, and until the 19th, several other sexual utopias erupted in China. An imperial edict of 1839 alludes to one of these religious movements, a cult called *K'oen-tan*. Only men and women are admitted who practiced (as a couple) the love disciplines prescribed. "They come together in the evening, they all go into one room, and the lamps are not lit. Then, they have carnal trade in the darkness."

This tradition of obscene subversion is so profoundly deep-rooted in the history of China that it sometimes still reappears today. At the end of 1950, the popular Maoist Republic tried to fight a secret Taoist cult called Yi-koan-tao. Its members opposed the Communist regime and sacrificed to in ritual orgies. On this subject, van Gulik quotes the newspaper *Koang-ming-je-pao*, November 20, 1950. "The heads of this cult, these shameless lechers," it reports, "organized a 'beauty contest' with the female members of the cult, and during the 'Taoist study classes' incited the members to engage in carnal trade, with complete promiscuity, promising the participants immortality and relief from disease."[7]

And has anyone forgotten that, during the "Peking Spring" of 1989, *dazibaos* calling for open sexuality were displayed on the walls of Tien-An-Men Square where the students were protesting?

Under the French Revolution, the denunciation of the real or supposed depravities of the aristocracy went hand in hand, as we have seen, with all kinds of specific complaints regarding the liberalized conduct of, for example, the homosexuals. A curious text was written in 1790 by a group calling themselves the "Knights of the Cuff," under the title, "Children of Sodom at the National Assembly, or a delegation of the Order of the Cuff to the representatives of all the orders taken in the sixty districts of Paris." There, certain freedoms were claimed on behalf of all the "knights," in particular in the red light districts of Paris. In the preamble one may also read a speech by the Duke de Noailles, who was part of the group. "Anti-physics, which its detractors have derisively called buggery and which the ignorance of the centuries had caused to be considered until our day as an illicit game of lubricity, thus in the future will be a science known and taught in every class of the society." A list of the deputies follows, wherein one finds the entire lot of the sodomite society of the time.

But people really abandoned themselves to desperate pleasures and ostentatiously libertine behavior only under the *Directoire* (after the end of the Terror, which had been dominated by a Puritanism that tried to stamp out all such transgression) and in spite of the fact that the Penal code of 1791 abolished the concept of conduct against nature. The activity was all the more frantic as an antidote to the horror of the guillotine. In fact, it seems that indeed it was in connection with *violence to children* that the first notes of alarm were sounded. Libertine conduct in Paris, in any case, was short-lived. One of the eye-witness documents that we can quote here is a police report made by Citizen Picquenard, Commissioner of the Executive Power, to Citizen Merlin, President of the Directoire Executive — known as Merlin from Douai — and dated Prairie (the name of a month) 5, Year VI. This report expresses alarm at the climate of general dissolution and public depravity. It refers to "pederasts" at the Palais Royal and affirms that male children with venereal disease are continually being brought in to the district police station; the oldest of them was barely six years old. The matter was soon taken in hand. From 1810 onward, the Napoleonic Penal code restored severe prison sentences for indecent assault with violence to a minor of less than fifteen years.[8]

The October Revolution and "Sexual Chaos"

A comparable scenario was recorded in Bolshevik Russia. From 1917 to 1922, revolutionary effervescence and the civil war, added to the three years of international war, led to a social and family disintegration that went well beyond what the Communists wished. There are poignant descriptions of thousands of families wandering on the roads, of whole villages seeking far and wide for food. Women giving up their children, prostituting themselves occasionally, then regularly, to survive, while teenagers of both sexes also became prostitutes; the formation of "gangs of children," left to their own devices or to unscrupulous exploiters; rape and recurring violence. At the end of the Twenties and in the early Thirties, the expression "sexual chaos" became current in the Communist press. This frightening rise of disorder and private violence, often spurred by sexuality, was blamed on young people giving themselves up to the most immoral excesses and adults having lost all sense of morality responsibility. This topic of generalized sexual chaos was picked up and hammered home; it was used to justify, in the interests of the community, the legislative neo-moralism of the Thirties.

In *The Sexual Revolution*, Reich affirmed that he, for one, had deliberately exaggerated these disorders with the aim of making a return to the old order more acceptable: the prohibition of homosexuality, pro-family and pro-birth support. But he would also tell (without seeming to be overjoyed about it) how certain "communes" of young Russians spontaneously reinvented mechanisms of voluntary regulation in order to prevent "sexual chaos." Thus these young commune members of Moscow voluntarily lived by the following rule: "Sexual intercourse is undesirable among members during the first five years of the commune."[9]

During the French and Russian revolutionary periods, violence and disorder that were threatening for the group led to the failure of the utopia. But the ambivalence of Revolution itself also stands out. Two contrary principles come into explosive conflict in those moments. Revolution is essentially a mechanism of devastating disorder. It comes up as a furious spasm, seeking to throw down morality and accepted behavior. Much has been written on the sexual fury that gripped the people of Paris in 1789, a twilight episode in which the people were out to attack the old world, the shipwreck of a corrupt and debauched aristocratic order that *made them sick but envious at the same time.*

Bataille relates an extraordinary scene that took place on the eve of July 14, 1789, when the Marquis de Sade, the lively and sulfurous symbol of this glut, was to be moved from the Bastille to another prison. De Sade, indeed, more sensitive than any one else to the intoxication of the moment, had tried to attract passersby by shouting from his window: "People of Paris, they are cutting the prisoners' throats!" "He was not allowed to take anything with him," Bataille writes, "and the manuscript of *One Hundred and Twenty Days of Sodom* was lost in the plundering that followed the fall of the Bastille. Scavengers retrieved whatever looked interesting from among the objects that strewed the courtyard, and the manuscript was found, around 1900, in a bookshop in Germany. De Sade himself said he 'cried tears of blood' for a loss on behalf of everyone, on behalf of humanity."[10]

But while it is the deliberate purveyor of sexual upheaval, any revolution also carries within it a dream of purification and virtue that is diametrically opposed to license, a dream which, generally, turns out badly. *There is a direct relation between terror and virtue.* It was as the leader of an army of *saints* dreaming of a moral renaissance that Cromwell conducted many massacres. "Who will say it? Even virtue needs limits,"[11] wisely wrote Montesquieu.

Georges Nivat points out that this paradox within the idea of revolution is illustrated by Tolstoy. In *Resurrection* (1889), there is a scene where a number of revolutionaries and terrorists condemned to prison discuss violence and sexuality. "Tolstoy, apostle of non-violence, takes an ambiguous and none too straightforward stand toward them: he tries to divide them into good and bad, to relate their violence to a sexual problem (this is more clear in the draft manuscripts, but can still be seen in the final version), and it is remarkable that he treats the women as a separate case entirely, attributing their 'entry into terror' to a sexual deficiency comparable to that which justifies 'entering a convent' (see the character of Maria Pavlovna). Chastity is the other face of terrorist asceticism. . ."[12]

One thing is certain: until things are put back under control, the turmoil (real or imagined) that threatens the cohesion of the group generates a vague anxiety, an obscure call for order that serves demagogues and "restorers" of any type. "During most of Western history," observes Boswell, "it seems that the catastrophes could be explained easily as the result of the evil machinations of certain minority groups; and even if no specific relationship were to be suspected, anger and anxiety often compensate for a personal uneasiness by attacking anything eccentric, anything out of the ordinary, any exception to the social standard. . . .In 4th century Rome, at the hour of collapse and peril, as in 14th century Paris, any variation from the norm had a sinister, alarming air, and seemed to be emanating from a constellation of evil forces plotting the destruction of the established order."[13]

After the Death of a King

Nowadays, we have gotten in the habit of asserting greater permissiveness not only during a revolution, but as soon as any authoritative (or, rather, conservative) power is removed. That was the case in
Quebec, after the "silent revolution" in the early Sixties, which put an
end to the Catholic Church's educational monopoly. The same thing
happened, after 1975, in post-Franco Spain, which shortly abandonned
itself to the beautiful libertarian and libertine festival of *Movida*. In the
countries of Eastern Europe as in those of the former USSR, the end of
the communist dictatorship was accompanied by an explosion of sexuality, especially pornography and prostitution.

More recently, our attention ahs been drawn to South Africa.
"Twenty months after Nelson Mandela's election, could one read in the
International Courier weekly magazine, brothels were proliferating in the
country's major cities. In the fashionable suburbs of Johannesburg,
clubs sprang up with more and more evocative names: Erotica, Orien-
tal Palace," wrote *The Independent,* which visited largest cat house in Johannesburg. "The Quirinale hotel has fourteen floors. Downstairs,
there are four levels with bars and sofas. Upstairs, there are so many
girls it seems to be raining them. They come from Mozambique, Swazi-
land or beyond. Their customers are, for the most part, middle class
Whites. They pay less than a hundred francs to be satisfied. And to ask
for more. 'Going to the brothel is a little like going hunting. If you've
never killed an antelope, you absolutely must try it. And once you've
done it, you only want one thing — to do it again.' That's the analysis of
an officer from the vice squad."[14]

The merry revenge that the free individual takes on the group,
that freedom takes on regulations, and greedy anarchy on austere order,
these hedonistic "crises" that societies allow themselves do not last
much longer than the excesses that accompany revolutions. Sooner or
later, a minimal holism comes to the fore once again and, of course, we
are tempted to interpret them in political or ideological terms: the victory of progress, the revenge of conservatism, various plots, etc.. That
may be a little short-sighted. Anthropology and ethnology — which
consider the long term — have much more to do with it.

In *L'Homme et le sacré* (*Man and the Sacred*), Roger Caillois proposes
an interpretation that appeals to Bataille. In several of his books, the

author of the *History of Eroticism* refers to his friend Caillois' reflections on the sexual license that flairs up in a given group. He says that it corresponds, actually, to ancient rites that are still imprinted in our collective memory. "Sometimes, when facing death, when facing the failure of human ambition, an immeasurable despair sets in. And then it seems that the heavy storms and urges of nature take over, impulses that man is usually ashamed to yield to. In this sense, the death of a king is likely to unleash dramatic effects of horror and wild behavior. . . . As soon as the macabre event is announced, people start running, killing everything they meet, plundering and raping at will. 'Sexual license,' says Caillois, 'then takes on an aspect corresponding to the catastrophe which has occurred ...There is never the least resistance to popular frenzy. In the Sandwich Islands, when the crowd learned that the king had died, it committed all the acts that are considered criminal during ordinary times: arson, plunder and murder; and the women were made to engage in public prostitution. . .'"[15]

This idea of periodic recreation disturbs us because it seems to convey a paradoxical wisdom that the common sense finds instinctively and expresses in numerous aphorisms: "it can't be Sunday everyday," "even the best things must come to an end", "the party's over," etc.. Even more, these permissive periods that bracket more conservative spells are understood to be temporary. They internalize by anticipation the illusory character of utopias and the obligation in which we will soon find ourselves to control our desire, rather than to leave it, dangerously, to take its course. The other side of this wisdom is the unspoken indulgence, the ongoing benevolence, expressed by human groups when transgressions do take place. Cultures, in other words, are wary of utopias but still celebrate, in great secrecy or in hushed tones, erotic audacity, be it symbolic or real.

Eroticism as a Constant

From the Egyptian and Mesopotamian civilizations to the modern age, not to mention Greco-Roman culture and the beginnings of Christianity, the Middle Ages and the Enlightenment, it would be possible to trace our entire history through licentious literature and artistic transgression. There is not one century, not one era, and not a single form of art that does not have its richly ornamented "hell." There, in infinitely varied forms, we will find the same science of the interdict, the same way of acknowledging it even while defying it. Clandestine or not, this erotic culture is like a hypersensitive photographic plate, the negative imprint of the official culture whose misadventures, waywardness and deviance it records.

That of the Middle Ages, for example, is infinitely more subtle — or cleverer, we might say — than is commonly imagined. It reinterprets the interdicts of the time and, from afar, helps us to understand how they shaped medieval desire. "The interdict," writes a medievalist, "produces fantasies, and dreams; it encourages transgressions. This gives rise to an imagination that one also sees in the cosmographies of that time, in the images of the world, the *Imagines mundi*, which were flourishing at the time and which show us the center of the world as the location of the values of civilization. If, by misfortune, one moves away from this center, one arrives at strange, fantastic regions where the monstrous reigns. This is why the cosmographers of the Middle Ages described peoples living at the edges of the universe — all the way to the East or the West — who practiced sexual interdicts: polygamy, sodomy, bestiality. . . ."[16]

Eroticism, the prolongation of desire, is also a counter-culture. Because it is suffused with Christianity, Europe of the Middle Ages readily made the Church and its clerics the butt of humor in its erotic *fabliaux*, but without, for all that, causing any very significant reactions. The Middle Ages, explains Alexandrian, which are often taken as a time of obscurantism, was full of original characters who were both learned and playful, good Christians but with a ready pen to evoke the effects of lust. Jean Molinet, author of parodies of sermons and liturgical prayers, like *Le Serment de saint Billouart*, was so much appreciated during his lifetime that Archduke Maximilian made him an adviser and gave him a noble title. "Upon his death in 1507, the great poet Jean Lemaire of the Belgians called him the chief and sovereign of all the orators and rhetoricians of our Gallic language. . . famed in every district of Europe where the aforementioned language is known."[17]

Spread far and wide from the end of 12th to the middle of the 14th century, recited in inns and châteaux by minstrels and goliards, defrocked monks, jugglers and giddy students, these *fabliaux* were known by all and appreciated in every class of the society. It is true that they demonstrated not only obscenity but poetic art, a handling of language and metaphor that was far from the commonplace provocation. This virtuosity in allusion and symbolic codes was largely lost after the Renaissance. "The Middle Ages were excited about the fact that language can say anything, provided that it obeys a code. *The Novel of the Rose* is not a history of gardening. However, since Descartes, we have endeavored to speak as directly possible, the least metaphorically. And sexuality cannot be described overtly . . . . For us, the language has been impoverished in a disturbing way."[18]

As for courtly love, celebrated since the 11th century, it was considerably less ethereal than we think. According to specialists like Rene Nelli, author of a work on *L'Erotique des troubadours* (*The Eroticism of the Troubadours*), it encompassed on the contrary a voluptuous code, refined, and erotic in the literal meaning of the word. After a series of tests imposed on the admirer before the conquest of his lady, there came a stage where matters ceased being platonic. "The supreme reward was the trial (*asag*), where the man's reserve was put to the test. This was to ascertain whether he was capable of the self-control essential to courtesy. The lady thus invited her admirer to share her bed; they stayed there naked together all night, with permission to caress, but without arriving at the "*finale*." If the man gave in to temptation, that was proof that he did not love enough; he was rejected, declared unworthy of the *fin's amors*; if he did not give in, he acquired Value. He could hope to be transformed soon into a carnal lover (*drut*)."[19]

According to the medievalist Howard Bloch, the *fabliaux* are not so different from the more courtly medieval forms, with their idealized women and the long-suffering waiting that the knights-chevaliers had to endure. Actually "both kinds, realistic and idealistic, have in common the obsession with eroticism; it is simply shown under different aspects in these so distinct literary forms."[20]

The Failure of the Censor

All this erotic literature was hardly repressed during the Middle Ages. It is known that, for centuries, certain authors of licentious poetry and certain voluptuarians were good Christians, too (Ausone, Sidoine Apollinaire, St. John of Damascus, Marbode of Rennes, St. Alfred de Rievault, Paul the Silent, etc.). The will to censor such writings really only began early in the 17th century, after it had become common practice to associate the idea of sexual vice with that of religious unbelief. The word "libertine" originally meant, in Rome, the free-born son of a freed slave. It was then used by Calvin to designate an irreligious man, a "humanist," opposing natural morality to revealed morality, and nature to Christian faith. Vice, then, was a different matter altogether.

"The repression of erotic literature came along when libertine behavior combined anti-religious ideas with pornographic descriptions. Priapean collections could have continued being published as freely as you please, if they had never become tinged with impiety. But there was a fear that by tolerating license of expression on sexuality, one might appear to be allowing blasphemies at the same time. Father François Garasse, a great adversary of the libertines (author of *La Doctrine curieuse des beaux esprits de ce temps* [*The Curious Doctrine of the Wits of Our Time*], 1624), said that the pundits' subversive doctrines comprised two branches, the libertine and the atheistic. . . . As libertinage was likely to degenerate into atheism, it was decided to prohibit the writings that incite the libertine pleasures in order to prevent a greater evil."[21]

Of course, these repressive inclinations and the censor had no effect. In fact, quite the opposite. From the 17th century on, erotic literature became richer, more talented and more popular than ever. In his famous *Lettre sur le commerce de la librairie* (*Letter on the book trade*), Diderot is ironical about the proven impotence of the critics. "The more severe the proscription," he wrote, "the more it increased the price of the book, the more it excited curiosity to read it, the more copies were bought, the more it was read." He revealed that many academicians and booksellers would have liked to tell the magistrates: "Dear Sirs, Please grace my manuscript with a small injunction condemning me." And that, at the print shop, the workmen would applaud the announcement of a judgment, happily shouting: "Good, print another edition!"[22]

Thus, at the very moment when bourgeois moralism was being invented, the France of the Enlightenment was publishing thousands of risqué books, poems, rhymes, tales and pastiches; in fact, pornography. It was as if this transgression accompanied step by step and *compensated for* the puritan constriction. The prudish 19th century and a good half of the 20th century were thus marked by the picturesque contentions between the creators and the censors. A law went into effect on May 17, 1819, trying to inaugurate a new restrictive climate; this led to the prohibition of certain works that had circulated freely until then, such as *Le Chevalier de Faublas* (*The Knight of Faublas*), by Louvet de Couvray.[23]

Moreover, England, the fatherland of Protestant Puritanism, was not idle when it comes to literary transgression. Periodicals like *The Rambler's Magazine*, *The Bon Ton Magazine* and, in 1795, *The Ranger's Magazine* published illustrations and texts that were more than a little smutty. A licentious poem, *The Plenipotentiary* (1788), was authored by a friend of the Prince of Wales, Captain Charles Morris. According to a historian, cited by Alexandrian, "Pornography flowed freely in England at this period. But in 1797," he continues, "King George III made a proclamation against vice, inviting his subjects to fight it in all its forms. The Society for the Suppression of Vice, founded in 1802, took on the mission of hunting down obscene writings and engravings. It had a big job to do... and, as soon as it put up obstacles blocked, licentious works proliferated in the shadows.   Queen Victoria, who died in 1901, never suspected that under her reign the British secretly had become the foremost pornographers of the world."[24]

It seems as though, ultimately, the principle of transgression was not only a prolongation of desire, and a counter-culture, but also a form of collective sagacity. To test that notion, we should consider the testimony of regional historians. In certain cases, controlled transgression, i. e. the careful management of the "borderline," is not confined to forms of expression. It becomes active.

Old Customs in the Vendée and Savoie

In the 19th century, while the Louis-Philippe prudishness and rigid bourgeois morality were in full swing, it was discovered that certain customs persisted in several French provinces that we would still judge daring today. They were directly intended to counterbalance the narrowness of official morality, while organizing — wholesale — the initiation of young people. Some of these traditions offer, to quote Jean-Louis Flandrin, "a model of sexual behavior *absque coitu*" which enables young people to relieve their impulses playfully.

One may cite the girls' fair in the Challans region, or the famous trial marriages of the Basque Country; but the *Vendéan maraîchinage* especially catches the attention. We know some details thanks to the testimony of a 19th century doctor from the Vendée, Marcel Baudoin, who, after long field work, published a well-documented book.

Maraîchinage — what we would call today "fooling around" and "flirting" — was tolerated between girls and boys, and practiced under certain conditions known and accepted by all: at the side of the road, at nightfall, or "sheltered under a red umbrella," in the back room of an inn or under the eaves of a roof. Baudoin's descriptions drop some of the scientistic rhetoric of the time and give evidence of a vague sense of offense — which makes them all the more appealing.

"They hold each other, they intertwine. They roll around on the bed! . . . Soon this little game, which at first is harmless enough, is succeeded by a nervous, localized erethism, which by the intermediary of the centers resounds quickly on the genitals of both sexes. It goes so far, when these are ardent Maraîchins and not yet jaded to the advantages of oral flirtation, that very often a voluptuous feeling follows, both for the woman and the man. They even claim that the man sometimes ejaculates, without direct contact nor local friction.

"Some say that at a given moment the aroused damsel no longer resists and that she is at the mercy of her gallant. He, under these conditions, would masturbate her on several occasions: for hours, and almost without let up. . . . It is also said that the girl allows herself some contact with her lover's rod; but I allow myself to doubt this genital masturbation, from the point of view of the general custom."[25]

The example of the maraîchinage is interesting in more than one way. Initially, it should be clearly understood that this tradition was observed in the heart of the very Catholic Vendée of the 19th century, a territory where the priest reigned but where the old local freedom was not completely eradicated by the Revolution. Thus it testifies to the persistence of a very ancient rural culture, the rich complexity of which we usually underestimate. We should also note that the effectiveness of the maraîchinage in terms of social and family balance is proven. Flandrin stresses that, in the 1830's, the rate of illegitimate births was much lower in the Vendée than everywhere else in France. One final but telling comment: it was the mayors of the Third Republic who, in the final analysis, prohibited this pleasant tradition.

The albergement practiced by the Savoyards originated from the same concern to share passions. It allows the girls to admit to their bed, to spend the night, one of the gallants who come to court her. Young people were authorized all forms of caresses other than coitus. Alberge-

ment, which was prohibited under penalty of excommunication since 1609, disappeared only very slowly.

Other areas seem to have known similar customs. They were widely practiced but remained surrounded by a relative discretion. Paradoxically, it is only thanks to those who were opposed to the customs that we even know of their existence. Thus, in 1877, a medical lampoon against female masturbation described the traditional — very thorough — flirtation — among young people of Pas-de-Calais. "During a matrimonial union between country folk of a relatively low class, the company of the wedding, girls and boys, two by two, after the bridal meal and before the ball, withdraw to a room, four, five or six groups together, and there, after kidding around in dubious taste, they are somehow find themselves in the dark. The young fellows then take their partners on their knees, and the girls, who would scarcely have given in to their lovers for a kingdom, give in, so elastic is their modesty, to groping and petting with great pleasure."[26]

Back to Georges Bataille

Bad news for utopias, good news for transgressions: is that the real lesson of history? If that is the case, we would still like to see how transgression ties in with pleasure itself, a linkage that matters deeply to our modern society that is so frightened to see the intensity of its desires declining in proportion to their liberation. On this subject, renewed curiosity about Bataille and the appreciably different view of his works today is no mere coincidence. In the Sixties, at the height of the sexual revolution, Bataille was honored as one of our great transgressors (with De Sade, Joyce and Nietzsche). That is not quite the case any more.

A former seminarian, haunted by Christianity and what he himself calls "the faith of his youth," Bataille is a proponent of the idea that the existence of the interdict and its transgression is the basis of desire itself. He is certain that desire has a tragic side. "If we observe the interdict, if we subject ourselves to it, we are no longer aware of desire. But we experience, at the moment of transgression, the anguish without which the interdict would not exist: it is the experience of sin. The experience leads us to commit transgressions, the successful transgression, which, in maintaining the interdict, maintains it *to enjoy it*."[27]

He has expressed on several occasions his deep terror that all the interdicts might disappear, while at the same time he preaches transgression and goes out of his own way to be provocative (for example by masturbating in front of his mother's corpse). In addition to repeated homages to De Sade and Nietzsche, under his by-line we find topics directly inherited from the very Christianity with which he intends to break.

For example, the half-frightened, half-fascinated observation that the essential characteristic of sexual desire is that it escapes the human will and reason. An idea come straight from St. Augustine and the meaning of which Bataille furiously shows the opposite. "What the act of love and sacrifice reveal," he writes, "is the *flesh*. The sacrifice substitutes the blind convulsion of the bodies for the ordered life of the animal. The same holds true for the erotic convulsion: it frees the many organs whose blind games continue beyond the deliberate will of the lovers. This deliberate will is followed by animalic movements of the organs inflated with blood. A violence no longer controlled by reason animates these organs, it squeezes them to the bursting point and suddenly it is the joy of the heart to yield to the surging wave of this tide. The movement of the *flesh* goes beyond a certain limit, without the will being involved. The *flesh* is this excess in us which is opposed to the law of decency."[28]

According to Bataille, pleasure is partly dependent on the despicable animality that it awakens in us. ("That which most violently revolts us, is within us.") He quotes Baudelaire (in *Fusées* [*Rockets*, an autobiographical essay]) affirming that "the single and supreme pleasure of loving lies in the certainty that one is doing wrong." In a splendid passage in *L'Histoire de l'érotisme* (*The History of Eroticism*), he particularly evokes the irrepressible reflex which, at the very moment of pleasure, impels us to grunt "dirty" words, as if to "shout out a discovered secret."

More significantly, he finds the vocabulary of the encratite cults of the first centuries of Christendom to describe almost word for word man's fear of the orgiastic and the relentless maelstrom of nature. For Bataille, the sexual interdict expresses man's refusal, a refusal to give in to the immense and proliferating *wastefulness* of nature, which ceaselessly recycles death to make new life, brewing beings and matter in a monstrous cauldron that makes death the condition of rebirth. Man's terror, and the "no" that he suddenly utters, proceed from the will to disobey this alarming cosmic movement.

"Sexuality *and* death are only the acute moments of a festival that nature celebrates with the inexhaustible multitude of beings, one and the other signifying the boundless wasting to which nature proceeds, countering the desire to endure that is innate in every being... As if man in one moment had unconsciously grasped the impossible condition of nature (what is *given* to us) requiring the beings that she produces to take part in the rage to destroy that animates her and that nothing will appease. Nature requires that they yield, what can I say? She requires that they throw themselves into it: and the human possibility depended on the moment when, being seized by an overwhelming urge, one being strove to answer *no*."[29]

Cambered in his Nietzchean revolt, Bataille denounced this refusal of primitive animality, a moralizing rejection that he described as a "moment of failure." He recommended eliminating from our world what the millennia had accumulated as the "order of thinking" and reintroducing disorder in its place. He urged us to "destroy in ourselves the habit of having a goal."[30] But, in keeping with his times (the 1950's), more sensitive than anyone to the immense revulsion after the war, at least he knew exactly *what the question was about* in all that.

CHAPTER 11

FROM A "PLAN FOR IMMORTALITY" TO DEMOGRAPHIC FEAR

Who wouldn't be upset, in the final analysis, by this immense flooding and ebbing tide of rigor, then permissiveness, that seems to set the rhythm of our history, forging then foundering our morality, building then razing our utopias, on and on since the earliest traces of civilization? Who wouldn't be agitated, upon reflection, about what turns out to be, in certain respects, a historical enigma? As soon as we step outside the usual approach to the matter — judging, denouncing, justifying, a grand curiosity takes over, but then it only ends in obscurity. Are there anthropological factors that govern this endless oscillation? Are these alternating patterns of rigor and laxity predetermined by an invisible logic or do they simply obey the random swings of ideology and the pendulum course of beliefs?

In theory, this question is absolutely fundamental, since a convincing answer would neutralize most of the superficial quarrels, fulminations and arguments that swirl throughout our era. Do you want to discuss sexual morality without considering its foundations? Examine the evolution of the symbolic representations without looking at the cycles of which they form a part? What would be the point?!

If we look closely at the sequence of the periods, we may of course discern an element of explanation, but we should be very careful how we interpret it. It is the *demographic constraint*, the will to perpetuate the species that Plato calls "the concern to create offspring" and that allows the human race "to participate, through generation, in immortality" (Laws, IV, 721). In other words, a society would always have, more or less, have the morality of its demography.[1] We can only state this possibility conditionally. Anyone who considers the question will be surprised to note that it has been studied relatively little. There are a few historical works from the School of Annals, some stimulating notes from Jean-Louis Fleming and Philippe Ariès, but much has been left unexamined. How many putative causalities remain unverified and how many conjectures are left unproven? Demographers are the first to underline the imperfection of their science. Alfred Sauvy, its founder, described it as "wild" in 1946. They often insist that their explanations are inevitably random, in particular when it comes to the successive cycles of growth and decline. Thus the infinite prudence with which they venture to articulate any laws on the matter. Not to mention the politicization of demographic questions, which is more a factor in France than elsewhere.[2]

Rome and the Anguish of the Decline

Ancient episodes are known where, judging from the evidence, some specific demographic accident resulted in a significant shift in sexual morality. That was the case for certain major epidemics, that decimated a population and thus exacerbated, for a time, the obsession with reproduction. As mentioned above,[3] Ancient China' relative unconcern was disturbed at least twice by this type of cataclysm, in fact by sweeping epidemics of syphilis, at the beginning of the 16th century and then around the year 1630. These events, basically, encouraged a renewal of prudishness and "family values," even though, to the contrary, some portion of the population may have reacted to this morbid anxiety by giving way to pleasures even more frantically.

During the first centuries of Christianity, the great theological and philosophical debates among pagans, Christians, Jews and Roman jurists were not as unrelated to demographic realities as one may think. Concern about the birthrate, negligible during the first two centuries of our era (which enjoyed strong demographic growth), would play an essential role from the 4th century onward. It is true that life expectancy in the Roman Empire at that time was under twenty-five years. To ensure the renewal of the population, every woman had to have, on average, five children. The marriageable age was approximately fourteen years.[4] Roman society was extremely vulnerable to any modification of the demographic patterns. Not to mention the need for soldiers for the Roman legions. To understand this type of situation, we might look at how, in certain countries of the southern hemisphere, the poor still have large families in order to provide "insurance" for their own old age.

Around the 2nd century, as we know, Christianity was still seeking to establish itself in contrast to the gnostic and Encratite movements, by praising — through Clement of Alexandria, for example — the praise of the marriage. At that time, there was no concern over the Empire's demographic situation. However, by the 4th and 5th centuries, a period of decline, tense debates opposed the Roman authorities to the Christian thinkers — in the inverse of today. The pro-birth concerns of the Romans and certain emperors, driven by anguish over the decline, adopted laws that should support population growth. The Christians, on the contrary, inclined to favor chastity and celibacy, defended themselves sometimes on considerations that anticipated Malthus. In his treatise *On Virginity*, St. John Chrysostom maintained that the earth was already fully populated and that thus it was hardly necessary any more to procreate. It is true that the pagan author Lucian of Samosat had used the same argument, in *Loves*, "to speak in praise of pederasty, the ultimate refinement of physical love in a society freed from the concern of procreating by too great a population density."[5] Aristotle, for his part, had called upon a possible invasion of the ground to support that "the multiplication of children was to be limited."

All in all, however, Rome's pro-birth concerns ran against the Christians' distrust for the flesh. According to certain historians, the demographic situation of the Roman world had become critical. However, Christianity was increasingly influential, so much so that "the Church claimed and obtained the abrogation of Rome's pro-population laws because they hindered the rise of chastity among the celibate and the married."[6] For Jean-Louis Fleming, there is no doubt that the Christian doctrines were thus in conflict with the demographic needs. (The French Church did not become pro-birth, as it will be seen, until modern times.)

The Wrong Time for Morality?

This face-off between a Church attached to the principle[7] of celibacy for the priests and a temporal power obsessed with the hazards of depopulation (analogous to a loss of military power) went on in practically the same terms for several centuries. With the great plague of 1348-1349, the urban population was cut to a third, engendering a long-lasting demographic crisis. The forceful pro-birth reaction was not unrelated to the moralistic crackdown that occurred: homosexuality and masturbation were denounced, etc.. But this reaction was more of lay inspiration than religious. And it aimed directly at the celibacy of the priests. "Early in the 15th century," notes Jacques Rossiaud, "certain lay authors began to denounce the celibacy of the clerics and the monks, and even to dispute the primacy of virginity . . . Look at the *Lamentation de l'humaine nature* written by Guillaume Saignet in 1412.   Moreover, in the 15th century, the French bourgeois families were much less ready to send their daughters to the convent. It's all part of the same trend: it was necessary to procreate!"[8]

We should underline, by contrast, that the easy-going 12th century, which had seen a softening of sexual morality, the developing taste for pleasures and the love of nature, corresponded to a period of demographic increase all over Europe. That increase started from the very beginning of the 11th century. Thus, the Church's struggle against continence and the Cathares, in favor of the procreative sanctity of marriage, did not by any means correspond to the temporal needs. In all lay logic, better birth control and more praise of celibacy would have been preferable. But one can also maintain (like certain historians who disagree with Flandrin) that it was the Church's reduction of the periods of continence inspired of the liturgical calendar (starting in the beginning of the 11th century) that encouraged the demographic recovery. At any rate, we should not ignore this disconcerting *coincidence*.

In the pagan communities of the early Middle Ages, the pro-birth concern was omnipresent given the high rate of infant mortality. This directly influenced sexual practice, interdicts and morality itself. Frankish society, to look at just one example, was completely preoccupied by the concern to encourage procreation. The child was regarded as most valuable of all the goods. The death of a child was an irrecoverable disaster; and it was severely punished, even in anticipation.

"Anyone who kills an available young woman of suitable age for pro-creation must pay 600 sous, as much as for a antrusion, but if a woman is killed after her menopause, just 200 sous! If she is attacked while pregnant and she dies, 700 sous of fine; only 100 if the child dies from an abortion related to the attack! King Gontran, at the end of the 6th cen-tury, promulgated an additional stipulation, probably because this kind of offence was increasing: from now on, the fine was 600 sous for kill-ing a pregnant woman, and an additional 600 sous if the dead child would have been a boy. One could hardly be more explicit."[9]

In the late 16th and 17th centuries, canonical and political argu-ments about the linkage between birthrate and sexual morality were not always that coherent. How could they be, in a society where the mechanisms of procreation were still not clearly understood and led to different interpretations (as we saw with Galen and Aristotle)? At that time, authors like Laurent Jobert (*Erreurs populaires*, 1587) thought that too frequent sexual activity would cause sterility. Such theories were all the more likely to be accepted since they combine the Aristotelian ideal of moderation and that of Christian chastity. They met several needs; first, they reconciled the pagan obsession with the birthrate and the Christian preoccupation with sexual discipline; second, they al-lowed the temporal power and the Church — which were frequently in conflict — to find an area of agreement. Christian morality was no longer perceived as a complete enemy of demography for moderating the couple's passion.[10]

The Inflation of Hopes

Thereafter, things become more understandable. Between the Enlightenment and the beginning of the 20th century, historians al-ways mention two great contradictory demographic trends: a sudden increase starting in the mid-18th century, and a decline that turned brutal toward the end of the 19th. It is tempting — and pretty well-justified — to tie these two shifts to the evolution of customs and legis-lation.

Concerning the first phase, Emmanuel Le Roy Ladurie uses a splendid expression when he talks about "an inflationary rise in hope." He sees the demographic expansion around 1740-1750 as a kind of blaze of optimism announcing the modern age. Suddenly, the birthrate tended to match mortality. The population increased and so did life expectancy. "People who married at around the age of 25 now had before them another 35 years of probable life, whereas their grandparents or great-grandparents had only 20 to 25 years. The epidemics that had long been decimating the population at more or less regular intervals seemed to have been vanquished. The last plague hit Marseilles in 1710. . . . In short, the biological conditions of individualism had been met."[11]

This phenomenon, profound as it was, can be interpreted in various ways. (As Philippe Ariès points out, we cannot be sure of the real explanation.) Various hypothese exist. In terms of its effect on the contemporary morality, one might suggest that this population boom, while reducing the obsession with reproduction, supported the tendency to asceticism that was present since the 17th century. That Jansenist asceticism, dominated by a preoccupation with self-control, in its turn would have paved the way for the second phase — the decline — that came at the end of the 19th century. Compared to its neighbors, France seems to be the forerunner when it comes to contraception — contraception which, at the time, rested precisely on "self-control." "Works on historical demography [underline] a unique feature in France: a very early inclination to limit births. Studies in the last few decades have made it possible to establish that French couples tried to limit their progeniture even before the French Revolution, a full century before their neighbors."[12]

If the initial causes of this long demographic springtime — from the middle of the 17th to the beginning of the 19th centuries — are not fully understood, its effects on the moral debate are it a little more clear. In France, the Church certainly opposed the re-institution of divorce,[13] but, in fact, it softened its doctrinal stand on marital sexuality. If there was any generally shared fear at that time, it was rather that of overpopulation. France was then the most populous country in Europe. Under Napoleon, her armies could stand at the head of enormous coalitions of the continent. France's crushing demographic superiority is even one of the keys to explaining the Napoleonic epic. The Emperor could easily call upon his reserves. And it is an understatement to say that he was generous with human lives. In 1812-1813, for example, the Russian campaign alone would cost the Grande Armée approximately 400,000 lives in just a few months (not all French, it is true). The cumulative losses of the revolutionary period and the Napoleonic wars far exceed a million deaths. France had enormous demographic strength.

The need to procreate was not yet regarded as a national emergency, far from it. The clerics thus often gave up strictly imposing the marital morality that focussed on procreation as the sole justification of pleasure. "The declining death rate made it hard to support the strict application of Church doctrines regarding fruitfulness. A large part of the French clergy appeared to be very much aware of the problem and had given up applying the principles."[14] We were on the road toward, under certain conditions, the Church's acceptance of contraception.

"The Danger of Depopulation"

In the last quarter of the 19th century, shortly after the war of 1870, everything was turned on its head. *Immediately following the disaster of Sedan* [ed. note: the decisive defeat of the French army in the Franco-German War, leading to the overthrow of the Second French Empire], the brutal inversion of the demographic trend, which had actually started at the beginning of the century, would cause a true collective anguish and would upset in just a few years the whole complex of attitudes relating to marriage, sexuality and procreation. Obsessed by the danger of depopulation, the political power and the Church would now compete in using pro-birth rhetoric that sometimes bordered on nationalist delusion. The decline of fecundity, indeed, no longer allowed for the replacement of generations. More serious still, France realized with a shock that it was lagging behind the other European countries — especially Prussia — in population growth. This awakening was the catalyst of a psychological trauma (the French "demographic fear," one researcher would call it) that would dominate French history for nearly a century. All parties were galvanized for a "national jump-start." In 1896 an Alliance for Increasing the Population was formed; it was followed in 1900 by the creation of a senatorial commission, and then of a parliamentary group, looking after the interests of large families.

On the secular side, science was once again enlisted to help. Sociological and political publications devoted to the new "threat" multiplied. Medicine, history, republican morality were pressed into service to invite the French to procreate. It was said that a woman would not know real fulfillment until she became a mother and, if possible, many times over. The Church was not to be outdone. For centuries, it had been reticent on the matter and refused to declare itself to be pro-birth. Those days were over. Now, the bishops joined their voices to those of the Republic in calling for more children. The air was filled with grandiloquent oratory. On July 14, 1872, in Beauvais, the Swiss cardinal Mgr Kaspar Mermillod addressed the people of France, saying: "You have, in a sordid calculation, dug tombs instead of filling the children's cradles; that is why you lack for soldiers." In 1886, Rome for the first time instructed confessors to question the penitents on their practice of contraception in the event of "well-founded suspicion."

At the doctrinal level, certain theological texts were used to support the pro-birth movement. Thus, in 1909, Cardinal Mercier called upon St. Thomas Aquinas who, in his *Summa Theologica*, sanctified procreation in these terms: "God has attached sexual pleasure to the act of human procreation, as he attached the satisfaction of taste to the consumption of food. With one as with the other delight of the senses, it should be said that it is legitimate only when it is performed according to God's design. Therefore sexual pleasure is legitimate when it is directed toward the procreative act, and it is wicked and guilty when it is pursued without direct nor indirect relation to the normal act within a legitimate marriage or in a manner which does not serve to generate offspring."

This pro-birth campaign is a first in the history of Christianity. Until then, Rome had shown itself relatively insensitive to the patriotic concerns. The Church from this point onward — and for a long time — aimed its sights at birth control. "The new rigidity of the doctrine regarding contraceptive practices, that began at the start of the 20th century and that grew more intense over time, thus appears to have been, originally, closely related to the French demographic situation."[15] The Church's effort was reinforced by some talented propagandists such as the Jesuit Joseph Hoppenot, and Charles Gibier, the priest of Ste-Paterne in Orleans and author of two books with evocative titles: *La Désorganisation des families (Families in Disarray)*, 1903, and *Les Berceaux vides (Empty Cradles)*, 1917.

The greater the confrontation with Germany, the closer we got to the Great War, the stronger became the pro-birth propaganda. Between 1912 and 1914, six *Letters of Lent* took depopulation as their central topic. Two of them (Angers and Verdun) refer to it explicitly as a "plague." In one of his pro-birth pleas, the priest Charles Gibier — soon to become Bishop of Versailles — stated that, according to his calculations, in fifteen years Germany would count twice as many conscripts as France. Paradoxically, the same demographic anxiety was recorded in Germany, although that was less well-founded. In 1915, Father H. A. Krose published in the Jesuit review *Stimmen der Zeit* (*Voices of Our Time*) an article where he wrote, specifically, "In the sharp literary controversy caused by the worrying decline of German birthrate statistics, one cannot emphasize enough the danger that this phenomenon represents for the global position of the Reich."

Let us note, in passing, that adding to this nationalist climate the link was already established between the diminishing French birth rate and the risk of "invasion" by foreign immigration, which would be a popular topic in the future, as we know. In 1903, Gibier wrote in *La Désorganisation des familles*: "If we still have 38 million, we owe it to the foreigners who send their overflow to us. Yesterday, they were hundreds, today they are thousands; tomorrow, they will be a million. This is a danger, an immense danger. Our race is threatened by the increasing infiltration of a foreign element."

No to Marital "Onanism"

In retrospect, it is frightening to see how, between the late 19th century and the Great War, everything — literally *everything* — worked together to accentuate a procreative and puritanical moralism in sexual matters; this would prevail in France until the early 1960's. There was no place for pleasure nor hedonism. It was the of the Rooms of the blue horizon, of Alsace-Lorraine, of colonization and the dreams of "grand revenge"[16] on Germany. The Republic called for children, that is, for workmen and soldiers. This spurred the moralizing flights of rhetoric, which brought together the secular Right *and* the Left in the same holy union around the nursery. From the economic point of view, the industrial revolution had already consolidated a kind of bourgeois-inspired sexual morality, cautious and austere, at least in public. It went further still. The Church, which did not accept the republic, did not intend to be left behind when it came to patriotism and demography. Therefore, it tried to go even further in encouraging more births, demonizing birth control and what began to be called "marital Onanism."

This twofold pro-birth injunction gave rise, in reaction, to a Malthusian current, which called for "the strike of the bellies" in 1909 and planted deep roots in the French political landscape. (It reappeared, for example, in 1968.) Among the clergy, the new message from Rome intended for married couples was so heavy-handed that it caused a real embarrassment. The priests and the confessors were confronted with the following dilemma: either to condemn firmly any "marital Onanism," to ask for confession but to lose contact with the majority of Christians who were not about to give it up; or to remain silent on that issue, maintaining contact with the public but appearing excessively tolerant or lax. Catholic reviews like *L'Ami du clergé* (*Friend of the clergy*) echoed these painful debates of conscience, on a background of culpability and distress. Until the middle of the 20th century, this procreative injunction that precluded any form of contraception would be regarded as "the cross of the confessors." The sex act was supposed to conform to the elements required by moral theology: penetration in "the appropriate vessel" (*Penetratio vasis debiti*), ejaculation of the seed "so that it can be attracted in the uterus and fertilized in good time."

At that time a very rigorous interpretation of St. Augustine came into play, and the treatise on marriage and concupiscence was a favored section to quote (*De nuptiis et concupiscentia*). "If the two who are united are such, they do not deserve to be called husband and wife; and if, from the very beginning, they were such, they have not come together to marry, but rather to give themselves up to fornication: if they are not both, I dare say, then either the one is in a certain sense her husband's prostitute, or he is an adulterer with his wife."

The Great War, which would bleed the French population, could only aggravate this obsessive Puritanism. The hecatomb and the military setbacks of the first years of the conflict were blamed, in retrospect, on France's demographic weakness, just as the rout in 1940 would be blamed on the "immorality" of the Popular Front. A bishop, Mgr de Gibergues, wrote in 1919, in a work entitled *On the Birthrate Crisis in View of the Catholic Conscience*: "If the fathers and mothers had done their duty, Germany in 1914 would not have dared to declare war. So immorality is the primary cause of the present war. . . . We had to retreat, from the beginning, before a crushing numerical superiority."

From this date forward, "demographic deficiency became the

scapegoat on which France, its unconscious, blamed the defeats, the loss of preeminence in the world and then on the continent, [and soon] that of an empire, and the inexorable decline of its power and its influence. [This state of mind] became a defensive reaction, primal and instinctive, quasi-biological like that of an organism fighting for survival."[17]

In September 1919 the first National Congress on the Birthrate was organized in Nancy, on the initiative of the Chambers of Commerce. What is more significant, the following year, the parliamentary assembly approved with a crushing majority (500 votes to 73) the famous law of 1920 that prohibits using any direct or indirect means to provoke an abortion, *and even suppresses any information on contraception.*[18] This law would remain in force until 1967, the year the Neuwirth law that authorizes contraception was adopted. The anticlerical parties were not the last to give their votes to the law of 1920, just as a Chamber where the Popular Front held the majority would approve, on July 29, 1939, the Family Code that was later wrongly ascribed to Vichy. Demographic voluntarism was the consensus, a specifically French condition.

Sexual morality, compared with the of the preceding centuries, became more stifling than ever. Now it was not only the Church that identified the contraception that the French had practiced for so long (including the Christians) with "Onan's crime." In the eyes of the Republic itself, it becomes a potential criminal offence. This time, population trends and the fantasies that were associated with them led to direct consequences on public morality.

Catch the Cheaters!

The inter-war period, under Vichy, definitely marks the apogee of this moralistic phase. Looking back, these excesses seem hardly credible. On the lay side, medical discussions took on apocalyptic tones whenever it referred to women without children; all kinds of diseases were predicted for them. In the 1920's, a doctor from Bordeaux (Lauret) claimed at a regional congress on the birthrate that "women only experience physiological plenitude during pregnancy and lactation." In 1929, the Brussels doctor R. de Guchteneere announced, in his work entitled *Birth Control*, that contraception is likely to lead to complete sterility in women, that it predisposes them to fibroids and to nervous problems. In 1930, Doctor Jacques Sédillot introduced an even more fantastic concept: "The Cheaters' syndrome." He explained that gynecological and nervous disorders come from a spermatic deficiency in woman having an active genital life. As for the above-mentioned Dr. Guchteneere, in 1931 he advanced a new hypothesis: non-conception would lead to female genital cancer.

On the part of the Church, the fight against marital "Onanism," from the 1930's to the 1950's, took the form of a crusade. The debate on birth control took center stage, and Rome became ever more intransigent. There was talk of the "honesty" of the marital bed and the possibility of profaning it. Certain Christians, especially the intellectuals, began to protest and to plead for a theology that gave more attention to happiness and the freedom of the spouses. In the early 1930's, two gynecologists, Ogino and Knauss, published the preliminary results of their experiments with a new method of contraception, based on the variations in temperature according to menstrual cycles. A significant detail: it was the prior of the convent of Coublevie that distributed their booklet. That was pretty audacious, especially since it falls in theory under the law of 1920 and could lead to prosecution for its authors.

But the publication by Pius XI, December 31, 1930, of the famous encyclical *Casti Connubi* rang the death knell for any liberal hopes that may have lingered among the Christians. The encyclical reaffirmed the Vatican's hostility to any contraception. The battle cry was still: "Be fruitful and multiply!" It was twenty more years before a pope, Pius XII, would half-accept the principle of birth control.[19]

Don't underestimate the disastrous consequences of this Roman conservatism. Many Christian couples felt torn between their religious faith and their desire to limit childbirth, while having a harmonious sex life. The testimonies accumulated at that time, the letters addressed by parishioners to their confessors, contain pathetic confidences.[20] How many intimate sufferings, hardships taken on, pleasures foregone and loves lost? "These questions," Martine Sevegrand says, "are evidence of a clandestine revolt against an 'intractable' Church that was demanding the impossible, the unrealizable, and confronting the most devout Christian homes with absurd choices. A father of three children wrote in 1936 to the abbot Viollet 'to ask for help. . . . For the moment, I know that I must not have any sexual relations, but in spite of my efforts I cannot manage to do that, or rather when I do, I am filled with a great sadness, and as a result I completely stop enjoying life. . . .I summarize: on the one hand, when I obey the divine law, it wrecks my family affection and the taste for living. On the other, if I disobey by having fraudulent relations, everything else is fine.'"

As an irony of history and a new resurgence of "transgression," statistics from that era indicate that in spite of the Vatican's intransigence, Christian couples continued to practice contraception. The decline of fruitfulness persisted in the 1930's and, more significant still, the overall birthrate of the regions with a strong Catholic influence was similar to that of the lay areas. It is true that, paradoxically, the wish to limit the size of the family does not always mean that attachment to the family is not a fundamental value, as Philippe Ariès has shown. The role model of the time, he explains, was that of "the prudent, calculating family, looking ahead, absorbed in preparing a better future for one or two children. Under these conditions, the reduction of births did not correspond to some form of hedonism. On the contrary, it corresponded to an ascetic concept of life where everything, including sexual pleasure, was sacrificed to the patient upbringing of the next generation."[21]

The pro-birth ideology, the worship of the family, the puritanical rigor about sexuality: it all created (or at least it was a collaborator!) a Vichyist atmosphere before the fact. After the rout of 1940, Philippe Pétain's French State, with its slogan, "Labor, Family, Fatherland," by no means went against the grain in France. On this matter at least, it coincided with a general climate that predated him. Petainism, from this point of view, largely preceded Pétain.

At that time (1938), *L'Amour et l'Occident* (*Love and the West*) appeared, an admirable work and, on many points, prophetic. The Protestant author Denis de Rougemont considered, in particular, the very Western idea of passion, embodied by the character of Tristan in love with Iseult, a passion whose morality is contrary to that of marriage which postulates stability and permanence. Rougemont's analyses heralded the great individualistic debates of the 1960's.[22]

1942-1943: An Unforeseen Reversal

Extraordinarily enough, it was in the blackest time of the German occupation, in the middle of the Second World War, that French population trends reversed again. The slow decline that had started at the end of the 19th century and had been statistically worsened by the slaughters of 1914-1918 gave way to a spectacular new wave of births. The trend started in 1942. It would intensify, as we know, for the two years following the Liberation, and so abruptly, on so wide a scale, that a new expression had to be coined to indicate the phenomenon: the baby-boom.

This new — and enormous — demographic reversal would determine the destiny of French society for several decades. Its consequences are still being felt today.[23] It is not as simple a phenomenon as one might think, and is not tied, for example, to the return of war prisoners. Philippe Ariès talks in this connection "about the surprising interruption of a secular evolution." "To date," says Jean-Marie Poursin, "the baby-boom remains an enigma for the entire field of demographers."[24] "It is undoubtedly the result of a complex evolution of collective mentalities (for example, how people felt about the future), that started long before. The parents of the baby-boom, should it be pointed out, belong to the generation born in the 1920's. Thus it makes sense to see this revival as the cultural consequence, shifted forward, of the pro-birth campaign at the beginning of the century.

As for sexual morality, many generations' view of the future, in the immediate post-war period, logically would have modified the terms of the debate since "the demographic threat" had been warded off. However, that was not the case. Culturally, the post-war climate remained very pro-birth. France admittedly had to be rebuilt, and the miracle of economic growth ("the glorious thirty [years])" brought a renewed confidence in the future. General de Gaulle won the majority when — in 1962 — he proclaimed a France of 100 million inhabitants. The parties on the Left, including the most lay, the Communist Party, were no less concerned with the birthrate and family morality. Jeannette Vermeersch finds the Communists echoing the accents of Conventioneers of the French Revolution or those of the Russian Bolsheviks in the 1930's, calling abortion a "vice for women of the grande bourgeoisie." The influential sociologist Alfred Sauvy weighed in, as well. In 1956, he stated that he was concerned that an abrogation of Articles 3 and 4 of the law of 1920 repressing anti-conceptional propaganda would jeopardize France's demographic recovery.

Other experts from the National Institute of Demographic Studies (the INED, created in October, 1945 by Gaulle), held similar opinions. Paul Vincent, in 1950, went right to the point: "In the current state of our society... the demographic equilibrium... can only be precarious, for it rests primarily on the existence of large families that are, for the most part, involuntary."[25] Thus, this exceptionally repressive law remained in force.

So, the 1950's and the beginning of the 1960's were times of family and not of sexual hedonism. The Cognacq-Jay prize, created in 1920 to reward large families (more than nine children), increased in prestige. It gained even more popularity, thanks to television. Admittedly, the family was glorified for reasons appreciably different (and less distressed) than in the 1920's or 30's, but the result was about the same. "The baby-boom," writes Ariès, "shows how much the attitude toward life is a matter of mind-set. The contraceptive attitude of the 19th century had developed in one particular psychological climate, which disappeared in the 1940's. Another climate succeeded it, where the careful calculations of the former period were no longer necessary, dissipated by a climate of confidence in a future of plenty. So nothing stood in the way anymore of making the family a little bigger, a family that had become the place of happiness: 'the happy family.'"[26]

The Triumph of "Family Values"

This consensus in favor of family values was not unique to France, and thus it is not related to any particular political situation. All of devastated Europe in the post-war years seemed to obey a formidable instinct for recovery. It was the golden age of the institution of marriage. "All of Europe," observes Évelyne Sullerot, "felt the fever of marriage. Of course, people were making up for the deficit of the war years, during which many unions could not take place or were broken by death. But, even after 1950, and until 1965, the marriage rate smashed all the records in France, Great Britain, Belgium, the Netherlands, Sweden, Germany, Denmark, Italy. . . .Even in Ireland, the single people were melting like snow in the sunshine. Everyone was getting married, and getting married earlier. At the time, that was called the 'modernization' of the family."[27]

This state of mind went beyond the borders of Europe and to tell the truth it affected all of the developed countries. In the United States, the feminism of the pre-war period seemed out of date. Nothing was exempt from the imprint of this climate, even the Universal Declaration of Human Rights of 1948, the first subparagraph of which evokes institution of the family as the fundamental element of society. Until the beginning of the Sixties, well-known American commentators like David Riesman spoke of the prevalence of a "pro-family" sensibility in the Western countries."[28]

In France, the debate over contraception continued, and continued to divide Christians. It was then complicated by an additional parameter that had hardly been counted until then: the vague feeling that the planet was overpopulated, a feeling exacerbated by the discovery of the underdevelopment of the former colonies. The partisans of birth control would be accused more and more often of Malthusianism — including by the Left — while the pro-birth doctrines of the Church would be held to be favoring the poor countries. Thus, after the publication of the encyclicals *Mater et magistra* (1962) and *Humanae Vitae* (1968), both very hostile toward contraception, certain Christians from the Third World would be pleased by this priority granted to life, including for poorest.[29] In November 1968, the monthly magazine *Growth of Young Nations* celebrated Latin America's warm welcome for the encyclical *Humanae Vitae*, for "Paul VI defends the poor. At the banquet of life... the poor have a right, too, to have their place; first of all, to be born and to live. Life must not be controlled by financial interests, but the latter must be put to the service of life."

The Church's stand was most spectacularly unyielding and had the greatest impact during the two decades following the Liberation. Among the Christians, indeed, revolt was brewing. The signs of a deep moral crisis began to show. The rigid positions of the Vatican were less and less accepted. Confidential reports written by priests underline how widespread this resistance to Rome's conservatism had become among the believers. Early in 1950, in the magazine *The Priest and the Family*, Belgian moralist Jacques Leclerc described the crisis with a sensational candor. The same year, a report by the Abbot Dantec maintained that Catholic morality relating to marriage was causing a desertion from the sacraments. In 1951, Father Boigelot's report made the same claim. "The great masses are leaving the Christian practice for reasons of Onanism." Progressive young abbots, like Marc Speech, published books relaying this protest and opposing more conservative clerics like Father Carré.

Nothing changed. Pius XII intervened again, in 1951, to denounce all Catholic sex education literature, which he suspected was no longer any different from the erotic and obscene press that "exploits the basest instincts of a fallen nature." A work by Oraison, *Christian Life and Problems of Sexuality*, was blacklisted in 1955. Even a position as moderate as that of the Christian Paul Chanson (his 1951 book, *The Art of Love and Marital Continence*, preaches contraception based on the reserved pressure practiced by the Buddhists, *copulata reservata*) made a scandal in the Catholic hierarchy. The method recommended by Chanson was the target of a *monitum* (warning) in June 1952. "The accumulation of repressive measurements launched by Pius XII," says Sevegrand, "testifies not only to an obsessive fear of hedonistic tendencies, but also an uneasiness, even distress, at descriptions of sexuality."[30]

The Church gave the strong impression, during this long period leading up to the Vatican II council (1962), to have lost its memory and, confronting the post-war world, to pick up the same concerns as Pius IX who, in his *Syllabus* of 1864, condemned modern ideas.

The Great Rift of 1965

This was the context in which a new demographic shift occurred, in the mid-Sixties. It was broader and more fulgurating than the two that preceded. Demographers are still speculating today about this powerful "signal" that cut across all the Western countries in 1964-1965. The statistical cataclysm stunned the sociologists. All the demographic parameters suddenly reversed at the same time: the birthrate and marriage rate dropped, women married later, there was a striking increase in the divorces, families had fewer children, etc.. In a few years, the birthrate fell to a new low. In 1975, the fertility rate dropped below the threshold of population replacement.

Once again, the phenomenon touched all the Western countries and was striking in its simultaneity. "In 1964," writes Sullerot, "an amazing shift occurred. For the first time in twenty years, the birth rates began to lose ground and then began to plummet — in the same year — in the FRG, Belgium, Denmark, Spain, France, Greece, Italy, Netherlands, Portugal, the UK, Sweden and Switzerland. . . . In the next three years, from 1964 to 1967, France, England and Germany lost

1.3 birth per 1000 inhabitants; the Netherlands and Italy 1.8; Belgium 2.0."[31]

What really happened? Countless explanations were advanced. Some point to the progress of feminism and women's entry *en masse* into the labor market. Some emphasize the scientific — and sociological — of contraception. (But that does not help us understand the general decline in "wanted children," that showed up in studies.) Some blame the massive urbanization of the late Fifties. Certain authors like Richard Easterlin propose a theory known as the long cycles, which suggests that demographic trends reverse in an almost mechanical way every two generations.

Actually, none of these analyses it sufficient on its own. This reversal was the result, and the herald, of a far greater cultural jolt. It follows long term anthropological patterns that will take years to measure. "This pivotal year (1965) marks the moment when the generations born at the end of the war, or immediately after, became adults and engaged in the formation of their own families. These groups did not experience the war or, if they did, then only very briefly. Their childhood occurred in a climate of relative security and social promotion. They suffered neither catastrophe nor deprivation. The job market was mostly open to them. . . . They started to build a family biography that was different from their parents'."[32]

Thus a bracket was closed (that of the Fifties). One could already feel a presentiment of the gradual decline of public values in favor of private values. The baby boomers, a numerous and impatient generation, were arriving at adulthood in all the industrialized countries. They rejected instinctively the values shared by the preceding generation that remained haunted by the idea of war, collapse, shortages, destruction.

Western society in the mid-Sixties benefited culturally from two unprecedented innovations. First, extraordinary economic enrichment that no human community had ever known, not even Spain in the 16th century, artificially enriched by gold from the New World. The prosperity of these post-war years amounted to a quadrupling of purchasing power in less than thirty years. This growth was so miraculous that it was thought to have been established for ever. The view of the future, more optimistic than ever, justified Keynesianism and the inflation that controlled how the Western economies operated. Both phenomena were, in fact, borrowing from the future, favoring youth, movement, and hope, against any idea of prudence and saving. Inflation, said the economists, is "the euthanasia of the independently wealthy," meaning that tomorrow is coming, to hell with the old world! This era gave wealthy Europe the gift of a cultural (and moral) luxury never before imaginable: improvidence without risks.

The second innovation was that the countries of Europe imperceptibly settled into a very long period of military peace, made compulsory by the fact of nuclear weapons. War is already nothing more than an epi-phenomenon that devastates the countries of the South, which we still call the Third World. Europe not only is at peace, but it is expunging the very concept of war, and all the prudence that it implied, from its collective conscience. What is happening, ultimately, is that the consciousness of others is being reduced spectacularly, a concession made for the cohesion and the survival of the group, in favor of a new "imperialism:" that of the individual-as-king.

Looking back, the incredible change of 1964-1965 gives us food for thought, in more than one way. First, the near-immediacy with which the changes were locked in at the legislative level. The majority of the reforms (contraception, abortion, marriage, divorce, etc.) that upset the social and family "givens" were introduced at this time, in the space of just a few years. The big lawyer Jean Carbonnier, who was one of the craftsmen who rewrote the French civil law, suggests that France had an extraordinary "legislative spring." "The turning point in the evolution of conduct," he says, "was not in 1968, it was 1964."[33]

Then, it is striking to note that the properly cultural and political expression of this immense change would come only afterwards. The student uprisings of May 1968, the rediscovery of Wilhelm Reich and Herbert Marcuse, sexual hedonism and assertive permissiveness, the querulous aspiration to immediate pleasure: the whole devastating ostentation of the revolution of manners actually followed its effective achievement, rather than preceded it. In May 1968, we set off on an intrepid voyage; at least we already had a ticket.

Now, we don't have any ticket; will there be a way to get back?

PART 3

A LOGIC OF LONELINESS

"Today's talk of love is extremely lonely."
Roland Barthes, 1977

.

CHAPTER 12

BETWEEN THE JUDGE AND THE DOCTOR

Thirty five years later, we are trapped by a bizarre contradiction. For having dreamed (too much?) of freedom yesterday, today we butt up against an unreasoning fear. We are all submerged in the repressive obsession that accompanies any fear. Society suddenly feels inhabited by violence, threats, unimaginable dangers. Children are no longer safe from perverts; women are exposed to beatings and rape; permissive-ness turns into a nightmare; and our closest neighbor, such and such teacher or youth group leader, *might* possibly be a sexual criminal from whom we need to be protected. This violence can be seen in the spec-tacular increase in criminal statistics.[1] But it shows even more in the public's imagination, where it supplants little by little all the other fan-tasies.

Everything having to do with sex has become a major topic for today's media. We should pay attention to the disturbed haste with which we turn to gobble it up. Any collective fear induces the same fas-cination for that which feeds it. Every new means of communication spreads this dreadful tension further and faster. After the Minitel, where call girls and crime quickly established themselves, the Internet has taken over as the great "broadcaster" of anguish. Now, we read the Marquis de Sade perfectly openly; now, we hear about sadistic crimes "for real," every day. These are crimes that keep driving back the boundaries of what the media can call a "horror" or "nightmare." On August 13, 1996, the Munich police opened an inquest after a series of photographs was displayed on the Internet, showing a naked woman using a saw to decapitate a man. According to the caption on these photographs, broadcast on an Internet chat from Honolulu, the scene was taped in the early Eighties by a couple of sex perverts who had just killed a man in the United States.[2]

"Thanks to the technological wonders of the Internet and the Minitel, we can now place an order for a minor," explains the director of the French Committee of UNICEF, Claire Brisset. "Pornographic cassettes circulate throughout Europe, showing infants, some of which died after undergoing such treatment."[3]

Fear and curiosity feed off of each other.

Decades later, with all the sense of getting away with something, we thought it was a big deal to read about the great perverts of history, like Gilles de Rais, our Bluebeard. Now, in fact, the media, detail for everyone's consumption all the comparable cases, day after day. Just to judges from the admissions of Gilles de Rais himself, during his trial in autumn 1440. "The child having been brought into Gilles' room, things went quickly. Taking in hand his 'male member,' Gilles 'rubbed it,' 'erected it' or 'pressed it' on the belly of the victim, he placed it between his thighs. He rubbed himself against the belly of. . . the children. . . , and was so aroused and enflamed that sperm spouted out on the belly of these children, criminally, and not the way it should. With each child, Gilles achieved at his ends only once or twice, after which he killed them . . . or had them killed."[4]

Descriptions like that are too bland, any more, for provocative writers, but they keep the court reporters busy. Identical confessions may come from a Marc Dutroux (the Belgian pedophile of the 1990's), or another such "monster." Yes, an indefinable fear inhabits Western societies today. As in Paris at the end of the *Directoire*, Moscow in the Thirties, and Rome of the late Empire, sexual utopia is crashing against the idea of violence and the psychosis that goes with it.

Making Everything a Criminal Offense

Psychosis? One thing is clear: sexual violence, real or fantasy, is already leading us into what would have to be called a tendency toward criminalization. We are constantly talking about having a strong police force and spectacular raids, merciless punishment, life sentences and community notification programs. This increased, reinforced, immediate protection requires that the judge and the legislator deal with our media-driven fluctuations of emotion. We get the protection, more or less, but at the price of serious legal and penal setbacks. "The law is more and more often relying on detention as the last resort to define and to set moral parameters on a given field of activity or a sector of public life, to affirm the importance of the general standards that have been spelled out, and to try to provide the means of having them respected. [There is a noticeable] conflict between the progress of the Western democracies, that offer more protection of freedoms and physical integrity of the individuals, and, at the same time, increasing use of imprisonment."[5]

Henceforth the law, and only the law, is charged with making us feel safe. We certainly want to live together, but under the condition of being protected from *other people*. We are less in a hurry to change society than to *make it secure*. The deterioration of the social consciousness, the fading of ethical standards and the sense of community lead to what Antoine Garapon and Denis Salas call "the criminalization of society." That means that we are relying on the courts of law to determine what is legal and what is illegal, to ensure social peace and to manage the boundaries of acceptable behavior. While they were founded on freedom and individualism, our postmodern democracies are thus becoming, even in sexual matters, more repressive than were most of the traditional societies. Here is a reality that we do not like to face up to, it contradicts our beliefs so harshly. We continue to talk in a superficial way about the terrible punishments of the olden days, and the alleged medieval cruelties. But it is *our* prisons, today, that are full!

According to the official statistics of the American prison authorities, the United States counted 1,630,940 prisoners in 1996, or 615 prisoners per hundred thousand inhabitants.[6] Not only does this ratio blow away all previous records, it marks an unprecedented expansion of the American prison population. The U.S. had only 290,000 prisoners in 1960, 494,000 in 1984 and 744,000 in 1985. Their *number went up 5.5 times* in less than forty years. At the same time, the severity of the sentences was sharply increased, especially for sex cases. Now they talk about *tough penalties*. Since 1994, in the United States, the recidivist sexual delinquent is liable to twice the usual sentence for the same infraction. In May 1996, *Megan's Law*, which provides that the community should be alerted when a sexual delinquent is released, was extended to the federal level. A federal register of sexual delinquents is being compiled. In August 1996, California was the first state to authorize the chemical castration of recidivists. The Middle Ages didn't do that.

In France, of course, the situation is somewhat different, but there the trend is also toward greater severity. "It is now a fact," say the magistrates, "that the prison population is going up due to longer sentences more than because of a higher number of incarcerations. And these longer sentences are to a great extent tied to incest and sexual violence."[7]

Isn't this bizarre situation disturbing, when you consider our recent past? In the mid-Sixties, we dismissed the priest, the moralist, and the politician who had been expected to look after the common good. We thought we could allow the individual to take precedence over the group (an unprecedented situation). We thought we had acquired the ability to challenge the immemorial prudence, the acceptance of limits, the infinite social ploys and of all kinds of compromises by which human societies after a fashion combined the aspiration to pleasure and the needs of the community. A few decades ago, we were, when it comes to sex, more intrepidly constructivist than any society had ever been before us. The apotheosis of the individual, his complete emancipation, seemed to be the greatest accomplishment of Western modernity. Now we were rich enough, smart enough, rational enough to reject the superstitions of the past. And free enough, finally, to denounce the tyrannies of the intimate life.

Didn't reason cancel out religion? Didn't democracy render inoperative the political perpetuation of restrictions? Didn't knowledge give us mastery over what used to be our fate? Didn't science give us the keys to procreation itself? Didn't the certainty of progress free us from the timorous faith in traditions? Didn't faith in the universal, finally, allow us to measure the "specific pathos" of human cultures as if they were pleasant folk tales, with their holistic taboos and their cares? This right to pleasure, we granted it to ourselves like an extraordinary historical reward. And so it was. We shouldn't laugh too much, looking back at this optimism.

If we are disturbed, today, it is by seeing this great plan finally running up against the same obstacles, the same contradictions and, especially, the same mortals risks as all the utopias that had preceded it. Today's "climate," the lurking threats and fears bring us back very close to past history. The many-faced violence that rightly or wrongly we feel all around us, the giddy sense of insecurity that virtually leads us to legal panic, are exactly what past societies kept trying to manage. We have to admit that the traditional cultures, from which we proudly want to dissociate ourselves, understood pretty well the indissoluble intricacies linking sexuality and violence.

One should remember René Girard's remarks about the taboo around women's menstrual blood, a taboo observed in most cultures. Why was it considered impure, he wondered. "We should consider menstruation in the more general context of bloodshed. Most primitive men took extraordinary precautions not to come into contact with blood. . . . Ritual impurity is found everywhere where one might fear violence. . . . It is easy to believe that violence is impure because it re-lates to sexuality. The reverse proposal is only valid in the field of known cases. Sexuality is impure because it is related to violence."[8]

The violence that has suddenly returned in our societies seems to prove his point. And in the same chapter of *La Violence et le Sacré* (*Violence and the Sacred*), Girard observes with a touch of irony: "The idea that the beliefs of all humanity are only a vast mystification that we have been the only ones to escape is, at the very, least premature." Today, in any case, the situation is outrageous in more ways than one. By dismissing the priest, the moralist and beliefs themselves, we have been refusing to internalize the interdicts any longer. We have been rejecting them to the outside, "externalizing" them, as the economists say in connection with monetary constraints. Now, here we are, precipitately forced to entrust the management of the limits to two new authorities, authori-ties who have none of the finesse of Seneca, Maïmonides nor St. John of the Cross: the judge and the doctor. It is to them that we have ulti-mately agree to hand over, with eyes closed, our fears and even our free-dom. They weren't really ready for such a gift.

At this stage, talking about the tendency to criminalize sexual delinquency is no longer sufficient. Beyond their sometimes shocking aspects, this siege mentality and the resulting quest for security are changing our very concept of justice and law. This enormous legal chal-lenge was avidly pondered, with great perspicacity, at the Institute of Advanced Studies on Justice.[9]

Risk Phobia

An observation: in the last few years, two concepts have taken over the universe of the law: *violence*, and *security*. France's New Penal Code, promulgated in 1993, bears witness. "The title of the chapter on sexual violence in the new Penal Code has been changed: it is no longer 'attacks against manners,' as it was called in 1810, but 'sexual aggression,' no longer alluding to decency but exclusively to violence."[10]

A sign of the times: sexual questions were a priority in the French parliamentary debates of June 1991, at which this new Penal Code was discussed. Admittedly, the spokesman for the draft of the law, Michel Pezet, had declared from the start that, "We need to distinguish which aspects of sexual behavior concern the moral or religious law and what relates to criminal law." In fact, however, the repressive aspect largely carried the day. Would be this only because of the increasing difficulty of agreeing on a set of shared beliefs? "The parliamentary debates on the subject [were] symptomatic of today's difficulty in locating a standard to which we can refer, in a historical moment when the respective places of men and women have been mixed up and their relations have become a question without any clear answer."[11]

In spite of Jacques Toubon's protests (he was Minister of Justice) on principle about the article dealing with sexual harassment ("I have much more faith in human comportment than in legal penalties)," this new Penal Code conveyed a powerful truth, underlined by Alain Ehrenberg. "Criminality is occupying a greater and greater place in French society."

The philosopher Philippe Raynaud goes still further. Behind this obsessive will to *use the penal system* to eradicate any form of violence and insecurity (and not only when it comes to sexual delinquency), he thinks he sees something that he calls "a new sanitarianism." He uses it to indicate "a new approach, in which standards are set independently of any 'traditional' or 'authoritative' moralistic injunction. They are based on public interests that are obvious in themselves and on universally acceptable values. The interdict arises from an objectively seen danger, from the victims' point of view."

So, now we are expecting the same thing from criminal law that we are counting on from medicine: a maximum guarantee of security, a hypothetical zero degree of risk, insurance against every conceivable harm. Because we are afraid. Here, in terms of law and order, we are matching the contemporary obsession with "perfect health" mentioned above. Lucien Sfez has analyzed the utopian and *ideological* — in the literal meaning of the term — qualities of that obsession (like "communication").[12] The *safe* society, from any point of view (sexual, etc.), is the new goal we are striving to attain. The repressive arsenal will be built up to help us get there faster. The penal code, the law's blunt instrument, thus becomes "the only code of conduct in a disorientated" and more anxious society every day. With the help of media exposure, the public life is taking on the form of an interminable plea to the authorities, who are urged to punish, to compensate, to reassure, to take care of us on every front where the danger could emerge. Seen in this light, Antoine Garapon's and Denis Salas' reading of the new Penal Code, vehicle of what they call "the new signs of insecurity," is more worrying still.

They say that the doctrines of the new Penal Code could be summarized like this: "Children, watch out for your parents; they may mistreat you or misuse you. Wives, look out for your husbands, who may be violent. Employees, keep an eye on the owners, who may harass you; restaurant-goers, make sure your table-mates don't smoke. Be careful of your sexual partner, who may infect you, of the driver who can kill you, etc.. We are at war against a faceless enemy .... The new Penal Code involuntarily shows the link between two contradictory schools of thought as to contemporary individualism, that of the claim to infinite rights and that of the demand for protection."[13]

This heightened anxiety about violence, this pervasive phobia of the public danger in whatever form, are related to the oft-denounced social rifts and the progressive crumbling of "the common good." A society of isolated individuals, disjointed, lacking strong family, political or social ties, tends to become an endless confrontation of competing desires, the generator of innumerable "damages" that each person seeks to have compensated. "Living together" sooner or later leads to endless territorial "disputes" which the so deeply revered law will have to arbitrate, day after day, under the glare of the media. This starts to look like an example of what Girard called "the mimetic crisis" or the war of all against all.

Even worse than this insecurity that is little by little taking over our lives is the social inequality that is enjoying a comeback in our de-mocracies. In the last few decades, as we know, the inequalities in Western societies have widened, but they have also become much more visible. Fear is now accompanied by an insidious sense of injustice, of envy and of not being treated rightly; as a consequence protests are mounting. The exaggerated reliance on the penal system is seen like a final recourse, a consolation prize. The intrepid little judge and the business owner standing trial (or better still, imprisoned) become char-acters in a theatrical confrontation that replaces yesterday's social struggles. The law books will avenge us against society. Society as a whole is perceived more and more as a jungle dominated by two risks. "First, obviously, we see the weakest ones abandoned to the private relations of forces, and the number of victims of freedom keeps going up. Second, we see the [vertiginous] increase of each person's responsi-bility, which is the other side of the coin of the freedom of morality; and no one knows where it will end."[14]

Conversely, the obsession with an omnipresent and unforeseeable public danger, this time coming from the bottom of society, literally undermines what is commonly called the "privileged classes," in truth the so-called silent majority. The housing projects, the unemployed and the homeless already fill the role held by the "dangerous" classes in the imagination of the 19th century. The "haves" feel besieged by the "have-nots." The sexual pervert, hunting down isolated women or children, is always just but one aspect of this all-surrounding threat. In the end, everything conspires to make the concern for security override any other consideration. Just think, France had 120,000 police officers and 90,000 gendarmes already, in 1996, and 100,000 private security agents.

It's a safe bet that these numbers will go up further.

The Return of the 'Bad Guy'

The first consequence of this fear is quite evident: our societies are gradually getting used to thresholds of repression that, until recently, would have scandalized anyone who heard about it. Today, people not only call for the culprit to be punished, but to be put away for good, i.e. his expulsion from society, without appeal. In the United States, an incredibly severe law has been put into effect. It picks up the old rule that used to be practiced in Europe — a life sentence for anyone who commits three serious crimes of similar nature. It's called, "Three strikes and you're out."

In France, this required expulsion is particularly clear in sex cases. "All the debate on sexual delinquents, for which many countries are establishing very long sentences," reckons Claude Faugeron, "is for no other purpose than to find a place where they can be put away in a more or less forever."[15]

Admittedly, the fear of sex-related murders of children is both comprehensible and legitimate. One can never discover the extent and the baseness of these crimes without feeling a distress that nothing can mitigate. The immense protest marches in Belgium during the summer of 1996, after the arrest of the pedophile murderer Marc Dutroux, are a sign of that. Nonetheless, this impulse, like it or not, is related to a vengeful view of justice, which the legal system strictly has tried to avoid. Isn't justice, in the civilized meaning of the word, a voluntary and codified renunciation of private revenge? This vengeful aspect is making a big comeback today, helped by the ostentatious and emotional character of the new "media justice," carried out under the glare of TV cameras. How can we deny that these televised exhibitions of the suspect, finally flushed out, mimic a ritual lynching whose function is to alleviate the crowd's fury by directing it toward an individual promised as a sacrifice?

The sexual pervert embodies the ideal culprit in more ways than one. First, because his crime is inexcusable — and especially when the victim is a child, our last taboo; then, because it is the wrong to take literally all the sexual licenses that society has granted verbally or in fantasy. He is implicitly burdened with a kind of remorse or inadmissible collective disorder. The intensity of the demand for punishment that is heaped upon him is commensurate with this disorder. It is powerful enough to break the traditional limits — moderation, concern for reintegrating the offender into society, compassion, etc. — that society considered essential in normal times. Only punishment and eradication matter, now. In demanding that, our societies trap themselves in a strange contradiction since they continue to call just as loudly for maximum freedom and maximum repression.

It is true that this ritual of lynching by the media and the legal system has the same extenuating virtues as sacrificial murder had in primitive societies. For the inchoate and distressing notion of public violence, it substitutes the clear and reassuring scene of the culprit punished by all the decent folk. That is exactly how the penal system comes to be substituted for the political. "The democracy of opinion prefers stories that are easy to grasp, like lawsuits, where it is easy to see who is good and who is bad. When the political no longer offers guideposts for judging the experience of society, the crude figure of the 'bad guy' makes his return in democracy. When there are no more external enemies, crime and the criminals provide the repulsive figures around which unity can be forged, the sacred union, even, and which the political requires to justify its actions. Thus the importance taken on by the murder of child (the incarnation of absolute evil, often compared to Nazism), or to a lesser degree, mistreatment of children, which in all our democracies has become a 'great national cause.'"[16]

It doesn't take much effort to see how greatly this state of mind differs from that of the Seventies, years during which people still wondered about the effects of imprisonment, the symbolic scope of criminal law and the role prisons play in society. Garapon and Salas have insisted, rightly, on the course of these "humanistic" years or, more precisely, how far we have allowed ourselves to regress without actually realizing it. "Prison isn't very interesting any more," they write, "since public opinion seems to have become resigned to this necessary evil. How far we have come from the time when Foucault and other intellectuals called attention to the scandal of the prisons! And worse, security now gets top billing in political speeches and one might even say that, aside from a bit of tut-tutting in the evening news, not only is prison no longer shocking, but now it goes hand-in-hand with a new discourse on moral responsibility that is less concerned with understanding than with reparations."[17]

Private Despotism

Moreover, the expression "the criminalization of society" could easily be misconstrued. Beginning with sex cases (pedophilia, incest, sexual harassment, etc.) the fundamental phenomenon is not only that the Penal Code is being substituted for the social contract, but this substitution implies *the gradual investment by the law of what used to be called the private space.* Remember the beautiful formula from the senior Carbonnier, who articulated a general principle that is now repudiated. "Where the private, intimate life, is concerned, the prevailing wind is the renunciation of the law." He meant that the law was to be applied more lightly, less heavy-handed and directive, as it approached the hard core of private space, that is, our intimacy. The latter was to be left, as much as could be, to the free regulation of consensus, affection, domestic autonomy. That was one of the oldest axioms of our consensual legal philosophy inherited from Roman law. Things have really changed. Now we have the law, including in its most severe version, i.e. capital punishment, bursting forth in the private sphere.

There are reasons for that. Our era has lost its equilibrium, now that neither morality, traditional affiliations, the family as an institution nor, of course, shared values can dominate the private sphere. An open vacuum that feeds our insecurity is gaping ever wider, even in the heart of our intimate lives. A vacuum that Boris Cyrulnik describes as follows. "The culture where we find ourselves is no longer shaping family roles: fathers feel less like fathers in the company of their daughters, and mothers start to feel less like mothers with their sons. The increase in mixed marriages, the higher incidence of rape, the banalization of pregnancies outside of stable families, all reflect the same phenomenon: our culture, traditionally mediated by affective relations, is no longer shaping our behaviors."[18]

The boundaries between public and private have become blurred. In the contemporary imagination, the private space tends to become a dangerous zone where the weak is all the more threatened by the powerful since violence can take advantage of the fact that the law is hesitant to interfere. "The risk that the relations will be based on relative strength, in closed spaces, [means] the retreat of public space, that is, the haunting fear of an intolerable society where each one is at the mercy of the other. Thus the temptation to use the criminal law to maintain the interdicts, to confine the balance of forces in all areas of human activity within reasonable limits, in a word, to maintain the distances necessary so that each one stays in his place. But it is no longer clear where that place is."[19]

That is the other side of the progressive deregulation of our societies: a continuous retreat of the public space (and the public services), a weakening of the collective in favor of the private, a continuous retreat of the State vis-a-vis the market, the obliteration of the good common in favor of personal interests, etc.. The automatic side-effect of this vast privatization of society is the invasion of our private space by the legal system. The law is now summoned to protect the wife against her husband, the child against his father, the pupil against his teacher, the sister against her brother, etc.. The legal system has become a permanent referee for domestic disputes.

This is the main topic of the mass media, after day *ad nauseum*. The media tracks "the bad guy" right inside his private bunker and is pleased that justice can, in such and such case, hunt down what might be called domestic despotism. People are encouraged to cross the borders of their own private lives to flush out problems that these boundaries could disguise. The right to interfere, so dear to the militant humanitarian, has been extended to the family domain. The social worker and the examining magistrate have been promoted to Doctors of Moral Prevention.

As the legal code, the police force and the judge invade the territory of intimacy, the phenomenon is portrayed as a victory for the individual, so well endowed with rights and prerogatives, a victory achieved against the antiquated and barbarian impunity of the group. One can, certainly, regard that as progress for humans right and civilization and, in certain cases, it indubitably is such. Suddenly, that which "was rather shamefully tolerated" no longer is, and a notorious injustice that used to be sheltered behind a wall of privacy is now being addressed. However, we have yet to consider how this affects the family institution.[20] Suffice it to say, for the moment, that our concept of the law has been reduced to a tangled skein of contradictions and even of nonsense. Too much law destroys freedom.

Legal Distress

Thus the legal system — the law itself — is brought to bear on matters where it used to have no bearing and for purposes that were not within its area of competence. "The legal field suddenly acquired an elevated status in our democratic societies. Whereas it used to be expected to smooth out social relations, to serve as a link to the actions of the State or to protect morals, now all of a sudden it is expected to manage everything in the world. When the religions have deserted the democratic scene, when the ideologies fall far short of utopias and the welfare state is at the end of its resources, we turn to the law to demand justice."[21]

In the United States, the tougher stance on sexual harassment corresponds to this same phenomenon of defining the private space in criminal terms. For the criminalization (of harassment) goes well beyond simply defining behaviors and practices that clearly should be punished. "The gradual generalization of the concept basically aims to abolish any form of ambiguity in social relations; it *represents a need to encode in law the most private conduct.*"[22]

We all are witness — directly or via the media — of Rocambolesque situations where judges and police officers implicated, against their will, in private disputes where the conflict is not between legally identifiable interests but between irreducible beliefs, between incompatible world views and moral systems. Then they are required not just to recite the law but to enforce a value, to set a moral or philosophical standard. They are promoted to guardians not only of the law but of the meaning, supermen in spite of themselves, charged with "performing miracles." Society has tossed off onto them the job of producing the necessary symbols. "The legal ensemble" thus conceived, i.e. diverted from its natural role, is supposed to mitigate the inadequacy of the collective standards.

And the legal sector will have to do the job within an acrimonious context, made mercilessly confrontational, with a rigid list of fines for various infractions. These "fines" are likely to cause more and more countries to fall into the same pattern as the U.S., where the systematic penal treatment of sex cases has accelerated the growth of sex-related business. In the U.S., indeed, the new interpretation of the concept of sexual harassment has made the lawyers rich. Since 1990, the number of complaints for sexual harassment has tripled, from 5,000 to 16,000 per annum. And the number of specialized law firms has gone up, too. A new business was born. Since 1992, at least 2,000 have added sexual harassment to the list of their best sources of income, along with civil liability and medical malpractice.[23]

But let's not miss the forest for the trees. In America as in Europe, the business side's jubilation hardly masks the intensity of the distress. Confronted with the breakdown, even the disappearance of all standards, the Western individual feels crushed, overwhelmed by the weight of responsibility in a realm with no guidelines. As Marcel Gauchet said in 1985, libertarian individualism has been transformed into timorous individualism, for "we pay for the decline of religion by the difficulty of being oneself." And he added more precisely, "Now we have vowed to live our lives stripped naked and in the anguish that was, by the grace of the gods, more or less spared us since the beginning of the human adventure. Each person has to work out the answers for himself."[24] Pierre Legendre, coming from another direction, arrived at the same conclusion but expressed it with jeering rage. "The supposed conviviality, de-theatralized, de-ritualized, breaks humanity, destroys the individuals by leaving them alone face to face with nothing. Muddle through, take drugs, commit suicide, it's your business. There are mechanics who will repair if it is reparable, and cops if not."[25] We've already spoken about the cops. We'll look at the "mechanics" in a bit.

Misery and fragility of the individual, indeed! Ehrenberg expresses the same idea when he notes that the new freedom of manners, the limits of which can no longer really be specified, "results in making the individual bear increasingly heavy responsibilities, and exhaust himself psychologically with constant self-questioning."[26] Irene Théry sees this "duo of isolation and solipsism... [as] the flip side of individualistic emancipation."[27] This individualism is all the more difficult to assume when it comes to morés since, in their casual inconsistency, our societies continue to display that which they claim to repress and to sell to the highest bidder the things they ostensibly prohibit.

Judges and police officers have been assigned the (inherently impossible) mission of dealing with this inconsistency. Panicky — and ineffective — reliance on the law has made the law less meaningful; especially since, as a result of the liberalization of morés, "the law has lost any meaning."[28] Théry, a specialist in family law, makes a remark concerning divorce which could apply to all private questions. "Now the law is nowhere and everywhere, having lost its meaning but become inflated in its power."[29]

How the judge escape this ontological trap? Quite simply: by palming it off, in turn, onto another protagonist, the psychiatrist or the doctor. The judge, constrained and backed into a corner, withdraws more and more from the task of judging, in the literal meaning of the term. "He gives the impression of being a powerless power, who delegates to the parties themselves and to their counsel, or sometimes to an expert, the task of coming to a decision.... This is further confirmed every year, through the debates on guardianship of children, the paternal and maternal roles... it de-legitimizes all the principles of justice and the fictions of the law, in favor of a standardization of morals allegedly founded on the "facts" of social science, justifying the use of psychosocial techniques to regulate the conflicts."[30]

Should "shrinks" be charged, like the cavalry in western movies, with riding to the rescue of our besieged justice system?

The Return of Scientism

The growing role played in the courts by "experts" of all kinds, sexologists, psychiatrists, sociologists and neurologists, is a very worrisome phenomena, and it is further worrisome that it is so rarely denounced. It is a sign of "psychologizing" the law, of slipping toward interpreting the law as a matter of psychology, which the lawyers are the first to decry. And, this bewildered reliance on an alleged scientific rationality testifies to a paradoxical naiveté. It is more dangerous than most people think.

Although we are impatient at any talk of setting moral standards, and instinctively rebel against any ethical judgement founded on belief and responsibility, we have no problem capitulating before the false majesty of medicine. While we are suspicious of political or social institutions, we superstitiously idolize the "wise man" who states his conclusions. His knowledge impresses us. We lose our critical thinking in his presence. We accept his diagnoses with docility. We even ask for this therapeutic solicitude. Think how easily the verdict of one of these experts is accepted, how piously their decisions about family or personal tragedies are welcomed, and given precedence over any other consideration. Scornfully rejecting the moralist, the philosopher and the priest, we thus agree to make Hippocrates our new spiritual adviser.

Admittedly, one might object that the expert's counsel is only advisory, and that the decision still rests with the judge. We know very well, however, that it is not how things turn out. The medical categorization of a defendant is, in itself, a sentence that has to do with his being put away where he can do no harm, that is, with "getting rid of him." Science is thus used as another means of putting someone behind bars. We count on both the prison *and* the "shrink's" verdict to protect us from people who scare us. "Society is losing all distinction between treatment and punishment, between prison and alternative measures. The evil is so great that prison is the only choice and life sentences are the only possible duration. Given that we cannot actually act on an unverifiable sexual instinct, this is yet another field where there is only one socially-acceptable line of thought, and it comes down hard on our worst enemy, the pervert."[31]

This hasty recourse to knowledge (which we prefer to forget is random, contestable, falsifiable in Karl Popper's sense [32]) is literally a superstition. It is terrifying. It perpetuates antiquated and cruel legal traditions linking sexuality and criminal law to medical theory. For centuries and centuries (since ancient Rome), judges, politicians and tyrants have claimed a medical basis to justify their judgments. When it comes to sex, history offers us deviance, perversion, normality, the most extraordinary collection of medical bloopers ever. And each epoch stigmatizes the ignorance of the earlier days.

Thus we laugh when we hear that Doctor Julien Virey, to cite one case out of a thousand, learnedly demonstrated in 1880 that it was "the energy of the sperm" that protected the married woman. "It is certain," he wrote, "that male sperm impregnates the woman's organism, that it revives and catalyzes all its functions."[33] We are revolted, rightly, by the scientific "vilification" of Onanism by the doctors of the 18th and 19th centuries. We are frightened, rightly, to learn that Stalin had appealed to the "certainty" of another doctor, Zaldkin, to justify the return to a strict sexual morality 1932. This Zaldkin declared — believing in it himself, no doubt — that feeling "sexual attraction for a person of the enemy class is as perverse as feeling sexual attraction for an orangutan or a crocodile." He also considered that it was extremely detrimental to the health and "the citizen's creative energy" to repeat the sex act too often.

On the other hand, we don't say a word after the often rather Molièresque tirades of the "sex experts" that our courts listen to, for want of anything better, and that television echoes into every living room. Especially when they are talking about a completely irredeemable pervert.

Why are we so docile?

The "Monster" Character

Fear is what most inclines us toward this positivist regression. Making legal problems into medical problems allows for the oldest figures of criminal science to stage a comeback. That is, the alleged "criminal nature," that old saw in criminology, which is to criminal law what the reference to "the strong sex" is to anthropology. And that of the "natural-born criminal," inherited from Italian criminologist Cesare Lombroso, author of The Criminal Man (1874). A disciple of Darwin and a radical believer in evolutionary theories, Lombroso reckoned that devi-

270

ance and crime were purely biological phenomena. In his eyes, the natural-born criminal (who could be identified by certain anatomical and physiological characteristics) was only an accidental survival of the primitive savage. That medical experts should say what constitutes a sexual pervert is clearly as obsolete and off-base as were Gobineau's theories on the inequality of the human races or the Nazis' view of the morphology of the Jew. True, it makes it possible to justify irrevocably eliminating the new "monster," that is, danger. How can we be so careless about the gravity of these retrogressions?

The judges from the (French) Institute of Advanced Studies on Justice comment nervously on this trend of contemporary criminology in the field of sexual delinquency. "We are at the far end of the spectrum from the notion of responsibility, which holds that everyone is accountable for his own decisions or, at the very least, promptly recalls him to this accountability. How can we sentence an individual in this state? Only a flexible sentence, subordinated to the relevant expert opinions, becomes relevant. The expert becomes the judge, due to a positivism that one would think was void of psychiatry. The idea of being dangerous makes the sex pervert the scapegoat of our fears, and precludes any possibility of rehabilitation and reintegration into society."[34]

The mechanical way in which we, in all good conscience, draw the line between normality and perversity thus has the advantage of making it easier to put delinquents away for good. The figure of the "psychopath" or the "monster" who can be treated with chemicals, with a medical regimen, or by being quarantined, has become omnipresent in the media. But that is not all. Medicalizing the problem voids the idea of responsibility, freedom, repentance and reintegration. It conveniently enables us to circumvent any moral debate. As far as sexuality, society is made up only of "normal" people and "abnormal" people. It is regulated by medical criteria, which can be identified and dealt with as such. Accepting the notion that human freedom is constantly confronted with the temptation to commit the act, confronted with complex and unforeseeable impulses that a minimal structuring of the personality enables us to resist — the idea of an individual facing up to and taking responsibility for his free will — all that is swept aside by the hypothesis of some kind of hormonal predestination. This not only does away with the idea of each person choosing between Good and Evil, but in the extreme, it does away with the concept of humanity itself.

Through a pathetic irony of history, we are reintroducing in this way something that we had so much difficulty to vanquish (for example in terms of homosexuality): the idea of a physiological abnormality of nature, instead of a free choice taken in all consciousness. Wrongfully reassured by the false majesty of the scientist, we fail to guard against the insidious standards that will be set if we allow the question to be considered as a medical issue. In the United States, a too intense sex drive is sometimes regarded as a dysfunction or a dependence (addiction), which can be addressed in a private clinic. The moral order is at risk of being replaced by a medical order; we will regret it.

Foucault, in all his honor, had suspected this type of Orwellian evolution. He suggested that we could very well find new — and very effective — ways to control our desires; a certain form of order would be maintained not by institutions, but by blackmailing each other with normality and by manipulating desires according to an alleged *scientia sexualis*.[35] In place of regulators, we would have widespread publicity campaigns and a *doxa* wrongly considered to be benevolent. He traced the emergence of this positivist-inspired Inquisition to the 19th century.

More surprising is that the doctors themselves, in particular the "shrinks," are not always happy with the crushing burden they are charged with in connection with sexual delinquency. That can be judged by this protest, *inter alia*, from a psychoanalyst. "Why call on psychic questions and "specialists" if it is really a social vision, a security and medical issue that puts the subjective dimensions in second place and considers endocrinology the driving force.... The shrinks, in spite of themselves, are set up as both wizards and arms of justice: for this reason, they can only fail. If this trend continues, in the medium term, witch hunting is likely to start very soon. Especially if the shrinks, giving in to the temptation of absolute power that is being offered to them, do not make clear that they are neither wizards nor magicians."[36]

*
* *

Believing we obey Dionysiac promises of freedom, refusing any concerted codification of our desires, we have exposed ourselves to an extraordinary snarl of contradictory meanings. The moral responsibility that we refuse to internalize anymore since it is the sign of "alienation" (what a furor that word made in the 1970's!), now we humbly give it to the judge and the doctor. Entirely lost, we are looking for their science to provide with at least minimal guideposts, thin substitutes for the ethical and religious beliefs of yesteryear. The damage, the risk, the cost, the pathology, the penal code, the emotional and televised revenge: such are the new regulations whose tyranny we accept henceforth.

With such humility! And such improvidence!

CHAPTER 13

HOMOSEXUALS AND FEMINISTS, STILL CRUSADING

Few debates today are as spontaneously combustible as those on homosexuality and feminism. The passions that flair up at once, the polemic that is unleashed, the excommunications pronounced on both sides, all contrast with the persistent anemia of the usual social quarrels, the discouraged resignation that reigns — except for sporadic exceptions — on the labor front and at the factory gate. It all seems as if the combative and militant capacities were (temporarily?) expatriated, from the plant into daily life, from the trade-union meeting to demonstrations of Act Up. Abortion, condoms, AIDS, Gay Pride, gender equality, ordinary racism — such are, for the moment, in the West — the territories of the conflict and the principal objects of what Pierre Bourdieu calls "the dissensus." Verbal violence and fortifying mobilization on one side; trade-union misery, political correctness and resignation disturb the other. That's how it is.

Hardly a week goes by, in any case, without a debate in the United States or in Europe, that ignites the media about morality. With a violence that, *mutatis-mutandis*, prolongs and replaces that of the social and political struggles of the 1960's and 70's. Having disappeared from that arena, the constructivist energy re-appears here; disparaged in the realm of political economy, activism still has a role in the other one. Think back, over the last several years, on the virulence of the verbal conflicts over the inadequate public health policies concerning AIDS, the sexual compromising of male politicians in the Anglo-Saxon world, the innumerable legal episodes tied to sexual harassment, and the inexcusable confrontations about building a gay community in France. These texts, vengeful official statements, petitions and press releases, irresistibly recall (albeit in a different form) the virulence of yesterday's ideological confrontations over totalitarianism, nationalization, the Cold War, imperialism and the Vietnam War. The same parochialism, the same meticulous hearkening back to fundamental texts and to the struggles of those who went before, the same generous but vague lyricism in the argumentation. The traitor to the community and the hetero-fascist have simply replaced the class enemy, the exploitative bourgeoisie.

The private domain, that of the body, of self expression, of gender relations, has become a battlefield. How can we complain or pretend to be surprised? The apotheosis of individualism, the priceless heritage of the "revolution within the revolution" of the 1970's, logically indicated that liberty as the principal goal. A goal that is all the more crucial since the recently achieved individual emancipation is still not very secure; it is haunted by a thousand contradictions, and undermined by the famous difficulty of being oneself (evoked by Gauchet in connection with modernity). We are emancipated but abandoned to our loneliness, after the great retreat of the community; we are inclined to make this triumphant Me into an asset to be defended.

The metaphor of the asset is quite apt. If the polemic is so harsh, that is because the achievements of the 1970's touching on individualism — the acceptance of homosexuality, women's liberation, etc. — are more fragile than one would think. The media consensus on this subject — almost unanimously favorable — cannot mask things for ever. While the risk of going back to the bad old days of the moral order is just nonsense, still homophobia persists, antiquated machismo lingers, and repressive nostalgia is still with us. You can easily verify that by listening to or reading the leaders of the far Right (and sometimes of the Right, or even of the Left). They don't accept the liberalization of mores, including the most legitimate aspects, any better than the same parties accepted the Republic at the beginning of the century. In spring 1997, after the exaggeratedly publicized cases of pedophilia, posters were displayed throughout Paris denouncing all French homosexuals in a tone and with an aggressiveness that one would have thought we were through with. All things considered, it follows that homophobia and machismo must be treated like racism and anti-Semitism: we must not lower our guard. "The reduction of social guilt" for homosexuals does not mean there won't be any possibility of discriminatory back-sliding.

But does maintaining our vigilance preclude any further reflection? Must we hold back our objections and criticism under the pretext that the enemy is at the gates? Must we remain paralyzed, as before, by the maddening fear of doing our cause more harm than good? Not only would that be nonsensical in principle, but such a capitulation would be even more regrettable since the virulence of the polemic hides a beautiful richness of reflection in this field; reflection which, starting with sexuality, opens out onto far broader prospects.

Homophobia and the Gay Community

On the "gay" front, most militant organizations in France and elsewhere insist that what they call "the homosexual community" is highly vulnerable. Successful repetitions of the Gay Pride parade, the wealth of the gay market, the undeniable influence of the gay lobby should not give us any illusions, they say. Like racism, like authoritarian tendencies, homophobic reprobation continues to flourish. In certain social milieux, in certain families or regions, it is as hard as to be openly gay as it was years ago. Brandishing the achievements of gay sensibility, including legislative victories, cannot erase the myriad sufferings that persist, the myriad dangers that remain. The battle isn't over.

This fragility provides the justification for the existence of a community, in the social and cultural sense of the term, and its role as a haven. Just as anti-Semitism contributed to the ghetto, just as ordinary racism encourages cultural differentiation, ambient homophobia produces the automatic inclination toward a distinct tribalism, with its special neighborhoods, its hangouts, its shops, its codes and, finally, its claims to an identity. All the campaigns that noisily assert a difference and what is known as gay pride are based on this inconsolable concern: no victory is ensured, nothing is ever fully achieved.[1]

For advocates of this defensive militancy, certain debates

(imprudent? hasty? unjust?) concerning the homosexual question run the risk of weakening the freedom that so laboriously has been gained, by giving weapons to the adversaries. As proof, they pint to the jubilant haste with which the extreme Right press picks up every criticism levied, internally, against the communitarian ideology or the original imprudence of homosexual associations in connection with AIDS.[2] Traditional demagogy and a message that has been diverted on the topic: a gay intellectual recognizes it, you know — and so on.[3]

Challenging the charge of communitarianism that is sometimes imputed to them, the defenders of the right to be different dispute, furthermore, that — at least in France — you could make the homosexuals out to be an arrogant group of individualists that threaten national cohesion and the Republic. For them, the community remains threatened, in abeyance, more tolerated than accepted. It consequently requires defending, not criticizing. "The community," points out Philippe Mangeot, an Act Up activist, "is also built on a common experience of discrimination. Every homosexual teenager has had, at one time or another, the feeling of not being at home, not being where he belonged. However, learning not to be afraid, that too comes with being part of a group."[4]

Should these things be discussed completely openly, or should people militate while keeping quiet about the rest? This dilemma coincides on many points with the quarrel which that, toward the end of the Eighties, set the militant antiracists against certain sociologists and intellectuals who were frightened to see a media-fed antiracism that rallied around a thoughtless cultural differentiation, a differentiation which, paradox of paradoxes, belongs as much to the ideological baggage of the new Right.[5] Disastrous thoughtlessness, superficial good intentions, the rhetoric of finer feelings: this "sympathetic antiracism," more or less used by the French government in the mid-1980's, was officially criticized rule by researchers like Pierre-Andre Taguieff, who is certainly on the Left. At the time, these criticisms were criticized, using the argument that what was most urgent was above all to fight racism, to avoid being mistaken for the enemy, to avoid giving the adversary any weapons, etc..

"You criticize anti-racism," objects one side, "but racism has not disarmed. You must be mad! You don't like to emphasize cultural differentiation, but you forget that the alleged racial differences continue to cause hatred and rejection, day after day. Much effort and time were required to bring together a debate over antiracism, a delicate issue whose relevance is recognized today. All critical questioning about the homosexual difference runs up against a difficulty that is in all points comparable to this, which can be boiled down to one simple question: that of opportunity.

This is an urgent matter, requiring very astute handling. But debates that are put off always return, sooner or later, and usually under the worst conditions.

The "Invention" of Homosexuality

All this justifies caution when it comes the notion of the "gay community." Why? Because militant good intentions in relation to homosexuality, as with anti-racism, can lead to fatal conceptual blunders. This mistrust of building a separate community has been articulated very lucidly for several years, especially by Michel Foucault and Gilles Deleuze.6 Deleuze and Foucault were among the first to be concerned about the snares that lie hidden within the demand for homosexual rights — a demand that they did support, in principle. They were concerned, for example, that the perception of systematic victimization can gradually induce a defensive and hurt attitude, which is not consistent with self-assertion. Likewise with the campaign in favor of acknowledging being gay, of coming out of the closet (which was very popular in the 1970's and 1980's). Wasn't this excessive tendency toward public confession, which Foucault resisted, likely to feed a kind of reverse dogmatism and create a new form of alienation?

After all, why would one impose this declaration of sexual identity as if it were of a collective duty and a personal achievement? Those who obstinately refused to make the public avowal that the dominant thought seemed to make compulsory were not necessarily cowards. They were taking a different stand.

But what appeared most dangerous to Foucault was the consideration of a sexual preference as an *essential* characteristic. Would homosexuality alone determine one's identity? The ancient Greeks would have found the question absurd. As we know, Greek public opinion did not condemn homosexual practices. On the other hand, making such a preference absolute would have been a completely alien idea. In Athens, various practices were freely accepted; there was no homosexuality as such, that is, final, and exclusive.

"Loving one's own sex or loving the opposite sex," Foucault wrote, "did not appear to the Greeks to be two exclusive choices, two types of radically different behavior. The dividing lines were not so clear. The distinction between a temperate man who was master of himself and the one devoted himself to the pleasures was, from the point of view of morality, much more important than the distinction between the categories of pleasures in which one most readily indulged. Having loose morals meant being known to resist neither women nor boys, it didn't mean having a preference for one or the other. . . . We might call them "bisexuals" since they were open to choosing either of the two sexes, but they did not see it as a dichotomy. In their eyes, what led one to choose either a male or female lover was the general appetite that nature had established in the heart of man for those who are "beautiful," whatever their gender might be."[7]

Today's claims to a special identity literally would be incomprehensible for an Athenian. Would you (if you did not have to) assert a status that, once obtained, would lock you into one role as narrowly as does one's marital status? Why would one claim "the right" to be seen and identified only on the basis of gender preference? Can a person be summarized by his or her sexuality? That would not only seem absurd to Plutarch's contemporaries but it is shocking even now. Doesn't it amount to giving in to the injunctions of the critic? Isn't it like inviting everyone to wear a pink triangle on his chest? The Greeks were not the only ones to shy away from such a possibility. In the Middle Ages, no one who engaged in buggery would have accepted being labeled once and for all as a "bugger." Later figures such as Louis XIII (tempted for a moment by the brilliant Marquis de Cinq-Mars, whose real name was Henri d'Effiat), Louis-Armand, Prince de Conti, or Gaston d'Orleans or the Prince de Guéménée, were all sensitive to the allure of young men, but they would not have agreed to be defined as sodomites and members of a community that was defined by its sexual practices.

One should bear in mind a chronological detail: it was in the 19th century, at the apotheosis of middle-class puritanism and the most standard-setting scientism, that the homosexuality was defined as a category of its own. That did not happen by chance. Foucault pointed out this coincidence and emphasized the dangers that it heralded.

"Sodomy — that referred to in old law, whether civil or canonical — was a type of prohibited act; the person who committed the acts was only a judicial entity. In the 19th century, the homosexual became a person, with a past, a history and a childhood, a character, a lifestyle; and a morphology also, with an indiscreet anatomy and perhaps a mysterious physiology. No aspect of his being was separate from his sexuality. . . . The sodomite was a backslider, the homosexual now became a species."[8]

It is not only the culture of the ghetto that we should avoid, but the alienating categorization of desire, the eagerness to state a *definition* that will then be used to set up a conflict with oppressions supposedly coming from the outside. This fetish for declaring an identity is, it is true, much more pronounced in Great Britain and the U.S. than it is in Europe. A recent scientific event proved that. In the early 1990's, the separatist leanings of the American gay community led many of its members to greet rather favorably the fairly eccentric (and since contradicted) notion that there could be a "homosexual gene," Xq28, a hypothesis advanced by Dr. Dean Hammer, of the National Institute of Cancer in Washington.

This researcher thought that homosexuality originated in a genetic characteristic present from birth. In spirit, the discovery of this biological marker was providential since it anointed the gay community with an irrefutable legitimacy, founded on *both* science and their status as victims. If homosexuals are genetically different, people said, then that means they are not responsible, neither they nor their parents. They cannot be reproached for the nature of their desires, any more than one might oblige a person to answer for the color of his skin. The alleged homosexual gene allowed gay Americans scientifically to attain the "privileged minority" status so gratifying in America. And that made it all the more legitimates, they added, if they wanted to display their difference and take pride in it.

In France, on the contrary, Hammer's hypothesis alarmed most homosexuals, and with reason. Most of them saw it as a genetic theory that might be compared to the eugenics delusions of the Nazis. This reaction shows that the idea of building a special community continues to run counter to the anthropological and cultural orientation in France, which is profoundly infusedwith universalism. Compared to the Anglo-Saxons, the French have less instinct to a reflex of categorical classification, and are less inclined to emphasize our differences. But that does not mean that such a tendency might never gain momentum. The temptation to separate into communities, as we know, is gaining ground in the Mediterranean provinces, whether in connection with homosexuality, religion, ethnic group, language, etc.

These discussions, definitely, are not merely anecdotal.

Identity with Indetermination

Sometimes, it helps to take things back to their beginning. In the final analysis, what was the original intention of liberalizing morality? To increase personal freedom. If we assume that that was desirable, the next question is to determine how personal freedom best could be en-sured concerning homosexuality — by asserting the difference, or by minimizing the difference? One has to acknowledge that those who are against the community idea are arguing from a strong position.

Let us risk a hypothesis: it is because the modern world refused to exert personal control over desires, because it avoided seeing this self-dominion (recognized by the Greeks) as the only true criterion transcending preferences, that modernity was led to categorize these same preferences. There was nothing left to do but to classify people, substituting their alleged nature (homo, hetero, bi, etc.) for the former classifications, which had been *largely related to free will*. For some thirty or more years, the permissive general populace saw unbridled self ex-pression, passion, and bewildered satisfaction as the only real value. Whoever enjoyed freely was modern; whoever resisted the "tyrant Eros" or remained faithful to any convictions was out of touch. Hence-forth, people were not categorized as chaste or libertine, self-disciplined or driven by impulses, willful or sensualist, ascetic or is de-bauched, etc.. People were categorized only by the characteristics of their desires.

This juggling act was considerably less liberating than expected. In exchange for this new license, it was tacitly acknowledged that from this point forward, everything would be linked to the specifics of one's pleasure. It was even agreed that that was OK. Anyone would yielded to an inclination in love — homosexual or otherwise — was called upon to *admit* it and to acknowledge his status. A sentence with very little room for appeal. If one rejected it, he was condemned for being

282

ashamed or for being a coward; if he went along, the community of like-minded people would be at his door to defend him. . . and to absorb him. That's a terrible choice, if you think about it. But still! How many literary variations have been published on this obsessive topic of accepting one's sexual orientation? How many testimonies have embroidered on the idea of "a victory over shame" or "a truth" that one had the courage "to look in the face." I finally could accept myself as a homosexual, etc..

No one really asked whether liberty was gaining from these changes. It was not recognized that such a distinct — and public — classification of the desires was likely to become quite simply totalitarian. Ideally, wouldn't true freedom consist in living unfettered and flexible lives, changing in response to choices that are not irrevocably limited, always negotiable, requiring neither justification nor conformity? Freedom that would include, hopefully, that of not being "only" homosexual. Isn't the most cogent utopia did not to live as a bisexual (still another category) but as supreme master of one's inclinations, including the will to resist them.

In other words, freedom proceeds more naturally from the improbable, from the random, than from stringent identity definitions. True emancipation consists less in being dissolved in one category than in escaping categorization altogether. Suggested already a quarter century ago by Deleuze and Guattari, the famous metaphor of "wishing machines," unstable and wandering, neither rigid nor even characterized, probably came closer to this ideal freedom. "We must think in dubious, improbable terms" (Deleuze). These remarks, in retrospect, seem like simple common sense. It is quite possible to detest homophobia and still feel uneasy about the aggressively community-centered claims and the festive but not very well thought-through Gay Pride marches.

Let us remember too, as Frederic Martel[9] invites us to do, that in the early 1970's, some of the slogans in the fundamental militant texts, like the *Rapport contre normalité* (Report Against Normality)[10] and *Trois Milliards de pervers* (*Three Billion Perverts*),[11] preached the indeterminate and fluid nature of sexual choice. They alluded to bisexuality, and the "wishing machines" of Deleuze and Guattari, rather than a fixed homosexual identity. These warnings were quickly forgotten.

And then? In June 1997, without denying the legitimacy of the gay pride street marches, two journalists from *Liberation* expressed a rather convincing reservation. "To be gay or lesbian," they wrote, "is not to testify, either before the court of history, nor the tribunes of the media. And even less 'to acknowledge' one's difference. To be gay is one current among others and it does not take any precedence over others, it only creates waves, swirls, a groundswell and underground disorders. . . . To be gay, to be lesbian, is rather simple. It means enduring and at the same time disappearing, persisting and desisting, creating and destroying oneself, staying and going."[12]

The Promises of "Queer Theory"

Here, however, the matter touches on something that was not anticipated. The adherents of queer theory (who are more and more active on American campuses) intend to put to rest once and for all this interminable debate between identity and indecision, communitarianism and universalism. Let us try, in few words, to explain is going on. A few years ago, the American homosexual movement was still fighting for more courses in gay and lesbian studies. They wanted to mark out a specific field of knowledge, in the name of their claims to identity. They, and the other American minorities — African-Americans, Indians, Chicanos, bisexuals, etc.. — were ardently defended by the "politically correct." This claim to an identity amounted a challenge to the universalist claim of the WASP and heterosexual culture, to make room for "other" cultures (including gay culture), that historically had been oppressed and even hidden.

In short, they wanted to make it possible to study literature, sociology or music based on works by gay or lesbians artists, to the exclusion of all others. In this way, a whole block of culture would be rescued from the injustices of oblivion, conveying a sensibility and a world vision that were irreducible. In the 1980's and early 1990's, university departments devoted to gay and lesbian studies multiplied in the United States (along with departments focusing on other minority cultures). The department founded in 1995 at Berkeley is called "Lesbian, Gay, Bisexual and Transgender Studies." These specific disciplines are starting to make an appearance today in France, but prudently, through certain conferences and specialized libraries. In France, indeed, people are wary of "the possible ghetto-ization of gay and lesbian studies, which would be prejudicial not only for those studies but for all research."[13]

The progressive ideas that make up queer theory may be quite different from what one imagines. The word queer means "strange" but, in its familiar meaning, of course, it corresponds to an insult like "fag" or "nut." By turning it away from its current meaning, and using it against its homophobic users, gay academics took it over. To simplify, let us say that queer theory proposes to revisit historical knowledge from a particular perspective, bringing out into the light of day a homosexual dimension that the dominant culture had been accustomed to glossing over. The plan makes some sense. Our culture, clearly, is full of blind spots, blank spaces, and dead ends. Modesty and the interdicts of the part have turned our memory into a sieve. The taboos are, characteristically, retrospective. As for Puritanism, especially Anglo-Saxon Puritanism, it has always been very careful over the centuries to make sure that certain silences were respected. History, inevitably read through a particular prism, dependent on a given time or culture, is thus never through with revisionism (in the noble sense of the term). Let us say that it remains in play.

It is legitimate to strive to show what effect the homosexual dimension might have had on a given event or character. It has the merit of throwing suspicion on the over-simplification and dissimulation that have led to a too strictly heterosexual view of history. This is a vast undertaking! The universities that are most advance in this field are Duke, John Hopkins and Berkeley. The principal academic proponents of queer theory are Eve Sedgwick, Judith Buttler, Jonathan Goldberg and Michael Warner.

In truth, this effort was started long ago. The principal initiator of queer thought was the gay historian John Boswell (who died of AIDS in 1984); he has been cited several times in the preceding chapters. The fundamental book outlining its principles — Christianity, Social Tolerance and Homosexuality — published in the United States (by the University of Chicago Press) in 1980 and translated into French in 1985. The paradox is that Boswell, throughout a massive militant work of five hundred pages, ends up rehabilitating the Christianity of the first centuries and the Middle Ages by showing that it was far more tolerant of homosexuals than is commonly acknowledged.

Sometimes queer theory is compared to the differentialist approach and identity politics. That's going a little too far. In fact, setting out to intrude on every sector of knowledge, to stubbornly revisit every field of study is, rather, a universalist approach, isn't it? It aims to get away from categorical and communal restrictions, a shortcoming of which gay and lesbian studies are accused, with some reason. Some got it right. "The *Queer* movement," wrote François Cusset, "stands tall, full of optimism, willingly, on a universal ground that had long been abandoned. . . . The universal is no longer the curse word that it had become under 'political correctness;' now it is the target of an underground redefinition, an appropriation — of a framework of underground reinterpretation and without adversary. . . . By a curious reversal, the universal driven out of America by the cantors of identity comes back to offer to share the difficulties of ambiguity."[14]

And if queer theory heralded, in its own way, a return to the Greek approach and the end of the ghetto? That would really be an unforeseen reversal of the "sexual revolution."

The Vitality of Feminism

There are some grounds for suggesting that within the American feminist movement a similar groping rediscovery of the universal is beginning to be felt, and a similar relearning of the voluntary control of desire.

First, let's address some misunderstandings. In France, the cult-like excesses of American/British feminism are viewed with irony — the ridiculous quarrels between radical lesbians, sadomasochistic lesbians and the militant antipornography lobby. The hyperbole and the outdated battles are not taken seriously. From a French point of view, American feminism today embodies some kind of ideological neurosis or, worse, a resurgence of castrating puritanism. It is true that in France this feminist identity — a tiny faction — never gained much of a following, even in the most militant milieux.

Monique Wittig, an emblematic figure of French feminism and author of the book *Guerillères (Women Guerillas)* in 1969, was the first to recognize it, retrospectively. She now lives in Arizona. "In France," she says, "the feminists did not want any lesbian groups to be created, I was always a thorn in their sides. . . . There, even intellectuals like Barthes and Foucault were ashamed of their homosexuality."[15]

Wittig admittedly feels alien to the dominant French sensibility for the good reason that she is an unabashed adherent of Anglo-Saxon communitarianism. The vaguely bitter irony that her remarks betray today could thus be directed to her, as well. Were political correctness and the accompanying tribal obsessions any better?

But it would be wrong to confine ourselves to this mocking universalism that we champion. In spite of the excesses, adventures, fragmentation and inexcusable exclusions, the reflection carried out within the American feminist movement on desire, pleasure, men and love are of considerable interest. Including — if you'll forgive me — for a "male" who is very French...

We should quickly summarize the dynamics and the history of the movement, since they present so rich a lesson.[16] At the start, that is in the early 1960's, feminist demands were one of the sensitivities that were expressed, in particular, on the university campuses of California and then within the Students for a Democratic Society (SDS). As their homologues would soon do in Europe, American coeds denounced the alienating character of middle-class marriage with its possessive and monogamist dimension. They intended to fight for the sovereignty of desire, the innocence of pleasure. They demanded, more simply, the right to free love.

As of this time, however, two sensitivities, two strategies came up among them. For some, the fight they were undertaking must allow women (who had been exploited and viewed as inferior for centuries) to break their chains and to catch up with men by obtaining equality of rights and station. For the others, equality with men was neither a sensible nor sufficient objective. More ambitious, they believed that it would be necessary to assert the existence of a distinct female culture. Admittedly, modesty, constancy, and the inextricable bond of desire and sentiment are cultural values inculcated in women by men, and in men's interest. But these values fostere a female approach to love, different from men's approach, more civilized, of higher moral standards and *deserving to be defended as such*. We'll have to reform men, they added, by liberating them from their own crude and brutal mode of sexuality.

The great figures of Sixties feminism are Betty Friedan, author of *The Feminine Mystique* (1963) and, of course, Kate Millet, who would publish *Sexual Politics* (1969). These two embody a very "radical" feminism (in the American meaning of the term) that would soon espouse the second tendency mentioned above.

Generally speaking the feminists, in the beginnings, shared in the permissive, hedonistic, even "Reichian" climate of the time. The advent of free sexuality seemed like a victory. And a festival. It was an example of a traditional permissive utopia which — temporarily — was actually being lived. It only took a few years, however, before the radical feminists themselves began to criticize the "sexual revolution" as it was conceived. Without realizing it, they were taking up the same concerns and objections expressed throughout history in comparable circumstances.

Simple liberation of the desires as a whole, they said, generates anarchy, a jungle, a market operating to the benefit of the strongest and to the detriment of the weakest. In fact, women were sacrificed to male desires even more crudely and brutally than before. The feminists thus denounced the supposed sexual revolution as a stratagem (conscious or unconscious) of the male culture. One of them, Shulamith Firestone, made the commonsense observation that if men were willing to give up the assurance of having a legitimate wife, it was because they "prefer from now on to have the means of consuming more of them, without having to take on their economic and sentimental maintenance." Men found it more advantageous "to increase the sexual supply while reducing the costs." Women should thus look on desire like a plague, of which they are only the victims.

More significantly still, Robin Morgan, another militant, was eager to denounce the sensualist and purely carnal vitalism that led to the pansexualism of the 1960's and 70's. "The importance attached to genital sexuality, treating bodies as objects, promiscuity, emotional detachment —" she wrote, " — all that is part of the male style, whereas we, as women, attach far more importance to love, sensuality, humor, tenderness, commitments."[17]

It is paradoxical that these militant libertarians who, as feminists, thus arrived, by roundabout ways, at positions fairly close to the most traditional moral objection (mistrust for pansexualism), even a Christian interpretation of sexuality. American university feminists would be put down for this moralism, or this neo-puritanism, especially in Europe. It is true that in their pitched battle against pornography, some of them (such as Catherine MacKinnon, Kathleen Barry and Andrea Dworkin) even allied themselves with the very far Right "leagues of virtue." This type of alliance was highly criticized within the feminist community.

In the United States, it should be said, the leagues of virtue seldom bother with nuance. The knee-jerk reference — in France — to Protestant Puritanism as a framework to explain American is suspiciously systematic, but the Puritan cultural foundation is nonetheless a reality. The first penal codes written by the founders of America were drawn from the Bible; they specified capital punishment for adultery, rape and homosexuality. Tocqueville, in *Democracy in America*, was astonished by such severity. "Simple commerce between unmarried people," he wrote, "is severely repressed by the fine, the whip or by marriage."

It would be well to remember this, if one wants to understand the extraordinary violence of the confrontations around sexual questions, in the United States.

Between Apollo and Dionysius

The paradoxical convergence between the most radical feminists and the canons of traditional morality did not stop there. Gradually, the more extreme currents within the movement headed toward a kind of neo-Encratism, a defense of continence.

Initially under the influence of the radical lesbians of the National Organization of Women (who were soon expelled) and then from their own leader, the heterosexual feminists soon came to preach a radical separatism between women and men. They would push to its logical limit the fight against sexual harassment, popularized by the famous slogan: "No means no!" Andrea Dworkin even compared the heterosexual act to an "occupation" of the woman's body and called anyone who allowed it "a collaborator."

"Many were led to conclude," wrote Michel Feher, "[that] sexual intercourse itself was an instance and an preeminent example of subjugation of women; so that a secession, at least temporary, seemed to be essential. . . .Defining the gender differences in these terms (based on Oedipal considerations) consequently forced women to adopt a moratorium on the pursuit of heterosexual relations. This interruption was necessary anyway to hasten the breakup of the patriarchal family, which functions only to continue the subjection of women by restricting both parties to their respective gender roles."

At this stage, after eighteen or nineteen centuries, the convergence with Christian Encratitism is striking: the same mistrust for the violence of desire (conceived as "a factor of dependence no matter what its object," Feher), the same will to find a way to finally invent pacific relationships, the same will to subvert the traditional family which perpetuates the subjection of women in general. In the first centuries of Christianity, it was *also* in search of emancipation from marital violence and domestic tyrannies that certain Greek and Roman ladies converted and chose chastity, to the general dismay of all the right-thinking people of the time. The *Actes de Pierre* (third century) spells it out. "But many other women," he wrote, "taken with the preaching on chastity, separated from their husbands; and men even stayed far away from their own wives' beds. . . and so a very great tumult went up in Rome."[18] In the 4th century, it was also in reaction against the male authority of the father and to escape "arranged" marriage that young Roman aristocrats chose chastity, and bequeathed their fortunes to the monks.

Strange convergence, indeed; except that neither the motivations of the feminists nor their vocabulary are comparable with those of the first Christian women. Here are some quotations randomly chosen. "Sexual relations with men such as we know them are increasingly impossible," (Andrea Dworkin). "It is enough to compare the victims' description of rape with women's description of the sex act: it is very similar," (Catherine MacKinnon, in her book *Only Words*). "Love is rape, embellished by eloquent glances. In the game of seduction, the rapist simply takes the trouble to buy a bottle of wine."[19]

In the 1970's and 80's, a great deal of reflection turned on looking further into the supposed ontological difference separating the male universe from that of women — from a feminist point of view. This phase was called "cultural feminism." It has some interest. "The cultural feminists," notes Michel Feher, "define a male culture founded on performance, competition, the will to dominate, and cold reason; but also aggressive male sexuality, objectifying, extended to promiscuity and the dissociation of desire and feeling unceasingly. These emblems of masculinity are opposed by a basically monogamist female culture, that seeks sharing and emotional intimacy, as well as a female sexuality that is diffuse more than strictly genital, and is centered on the person rather than on the body."[20]

Much has been written on the topic of the incompatibility of the male and female cultures and the difficulties in communicating across the gap; and much is still being written. One of the best-known (written from a conciliatory standpoint) is Deborah Tannen's *You Just Don't Understand.*[21]

The most extreme of these militant "culturalists," women must liberate themselves from male fantasies, once and for all. A female community has to be forged that can resist men and cultivate its own values. While Françoise Héritier denounced this notion of difference, far from rejecting it the cultural feminists assert it on their side, and credit the female mental universe with being "better," of a higher civilizing value.

This distinction actually goes along with the famous anthropological classification developed by Jean Cazeneuve (and others), contrasting Dionysiac civilizations, founded on more or less male values (competition, nomadism, risk and conquest), with Apollonian civilizations, those that give precedence to values considered, wrongly or rightly, female (stability, security, non-violence, economic growth).[22] Accordingly, the ambiguous position of the feminists vis-a-vis the "sexual revolution" isn't surprising in the least. Didn't its vitalistic, Nietzchean and Reichian version — exaltation of the state of nature, the will to release the "torrent-like floods of desire," implicit machismo — have more to do with Dionysius than with Apollo? Didn't it express, essentially, a male pathos, at the very time that a good share of the contemporary sensitivity of the society was inclining toward feminization? For three decades, the dominant train of thought hardly took the trouble to think of this contradiction, however essential it might be.

However, aside from their excesses, it is on this very question of dominant values that the cultural feminists and the gay intellectuals promoting queer theory jointly made a positive contribution.

A New Art of Loving?

Certainly, by now wee can afford to make fun of both sides. What? The homosexuals want to re-examine the entire culture to expose what has been dissimulated! Women, unleashed warriors in the battle of the sexes, recommend a moratorium on heterosexual relations until masculinity in all its arrogance turns in its weapons! Thirty years after the beginning of the Western "sexual revolution," feminists "invited women to protect their independence by protecting themselves from the fires of desire!" There is no point in going on about all the comments that such excesses caused. And still cause.

Upon reflection, despite everything, many of the claims — even if only in a confused, inarticulate way — stem from a more attractive and perhaps more reasonable world view than libertarian utopias like Wilhelm Reich's. Isn't it a question, ultimately, of enriching our collective representations about history, culture, love itself? Isn't it a matter of reintroducing into our practices and our rigid representations some elements of indecision, play and tolerance? Aren't we looking, beyond the ignited slogans, to dismiss the most violent tropisms and the most dominating behaviors?

None of that necessarily lends itself to mockery. The march of history, like that of ideas, sometimes goes by circuitous routes, and reason, as we know, plays many tricks. Isn't it a trick of reason, for example, that homosexuals have rediscovered (through their contracts of civil union embodying the fidelity, stability, and solidarity, values that were derisively rejected by the hedonism of the 1960's? Isn't it another trick that led homosexuals, in the 1970's, to bring back a reassuring and uncomplicated image of virility that conflicted with the heterosexual emancipation founded, as Michael Pollack underlined, on "the lack of differentiation of male and female roles"?[23]

Other periods of history — the Renaissance, for example — grew rich, after all, on comparable contributions, rediscoveries and reinventions that were equally unexpected.

Gay and feminist folklore, the dazzling parade, the media campaigns and the rhetoric that sometimes borders on the ridiculous — none of that must disguise what remains. Homosexual intellectuals and artists proclaim their will to invent new types of relations, breaking the contemporary prison of loneliness and harshness. They are keeping up rather nicely a sense of festival. They are portrayed as pioneers and, in certain cases, they are such. If it happens that these dogmatic territories are crawling with foolishness, denial of access and irresponsibility, let us acknowledge that those faults are found everywhere. "It could be that, reluctantly," Feher imagines, "the cultural feminists are supporting nothing less than the advent a new art of loving."[24]

This resolute optimism is not entirely groundless. And the immense distress in which today's "discourse about love" makes us look forward to the invention of a new happiness together more eagerly than ever.

CHAPTER 14

RE-MAKING THE FAMILY

And finally, let's talk about the state of the family.[1] That is harder to do than one might think. There are some questions that are so heavily politicized that they become cursed. The family is one of them. For decades, any reflection on this topic has been reduced quickly to the despairing confrontation between a nostalgic Right, brandishing "family values" and calling for their reinstitution, and a valorous Left, stalwartly defending the individual, resisting domination by the family. The "sexual revolution" of the Sixties only exacerbated this Manichean conflict; it existed long before.

In France, the very idea of family carries heavy connotations. In the contemporary political imagination, it is associated with some kind of vague Petainism. This mistrust is encouraged by the way the parties on the Right and the special interest groups ritually evoke the need for returning to the "true family." In response, we hear an almost symmetrical virulence defending the individual. Ambient progressivism — to speak like Jean-Claude Millner,[2] — instinctively impugns any reference to the family with the same over-simplification. Both sides get on their soap boxes, no one stops to reflect. Irene Théry is alarmed that the debate has become so rigid; it certainly won't help us find new answers.

"If we are not careful," she writes, "I fear that we will not be able to stop locking horns between the defenders of the Family and the defenders of the Individual. This anachronistic coupling still provides the invisible and inevitable backdrop to all our debates. . . . How can we explain this paradox — the never-ending force of an obsolete distinction, as if we had to choose what is the 'real' basic cell of society? As if the family the traditionalists have in mind was the only family, so much so that the word seems to belong to them. As if freedom existed only without limits, and the individual only in the assertion of absolute power."[3]

This endless antagonism is short-sighted. And lacks memory. It is founded on an inaccurate postulate: that the family, for all time, has been a conservative and Catholic value, and resisting it would inevitably be "Leftist." Actually, the family was a *transhumant* value, like, for example, the nation or cultural differentiation.[4] Historically, it was sometimes on the right, sometimes on the left. At the end of the 19th century, the exploited proletarians of the industrial revolution saw it as a structure of refuge, threatened as they were by the capitalist bourgeoisie, poverty, urbanization, child labor, etc.. In the Fifties, in the United States, this vision of the family as the ultimate shelter for interdependent personal relations and as a counterweight to the harshness of industrial capitalism was defended by certain authors like Talcott Parsons.[5]

For Parsons, "the principal function of the family was to constitute a space where personal relations remained possible, i.e. where the preoccupation with efficiency was not more important than sentiment. There each one found, whatever his behavior and his merit, the assurance of tenderness which redounded to him just because of his position inside the family, whether one of the spouses or a child. In a society where social progress required the disappearance of status, only the family still offered statutory and thus unconditional relations. Thus the happiness of the family was necessary to the proper functioning of the society."[6]

Christianity, as we have seen in the preceding chapters, consistently favored the individual over authoritative and family logics. The Catholics, in favoring celibacy over marriage, were distinguished from the Protestants who, according to Luther, saw marriage as "the state which is pleasing to God." In the first Christian centuries, explicit criticism of the family contained in the New Testament (in *Luke* and *Matthew*,[7] for example) scandalized the Jews. Indeed, Judaism resolutely places priority on family cohesion and the raising of the offspring. (That is still one of its greatest assets).

Finally, let us recall that the Nazi ideologists, far from praising the traditional family, proposed to dissolve it into the broader solidarity of the nation.

A Quarrel that Has Gone Too Far

To call the idea of family a fundamentally Catholic value, conservative, even Petainist, is to confuse recent events with history. It is to sin by amnesia or ignorance (which amounts to the same thing). Actually, a minimal distinction must be made. In stable societies, obeying an authoritative and holistic conformity, the family, as a place of transmission and social "reproduction", is indeed an instrument in service of the established order. It is, the obviously, the place for training in obedience, conformity and tradition. On the other hand, in periods of major disruption, where entropy, disorder and social fragmentation prevail — that is, where any capacity to transmit values is extremely weakened, it cannot provide that function.

The family then becomes a breakwater for humanization and resistance to solipsistic cruelty. It serves as the last haven where a minimal representation of the future still prevails, something greater which "any individual and any family can reference themselves by, as with what founds them, legitimates them by tying them to the law of the species, branding them as part of humanity by registering them in the culture."[8] It represents an instance of "progressivist refusal" to that which Irene Théry calls "the insignificance of a present without ties."

That, obviously, describes our contemporary societies. In its ideal radicalism, the market, ultra-liberalism, and consumerism at this bridge to the 21st century prefer to deal with consumers — and employees — without ties nor obligations. They have only to make whatever regulations they like. However, the family structure and loyalties constituted such a tie. The family, in theory, was the exemplary site of gratuitous action (in many senses). It was opposed, by definition, to the commercial order. After thirty years of "sexual revolution," radical individualism, disaffiliation, now we are stunned by the final disintegration of the "basic cell of the society." In this crisis, the old Right vs. Left quarrels around the family are out of place, just as it is no longer acceptable to pretend that talk about sexual permissiveness, the right to nomadic pleasures or enjoyment without restrictions has nothing to do with the family question.

But let us be fair. If this polemical drivel between the Right and the Left — the bombastic confrontation between those who defend the family and advocates of the individual — is still pervasive, it is in its least thoughtful version, that is at the level of media blather and electoral invective. At another level, everyone has understood that the house was on fire. All and sundry have learned how to get beyond the narrowness of their original ideological catechism. "The liberal Right has stopped being hung up on nostalgia for the 'real family,' a model that it had itself contributed to demolishing when it revised the Civil Code. . . . And the Social Left has ceased promoting a kind of triumphal proselytizing for a change of mores....The fragility of the family, in a context of social crisis, is now recognized as a new source of inequality."[9]

A telling detail: among intellectuals and within the social sciences, this awakening seems to have happened first among women. We must give them their due. The most lucid and most elaborate reflections on the need to "remake the family," the most serious analysis of new family structures, have mostly come from female authors and researchers. That would be a shock to those who protest that defending the family means wanting to send women back to the kitchen! When they reflect upon the consequences of the destruction of the family institution and how to remedy the situation, commentators like Christiane Olivier, Genevieve Delaisi de Parseval, Évelyne Sullerot, Irene Théry, Catherine Labrusse-Riou, Caroline Eliachef (to name just a few), they are not being reactionary or endangering women's emancipation, of which they are, to tell the truth, the living incarnation.

However, each one in her own discipline — psychoanalysis, sociology, philosophy of law, civil law, history, etc. — and each in her own way expresses the same fear of the present situation. "I make a point of testifying," writes Sullerot, pioneer of the fight for free contraception, "that we had no idea what was waiting for us behind the door of sexual freedom, when it was finally opened. Some, yes, dreamed of a paradise without sin, but could not picture it. Others were sure that the liberation of their sexuality would bring them psychic health — they prophesied the end of female neuroses, anxieties, depressions, the moment they could be protected by effective contraception. Others expected it to be the miracle cure to make love last and thus save their marriages."[10]

A Society without Fathers

Let us remember. In the last thirty years, we not only lived through a revolution of manners and a cataclysm of our shared notions about sexuality. We not only lived through a record collapse of demography, the decline of marriage, the banalization of divorce and an unprecedented extension of permissiveness. In a more concrete and more lasting way, a *legislative* revolution was accomplished during the same period. And that is what is most tangible today. And that is significant. The civil law (marriage, children's right, the status of woman, parental authority, etc.) inscribed in the laws — and almost in real time — this cultural convulsion, by making it permanent.

However, while this legal revolution may have represented indisputable progress in terms of personal freedom, it entailed infinitely more ambiguous consequences, consequences that we have long refused to consider. One of most painful is the quasi-disappearance of the father, the ruin of paternity. This has created an insidious imbalance about which, over the years, we have pretty much kept silent, because it was not "politically correct" with regard to the new morality. We really had our heads in the sand! "The silence about what is happening with paternity," acknowledges Sullerot, "on what has happened to fathers, on something that is likely to have a profound impact on sons, astounds me. . . . We neglect doing conducting the research and the polls; paternity is not a topic."[11] As for the psychoanalyst Christiane Olivier, she says it even more bluntly. "Since feminism came along, women have become the heads of the household, and it does not seem that they are ready yet to call this new power in question. Even while men continue to gain ground everywhere on the social level, women have conquered and occupy all the terrain of child-rearing. The social workers support the lawyers who have the ear of the woman-judges: it looks like an enormous female trust that gets into action as soon as anyone talks about a child anywhere."[12]

In fact, the ousting of the father and paternity were not, as is sometimes believed, an invention of the Sixties. It was the final stage of a evolution started two centuries before. The French Revolution, first, attacked the father figure. In the literal meaning as well as in the metaphoric sense. The golden age of the father and of patriarchy was during the three previous centuries. In 1789, they were regarded as the very symbol of the monarchy. Balzac would write that in "beheading Louis XVI (on January 21, 1793) the Republic beheaded the fathers of every family." And Cambacérès, one of the drafters of the new French legal code, exclaimed before the deputies, "The imperious voice of reason has been heard. It says: there is no more paternal power." The Revolution intended to break the indestructibles bonds of the family in the name of the sovereign freedom of man and woman. But it was the father that it targeted.

Thereafter, in spite of some set backs (when the Restoration, for example, abolished divorce, which was authorized again only in 1884 by the Third Republic), a slow, irreversible *degradation of the father's status* took place. Sometimes in fact — industrialization and proletarianization injured fathers by transforming them into absent semi-slaves — and sometimes in the law: the abolition of the right of correction (1935), the substitution of *parental* authority for *paternal* authority (1970), and laws on natural filiation (1972, 1987, 1993).

In the Sixties, as we have seen, the permissive utopia — Reich's obsession — branded the family as a place of constraints, the school of middle-class obedience and sexual repression. The Frankfurt School philosophers took the same clearly anti-paternal line. "On the basis of Adorno's and his collaborators' research, the father is at the center of the debate on authority, as the element that welds together two forms of power, one that is exercised by consensus and one that is exercised by the threat or the use of force and coercion. . . . The *Vaterlose Gesellschaft*, the society without fathers, to be created, should be a society of freedom (sexual freedom, among others), — hadn't they just legalized contraception? — in which the teenagers will speak, they who represent tomorrow as it is being made, and will impose silence on the 'old,' on those who claim to know, to teach, to govern, to control; on the fathers, the teachers, the ministers, and on the preeminent Old man, General de Gaulle."[13]

The Pill and "Fire from the Gods"

In same time, as we know, the widespread access to contraception gave women the power to decide the most important question of all:

that of giving life, the choice of "yes" or "no" and "when." Thanks to the pill, says Sullerot, "woman stole from man the fire of the gods." Other scientific achievements — condemned by the Right —would further increase women's omnipotence, even in the area of paternity. For example, the famous Jeffreys genetic test of 1984, which made it possible to identify the biological father with certainty. Thanks to this, a married woman can, in extreme cases, make her lover recognize the child of which he is indeed the father but that the legal father believed was his (and loved!). And in vitro fertilization, which straightforwardly limits the paternal figure to a drop of seed available to the woman. (The father? "We are interested in his sperm," wrote Genevieve Delaisi de Parseval, "we don't give a damn about his heart."[14])

Little by little we are getting used to the spectacle of these dispossessed fathers, battling from trial to trial, running from one court appearance to another, begging, in a context of polite indifference, for "permission" for something that, just yesterday, went without saying: the right to see their children, to take part in raising them, to exist even for a brief moment in their eyes. The image of the father cruelly separated from his offspring soon replaced that of the indifferent father we used to see: the eternally absent, distracted parent, the egotist so stingy that he could be accused of abandoning his family, a man who is cavalier and negligent in his responsibilities. An archetypal figure of the dime-store novel, that now seems as dated as a man in a top hat. In 1991 one of the first "fathers' groups" was created, whose name alone was a signal: SOS-Papa.

For their part, literature, songs and movies have been populated by depressive and disconsolate dads, sympathetic losers. Fathers who do not hide from their paternal roles but assert it, in vain.

Ruined by the law, science and statistics, traditional paternity thus suffered from a shift of public opinion and fashion. As Élisabeth Badinter has said, the hard man was gave way to the soft man. Dustin Hoffman, stammering and myopic, replaced Robert Mitchum just like that. The male character has become softer and more fragile, less imposing, more like a grown up child that needed to be comforted.

In Europe, the accelerated creation of single-parent families is also inseparable from social breakdowns, the many ways in which the democratic fabric and traditional loyalties have been torn; this phenomenon, since the beginning of the Eighties, obviously ascribable to the economic crisis, insecurity and unemployment. Men and women today endure, more than choose, the insecurity of the family. Hundreds of thousands of children, in the same way, suffer through (without having chosen it) the exile of the fathers, which some people compare to the suffering caused by the industrial revolution of the 19th century.

The most immediately quantifiable consequence is the fortune of the contemporary configuration that we call by the slightly barbarian term of "single-parent family" and which, in nearly every case, means a family without a father. The statistics are food for thought. In the United States, the Population Council generally estimates that approximately 24% of households with dependent children are led by only one parent, the mother. In the black community, the proportion is traditionally far greater: 57% of the children grow up in a single-parent home. But, today, the shift toward more single-parent families is affecting the whole population, especially in the poorer segments.

According to 1995 figures from Eurostat, the proportion of single-parent families increased by 25 to 50% in most European countries since the beginning of the Eighties. The single-parent unit now accounts for approximately 18% of families. The hardest hit are Norway, Finland, Great Britain, Belgium and Austria. In France alone, Évelyne Sullerot calculated in 1993 that 2.5 million children were living with only their mother.

This phenomenon is often brandished (especially in the United States) by the ultra-liberal adversaries of the Welfare State, who reproach various family support programs for encouraging the loosening of moral standards, idleness, immorality, etc.. But as usual, it would be a mistake to stop at these superficial polemics. Psychoanalysts themselves are divided today by a debate about the father, which reveals quite a different story.

Psychoanalysis Gripped by Doubt

When entering the realm of psychoanalysis, certain precautions must be taken. That field of knowledge is precise, rigorous and particular as to what interpretations one can make. It has produced, moreover, its own language, its codes, its ritualized polemics, and it tolerates what one might call an endogamous perspective. Like certain religions, it puts up with quarrels between different schools of thought, on the condition that they are conducted behind closed doors, within the tribe, without too many public incidents. Freudians, Lacanians, post-Lacanians debate each other freely, but they do not like it when their disagreements — sometimes Byzantine — are taken up by the layman. This leads to hopelessly incestuous "reflections" and discussions closed to outside influence, exiled in the protected space of seminars and conferences.

It is time to stop this type of intimidation.

The paternity/maternity question, indeed, was always at the center of the psychoanalytical method. Freud, in his time, boosted the value of the mother's role, which had already been strengthened historically and sociologically. He posited that the child's sexual instincts were based on his relationship with his mother, the father having only a very minor influence. Thereafter, psychoanalysis would continue to grant to paternity only a very modest share in the educational process. In the Sixties, for example, a psychoanalyst could coldly write: "The father is unable to derive pleasure from the role he must play and is not competent to share with the mother the great responsibility that a baby always represents."[15]

As for Lacan, he took the father from being an object to being a "metaphor," i.e. a "a signifier that stands in for another signifier." The father, in other words, is not only an intruder disturbing the close bonding between the mother and the child, he is the word that dictates the law (and especially the interdict of incest). For this reason, he is nothing, indeed, but a metaphor of the interdict. And still, to reach this status, he has to be designated "father" by the mother. This, in simplified terms, is the significance of the famous Lacanian expression: "the name of the father." The mother holds all the power, including that of investing the father with his own status. He is father only in so far as the mother wants it, only as long as his word is recognized by her.

Most Lacanians — from Bernard This to Aldo Naouri,[16] — took another look at this identification of the father as a metaphor. "It is by designating his/her father to him," Naouri wrote, "that mothers introduce her children to the symbolic world." According to the Lacanian view, the biological ties and physical demonstrations of paternity (tenderness, physical presence, etc.) are relegated to a subordinate, not to say negligible, rank. The father as a "metaphor authorized by the mother," or as a symbolic representation of the interdict, does not need to be the biological father. Neither does he have to venture onto the mother's territory, impelled by the desire to "be a father" by aping the mother, as was the fashion for new fathers in the Eighties.

Francoise Dolto repeats that it is not by the caress, the touch, the attentive handling of the baby bottle that the father could differentiate himself in the child's view, but by his word and his image. In other words, in her eyes, the new paternity could not be reduced to pure and simple mimicry of maternity. The image of the father could not be rein-vented within the context of physical relations reserved for the mother.

This disincarnated interpretation of paternity was perfectly ap-propriate to the famous new families compositions, in which the role of the father was held — minimally — by the new friend of the divorced mother. "Those who defend the new family structures," adds Sullerot, "are [wrongly] convinced of a principle, that of the interchangeability of the 'biological parent' who has left the home, and the 'sex-partner-of-the-remaining-parent.' The sexual bond which founds the couple, in that it expresses a personal freedom outside of any institution, seems to them to take precedence over the bond of filiation which is the basis of parenthood."[17]

Today, several post-Lacanian psychoanalysts hold this impover-ishing image of the father-metaphor as partly responsible for the pater-nity crisis, since the image legitimated the trend on the theoretical level. And it did so all the more effectively given that, for at least three decades, many fathers *consented to being ousted*, which released them from an oppressive responsibility. "I am among those who think that the disappearance of the fathers is a catastrophe for the children," wrote Christiane Olivier, "but that the fathers themselves have contributed much to this disappearance by not taking their share of responsibility in the life of the baby, majority of them stepping aside, believing the mothers to be hereditarily more gifted than them as nurturers."[18]

This devalued figure of the father-metaphor, designated by the mother, is fraught with consequences in societies undermined by di-vorce. In the event of divorce, indeed, the children usually go with the mother; the judges generally entrust them to her. However, if the fa-ther's status is only a kind of right derived from maternal recognition, it obviously disappears in the event of divorce. Not only will the child be separated from his father, but he/she will have literally lost him, in fa-vor of a surrogate father which the young divorced mother will designate. The single-parent family will no longer be a mishap but will become a concept based on faulty logic.

Critical psychoanalysts rightly qualify this as a trap. The most interesting thing about this criticism that comes from the inside is that it is not founded on a moral, political or ideological reaction that would reduce its theoretical impact. If it disputes the Lacanian theses on paternity, it does so on their own ground.

How Do You Manufacture a Misogynist?

Christiane Olivier, for example, persistently contests the idea that the father-child bond is developed by carnal proximity. She rests her arguments on the concept of *attachment*, as proposed by researchers like Rene Zazzo, Boris Cyrulnik and Hubert Montagner.[19] She stresses that it is quite likely that the attachment is not inevitably formed on the basis of carnal needs, such as food and sex, contrary to what Freud had thought. In her view, this theory of attachment "could raise the question again of the baby's establishing a *unique* relationship with only *one* person — the mother or her female substitute — and lead to a revision of Freud's thought concerning the 'relational object.'" Then we would have to reconsider the place of the father, from start to finish, including the importance of his *physical* presence during the child's first days of life: his voice, odors, caresses, etc.. "This is a far cry," Olivier writes, "from the 'Name of the Father' to which so many analysts persist in clinging, not daring to alter Lacan's writings and remaining indifferent to the fact that the child sometimes goes from his biological father to his father of attachment."[20]

We don't need to go any further into the details of this critique (fascinating as they are) to understand what kind of theoretical revolution it ignites. In the final analysis, we are rediscovering, through the question of attachment, the function of tenderness, including specifically paternal, in structuring family relations. And thus to admitting the consubstantial weakness of the single-parent family, whatever the devotion and the merit of the solitary mother. This is not a matter of moral judgement.

But Olivier's criticism is more disconcerting still when it blames — partially — the disappearance of the fathers for certain aggravated forms of chaos in modern society. For example, the obsessive sexual violence, which has so often been mentioned in this book, especially violence against women: rape, aggression, contempt, persistent misogyny, etc.. From a psychoanalytical point of view, we could hypothesize that absolute maternal power and the solitude of the mother and child are not unrelated to the background of aggressiveness that we take — wrongly — for a surviving residue of a bygone era. The impulse of the rapist could be analyzed as a revenge, taken in adulthood, on the new maternal — and mothering — hegemony of women.

To become a subject, indeed, the child must assert himself against the adult in relation to whom he feels like an object. In the traditional family, this revolt as an obligatory passage faces two parents between which it is possible to navigate dialectically. In the single-parent family, this same revolt confronts nothing but one protagonist, the mother. For a boy, this confrontation of the mother alone, whether assumed or refused, leads to dead ends. It can lead the child, whose development was derailed this way, to reject all women. The rape and violence in our societies would in that case be aimed, to a certain extent, at all the women who, in the man's mind, take the place of the Oedipal mother that the little boy never dared to attack.

"The Oedipal love of the mother which always disturbs the adolescent, even under normal circumstances," writes Olivier, "here becomes even more pregnant, and can thus give way to a brutal rejection against a mother who was far from expecting it! Obviously, that which was already difficult between mother and son when the father was with the family becomes impossible here in any way but through *counter-identification* with the mother, which comes to take to the place of the *identification* with the father. The boy has only one solution and can draw only one conclusion: to be man, *all it takes is to not be a woman.* The early signs of misogyny and all its corollaries are there, and the woman who will follow the mother will only feel the consequences."[21]

While it may be debatable, this hypothesis is interesting in more ways than one. It underlines an almost perfect example of what I would call a paradoxical achievement, that is, a step forward that generates its own negation. That step forward that no one would call into question is, obviously, the liberation of the woman, including liberation from the chains of the traditional marriage. Along with equality in the work force, the banalization of divorce, independence as a mother and the full exercise of educational sovereignty are its principal elements. That is why the single-parent family is so seldom criticized by the Left. It is undoubtedly perceived as a relative failure but also, confusedly, as the very symbol of women's emancipation. Some even see it as the positive sign of a final evolution in procreation, and perhaps even as the cradle of the 'new man' . . . . Think how media reports and television programs, innumerable and impassioned, ingenuously credit the single-parent family with such an ineffable progressive aura!

If it is shown, in the final analysis, that this solitary mother structurally leads to misogyny and machismo in the future adult, that would means that an alleged sign of progress has led, in fact, to regression. And on the very ground that was intended: the real and symbolic status of the woman. Modernity, standing up to misogyny and violence, arming itself with an ever-growing repressive arsenal and a whole moralizing system of rhetoric, would actually be in the ridiculous position of manufacturing the very evils about which it complains. A little like hitting oneself in the head and then cursing an invisible enemy.

"The longer the mother-son relation is unique and prolonged," adds Olivier, "the more violent will be the reaction of the man. The single-parent family is thus not at all the ideal place from which the new man will come. Quite to the contrary, the fact of having been raised solely by a woman can only increase boy's reaction against women. The new man, who will be the equal and the complement of the woman, can only come from a family where all the powers are not in the hands of a woman alone."[22]

A Duty of Happiness?

Parallel to this serious debate among psychoanalysts on "the family disaster," another, radically different one is developing. This one is located on the terrain of sociology and ethology. Researchers from these different disciplines express an equally strong concern, but justified this time, by the ruin of *the family as an institution*, where the word "institution" is used in its etymological sense. The Latin *instituere* means to indicate, to create, to found. In this sense, the family is the instrument by which the community institutes its new member — the child — as a human being. "It is characteristic of humanity," observes Irene Théry, "*to institute*, i.e. to give significance to its reproductive capacity as a living species, inscribing every little member of mankind as a newcomer in the world of men, and registering him also in the chain of generations."[23]

But, what has actually happened, from this point of view? Completing a shift in meaning introduced by modernity itself, the "sexual revolution" led to the triumph of quite a different concept of the family. It came to be seen more and more often as the free, voluntary and temporary meeting, of two consenting lovers. The idea of the couple defeated the idea of institution. The family, in this view, *primarily* looks like the space for emotional and sexual flourishing, the exclusive territory of love. The institutional dimension, inevitably referencing the long term, stability, and permanence, became secondary.

This gradual erosion of the family, from an institution toward a contractual union, a decline inseparable from the democratic adventure itself, had been presaged by Tocqueville. In *Democracy in America*, he demonstrated an extraordinary sagacity on this subject. "Among democratic people," he wrote, "new families unceasingly come out of nowhere, others unceasingly fall apart, and all those which remain change their faces; the continuum of time is constantly being broken, and the trace of the generations is erased. Those who came before are as easily forgotten as those who will follow you. Only close relations are of interest."

From a certain perspective, this colonization of the family by love, passion, and desire marked a definite progress. It corresponded to the triumph of what one might call a morality of happiness, breaking away from the austere ethics of the holistic societies, founded on duty and the need for perpetuating the species by raising children. Since the 1970's, after the recasting of family law (divorce, contraception, etc, this perception of the couple as sovereign, managing its affinities in love, prevailed even more exclusively still. Within the couple, duty was no longer interpreted in terms of sacrifice, patience or giving things up, but *being true to oneself*. If love-passion alone founded the couple, individual morality required that the couple be dissolved when passion was no longer there.

The morality of personal happiness thus implied, *ipso facto*, a morality of divorce. Divorce became the straightforward consequence of an absence of love, or desire. It was not viewed any more as a simple failure but as a sign of courage, freedom and, in the final analysis, hope in the future. It rejected the idea of resignation. It expressed, in the name of individualism, a decisive repudiation of the spirit of duty that had consisted, for centuries, in sacrificing the aspiration to happiness on the altar of the institution. Divorce became the refusal to "pretend," the rejection of resigned cohabitation, of churning resentments and of keeping up appearances (as one used to say) "for the children's sake."

"The overvaluation of the couple compared to the family," notes Sullerot, [has] transformed marital mediocrity into so many dramatic personal failures. The women think that it is necessary, that they must, that *they owe it to themselves* to get out of what they regard as a dead end. If not, the modern ideologies which are constantly measuring and classifying people, condemn them to the bottom rows, almost with opprobrium."[24]

Modernity, in its ultimate achievement, thus did not abolish morality. It substituted one morality for another, while profoundly transforming its collective categories and representations. What used to be judged as right or meritorious no longer was; behaviors formerly celebrated as evidence of courage, self-abnegation, sense of duty would be given a negative mark. True duty, in other words, consisted not in staying but in leaving. The institutional needs of the family would be challenged in the name of another need that was considered to take precedence: that of individual happiness. And immediate happiness. "The family, like the couple, will be a fusion, or it will not exist at all. Insofar as it retains as a criterion of legitimization only the evidence of the bond of love, marriage will no longer constitute the basis of the family nor a significant moment. . . . That will result in an increasing frequency of breakups and a growing number of successive unions."[25]

The Age of Uncertainty

Thus the family ceased being an institution, or more precisely, as Théry says, "it became an unthinkable institution." This matrimonial revolution leaves entirely the question of children, that is, of filiation, up in the air. The legislative shift did more or less the same thing. France instituted a law in 1972 on filiation (favorable to the natural children), which served directly to detach the question of marriage from that of filiation.

"This shocking redefinition of the bonds of conjugality as something fundamentally individual, private, contractual and from now on more precarious, had sociological and legal consequences. [It] can also be perceived as the end of a very long subservience of the conjugal ties to the imperative of the security of filiation (in both senses: security of the identification of the father, security of the permanence of the bonds in time). It would not be so problematic if it did not, in turn, open a new breach: how to articulate the difference between the sexes and between the generations? How to link together conjugality and filiation?"[26]

That is the immense challenge to Western modernity. Now two requirements have to be articulated, which in theory are mutually exclusive: that of love emancipated from constraints (especially the constraint of duration) and that of transmission, i.e. children humanized, little by little, by the complementary support of a father and a mother. This need to face a double constraint, to reconcile the irreconcilable, is a new situation in the history of mankind. It is an impossible situation, the consequences of which we are only starting to see today.

"Now it is at the anthropological level," writes Théry, "that we see the principal debates on the family. In what universe of meaning do we locate the feelings and the bonds, when the ideals of conjugality and filiation are in conflict? The family is no longer thought of as an institution, because it has become an unthinkable institution. Such is the conundrum obscured by the public debate."[27]

As soon as one looks a little harder at the analyses, the studies and the writing devoted to this question, one reads between the lines a certain vague uneasiness. The situation is described as intolerable, but a reversion to the earlier ways would be just as untenable. Indeed, no one imagines that it would be desirable, or even plausible, to retrogress. Neither freedom, nor the taste of individual happiness, nor the liberation of the mothers seems to be renegociable today, at least not within the framework of a democratic system. Those who defend the traditional family, driven by a rather simplistic nostalgia, must understand that. Why? Because a society cannot be made, if its own volition, to take back on a system of constraints that has become unacceptable once all the symbolism that gave it meaning has disappeared.

For a Roman citizen, it would have been downright obscene to expect to experience passionate love within the marriage, it was incongruous to confuse the two. For a man of the *Ancien Regime*, it would have been just as extravagant to mix the will for personal (and sexual) fulfillment with the matter of marriage and with the family institution. Love as the goal of marriage is a very recent invention; and the famous matrimonial *constraints*, the tyranny of which we reject today, were not experienced as burdens in earlier times. They were internalized, taken on, and legitimated by the collective representations of the age — such as the Christian faith, which placed great emphasis on the idea of commitment and having given one's word. Louis Roussel expresses this historical difference extremely well:

"Did it take a great effort of will for our ancestors to submit [to the constraints of the traditional family]? Probably not, at least under ordinary circumstances. The institution seemed like a fact of nature. Effective socialization and everyday practice made it a kind of unconscious 'habitus.' And then, one's contemporaries unanimously anticipated that each one would conform to the collective standard, and behind these contemporaries, invisible but always persuasive, stood the innumerable and confused crowd of the ancestors."[28]

The Limits of the Recomposed Family

Today, we do not imagine for a single moment that we could reconsider our perception of freedom, sexuality, passion or even of breaking up without a degree of drama that we have, in its turn, also internalized. And furthermore, nothing indicates that such would be desirable. That freedom and renewed assent now prevail within marriage is not all the sign of retrogressive values as those who are nostalgic about the old order might claim. It is, above all, an enrichment of marital love itself. This is "the upsetting redefinition" (Théry) of the bonds of marriage: the free and joint responsibility of the man and the woman engaged in renewing, day after day, the attentive dialogue, and in reweaving the everyday existence that Jean-Claude Kaufmann indicates with a beautiful metaphor: the marital screen.[29]

The fact remains that the family as institution is not only "unthinkable," it *becomes both necessary and impossible*. The expressions used to characterize this situation are revealing. "We have entered into uncertainty," writes Théry. The British historian Peter Laslett, evokes "the world that we have lost." Alain Ehrenberg blames the de-institutionalization of the family for "the private sufferings and the new forms of vulnerability that are flourishing all over, today."[30] The lawyer

Catherine Labrusse-Riou enumerates the "anchorage points that one could not shake or worse yet, give up, without major risks."[31] She even speaks, as a specialist in filiation, of "a shock to the foundations."

It's no surprise if the hazardous, obstinate, disappointing and difficult search for a new family order has become one of the great concerns of the moment. In spite of the slogans and declamations, everyone has a presentiment that the solutions lie not behind but before us. No resurrection of the past will free us from the need to invent something new. Like all quests, this one is conducted through various attempts, disappointed hopes, passing fancies and even fads. For example, we have already been trying for several years to conceptualize what is already a massive statistical reality: the so-called recomposed family, the kind that brings together in precarious — but often joyful —emotional balance a new couple and children from different beds.

Movies, literature and song have long popularized this Protean family, a heritage of the 1960's and 70's. But while the recomposed family may not inevitably be the catastrophe described by conservative moralists, it nevertheless leaves an immense challenge unresolved: that of filiation as a process of *institution* and transmission. Anthropologists know that human filiation — the "cascading flood of the generations" — must evolve under a system of bonds of alliance as complex as they are precise, bonds which marriage was supposed to create. It is not a question of some tradition that we might challenge, but quite simply the process of humanization. The family and the relationship, from this point of view, are not construction games where components can be recombined *ad infinitum*.

For this recomposition of the family through cohabitation "creates no legal bond of alliance, neither between the lover and the other person's parents, nor between the lover and the other person's children. So here we have, again, whether we like it or not, the burning question of what is the relation between family relationship and alliance, where the point of connection is marriage, the alliance of the sexes, which can ally themselves and generate life only because they are different and equal."[32]

Futuristic speculation on the techniques of assisted procreation, of *in vitro* fertilization, surrogate mothers and even (hypothetically) cloning, do not help to resolve any of the rather distressing questions raised by the weakening of the family as an institution that would guarantee enough stability and coherence for one human generation to suc-

ceed the other, perpetuating its *humanity*. The problem remains irremediably before us: how shall we remake the family?

This problem is so difficult that modern society is tempted to
avoid it. As in other fields, this evasion often takes the form of false
quarrels or one of those grandiloquent, gratifying and ambiguous debates that the media are so happy to pounce upon. Here is just one example: children's rights.

The Ideology of Children's Rights

The omnipresent violence in our societies, various forms of exploitation that are common in certain countries of the southern hemisphere, media coverage highlighting sexual delinquency (rape, pedophilia, etc.) in the private sphere, social dereliction: they all make children out to be victims. And very often, they are — defenseless victims
of all the chaos and insecurity. Thus it is logical that everyone would
jump to support the idea of protecting children. Don't our modern societies, in seeking to protect children by every means possible, feel they
are addressing an emergency by sheltering that which still can be sheltered? No cause is more legitimate and popular. Every passing week
sees a new story of violence against a child, even inside his school or his
own family, two "institutions" which in theory should be harbors of
safety for him.

In the name of this children's welfare, an International Convention on the Rights of the Child was drafted and approved at the United
Nations in 1989. Legitimate and even irreproachable in principle, this
convention, however, has gradually come to support the emergence of a
much more contestable ideology. An ideology that, like the humanitarian ideologies of the 1980's, finds eloquent propagandists and an echo in
the general public that is all the more resonant since it takes on the
tone of the war between Good and Evil. A judge, Jean-Pierre
Rosenczweig, has become a popular French media figure, as a vehement
advocate. However, this radical ideology is sufficiently irresponsible to
have scandalized many intellectuals and specialists in family rights,
including Théry, Éliacheff, Alain Finkielkraut, André Comte-Sponville,
and others — and for reasons that are easy to understand.

"The victimization of children," notes Éliacheff, "goes hand in
hand with the demonization of parents, which leads to disqualifying

the parental function in general. When somebody systematically iden-
tifies with the child as a victim, he has the illusion of taking the child's
side more firmly by deciding with certainty who is the attacker, and
who is attacked. It is wrong, and yet widespread, to consider that every
child is first of all a victim of his parents."[33]

Théry undoubtedly is the most resolutely hostile opponent of this
new politically correct view, which is drummed into the general public
every day. She denounces, with some reason, that which secretly fuels
this view: an ambient cowardice that still infuses democrats and progressivists any time family questions are raised. As if everyone were
afraid of being considered retrograde for defending the family! As if the
progressivists were looking to protect themselves against any suspicion, by brandishing "the scarecrow of an imaginary authoritarianism."
Thus they leave the terrain of family issues open to only authoritarian
and nostalgic demagogues, while the most urgent problem is not to
fight an institution but to avoid its complete evanescence.

"How can we miss the fact," Théry objects, "that the ideology of
children's rights lends support to one of the most worrisome tendencies of our democracies? For the rights that we used to think of as mutual relations, we keep substituting 'rights' that divide the parties into
so many separate lobbies. If you take that a little bit further, justice is
transformed into a simple field of confrontation, where the relations of
strength between the individualism of the ones competes against the
individualism of the others. Setting the 'rights of the ones' against the
'rights of the others' is a dilution of the principles that should make it
possible to consider the reciprocity of the social bond (rights do not
exist without responsibilities) and to abandon our concept of rights as
a regulating authority common to all."[34]

Let us risk a hypothesis: there is no pretence more emblematic of
our time, none more absurd than the immense evasion of responsibility
that masquerades as a humanistic activism. Children's rights follow a
direct parallel with humanitarian efforts. Originating as a splendid testimony of planetary solidarity, humanitarian aid has sometimes
evolved, as we know, into ideology — an ideology that is as misleading
as it is convenient, for it has enabled us to mask the diplomatic wait-
and-see policy behind the noisy ostentation of aid and urgency.

The same contradiction is at work in the ideology of children's
rights. In the interests of the child, we act against an institution theo-

retically charged with raising him to adulthood! This resignation, disguised as flagrant generosity, was best summed up by a judge who handles childhood and adolescent affairs: "'Children's rights' are a real gift for those who only want to get out from under the increasingly heavy 'educational burden,' in a world which, at least in the West, gives the impression of having given up transmitting to the child the means of taking his place in history."[35]

How can we ignore this warning?

CHAPTER 15

A CERTAIN IDEA OF TIME

And now?

After all this re-examination, one thing becomes clear: the theatricality of our debates too often masks their bankruptcy. Our daily indignities, our angry conflicts, our quarrels fall into the meager space of fugitive emotivity or empty gestures, and intoxicate themselves with their own repetition. Morality/amorality, permission/repression, hedonism/puritanism: in all good faith, we convince ourselves that decisive, urgent, risky choices are entailed and that they require, day after day, our engagement or, at any rate, our point of view.

Exaggeratedly presumptuous, we want to be convinced that Promethean confrontations are being held about morality, interdicts, and rules, and that we are free protagonists in the matter. Confrontations between a certain idea of Good and Evil; merciless quarrels over order vs. freedom; unremitting war between happiness and fear of chaos. In other words, we take *at face value* all these pugilistics whose din fills our era. In so doing, we lose sight of the fact that the lessons of history and anthropology (which should temper our rages and alleviate our feverish anxieties), indicate otherwise.

And why is that? Because the essential question is never addressed in these superficial polemics, nor anywhere else in the realm of what is commonly called morality, in the normative sense of the term. The moral question, that which supposedly pits one camp against another, *is significant only in relation to the underlying collective representations.* Sexual morality, in its usual meaning, *cannot be decreed,* outside of pure repression or a police state. It always figures within a symbolic process, which is either being built or chipped away little by little; it is founded on a corpus of representations that are largely shared and which always proceed from a long, slow logical process. Generally, we are not even conscious of these representations. These symbolic systems come and go, change and dissolve, are exhausted and rebuilt. They represent the true tide of history, whereas our cacophony is only a ripple. Behind the theatricality of our disputes lie more fundamental questions. Those are the ones to which we should devote the better part of our curiosity.

Not that we should scorn the backdrop of our daily existence, nor pretend to a haughty fatalism, standing above all the cries and all the furies of society. Let us say that, without abstracting oneself from all this turmoil, one might prefer to set oneself the task of deciphering them. When there is so much distress, there must be a better approach than the recurrent haste to "take sides." What is going on, what is at stake? What are the alternatives? Why is it urgent? How shall we go forward? While we can never completely understand history while we are living it, at least we must try to understand it as much as possible.

The Laughter of the Gods

Let us remember that we are trapped within our own era, far more than we imagine. It is characteristic of the famous Durkheimian representations that we are reluctantly driven by our own times. Because of that, our presumptuous clairvoyance and our superb perspicacity — especially in hindsight — are always a little bit laughable. Any thesis, wrote Kierkegaard, is laughable to the gods. Avid to affirm our autonomy of judgment and our lucidity, we remain no less mired, like it or not, in a time-specific cultural substrate. That is just as true today as it was yesterday. In reading Freud and Marx, for example, two of the great masters of suspicion, one notes in their writings the omnipresence of the petit-bourgeois culture that prevailed in their day — a culture from which both writers, however, believed they were emancipated.

Nietzsche is an even more revealing example. Today's libertines cite him as a bulwark against any lingering values, any crumbs of Puritanism that might threaten our appetite for life. However, calling on Nietzsche to support sexual freedom would make anyone smile who has actually read his works. Even with Nietzsche, indeed, one finds most of the 19th century bourgeois representations and prejudices about sexuality. You can find the leery distrust of pleasure: "The pigs wallow in pleasure; whoever preaches pleasure, check to see whether he doesn't have the face of a pig" (*Zarathustra*, a variation); and, "Sexual coolness among the superior minds is essential to the economy of humanity" (*Human, Too Human*). And the well-intended fear of the violence of impulses: "The sexual instinct keeps men apart from each other. It is a furious selfishness," (*Complete Philosophical Works*, IV, 472); and finally: "When a people degenerates. . . , lust is the result" (*Twilight of Idols*). Even the vicious misogyny, which literally signals the 19th century: "Woman constitutes God's second blunder," (*the Antichrist*); and, "One opens a book written by a woman and soon one sighs: another cook who strayed out of the kitchen!" (*Complete Philosophical Works*, XI, 419).[1] Not to Nietzsch's fear, so typical of the 19th century, of losing his sight from having masturbated too much.[2]

Yes, Nietzsche himself. But so much for polemics! We are only mentioning all this to underscore the extraordinary power of the symbolic representations, that can curb even the freest spirits. We must keep in mind, with a minimum of modesty, that we too obey to some extent ambient values which we cannot always identify. Of course, "to some extent" is the operative phrase, here. It designates the very leeway in which our freedom is found. We swim through our times without being absolute prisoners. However, the space of freedom available to us is always greater than we say it is, but more limited than we believe.

Greater? It is true, men are never completely prisoners of most of the prejudices of their time. Every one of us has a capacity for insolence, distance, separation, which he may or may not use, according to the circumstances and his temperament. Every period of history sheltered its own dissidents. No society was ever entirely standardized, even though each one did set standards. There were agnostics in the Christian Middle Ages, libertines in the 19th century, pornocrats in Calvinist England, pacifist sensualists on the eve of the Great War, Puritans during May '68, etc. In other words, the great evolutions of sexual morality that we set out to survey in this book never included the community as a whole. They were only of summary, overall, anthropological significance, could one say.

Whether to accept most of the values of one's time or to set one-self against them, to accept the weight of the holism or to go under-ground: there has always been this choice. It leaves each person to his irreducible freedom. The collective or imitative pressure, to quote René Girard, is always powerful — but never *absolutely*. One might even say that it is inside these interstices that human history plays out, in con-nection with sexuality as well as everything else.

On the other hand — and this is the very subject of this book — it was the incredible contemporary arrogance to believe that modernity could with impunity throw overboard the very idea of collective repre-sentations. It resided in the illusion that, now, the individual-as-king had not only the margins but the entire space; that he had been freed from any collective symbolism and now his imagination ruled the day; that he found himself blessed with an unbounded lucidity in a world that was entirely disenchanted, i.e. desacralized. What a disastrous and proud presumption! This arrogance blinds us to our fate and delivers us, consenting and disarmed, to our own superstitions. Very often, in-deed, at the very moment when we think we are acting autonomously, we are continuing to obey the new values of the group; and with the same docility that our ancestors adhered to theirs.

True human freedom always emanated from a dissidence from these shared values, never from blindness to them. Today, the collective values of modernity appear to be more imperious and less subject to critical analysis than ever before. This is a quite strange situation, tan-tamount to a capitulation of the critical mind. It is that paradoxical re-nunciation of true freedom in favor of a libertarian conformity (thundering, but docile) that these pages intended to flush out.

Idolatrous Fidelity

The alleged moral debate that takes up so much space and energy these days is just a caricatural expression of this misunderstanding. By holding to invective and denunciation, by refusing to really speculate about the significance of the new collective representations, we pre-clude any possibility of escaping Manicheism. We have reduced the discussion to a parlor game without much impact. Most of the time, it starts from the (false) postulate according to which modern society supposedly has done away with all moral guidelines, whereas in fact it has only made some changes. Thanks to the over-simplification of the diagnosis, right-thinking people will be afflicted by the purported amorality of the era, while the libertines will be delighted. And that is where the matter will be left, until the next time.

Actually, no true freedom has been substituted for the alleged tyrannies of the past. The constraints changed in nature, which is not the same thing. Traditional morality was rejected and replaced by another that is quite as normative, even if in a different way. A new morality, based likewise on representations that would deserve to be questioned as lucidly as were those of the past. But they seldom are. Why? All the signs are, indeed, that we have given up that freedom. We changed the fetishes but reinforced our fetishism. In other words, the first vanity of the era is our incapacity — or our refusal — to *question our own prejudices*.

However, the current era is invested with all kinds of new values, prohibitions and injunctions that are not seen as moral constraints because they are internalized like the air we breathe, and are charged with a powerful symbolism. They are accepted unconsciously — ingenuously — as the fundamental interdicts of traditional morality were at one time. The latter, on the other hand, are retrospectively perceived as repressive or constraining because they have been "de-symbolized." And it is against these values that are already dead that, with no danger and no glory, we continue to battle!

When we still exert our capacity of suspicion, when we unleash our criticisms, it is against something that was long since demolished. We are beating on doors that are already open. As for the new constraints, we cannot even identify them. As for the values, the modes, the fads and superstitions of modernity, we are as obedient as little children. Unprecedented mental idleness? Naive complacency? When the critical mind avoids analyzing the new sacred cow that controls us, it is not a good sign. It marks the end of the relentless self-questioning — the grandiloquently declared "state of crisis" that was, for 300 years, the very definition of the Enlightenment. It locks us, in our turn, inside the trap of a system of symbolics that we have not bothered to take apart. It distracts us from the perennial aspiration toward the universalist adventure that would require at least a minimal distance from all prejudice.

In this sense, we are becoming a tribe again.

A few examples spring to mind; the most commonplace are some-times the most significant. Here is one: when speaking about the past, we affect to be upset by the idea of bodily mortification which is, in our view, basically what the restraint of desires boils down to. We see 13th century Christians, devout Jews and wives from the 1930's as suffering beings, basically mutilated by the violence they have exerted voluntar-ily on their desires. The effort of physical restraint, the trial (in the car-nal sense of the term) that they consent to undergo, seems cruel to us in retrospect. In the extreme, the very idea of regulation and discipline of the body seems to us to be an antiquated barbarism that we are all cockily pleased to have put in the past. In our eyes, the principal merit of what we call the right to pleasure is precisely that we can finally leave the body in peace, let go the passions without constraint — as though that would be the very sign of progress. Rejecting the interdicts would be proof of a truce, finally concluded, between our body and our-selves.

Okay. At the same time, however, we accept without batting an eye other types of mortification whose harshness would terrify our re-mote ancestors. Dietary obsessions, the tyranny of "the figure," the tire-less concern with how we look, the categorization of the least activity as a medical problem, the obligation to play sports or go to the gym, professional conformity, the cruel prevalence of youth over any idea of maturity or wisdom: this all induces a physical cruelty towards oneself, that the magazines then innocently echo. Aren't these glorified forms of mortification about the same, in intensity of effort and pain, as the re-strictions that used to be exerted on sexual desires? On some of these questions, weren't the collective representations of the past more lib-eral, more fluid? One might object that today's are essentially voluntary and that they do not have the same goal. What difference does that make? In the past, self-control in matters of sexuality was similarly bal-anced on the ambiguous scale of free choice and cultural pressures. In one case, we are horrified at the thought of voluntarily exercising do-minion over ourselves, and in another case we develop it as a value.

So we have a new set of symbolic priorities. Why shouldn't we challenge its relevance?

The other example relates to the concept of fidelity. Spontane-ously, we see fidelity today as and anticipated attack on tomorrow's free will, a jail sentence compromising the impetuous unpredictability of the desire. We consider all the values that relate to constancy, commitment, the long term, as though the voluntary constraint they imply was scandalous. Pleasure, desire, happiness itself are now associated with nomadism, with wandering, with tribulation. Fidelity to another person appears to us to be an impoverishment that we angrily reject. A value that has lost its symbolic weight, fidelity in love is now seen as castrating. The symbolism has been reversed.

As we have seen concerning the couple and the family, "to give oneself, to forget oneself, to give up oneself, [now] relates to the slave mindset denounced by Nietzsche, to the neurosis that preoccupied Freud, to lack of character. Now it is morally dictated that we should leave the other when 'we don't love him anymore.' Fidelity is defined only as non-deception, not taking multiple partners simultaneously, in other words, the commitment to warn the one that we are leaving when we have found someone better. But fidelity over the time, faith in the word that was spoken yesterday when I was in a different mood than today, that form of fidelity is perceived as immoral."[3]

That is the contemporary point of view. Extraordinarily enough, however, we willingly subject ourselves to other kinds of fidelity that, in the past, would have been considered to too constraining. Fidelity to a career plan, for example; fidelity to oneself against all the winds and tides; fidelity to cliques or tribes and, of course, fidelity to our own inclinations. All these constraints to the spirit and to freedom were viewed by a Christian commentator (with some legitimacy) as "idolatrous fidelity" or even as new "idols produced by contemporary individualism."[4]

For the Ancients, indeed (whether Christian or Platonist), human freedom did not lie in this fidelity to the desires, but, on the contrary, in our capacity to disobey them. It was self-control and not abandonment to one's impulses that was equated with *active freedom*. Referring to the Greeks on this subject, Foucault said, "If it is so important to control desires and pleasures, if doing so is a moral goal of such great value, it is because we are seeking to preserve or rediscover some original innocence; it is not, in general (except of course in the Pythagorian tradition), to preserve purity; it is in order to be free, and to be able to remain free."[5]

We see the things backwards, today. Once again, it is all a matter of shifting symbolism and not of emancipation, strictly speaking. All

these shifts make sense, they follow a certain logic. They confrom confusedly to a plan or, at least, a vision of the world. They testify to a profound reversal of our approach to life. The true question is in what way.
There is no need to go far to identify some of the logic that governs this
new symbolic order.

"A Tool for Masturbation "

Uncommitted, uncertain, bulimic and anxious, contemporary
sexuality is above all solitary — to the point of sickness. It is as though
it had dismissed *the other* in its humanity finally to enjoy full but distressing autonomy. The fate of the word "partner" in loving relations is
revealing. It has made the other into a simple opposite number, a tool
for masturbation, an instrument that may be more or less satisfactory
and thus liable to ceaseless evaluations, comparisons, bench tests, etc..
The prevailing chatter about pleasure is like an interminable comparative audit, copied after the stock exchange report or the Olympic med-
als list. Locked up in this voluptuous loneliness ("There are no sexual
relations," said Lacan), having used the other, we wait impatiently, even
with exasperation, for the end of the final prohibition that still stands
in the way of our pleasure: non-desire for our partner.

In the first homosexual clubs of the 1980's, the famous "glory hole"
in pick-up joints was a striking symbol of this loneliness. An opening
bored in a wall at the height of the sexual organs hid the partner; this
made it possible to reduce sexual relations to simply trading organs,
with no meeting, however fleeting. Two sexual organs were offered, but
two bodies were hidden; two panting breaths might be heard, but no
words were exchanged. The dizzying solipsism of desire thus managed
to make commerce with the other while enjoying him. If the other were
erased, it is because one feared both meeting him and his otherness. The
same remark applies to the *backrooms* that were very much in fashion in
the 1970's, and not only for the use of homosexuals. Closed spaces with
no visual reference points, a darkness where bodies could be found, experienced and given, the *backrooms* not only make it possible to dissi-
pate in anonymity the last reserves or obstructions of decency, they
symbolically offer a presence-absence of the other, who is not identifiable, nor even visible. Can one imagine a more perfect metaphor of loneliness?

Roland Barthes already made the extreme loneliness of love the subject of his "fragments," in 1977. He underlined the strange permutation that made a new obscenity of the sentimental meeting, love, tenderness, taking responsibility for — and taking account of — *the other* person. "Discredited by modern opinion, the sentimentality of love must be assumed by the subject in love as a major transgression which leaves him alone and exposed; by an inversion of values, it is thus sentimentality that makes love obscene today."[6]

Two years later, it was Pascal Bruckner's and Alain Finkielkraut's turn to write a dissident and jubilant text, ironically commenting on the functional, medical, statistical and grimly gymnastic nature of modern "pleasure." "By reducing the male to his ejaculatory function, we are transforming sexual relations into something primitive, truthful, and literal, compared to which all the rest is only mystical lucubration or wantonness."[7]

Sexuality has finally been made into a purely biological function! Pleasure is becoming a purely anatomical, commercial and sporting matter (and cybernetic!). It is service, satiation, performance. Just when we were intoxicated with all the "potential" opportunities, contemporary individualism has remanded the overflowing voluptuousness to the rank of immediate predatory action, with no future — that is, to a bodily function that is now inevitably more solitary in principle than even eating and drinking could be. The "spectacle" and the contagious fear work together to set an unprecedented goal in the history of sexual relations: that of self-satisfaction. Safe sex, honors to Onan, and services rendered! In so doing, we not only testify to a rather timorous rejection of the other as a person, but we give up "linking the biological, the social and the unconscious subjective together," although that was precisely, as Pierre Legendre says, "that which constituted man as man and not only as living meat."[8]

Still dazed by all these new freedoms, we fail to take the true measure of the threats that they bring. Sexuality runs the risk today of being desocialized, disaffiliated, and dehumanized, even though, in substance, it is *culture* more than *function*. "Sexuality is dramatic," Maurice Merleau-Ponty once wrote, "because we engage all our personal life there. But why, exactly, do we do it? Why is our body a natural self, a given current of existence, so that we never know whether the forces that carry us along are ours or the body's, or rather that they are never entirely ours or the bodies'. There is no getting around sexuality; as there is no sexuality that is closed to the outside. Nobody is saved and nobody is lost entirely."[9]

Not much of this beautiful philosophical optimism remains; only the loneliness of a pleasure that "is not dramatic any more," because it has ceased, to quote Merleau-Ponty again, "to engage our personal life." While we may avoid actually looking into this vacuum, its quiet presence — the gaping void? — is has much to do with the neurotic attitude taken by modern society with regard to sex. It justifies these voracious arguments, ostentatious but unsated, that appear to stem from a kind of inconsolable lack. We thought we were finally grabbing something that had been forbidden, unobstructed pleasure, and here it slips between our fingers like a handful of water, leaving us frustrated and defeated. We are resolutely liberated, indeed, but alone and just as encumbered by our own pleasure that has been reduced to such a trivial thing. Thus we search, day after day, image after image, show after show, for that hypothetical "fabulous sex" of which Paul Ricoeur spoke some forty years ago. In the same work, he even added the premonition that: "Here man is engaged in an exhausting fight against the psychological poverty of pleasure itself, which is hardly likely to be improved, given its biological brutality."[10]

The general conversation around us does, indeed, seem to be obsessed by the imaginary pursuit of poorly defined and all the more disconcerting "sexual fairyland." This is an imaginary quest for a new holy grail of love, the constantly renewed (but never fulfilled) promise of an Omega point in the intensity of pleasure, heralding a forthcoming voluptuous achievement coming from who knows where. From a transgression never before dared? From a different technique? From more attempts and experimentation? From better performance? From a specific process? We like to believe that the ultimate pleasure, an opaque and unattainable mystery since the world was founded, would be within reach this time. And that is what secretly feeds all the nerve-wracking preoccupations and all the naivety of today.

We are far, indeed, from the supposedly decisive debate between the moral order that threatens and the freedom under threat.

The Fragmentation of Society

But the real significance of the anxious loneliness of pleasure, the consenting expulsion of the other, and the desocialization of sexuality only become clear in relation to a far more general phenomenon of so-cial fragmentation. What is going on in the realm of sexuality coincides and corresponds with what is happening in other spheres as well. The progressive desocialization, the weakening of institutions and the bonds of membership, the insecurity of individuals cast back upon their loneliness — these frightening breakdowns threaten the very cohesion of our post-industrial societies.

Work, to cite just one example, is also becoming desocialized in the sense that it is little by little losing its function of affiliation and integration. Similarly, the family is just one institution that is irrevoca-bly losing its role as a place of affiliation. The company is losing, like-wise, in the economic world. The evolution of liberalism in the late 1980's precipitated this institutional decline. The absolute preference given to shareholders over all the other stakeholders in the company (employees, executives, managers, suppliers, etc.) has led to a radically new design of an impoverished company-institution. The "values" es-poused are now of a different nature.

The *stake*holder values of yesteryear (i.e., the goals) founded the company as a communal institution, in which the leaders were the in-spirers of the community of social partners, between whom efforts and benefits were distributed. By contrast, according to *share*holder values, the success of which has become hegemonic in Western countries, the company is now only a contractual institution in which the leaders are simple agents of the shareholders and have only one objective, to maxi-mize short term financial gains. This means penalizing the other part-ners, if need be, for example through massive layoffs of employees to improve profits. Labor and the worker are in a weak position and no longer really constitute part of the institution; it's only the shareholders seeking a market against the consumers looking for products. The com-pany itself is not a community any more but a bunch of shares whose profitability is to be maximized.[11]

It may seem absurd to introduce micro-economic considerations into a reflection on sexual morality, the family and filiation. But the processes under way are quite comparable. And it is disconcerting to note that the pundits who describe the demise of the family as an institution are borrowing concepts coined in other realms to describe equivalent phenomena. Thus, for example, the explicit use of the concepts of insecurity and exclusion directly borrowed from a specialist in labor rights.[12] "In connection with the family question, we are in a situation similar to that recently analyzed by Robert Castel in connection with the social question. We have obstinately persisted in thinking of social exclusion as a kind of exceptional case, because we did not understand that it was the wage-based society itself that was damaged at its core; in the same way, we have persisted in thinking that the fragility of family bonds was a kind of increasing exception, because we have failed to see that the family institution has been struck to the heart."[13]

It is a fact that all the contemporary discussion of wage-earning, labor, the changes of value induced by the economic globalization and ultra-liberalism touches on questions equally relevant to the family and, in the final analysis, the new approach to love: a retreat of the institutions, rupture of the bonds of belonging, disaffiliation and a progressive crumbling of our societies into so many fragile bits of juxtaposed individual loneliness.

In contemporary industrialized societies, writes Philippe Engelhard, "each person is defined only by his aptitude to produce, consume and save. He is nothing more but the passive neuron of an economic and financial machine that has no other goal but itself. The consumerist pressure obviously contributes to the atomization of society. This pressure does not help flourish an actor who is responsible and free in his choices, but encourages the expansion of a corrosive form of individualism. The consumerist pressure has, moreover, the effect of increasing the cost of entry into the social/economic system and thus it generates exclusion and frustrations."[14]

Genealogical Power

This progressive fragmentation of human societies, this radical evolution of the disaffiliated individual, so total a triumph of individualism that exiles each one within his loneliness — it makes one wonder what is the significance of this transformation. The disillusioned but anxious loneliness of the individual-as-king is obviously the price we pay for the individual's emancipation. "The Ego gone mad" seems to be the ultimate result of a great historical rupture, recorded just over three centuries ago with the advent of the Enlightenment. If this triumph of individualism is now bordering on disintegration, in every field, is it any wonder why?

What has changed in our relationship to time? The individual, disaffiliated from any institution and without ties, is without a past. Taking refuge on a moment's notice, dedicated to a kind of feverish immediacy, he is also without a future, in the sense that he is not a part of any history any more. History such as he perceives it and experiences it is nothing but a random succession of present points in time, a sequence of fleeting moments all having the same value. That which our societies are beginning to mourn is what Pierre Legendre judiciously calls "genealogical power," that which used to organize human time in a continuity that gave the individual a context. Genealogical power is, essentially, that of institutions. One could even say that it defines them.

In the case of the family, this is obvious. Let us include here the entire sentence from Plato, which we cited above. "The human race has a natural affinity with all of time, which it accompanies and will accompany for the duration; that is what makes it immortal, by leaving the children of its children and thus, thanks to the perennial quality of its always identical unity, participating in immortality through generation." This attentive management of time is the precise vocation of institutions in general and of the family in particular.

That is where, ideally, the opposition is resolved between what one could call the brief time of the individual and the long time of the "immortal" collective. It is inside the family institution that these two contrasting temporalities are harmonized, after a fashion. The threshold of this arbitration — which favors one or the other — defines the degree of unity of a society. The traditional societies naturally gave precedence to the long time of the community, even at the cost of the individual. Today, we do the opposite. "The goal of tradition was for goal to maintain, against destiny, the survival of the group. It placed its confidence in the institutions that had proven reliable and could be defined as the best means for the present to stay as close as possible to the past. The constant sense of precariousness led to prudence, and prudence dictated that one reproduce what had succeeded earlier. One survived only by denying oneself as a singular being."[16]

But the necessary "prudence" and the will to ward off uncertainly are not the only objectives of the family institution. Mobilized in its entirety to resist the flow of time, the family constructs time by giving it meaning. It is through the family and its genealogical power as intermediaries that the human being, having arrived in the world, is inscribed in a system of relationships, a filiation, and therefore in time, and especially in culture. Humanization, in the final analysis, is inevitably achieved through the genealogical continuum.

Today, as we know, the weakening of the institutions favors the short view of time, that of the individual who is entirely occupied with the instantaneity of consumption, pleasures and competition. His loneliness, which is so much an issue today, is not only based on eviction from the group and the values that it used to transmit. Infused by "the obsessive illusion of personal authenticity as the source and the end of everything," this loneliness is also in mourning for the long-term view. Without genealogical ties and a representation of the future, we are confronted for the first time with what one might call "the uncertainty of time."

The vocation of the family institution — to triumph over time, to give some contents to the future — was in any case the inherent characteristic of all the other institutions, including the school, the company, the State itself. Institutions, by definition, carefully watch over the long haul. Concerned with anticipating, with protecting, with giving the future a chance, they are ontologically authorities of "foresight" charged with insuring the long term against the impatience of the moment. It is *this bias in favor of the future* which is called into question today, everywhere around us. The unilateral victory of the present is both the cause and the consequence of the vanishing future.

The Vanishing Future

This progressive fading of the future is particularly striking in the area of the economy. The new liberal perception of the company mentioned above — corporate governance — no only gives absolute priority to the interests of the shareholders. It amounts to a *de facto* bias in favor of instantaneous profitability, measured with the yardstick of the stock exchange, over longer term entrepreneurial visions. It places greater value on the present, to the detriment of the future.

But corporate governance is perfectly consistent with that alternative of capitalism, "the American model," that Michel Albert opposed to "the Rhenish model."[17] The first is based on stock exchange financing, the immediate maximization of profit, mobility and general deregulation. The second, founded on banks and family shareholding, placed its bets rather on the duration, on social cohesion, dialogue and consequently the long term. It favored the future. However, the last fifteen years' evolution has led to an irresistible extension of the American model. *Our perception of time* is behind this triumph,.

Still more striking: in terms of economic globalization, the financial policy choices made in the last several years by the Western countries (European especially) have also headed in the same direction. Certain economists, like Jean-Paul Fitoussi, have made a conceptual contribution by showing the extent to which this macro-economic orientation biased in favor of today has systematically compromised the future. The high level of interest rates, the obsessive fear of inflation, the resignation to unemployment (especially of young people), the encouragement of saving: it is all, at the level of the collective representation, a depreciation of the future.[18]

Let us add that habituation to mass unemployment in Europe and job insecurity are accompanied by new advantages that benefit revenue, especially of a share of the increasingly unfavorable value added to the wages. These new logics are advantageous for those who are not in the work force, retirees, investors, etc., but they are catastrophic for young people who are knocking on the doors of the community. It seems as if our aging societies have in some muddled way sacrificed the future in favor of the present; and of the past. In the 1960's and 1970's, by contrast, it was possible to show Keynesianism and inflation as a slow death for investors, in other words, a relative scorn for the past, compensated for by an immense collective projection toward the future. The symbolic representations have changed direction radically.

Devalued, the future has become especially indecipherable. That is a partial explanation. We must not be satisfied with interpreting this depreciation of the future in terms of pessimism, fear or timidity. It is much more profound. If the future is devalued, it is because we ceased having a plan, a collective ambition, even an ideology regarding it. In terms of representation, it became random, enigmatic, indecipherable. It ceased informing the present.

Thousands of symptoms bear witness to this groping temporal uncertainty. The ruin of the institutions is not the least of them. Think, for example, of the crisis of the schools (in the US, France, even Russia), a constant theme for hackneyed news reporting and an everlasting topic of debate. Ultimately, it comes down to a crisis of transmission, closely linked to our inability to identify with the future. What should we be transmitting? From which point of view? Toward what kind of collective goal? These are questions that it has become difficult to answer. Like the family, the school suffers from the uncertainty of times and is unable to assume its own genealogical power. It can no longer register the disaffiliated individual into the continuity of any history. It is as hard to transmit a heritage as to indicate a future. The effort is actually subverted by the dictatorship of the moment.

We should look at one more symptom, finally, that is equally revealing of the vanishing of the future: a rambling and invasive nostalgia, knee-jerk tropism, and an unadventurous fascination for the past. All these reflexes throw our era into an interminable looking back at a lost past. The fact is that we are living with our noses in the archives and our spirits drowned by regret. The value of the past goes up proportionately as the future is depreciated. We have become the librarians of our own history. Confronted with the tyrannical present, only one exit is still open: the one behind us. The only temporal mobility that remains available to us is that which allows us to go backward.

The Arrow of Time

This climate of retreating panic, of turning back, the interminable reappearance of the past basically calls into question the idea of progress. Isn't the very idea in trouble? Is progress in the process of disappearance as a fundamental concept? If the future is disappearing as a positive value, if we no longer know how to represent it and enhance it, if we refuse, therefore, to make the least "sacrifice" to it, isn't it because our perception of time itself has changed?

It is too much forgotten that the notion of progress that has governed our history since the Enlightenment was only the laicization of the Judeo-Christian idea of salvation. Its original basis was religious before it became scientific or ideological. Years ago, Mircea Eliade, the Romanian philosopher, highlighted the remote Western genealogy of progress, which was initially the expression of a heart in search of hope.[19] In that, it proceeded from a Judeo-Christian interpretation of time: time defined as "an arrow," directed in opposition to the cyclical or circular time of the pagan cultures, in particular of the Greeks in general and Plotinus in particular.

"Human progress," observes the Swiss essayist Étienne Barilier, "long before being a scientific or historical concept, was the Christian vision of a history of salvation, of a history directed by a higher sense, of the heart's judicious adventure in the world. It is only slowly, over the centuries, over the course of time, that this idea left the interior of the heart and moved toward Heaven to gain the externality of the material world."[20]

By losing the future, by wearily detaching ourselves from the idea of progress, we are breaking off from the "right time" that founded the West itself, and we don't even realize it. This rectilinear view of time, this directed continuity carrying all the promises — salvation for some, progress for others — directed our history and gave it meaning. That is what, for this reason, justified the voluntarist organization of our lives and our societies. It founded our choices and legitimated our concern for controlling destiny by countering the chaotic tyranny of pleasures with the free will of men and women who were on their way to the future.

A beautiful phrase comes to mind, by Emmanuel Lévinas, who observed in an interview that we, in the West, were "accustomed to the idea that time is going somewhere." And Max Weber's definition: politics is the taste for the future. We know very well that it is in the relation which we maintain with the future that the most decisive role is played.

Will this arrow of time be broken for good? If so, we would go back to circular time as before, the of the eternal return and the "natural" fates of the species. The question is whether that would not be a surreptitious return to barbarity.

NOTES

Chapter 1

1. See below, Chap. 11.
2. Michel Foucault, *Histoire de la sexualité*, t. I, La Volonté de savoir, Galli-mard, 1977.
3. Peter Brown, *Le Renoncement à la chair. Virginité, célibat et continence dans le christianisme primitif*, Gallimard, 1995.
4. Max Weber, *Le Savant et le Politique*, UGE, 10/18, 1979.
5. Somewhat earlier, of course, in countries like Canada and the United States.
6. *Infostat justice*, No. 44, March 1996.
7. P. Tournier, "Agressions sexuelles," *Questions pénales*, CESDIP, March 1996.
8. Denis Salas, *Esprit*, December 1996.
9. Antoine Garapon, *Esprit*, December 1996.
10. *Le Monde*, 29 April 1971.
11. One part of the Rightist press and the religious press did represent Louis Malle as having wanted, to put it bluntly, "to spit in the middle-class' soup," to use the expression of Andre Bessèges, chronicler of *La Vie catholique*.
12. Jean de Baroncelli, *Le Monde*, 29 April 1971.
13. See Chapter 13.

14. Frédéric Martel, *Le Rose et le Noir*, Seuil, 1996.
15. *Libération*, June 9, 1978. Today Rene Schérer, who has changed his point of view appreciably, remains an important and respected philosopher.
16. Gérard Zwang, *Lettre ouverte aux mal-baisants*, Albin Michel, 1975. The author relates the story of the time in 1975 when a group of FHAR militants in Vincennes obstructed a meeting of the French Society of Clinical Sexology which he had created.
17. *Le Nouvel Observateur*, February 25,1974.
18. *Libération*, April 10, 1978.
19. *Le Monde*, April 14, 1978.
20. *Le Matin de Paris*, March 27, 1979.
21. *Playboy*, July 1979.
22. *L'Événement du jeudi*, December 7-13, 1989.
23. Several other highly publicized events might be added to the Corral case, such as the dance class scandal in Cannes, in 1988, the assassination of Pastor Doucé, in 1989, and the missing children from Auxerre,
24. Gilles Lapouge and Marie-Françoise Hans, *Les Femmes, la pornographie et L'Érotisme*, Seuil, 1978.
25. In spite of his acknowledged crimes, some called his execution "an injustice" or an attempt to make an example of him. An anonymous and unpublished comedy, "Deschauffours' Shadow," 1739, even regarded the trial as a revenge of "the straights" against "the gays." (Maurice Lever, *Les Bûchers de Sodome*, Fayard, 1985.)
26. See Chapter 14.
27. Debate on France Culture (television show), September 20, 1996.
28. Peter Brown, *Le Renoncement à la chair. Virginité, célibat et continence dans le christianisme primitif, op. cit.*
29. Maurice Lever, *Les Bûchers de Sodome, op. cit.*
30. Philippe Engelhard, *L'Homme mondial*, Arléa, 1996.
31. *Le Monde*, August 29,1996. Bruno Latour explicitly borrows the idea of a "reflexive modernity" or a "second modernity" from two American essayists, Ulrich and Anthony Giddens, authors of *Reflexive Modernity* (Stanford University Press).

Chapter 2

1. On the critical importance of this watershed year, see Chapter 11.
2. The March 22 Movement, *Ce n'est qu'un début, continuons le combat*, Cahiers libres 124, Maspero, 1968.
3. Herbert Marcuse, *L'Homme unidimensionnel*, Minuit, 1967.
4. Actually, Wilhelm Reich was on the verge of madness and undertook

experiments with a mysterious substance, "orgon," or orgonic energy, which he claimed to have discovered, and with radioactivity. He wanted to commercialize supposed "orgon accumulators" to cure cancer and sexual impotence. At the instigation of the American Food and Drug Administration he was accused of being a charlatan and was prosecuted.

5. As testifies, like so many other examples, this short introduction of Reich in the preface to an article, in 1972: "Excluded from the German CP by the Stalinists, disavowed by the analytical movement, pursued by the Nazis, imprisoned by the American justice system, he was rehabilitated by the young people of the capitalist countries who have resuscitated his dream of life and who seek in his works an answer to the woes of life." (Jean-Michel Palmier, *Le Monde*, September 22, 1972).

6. The first two titles to be republished in France were the *La Fonction de l'orgasme* (Éd. de l'Arche, 1952, then in 1967) and *La Révolution sexuelle* (Plon, 1968, and UGE, "10/18,"1970).

7. Since the mid-Sixties, Reich had become the mastermind of the German SDS led by Rudy Dutschke. In France, he had influenced the situationists, and in particular Raoul Vaneigem who pays him homage in his own books.

8. Daniel Guérin, Marc Kravetz, Michel Cattier, Roger Dadoun, Jean-Michel Palmier, Constantin Sinelnikoff, Boris Fraenkel, Olivier Revault d'Alonnes and a few others.

9. Wilhelm Reich, *La Révolution sexuelle*, Christian Bourgois, éd. de 1982.

10. *Ibid.*

11. *Id., L'Analyse caractérielle*, Payot, 1971.

12. *Id., L'Irruption de la morale sexuelle*, Payot, 1972.

13. *Le Magazine littéraire*, March 1973.

14. A teacher at a coeducational school in Marcheille, Gabrielle Russier had become the mistress of one of her sixteen-year-old pupils in 1968. Accused of corrupting a minor, she was condemned in July 1969 to one year of prison with deferment; she committed suicide September 1 after the public prosecutor's office had interjected an appeal *a minima*. The Russier affair, which led to interminable polemics, several books and a movie, remains indissolubly linked to memories of May 1968.

15. Wilhelm Reich, *L'Irruption de la morale sexuelle, op. cit.*

16. Born in 1872 to a family of wealthy Generals, Alexandra Kollontaï, a famous lover and flamboyant personality who was called "the Valkyrie of the Revolution," published pamphlet after pamphlet arguing against the family and for sexual freedom. Cosying up to Lenin, she became, as a People's Commissar for Public Assistance, the first woman Minister of History. Gaining the friendship of Stalin, she was appointed Ambassa-

dor to Sweden and escaped the terror which struck her friends among the Mensheviks. (In this connection, see: *Arkadi Vaksberg, Alexandra Kollontaï*, translated from Russian by Dimitri Sesemann, Fayard, 1996.)

17. Preface to the third edition of *La Révolution sexuelle.*
18. See Chapter 8.
19. Raoul Vaneigem, *Traité de savoir-vivre à l'usage des jeunes générations*, reprinted with a previously unpublished preface, Gallimard, "Folio Actuel," No 28, 1992. Note that Vaneigem would publish, in 1992, a large booklet that was even more violently against Christianity, *La Résistance au christianisme. Les hérésies des origines au XVIII siècle*, Fayard.
20. See Chapters 7 and 8.
21. Ilse Ollendorf Reich, Reich's third wife, published a biography of him during the 1960's which focuses exclusively on his life in America. French translation: *Wilhelm Reich*, Belfond, 1971.
22. Preface to the third edition of *La Révolution sexuelle.*
23. *Le Magazine littéraire*, March 1973.
24. See especially James Lovelock, *La Terre est un être vivant*, Flammarion, 1993, and *Gaia*, Robert Laffont, 1992.
25. Luc Ferry, *Le Nouvel Ordre écologique*, LGF, 1994.
26. Georges Nivat, *Vers la fin du mythe russe. Essai sur la culture russe de Gogol à nos jours*, L'Age d'Homme, 1988.
27. *Ibid.*
28. Quoted by Alexandre Papadopoulos, *Introduction à la philosophie russe*, Odile Jacob, 1995.
29. Raoul Vaneigem, *Le Livre des plaisirs*, Éd. Labor, 1979.
30. Michel Foucault, *Histoire de la sexualité*, t. I, *La Volonté de savoir, op. cit.*
31. Wilhelm Reich, *Psychologie de masse du fascisme*, Payot, 1972.
32. Id., *La Révolution sexuelle, op. cit*, p. 331.
33. French translation published in *le Magazine littéraire*, September 1996.
34. Cited by Lorraine Millot, *Libération*, June 28-29, 1997.

Chapter 3

1. I borrow this expression from Albert O. Hirschman, author of a bracing essay, *Deux Siècles de rhétorique réactionnaire*, Fayard, 1991. Note that Hirschman ranks under this label the neo-conservative criticism of the welfare state that ended up triumphing in the United States.
2. Maurice Agulhon, *Histoire vagabonde*, Gallimard, 1996.
3. An example is David Cronenberg's movie, *Crash*, which explicitly assimi-

lates sex and death (that of other people!), and the admiring shivers that greeted it at the Cannes festival where it was shown in July 1996. Note, however, that some of the critics were not easily deceived. Consider this comment by Pascal Mérigeau: "To watch characters with the appeal of fashion models feeling up their neighbors, with their hands under their skirts, while watching road accidents, playing with the remote control on their video recorder in order to catch, in slow motion, some macabre detail that had escaped them at the normal speed, to listen to them protest that there is nothing more exciting than someone else dying (someone who hadn't asked anything of anybody) in his car that was hit by a lunatic – this is not so much disturbing as it is idiotic,"(*Le Monde,* May 19-20, 1996).

4. Albert O. Hirschman, *Deux Siècles de rhétorique réactionnaire, op. cit.*

5. Let us cite the example of Daniel Karlin's and Remi Lainé's filmed survey, *L'Amour en in France,* broadcast in 1991, the entire basis of which (very much disputed by psychoanalysts) consisted in openly going after "the tyranny of prohibitions" or "old social and sexist forms of alienation." As if that were, in 1991, still a problem...

6. Luc Pareydt, Editor in Chief des *Cahiers pour croire aujourd'hui,* in *Panoramiques,* No. 23, "Dépassées les valeurs catholiques?", Arléa-Corlet, 1995.

7. This is nicely clarified in Françoise Héritier's book, *Masculin/Féminin. La pensée de la différence,* Odile Jacob, 1996.

8. The adjective "unsurpassable" obviously refers to Jean-Paul Sartre's famous statement, "Je considère le marxisme comme l'indépassable philosophie de notre temps" (*Critique de la raison dialectique,* Gallimard, 1960).

9. I am intentionally using this legal term in its meaning of a general promise, a constant but not yet accepted offer, such as that of "the vendor" in a large self-service store.

10. At least six of the men questioned by the police in June 1997 in the context of an anti-pedophile raid committed suicide, even though two of them were not questioned.

11. Pierre Manent, on Allan Bloom's writings, *Commentaire,* No. 76, Winter 1996.

12. Here is a tragic irony: In France, the onset of AIDS (in 1982-1983) came *at the very moment* when most of the laws against homosexuality were abolished (between 1981 and 1983), in conformity with François Mitterrand's campaign promises. Especially the following: June12, 1981: the Defferre circular on limiting record keeping on homosexuals and identity checks at gay bars; June 12, 1981: the dissolution of the homosexual brigade within the police force; rejection of the WHO classification of homosexuality as a mental illness. August 4, 1981: amnesty law includ-

ing homosexual offences. July 27, 1982: abrogation (based on Robert Badinter's proposal) of article 331-2 of the Penal code which had set a different age of majority for homosexuals (18 years) and heterosexuals (15 years).

13. Michael Pollack, *Les Homosexuels et le Sida*, Métailié, 1988, and *Une identité blessée*, Métailié, 1993.

14. "In the few decades before or after the year 1300, the Jews were expelled from France and England; the Order of the Templars was dissolved on charges of sorcery and sexual deviation; Edward II of England, the last medieval sovereign who was openly homosexual, was deposed and not assassinated; interest charged on loans was equated to heresy and those who practiced it were submitted to the Inquisition; and lepers, every-where in France, were persecuted on the grounds that they supposedly poisoned the wells and debased themselves with Jews and witches,"(John Boswell, *Christianisme, tolérance sociale et homosexualité. Les homosexuels en Europe occidentale des débuts de l'ère chrétienne au XIV siècle*, Gal-limard, 1985).

15. Robert van Gulik, *La Vie sexuelle dans la Chine ancienne*, Gallimard, "Tel," 1993. An extraordinary figure, a great expert on China, Japan and Asian erotic art, Robert van Gulik was the subject of a biography translated into French: C.D. Barkman and H. de Vries, *Les Trois vies de Robert van Gulik*, Christian Bourgois, 1997. Later on, we will again refer to his works on sexuality in China.

16. In the complaints of "the Children of Sodom," presented in 1790, Article 5 makes this demand: "All doctors and surgeons, declared or not, assas-sins by patent of faculty, will be held to lend their ministry to the heal-ing of "crystalline, "under penalty of extraordinary prosecution by all authorized means." Reported by Alexandrian, *Les Libérateurs de l'amour*, Seuil, 1977.

17. Frédéric Martel, *Le Rose et le Noir, op. cit.*

18. Quoted in "Histoire d'une cause," in *L'Homme contaminé*, Autrement, No. 130, 1991.

19. Tony Anatrella, *L'Amour et le Préservatif*, Flammarion, 1995.

20. Some educational brochures and programs about AIDS don't worry much about delicacy. Thus, for example, the comic strip Toxico AIDS & Co., showing incest between mother and son, and Adventures of Latex, a picture book intended for children in which one of the scenes cele-brates the ménage à trois. (Examples cited by psychoanalyst Tony Ana-trella, *L'Amour et le Préservatif, op. cit.*)

21. *Le Monde*, 8 July 1995.

22. Sophie Chauveau, *Éloge de l'amour au temps du sida*, Flammarion, 1995.

23. Martine Sevegrand, *Les Enfants du bon Dieu. Les catholiques français et la procréation au XX siècle*, Albin Michel, 1995.

24. Statement by Monsignore di Falco, spokesman for the Bishops' Conference of France, to the *Journal des étudiants*, Paris-Sorbonne, April 1995.

25. Actually, the Church did so, on several occasions, but without really being understood. Comment by Cardinal Lustiger: "Sex and death: AIDS generates fear and guilt. That may explain why the Church is misunderstood," (*L'Express*, December 9, 1988).

Chapter 4

1. This is not true of the early Middle Ages. Under the Carolingians, i.e. between the VIIIth and Xth centuries, the discipline of marriage was reserved for the aristocracy.

2. We must insist on the adjective 'fantasy.' In reality, indeed, workers on the contrary gave a completely new importance to the family, in which they saw a refuge closed to the outside world that had become hostile. "Facing the 19th century society in full transformation, conquering, enterprising, but hard on the poor and the weak," writes a specialist on this question, "the couple, focusing on happiness, attached great importance to the family," (Louis Roussel, *La Famille incertaine*, Odile Jacob, 1989).

3. Karl Marx, *Œuvres complètes*, Gallimard, "Bibliothèque de la Pléiade" , t. I.

5. Sigmund Freud, *La Vie sexuelle*, PUF, 1995.

6. Wilhelm Reich, *La Révolution sexuelle, op. cit.*

7. "The most original was Alphonse Gallais, who, under his true name, published *Mémoires d'une fille de joie* (1902), "a mabulo-erotic novel," *Les Enfers lubriques* (1906), a study of sadism and masochism; various "chansons socials" dedicated to "comrades of the workers' Internationale" – Ma Faubourienne, Gloire à Ferrer,"(Alexandrian, *Histoire de la littérature érotique*, Seghers, 1989).

8. Quoted in an appendix to the book, *Internationale situationniste*, Fayard, reprinted May 1997.

9. More than 3000 copies of the brochure were distributed in various countries of Europe. In France, at least three pirate editions were printed.

10. Évelyne Sullerot, *Quels pères? Quels fils?*, Fayard, 1992.

11. These distinctions were clearly analyzed by Henri Weber, *Vingt Ans après, que reste-t-il de Mai 68?*, Seuil, 1988.

12. Michel Foucault, *Histoire de la sexualité*, t. I, *La Volonté de savoir, op. cit.* In another passage of the same work, Foucault begins another analysis of the 19th century. "Sex," he writes, "is not some part of the body that the

bourgeoisie had to disqualify or cancel in order to put to work those whom they dominated. It is an element of the bourgeoisie itself, which has, more than any other aspect of life, worried, disturbed, required and obtained care and attention, which the bourgeoisie cultivated with a mixture of fright, curiosity, delight and fever."

13. Reported in a special edition of the magazine *Autrement*, on California, dated April 1981.

14. Michael Pollack, "L'homosexualité masculine, ou le bonheur dans le ghetto?", in *Sexualités occidentales*, under the direction of Philippe Ariès and André Béjin, Seuil, "Points Essais," 1984.

15. Frédéric Martel, *L'Express*, June 19, 1997.

16. Raoul Vaneigem, *Le Livre des plaisirs, op. cit.*

17. *Le Point*, May 11, 1996.

18. This is explicitly emphasized in the June, 1997, report of the UNDP (UN Development Program).

19. Raoul Vaneigem, *Le Livre des plaisirs, op. cit.*

20. Interview by François Ewald for *Le Magazine littéraire*.

21. On this topic, see Philippe Van Parijs, *Qu'est-ce qu'une société juste?*, Seuil, 1991.

22. Amitai Etzioni, "Le paradigme du 'je' et du 'nous,'" *Krisis*, June 1994.

23. Quoted by Constantin Sinelnikoff, *Le Magazine littéraire*, March 1973.

24. Pascale Weil, *A quoi rêvent les années 90*, Seuil, 1997.

25. François Brune, *Le Bonheur conforme*, Gallimard, 1985.

26. *Le Nouvel Observateur*, August 29-September 4, 1996. François de Singly is a professor at the Université des sciences sociales at the Sorbonne and Director of the *Centre de recherches en sociologie de la famille*.

27. *Marianne*, June 30-July 6, 1997.

29. Évelyne Sullerot, *Quels pères? Quels fils?, op. cit.*

30. Robert Reich, *L'Économie mondialisée*, Dunod, 1993; Benjamin R. Barber, *Djihad versus McWorld*, Desclée de Brouwer, 1996.

31. For example Arthur Schlesinger, *La Désunion de l'Amérique*, Liana Levi, 1993.

32. Daniel Bélan, "La fin du Welfare State," *Esprit*, May 1997.

33. Allusion to a maxim of American journalism, having a deontological implication: defending the afflicted and afflicting the big guys

34. François de Singly, "Les habits neufs de la domination masculine," *Esprit*, November 1993.

35. Called "pointers" in prison jargon, criminal pedophiles were ostracized, even persecuted, by other prisoners throughout the entire period. In jail, they never enjoyed the least indulgence, contrary to what was the case outside.

36. Max Weber, *L'Éthique protestante et l'Esprit du capitalisme, op. cit.*

Chapter 5

1. Robert van Gulik, *La Vie sexuelle dans la Chine ancienne, op. cit.*
2. François Brune, *Le Bonheur conforme, op. cit.*
3. Raoul Vaneigem, *Le Livre des plaisirs, op. cit.*
4. Article by Libby Books published in *The Guardian* and translated in *Courrier international*, June 19-25, 1997.
5. Boris Cyrulnik, "*Éthologie de la sexualité,*" *Krisis*, No. 17, May 1995.
6. André Green, *Les Chaînes d'Éros. Actualité du sexuel*, Odile Jacob, 1997.
7. Peter Brown, *Le Renoncement à la chair, op. cit.*
8. On these questions, see Chapter 13.
9. Uta Ranke-Heineman, *Des eunuques pour le royaume des cieux. L'Église catholique et la sexualité*, Robert Laffont, 1990, and Hachette, "Pluriel," 1992; original edition: *Eunuchen für das Himmelreich*, Hoffman and Campe Verlag, 1988.
10. For a fairly recent French translation of Juvenal's satires, see *La Décadence*, Arléa, 1996. For Martial, *Épigrammes* (3 vol.), Les Belles Lettres.
11. Here is the exact passage in which Foucault uses the expression: "C'est le sexe aujourd'hui qui sert de support à cette vieille forme, si familière et si importante en Occident, de prédication. Un grand prêche sexuel – qui a eu ses théologiens subtils et ses voix populaires – a parcouru nos sociétés depuis quelques dizaines d'années, il a fustigé l'ordre ancien, dénoncé les hypocrisies, chanté le droit de l'immédiat et du réel; il a fait rêver d'une autre cité" (Michel Foucault, *Histoire de la sexualité*, t. I, *La Volonté de savoir, op. cit.*). [Today sex is used to support this old form, so familiar and so significant in the West, of preaching. A great sexual sermon – which has had both its subtle theologians and its popular voices – has been blanketing our societies for the last few decades; it harangued the old order, denounced hypocrisies, sang to the right to what is immediate and real; it made us dream of another city. "]
12. *Le Point*, October 12, 1996.
13. Michael Warner, "Pourquoi les homosexuels prennent-ils des risques?," *Le Journal du sida*, No. 72, April 1995.
14. "Sado-Maso," interview with Christine D., *Krisis*, No. 17, May 1995.
15. *Libération*, September 16, 1996.
16. Draft preface to *L'Impossible*, quoted by Alexandrian, *Histoire de la littérature érotique, op. cit.*

17. Georges Bataille, *L'Histoire de L'Érotisme*, in *Œuvres complètes*, Gallimard, t. VIII, 1976.

18. Georges Bataille, *L'Érotisme*, in *Œuvres complètes*, Gallimard, t. X, 1987.

19. Georges Duby, preface to the collection *Amour et Sexualité en Occident*, Seuil, "L'Histoire,"1991, and "Points Histoire."

20. William H. Masters and Virginia E. Johnson, *Les Mésententes sexuelles et leur traitement*, French trans., Robert Laffont, 1971.

21. André Béjin, "Le pouvoir des sexologues et la démocratie sexuelle," in *Sexualités occidentales, op. cit.*

22. *Ibid.*

23. Quoted by André Béjin, "Le pouvoir des sexologues et la démocratie sexuelle" , in *Sexualités occidentales, op. cit.*

24. Exact reference: Kinsey, Pomeroy, Martin Gebhard, *Le Comportement sexuel de l'homme* (French trans., Éd. du Pavois, 1948); *Le Comportement sexuel de la femme* (Amiot-Dumont, 1954).

25. Georges Bataille, *L'Érotisme, op. cit.*

26. Among the more recent, the famous "Simon Report," from1973, and the INSERM study from 1992, published under the title, *Les Comportements sexuels en France*, La Documentation française, 1993.

27. Allan Bloom, *L'Amour et l'Amitié*, Éd. de Fallois, 1997.

28. *Ibid.*

29. *Le Figaro*, 13 August 1996.

30. Quoted by Gilles Lapouge and Marie-Françoise Hans, *Les Femmes, la pornographie et L'Érotisme, op. cit.*

31. Gilbert Tordjmann, "Comportements sexuels et peines de sexe," *Krisis*, No. 17, May 1995.

32. Examples selected during a one-month period by *Le Canard enchaîné* in August 1996.

34. Statement by Dr. Giulinao during a colloquium entitled, "*Sexe et guérison*," held at the Sorbonne in early 1997. The erectile molecule in question was to be marketed under the name of *sildenasil*. A similar medicine, based on prostaglandine El, *Caverject*, was launched in November 1994. Marketed by Pharmacia Upjohn and sold by prescription, it has the unfortunate side effect of requiring to be injected.

35. In the guise of an introduction to René Girard's works and to his theory on mimetic desire: *Mensonges romantiques et Vérité romanesque*, Grasset, 1961, and *La Violence et le Sacré*, Grasset, 1972.

36. Roland Barthes, *Fragments d'un discours amoureux*, Seuil, 1977.

37. Quoted in *le Dictionnaire de sexologie*, J.-J. Pauvert, 1962.

38. Boris Cyrulnik, "*Éthologie de la sexualité, op. cit.*

Chapter 6

1. Louis Antoine de Bougainville, Voyage *autour du monde par la frégate "La Boudeuse" et la flûte "L'Étoile,"* La Découverte, reprinted 1987.
2. Paul Veyne, *Histoire de la vie privée,* Seuil, t. I, 1985.
3. Id., *L'Histoire,* No. 180, September 1994.
4. Alexandrian, *Histoire de la littérature érotique, op. cit.*
5. John Boswell, *Christianisme, tolérance sociale et homosexualité. Les homosexuels en Europe occidentale, des débuts de l'ère chrétienne au XIV siècle, op. cit.*
6. Mentioned by Georges Bataille, *Le Procès de Gilles de Rais,* in *Œuvres complètes,* Gallimard, t. X, 1987.
7. Restif of Bretonne, *Le Pornographe, suivi de État de la prostitution chez les Anciens,* Éd. d'Aujourd'hui, 1983.
8. Guillaume Apollinaire, *L'Œuvre libertine du comte de Mirabeau,* Éditions d'Aujourd'hui, 1984.
9. Friedrich Nietzsche, *Œuvres philosophiques complètes,* Gallimard, t. IV.
10. This is the title of a recent work by the historian Jean-Noël Robert, Les Belles Lettres, 1997.
11. As caricatured examples of the ongoing confusion between sexual interdicts and Christianity we may point to sexologist Gerard Zwang's irate texts; from book to book, he hammers home the same assertion: "Christianity has the sad singularity of founding moral criteria upon sexual deprivations," in "Dépassées les valeurs catholiques?", *Panoramiques,* No. 23, *op. cit.*
12. *L'Histoire,* No. 180, *op. cit.*
13. Michel Foucault, *Histoire de la sexualité, t. II, L'Usage des plaisirs, op. cit.*
14. Uta Ranke-Heineman, *Des eunuques pour le royaume des cieux. L'Église catholique et la sexualité, op. cit.*
15. *Ibid.*
16. Especially in his major work on this question: *Un temps pour embrasser. Aux origines de la morale sexuelle occidentale,* Seuil, 1983.
17. According to Marcel Détienne, *Les Jardins d'Adonis. La mythologie des aromates en Grèce,* Gallimard, 1972.
18. Pierre Braun, "Les tabous des feriae," *L'Année sociologique,* 1959, Quoted by J.-L. Flandrin, *Un temps pour embrasser. Aux origines de la morale sexuelle occidentale, op. cit.*
19. Paul Veyne, *Histoire de la vie privée, op. cit.,* t. I.
20. Note that the emperor Tiberius made a scandal by choosing, to be pro-

vocative, cunnilingus – and even cunnilingus with women.

21. Michel Foucault, *Histoire de la sexualité*, t. II, *L'Usage des plaisirs, op. cit.*

22. Quoted by Josy Eisenberg, *La Femme au temps de la Bible*, Stock-L. Pernoud, 1995.

23. France Quéré, *La Femme, les grands textes des pères de l'Église*, Grasset-Le Centurion.

24. Hesiod, *Les Travaux et les Jours*, new French trans. by Claude Terreaux, Arléa, 1995.

25. Pascal Quignard, *Le Sexe et l'Effroi*, Gallimard, "Folio," 1996.

26. Pliny, *Histoire* naturelle, VII, chap. 15.

27. Xenophon, *Tenir sa maison. L'Économique*, new French trans. by Claude Terreaux, Arléa, 1997.

28. Lucretiu, *La Nature des choses*, new French trans. by Chantal Labre, Arléa, livre IV, 1992.

29. Saint Augustine took up the defense of women in *La Cité de Dieu*, written shortly after the sack of Rome by the Visigoths.

30. Peter Brown, *Le Renoncement à la chair, op. cit.*

31. Paul Veyne, "L'homosexualité à Rome," in *Amour et Sexualité en Occident, op. cit.*

32. Plutarch, *Érotikos. Dialogue sur l'Amour*, new French trans. by Christiane Zielinsky, Arléa, 1991.

33. John Boswell, *Christianisme, tolérance sociale et homosexualité, op. cit.*

34. Seneca the Elder, *Controverses*, trans. by de H. Bornecque, Garnier, 1932.

35. Jean-Noël Robert, *Éros romain*, Les Belles Lettres, 1997.

36. Maurice Sartre, "L'homosexualité dans la Grèce antique," in *Amour et Sexualité en Occident, op. cit.*

37. Paul Veyne, "L'homosexualité à Rome," in *Amour et Sexualité en Occident, op. cit.*

38. John Boswell, *Christianisme, tolérance sociale et homosexualité, op. cit.*

39. Catherine Salles, "Les prostituées de Rome," in *Amour et Sexualité en Occident, op. cit.*

40. Uta Ranke-Heineman, *Des eunuques pour le royaume des cieux. L'Église catholique et la sexualité, op. cit.*

41. Paul Veyne, *L'Élégie érotique romaine*, Seuil, 1983.

42. Jean-Noël Robert, *Éros romain, op. cit.*

43. Paul Veyne, *L'Élégie érotique romaine, op. cit.*

Chapter 7

1. Évelyne Sullerot, *Quels pères? Quels fils?, op. cit.*

2. Michel Foucault, *Histoire de la sexualité*, t. II, *L'Usage des plaisirs*, *op. cit.*

3. John Boswell, *Christianisme, tolérance sociale et homosexualité*, *op. cit.*

4. Uta Ranke-Heineman, *Des eunuques pour le royaume des cieux. L'Église catholique et la sexualité*, *op. cit.*

5. Peter Brown, *Le Renoncement à la chair*, *op. cit.*

6. Alphonse Dupront, *Puissances et Latences de la religion catholique*, Gallimard, 1993.

7. Michel Foucault, *Histoire de la sexualité*, t. II, *L'Usage des plaisirs*, *op. cit.*

8. Josy Eisenberg, *La Femme au temps de la Bible*, *op. cit.*

9. Uta Ranke-Heineman, *Des eunuques pour le royaume des cieux*, *op. cit.*

10. Biblical citations are taken from *The Good News Bible, Today's English Version*, American Bible Society, New York.

11. Peter Brown, *Le Renoncement à la chair*, *op. cit.*

12. Quoted by Édith Castel, *L'Éternité au féminin. La femme dans les religions*, Assas-éditions, 1996.

13. Josy Eisenberg, *La Femme au temps de la Bible*, *op. cit.*

14. Peter Brown, *Le Renoncement à la chair*, *op. cit.*

15. I borrow these terms from Josy Eisenberg's interpretation.

16. I borrow this analysis from Jean Bottéro, Director of Studies at l'École pratique des hautes études (Assyriology): "Adam et Ève: le premier couple," *Amour et Sexualité en Occident*, *op. cit.*

17. Jean Daniélou, *L'Église des premiers temps*, Seuil, "Points Histoire," 1985.

18. After the clear separation between Judaism and Christianity, which did not come until the end of the First century, the first great Gnostic master was Basilide, who was active from 125 to 155 AD; he wrote 28 books of exegesis of the Scriptures.

19. Among the more recent works on this Judeo-Helleno-Christian confluence, see the passionate little book by an expert on the New Testament, professor emeritus at the University of Strasbourg, Étienne Trocmé, *L'Enfance du christianisme*, Éd. Noêsis, 1997.

20. Paul Veyne, *L'Élégie érotique romaine*, *op. cit.*

21. Peter Brown, *Le Renoncement à la chair*, *op. cit.*

22. Expression borrowed from the legendary *Acts of Thomas*, published in Syriac at Edessa, in 220 AD.

23. Jean Daniélou, *L'Église des premiers temps*, *op. cit.*

24. Peter Brown, *Le Renoncement à la chair*, *op. cit.*

25. Laure Aynard, *La Bible au féminin*, Éd. du Cerf, 1989.

26. Here, I take inspiration from Xavier Léon-Dufour's analysis, "Mariage et virginité selon saint Paul," *Christus*, No. 168, November 1995.

27. Jean Daniélou, *L'Église des premiers temps*, *op. cit.*

28. Peter Brown, *Le Renoncement à la chair, op. cit.*

29. Henri-Irénée Marrou, *L'Église de l'Antiquité tardive*, Seuil, "Points Histoire," 1985.

30. Somewhat astonishingly, this Egyptian tradition f fleeing into the desert survives to this daywith the *hijrat* ("rejection") that induces young people from the middle-classes of Cairo, breaking away from "impious" society, to take refuge in the caves of Egypt.

31. Henri-Irénée Marrou, *L'Église de l'Antiquité tardive, op. cit.*

32. *Ibid.*

33. *Ibid.*

34. One of the most atrocious cases of reprisals was the massacre by Emperor Flavian, in 387, of 7000 "seditious" inhabitants of Thessalonika, who had been gathered beforehand in the city's circus.

35. Henri-Irénée Marrou, *L'Église de l'Antiquité tardive, op. cit.*

36. Id., Saint Augustin et l'Augustinisme, Seuil, 1955.

37. Quoted by Jean-Louis Flandrin, *Les Amours paysannes (XVI-XIX siècles)*, Gallimard-Julliard, "Archives," 1975.

38. Saint Augustine, La Cité de Dieu, Seuil, "Points Sagesses," 3 vol., 1994.

39. These are Peter Brown's formulas, author of a monumental *Vie de Saint Augustin*, Seuil, 1971.

40. *La Cité de Dieu, op. cit.*, livre I, xvi.

41. Louis Dumont, *Essais sur l'individualisme. Une perspective anthropologique sur l'idéologie moderne*, Seuil, "Esprit," 1983.

42. *Ibid.*

43. Norbert Elias, *La Société des individus*, French trans., Fayard, 1991.

44. Louis Dumont, *Essais sur l'individualisme, op. cit.*

45. *Ibid.* Here, Dumont is referring to an analysis by Peter Brown.

46. Hannah Arendt, "Compréhension et politique," French trans., in *Esprit*, 1980 et 1985.

Chapter 8

1. Jacques Rossiaud (Prof. of medieval history at the University of Lyon II), *L'Histoire*, No. 180, September 1994.

2. Jean-Louis Flandrin, *Le Sexe et l'Occident. Évolution des attitudes et des*

3. *comportements*, Seuil, 1981.

4. John Boswell, *Christianisme, tolérance sociale et homosexualité, op. cit.*

5. Michel Rouche, *Histoire de la vie privée*, Seuil, t. I, 1985.

6. Twelve centuries later, in the 18th century, Pope Clément XIII ordered that the sex organs be broken off the statues with hammers, elicintg from the erotic poet Giorgio Baffo the following: "S'il se flatte de

détruire de cette façon / Tous les membres virils, je n'hésite pas à lui dire / Qu'il y en aura sur la terre tant qu'il vivra."

7. Michel Rouche, *Histoire de la vie privée, op. cit.*, t. I.

8. Noël-Yves Tonnerre, *Être chrétien au Moyen Age*, Seuil, 1996.

9. Jean-Louis Flandrin, *Un temps pour embrasser. Aux origines de la morale sexuelle occidentale, op. cit.*

10. Alphonse Dupront, *Puissances et Latences de la religion catholique, op. cit.*

11. *L'Histoire*, No. 180, *op. cit.*

12. Jean-Louis Flandrin, *Les Amours paysannes (XVI-XIX siècles), op. cit.*

13. *L'Histoire*, No. 180, *op. cit.*

14. Uta Ranke-Heineman, *Des eunuques pour le royaume des cieux. L'Église catholique et la sexualité, op. cit.*

15. John Boswell, *Christianisme, tolérance sociale et homosexualité, op. cit.*

16. *Ibid.*

17. *.Ibid.*

18. Michel Sot, "La genèse du mariage chrétien," in *Amour et Sexualité en Occident, op. cit.*

19. Jean-Louis Flandrin, *Les Amours paysannes (XVI-XIX siècles), op. cit.*

20. Christiane Olivier, *Les Fils d'Oreste ou la question du père*, Flammarion, 1994.

21. Jacques Berlioz, *L'Histoire*, No. 180, *op. cit.*

22. Here I base my comments on the notice on Galian in the *Encyclopaedia universalis*.

23. Jean-Louis Flandrin, *Un temps pour embrasser, op. cit.* On this question, J.-L. Flandrin relies on an 88-page dictated memorandum: *Les Théories de la génération et leur influence sur la morale sexuelle des XVI et XVIII siècles*, by A.-C. Ducasse-Kliszowski (Université de Paris VIII, June 1972).

24. Jacques Rossiaud, *L'Histoire*, No. 180, *op. cit.*

25. Alain de Libéra, *Penser au Moyen Age*, Seuil, 1991.

26. John Boswell, *Christianisme, tolérance sociale et homosexualité, op. cit.*

27. Jacques Le Goff, *Saint Louis*, Gallimard, 1996.

28. We owe homage to Condorcet's liberalism; on the basis of Voltaire's article, he made the following note: "La sodomie, lorsqu'il n'y a pas de violence, ne peut être du recours des lois criminelles. Elle ne viole le droit d'aucun homme." ["Sodomy, when no violence is involved, cannot be the domain of criminal laws. It does not violate the rights of any man."]

29. Alexandrian, *Histoire de la littérature érotique, op. cit.*

30. Quoted by Olivier Blanc, *Les Libertines: plaisir et liberté au temps des Lumières*, Perrin, 1997.

31. Quoted by Évelyne Sullerot, *Quels pères? Quels fils?, op. cit.*

32. See Michelle Perrot, *Histoire des femmes*, t. III, *XVIe-XVIIIe siècles*, Plon, 1991.

33. Olivier Blanc, *Les Libertines: plaisir et liberté au temps des Lumières*, *op. cit.*

34. Final edition, *Le Sycomore*, 1980.

35. Jean-Louis Flandrin, *Les Amours paysannes (XVI-XIX siècles)*, *op. cit.*

36. Roger-Henri Guerrand, "Haro sur la masturbation!," in *Amour et Sexualité en Occident*, *op. cit.*

37. Quoted by Henri Guillemin, *Regards sur Nietzsche*, Seuil, 1991.

38. Alain Corbin, "La petite Bible des jeunes époux," in *Amour et Sexualité en Occident*, *op cit.*

39. *Ibid.*

40. Max Weber, *L'Éthique protestante et l'Esprit du capitalisme*, *op. cit.*

41. *Ibid.*

42. Roger-Henri Guerrand, "Haro sur la masturbation!," in *Amour et Sexualité en Occident*, *op. cit.*

43. Michel Foucault, *Histoire de la sexualité*, t. II, *L'Usage des plaisirs*, *op. cit.*

44. Alain Corbin, "La fascination de l'adultère," in *Amour et Sexualité en Occident*, *op. cit.*

45. Michel Foucault, *Histoire de la sexualité*, t. I, *La Volonté de savoir*, *op. cit.*

46. Abel Hugo, *La France pittoresque*, quoted by Jean-Louis Flandrin, *Les Amours paysannes (xvie-xixe siècles)*, *op. cit.*

47. Louis Roussel, *La Famille incertaine*, *op. cit.*

Chapter 9

1. Jacques Soustelle, *La Vie quotidienne des Aztèques à la veille de la conquête espagnole*, Hachette, 1955.

2. Voir Jean Bottéro, "Tout commence à Babylone," in *Amour et Sexualité en Occident*, *op. cit.*

3. Georges Ballandier, *Le Sexuel*, No. Spécial des *Cahiers internationaux de sociologie*, 1984.

4. Jean-Louis Flandrin, *Un temps pour embrasser*, *op. cit.*

5. Gianfranco Poggio (born 1380 in Terranueva), the great Italian erotic poet who already heralded the Renaissance, in his *Facéties*, makes fun of the moralistic sermons of the Church. At the same time, he was appointed Apostolic Secretary of the Vatican by Boniface IX, in 1402.

6. Claude Gaignebet, quoted by Gilles Lapouge and Marie-Françoise Hans, *Les Femmes, la pornographie et L'Érotisme*, *op. cit.*

7. Albert Ducros uses this expression in an article cited in the collected works edited by Albert Ducros and Michel Panoff, *La Frontière des sexes*,

PUF, 1995.

8. Cited by Hanna Havnevik, *Combats des nonnes tibétaines*, Éd. Dharma, 1995.

9. Édith Castel, *L'Éternité au féminin. La femme dans les religions*, *op. cit.*

10. Françoise Héritier, *Masculin/Féminin. La pensée de la différence*, *op. cit.*

11. Albert Ducros and Michel Panoff (under the direction of), *La Frontière des sexes*, *op. cit.*

12. The question came up again in the United States in1994, with the publication of a book by two resolute innatists, Richard Herrnstein and Charles Murray, authors of The Bell Curve, which maintained that the influence of heredity is the determining factor in the transmission of intelligence and therefore that social assistance programs in schools are not useful.

13. Albert Ducros and Michel Panoff (under the direction of), *La Frontière des sexes*, *op. cit.*

14. See Chapter 13.

15. Albert Ducros and Michel Panoff (under the direction of), *La Frontière des sexes*, *op. cit.*

16. Françoise Héritier, *Masculin/Féminin. La pensée de la différence*, *op. cit.*

17. *Ibid.*

18. Robert van Gulik, *La Vie sexuelle dans la Chine ancienne*, *op. cit.*

19. *Ibid.*

20. *Ibid.*

21. This extraordinarily chaste conception of the kiss was the basis of a lasting misunderstanding. The Westerners arriving in China arrived at the false conclusion that the Chinese never embraced. For their part, the Chinese, seeing the Occidentals kissing in public, thought that all the women were prostitutes.

22. In fact, the Confucian School teaches eight virtues: Hsiao (filial piety), Ti (brotherly affection), Tchong (loyalty), Sin (fidelity), Li (rites), Yi (equity), Lien (integrity) and Tchi (sense of honor).

23. Robert van Gulik, *La Vie sexuelle dans la Chine ancienne*, *op. cit.*

24. *Ibid.*

25. Abdelwahab Bouhdiba, *La Sexualité en Islam*, PUF, "Quadrige," 1984.

26. This work, written in approximately 925 AD on the hegira of Sheikh Nefzaoui, an inhabitant of Tunis, on the request of a vizier, was translated into French for the first time in 1850. Maupassant became interested in this text, which was printed in a corrected translation in 1886.

27. Quoted by Philippe Aziz, *Le Point*, March 30,1996.

28. Quoted by Malek Chebel, *Encyclopédie de l'amour en Islam*, Payot, 1995.

29. Abdelwahab Bouhdiba, *La Sexualité en Islam*, *op. cit.*

30. *Ibid.*

31. Quoted by Josy Eisenberg, in *Maryse Choisy, La Survie après la mort*, Laber-gerie, 1967.

32. Abdelwahab Bouhdiba, *La Sexualité en Islam, op. cit.*

33. Malek Chebel, *Encyclopédie de l'amour en Islam, op. cit.*

34. Jean-Claude Guillebaud, *Sur la route des croisades*, Arléa, 1993, and Seuil, "Points," 1995.

35. Quoted by Édith Castel, *L'Éternité au féminin, op. cit.*

36. Germaine Tillion, *Le Harem et les Cousins*, Seuil, 1966.

37. Malek Chebel, *Encyclopédie de l'amour en Islam, op. cit.*

38. Quoted by Malek Chebel, whose magnificent encyclopedia was of great assistance in editing these pages.

Chapter 10

1. Georges Bataille, *L'Érotisme, op. cit.*

2. I borrow these few examples of sexual utopias from Alexandrian, *Les Libérateurs de l'amour, op. cit.*

3. *Ibid.*

4. The picturesque adventure of the Saint-Simonians in Egypt is a story very nicely told in Robert Solé, *L'Égypte, passion française*, Seuil, 1997.

5. Georges Bataille, *L'Érotisme, op. cit.*

6. Gilles Lapouge and Marie-Françoise Hans, *Les Femmes, la pornographie et L'Érotisme, op. cit.*

7. Robert van Gulik, *La Vie sexuelle dans la Chine ancienne, op. cit.*

8. Quoted by Maurice Lever, *Les Bûchers de Sodome, op. cit.*

9. Wilhelm Reich, *La Révolution sexuelle, op. cit.*

10. Georges Bataille, *L'Érotisme, op. cit.*

11. *L'Esprit des lois*, livre XI, chap. iv.

12. Georges Nivat, *Vers la fin du mythe russe, op. cit.*

13. John Boswell, *Christianisme, tolérance sociale et homosexualité, op. cit.*

14. *Courrier international*, January 4, 1996.

15. Georges Bataille, *L'Histoire de L'Érotisme, op. cit.*

16. Jacques Rossiaud, *L'Histoire*, No. 180, *op. cit.*

17. Alexandrian, *Histoire de la littérature érotique, op. cit.*

18. Claude Gaignebet, in Gilles Lapouge and Marie-Françoise Hans, *Les Femmes, la pornographie et L'Érotisme, op. cit.*

19. René Nelli, *L'Érotique des troubadours*, Privat, Toulouse, 1963.

20. Howard Bloch, postface to *Fabliaux érotiques*, Livre de poche, 1993.

21. Alexandrian, *Histoire de la littérature érotique, op. cit.*

22. *Ibid.*

23. Quoted by Emmanuel Pierrat, *Le Sexe et la Loi*, Arléa, 1996.

24. Alexandrian, *Histoire de la littérature érotique, op. cit.*

25. Extracts from Marcel Baudoin, *Le Maraîchinage*, quoted by Jean-Louis Flandrin, *Les Amours paysannes (XVI-XIX siècles), op. cit.*

26. Dr Pouillet, *L'Onanisme chez la femme*, Paris, 1877 (Quoted by Jean-Louis Flandrin, *Le Sexe et l'Occident, op. cit.*).

27. Georges Bataille, *L'Érotisme, op. cit.*

28. *Ibid.*

29. *Ibid.*

30. Interview with Georges Bataille rebroadcast in Jacques Munier's show on "*Georges Bataille, l'enragé,*" France Culture, August 3, 1997.

Chapter 11

1. This is Jacques Rossiaud's formula.

2. One may recall the extravagant and Byzantine public quarrel, in 1991, between a a somewhat Malthusian researcher at the INED (Hervé Le Bras) and the Director himself, who was more of a natalist (Gérard Calot).

3. See Chapter 3.

4. These observations are borrowed from Peter Brown, *Le Renoncement à la chair, op. cit.*

5. *Ibid.*

6. Jean-Louis Flandrin, *Un temps pour embrasser, op. cit.*

7. In principle more than in practice, as is known, and right up until the 12th century.

8. Jacques Rossiaud, *L'Histoire*, No. 180, *op. cit.*

9. Michel Rouche, *Histoire de la vie privée, op. cit.*, t. I.

10. Jean-Louis Flandrin, who evokes this ancient distrust ith regard to what would come to be called hyper-sexuality, ironically underscores the fact that we would be mistaken nideed to mock them today. Many contemporary doctors and demographers are leaning that way, to a certain extent, with arguments that are eminently scientific. "One of the explanations they give for the sterility of so many Western couples is the low sperm count of the husband. In addition, demographers have observed that beyond a certain limit – of about fifteen relations per month, approximately – the chances of conception are reduced due to the frequency of sexual intercourse. And one explains it by the reduced sperm count as sexual activity increases " (Jean-Louis Flandrin, *Un temps pour embrasser, op. cit.*).

11. Louis Roussel, *La Famille incertaine, op. cit.*

12. Martine Sevegrand, *Les Enfants du bon Dieu. Les catholiques français et la pro-création au xxe siècle, op. cit.*

13. It is accordingly that in 1880 Leo XIII published the encyclical *Arcanum divinae sapientiae*, as a reminder that marriage is a sacrament based on unity and perpetuity – and to denounce divorce.

14. Martine Sevegrand, *Les Enfants du bon Dieu, op. cit.*

15. *Ibid.*

16. This would be the name given to the 1915 promotion of the school of Saint-Cyr.

17. Jean-Marie Poursin, "La recherche démographique française: le tournant," *Esprit, January 1992.*

18. Article 3 of the law provides a penalty of one to six months in prison as well as a fine, for "anyone who, with an aim of contraceptive propaganda, will have, by one of the means specified in articles 1 and 2, described, or revealed, or offered to reveal, processes suitable to prevent pregnancy or facilitated the use of these processes."

19. Pius XII first made use of the expression "birth control" on November 28, 1951, in a talk before the Family Front.

20. See Martine Sevegrand's book, *L'Amour en toutes lettres. Questions à l'abbé Viollet sur la sexualité*, Albin Michel, 1996.

21. Philippe Ariès, "La contraception autrefois," in Amour et Sexualité en

22. Occident, *op. cit.*

23. Disponible en éd. de poche ("10/18") dans une version largement remaniée par l'auteur en 1957.

24. Notamment à travers le problème annoncé du financement des retraites lorsque la génération des baby boomers quittera la vie active, entre 2005 et 2010.

25. Jean-Marie Poursin, "La recherche démographique française: le tournant," *Esprit, op. cit.*

26. Quoted by Jean-Marie Poursin, *ibid.*

27. Philippe Ariès, "La contraception autrefois," in *Amour et Sexualité en Occident, op. cit.*

28. Évelyne Sullerot, *Quels pères? Quels fils?, op. cit.*

29. David Riesman, *La Foule solitaire*, French trans., Robert Laffont, 1964.

30. In 1962, in the encyclical *Mater et magistra*, John XXIII confirmed the Vatican's anti-Malthusian position by invoking scientific progress that made it possible to feed the entire planet: "God, in his goodness and wisdom, has given nature inexhaustible resources and has given mankind the intelligence and genius to invent instruments apt to procure for them the necessities of life...The technical and scientific progress already achieved opens unbounded horizons."

31. Martine Sevegrand, *Les Enfants du bon Dieu, op. cit.*

32. Évelyne Sullerot, *Quels pères? Quels fils?, op. cit.*

33. Louis Roussel, *La Famille incertaine, op. cit.*

34. Interview in the Nouvel Observateur, October 24-30, 1996.

Chapter 12

1. See Chapter 1.

2. *Libération*, August 14, 1996.

3. *Le Monde*, August 14, 1996.

4. Georges Bataille, *Le Procès de Gilles de Rais*, in *Œuvres complètes, op. cit.*

5. Claude Faugeron, "La dérive pénale," *Esprit*, October 1995.

6. *Le Monde*, August 13, 1997.

7. Antoine Garapon et Denis Salas, *La République pénalisée*, Hachette, 1996.

8. René Girard, *La Violence et le Sacré, op. cit.*

9. The following pages owe much to their analyses.

10. Georges Viragello, "Violences sexuelles, violences d'aujourd'hui," *Esprit*, August-September 1997.

11. Alain Ehrenberg, "Le harcèlement sexuel. Naissance d'un délit," *Esprit*, November 1993.

12. Lucien Sfez, *La Santé parfaite. Critique d'une nouvelle utopie, op. cit.*

13. Antoine Garapon and Denis Salas, *La République pénalisée, op. cit.*

14. Alain Ehrenberg, "Le harcèlement sexuel. Naissance d'un délit," *op. cit.*

15. Claude Faugeron, "La dérive pénale," *Esprit*, October 1995.

16. Laurence Engel and Antoine Garapon, "La montée en puissance de la justice, disqualification ou requalification du politique?," *Esprit*, August-September 1997.

17. Antoine Garapon and Denis Salas, *La République pénalisée, op. cit.*

18. Boris Cyrulnik, "Éthologie de la sexualité," *Krisis, op. cit.*

19. Alain Ehrenberg, "Le harcèlement sexuel. Naissance d'un délit," *op. cit.*

20. See Chapter 14.

21. Antoine Garapon and Denis Salas, *La République pénalisée, op. cit.*

22. Pierre Briançon, "La fragmentation de la société américaine," *Notes de la fondation Saint-Simon*, January 1993.

23. Statistics from *L'Express*, May 30, 1996.

24. Marcel Gauchet, *Le Désenchantement du monde*, Gallimard, 1985.

25. *Le Monde*, April 22, 1997.

26. Alain Ehrenberg, "Le harcèlement sexuel. Naissance d'un délit," *op. cit.*

27. Irène Théry, "L'homme désaffilié," *Esprit*, December 1996.

28. Catherine Labrusse-Riou, "La pudeur, la réserve et le trouble," *Autrement*,

October 1992.

29. Irène Théry, *Le Démariage, justice et vie privée*, Odile Jacob, 1993.

30. *Ibid.*

31. Antoine Garapon and Denis Salas, *La République pénalisée, op. cit.*

32. Karl Popper (dec. September 17, 1994), the German philosopher defended the legitimacy of "critical rationalism."The relevance of a scientific theory, according to him, was recognized with its possibility "of being falsified "(refuted).

33. Reference borrowed from Doctor Virey (who was a fanatical misogynist and whom Françoise Héritier cites in *Masculin/Féminin. La pensée de la différence, op. cit.*

34. Antoine Garapon and Denis Salas, *La République pénalisée, op. cit.*

35. Note that the expression *scientia sexualis* is used by Foucault as the title of the third part of Volume One of *L'Histoire de la sexualité, La Volonté de savoir, op. cit.*

36. Sylvie Nerson-Rousseau, *Libération*, August 8, 1997.

Chapter 13

1. In support of this concern, a report from Amnesty International entitled *Breaking the Silence*, published in June 1997 at the time of Europride, insisted that homosexuals continue to be victims of persecution throughout the World. It recalled for example that in the United States, only "twenty-eight of the fifty States have annulled the ordinances criminalizing sodomy."

2. In his book *Le Rose et le Noir*, Frédéric Martel re[rached the gay movements with having taken an attitude of "denial" between 1982 and 1985, in terms of the AIDS epidemic. Then, after a harsh and often unjust polemic, he admits that the word "denial," highly accusatory, could lead to misunderstandings and that it might be better to use the term "wait-and-see." He also conceded that he may have underestimated the persistence of homophobia ni French society. See "Retour sur une polémique," *Esprit*, November 1996.

3. Consider, for example, the way in which the press linked to the *Front National* wrongly seized upon the criticisms, in April 1996, contained in Frédéric Martel's book, *Le Rose et le Noir, op. cit.*

4. *Le Monde*, April 15, 1996.

5. I expanded upon this topic in *La Trahison des Lumières*, Seuil, 1994.

6. Notably Gilles Deleuze and Félix Guattari's "classic" *L'Anti-Œdipe* and also *Mille Plateaux: capitalisme et schizophrénie*, Minuit, 1973.

7. Michel Foucault, *Histoire de la sexualité, t. II, L'Usage des plaisirs, op. cit.*

8. *Ibid.*, t. I, *La Volonté de savoir, op. cit.*
9. Frédéric Martel, *Le Rose et le Noir, op. cit.*
10. Champ libre, 1971.
11. *Recherches*, March 1973.
12. Élisabeth Lebovici and Gérard Lefort, *Libération*, June 29, 1997.
13. *Le Monde*, July 17, 1997.
14. *Libération*, June 22, 1995
15. *Ibid.*, June 23, 1997.
16. Here, I rely on a long and remarkable analysis by Michel Feher – Director of the magazine *Zone* in New York – entitled "Érotisme et féminisme aux États-Unis: les exercices de la liberté" and publiée dans la revue *Esprit* en November 1993.
17. Robin Morgan, *Going too far*, Random House, 1977, quoted by Michel Feher, *op. cit.*
18. Quoted by Peter Brown, *Le Renoncement à la chair, op. cit.*
19. Remarks reported by Blake Morisson, *Sunday Times*, March 1996.
20. Michel Feher, "Érotisme et féminisme aux États-Unis: les exercices de la liberté," *op. cit.*
21. Published by Ballantine in 1991; French trans. under the title *Décidément, tu ne comprends pas! – surmonter les malentendus entre hommes et femmes*, Robert Laffont, 1993.
22. Jean Cazeneuve, *Bonheur et Civilisation*, Gallimard, 1970.
23. Michael Pollack, "L'homosexualité masculine," *Sexualités occidentales, op. cit.*
24. Michel Feher, "Érotisme et féminisme aux États-Unis: les exercices de la liberté," *op. cit.*

Chapter 14

1. "Re-Making the family" (and absolutely not "re-building the family"), which I have used as this chapter's title, is a direct transposition of the title judiciously chosen by Pierre Rosanvallon on the subject of the nation. Contrasting nationalism with the necessity of "re-making the nation" for reasons of social solidarity, Rosanvallon proposes an analysis that, in my view, is even better suited to the family. (Pierre Rosanvallon, *La Nouvelle Question sociale*, Seuil, 1995.)
2. Jean-Claude Millner, *L'Archéologie d'un échec*, Seuil, 1993.
3. Irène Théry, "Différence des sexes et différence des générations. L'enjeu de l'institution," *Esprit*, December 1996.
4. In *La Trahison des Lumières* (*op. cit.*), I devoted an entire chapter to various forms of migrations, between the Right and the Left, of differentialist

thought.

5. Talcott Parsons, *Family, Socialization and Interaction Process*, Glencoe Free Press, 1955, quoted by Louis Roussel, *La Famille incertaine, op. cit.*

6. Synthesis proposed by Louis Roussel, *ibid.*

7. Think of these three passages from the Evangelists: "Whoever loves his father or mother more than me is not fit to be my disciple," (Matthew 10:37); "And you must not call anyone here on earth 'Father,' for you have only the one Father in heaven," (Matthew 23:9); "Do not think that I have come to bring peace to the world. No, I did not come to bring peace, but a sword. I came to set sons against their fathers, daughters against their mothers, daughters-in-law against their mothers-in-law; a man's worst enemies will be the members of his own family." (Matthew 10:34-35).

8. Pierre Legendre, *Filiation*, Fayard, 1990.

9. Irène Théry, "Différence des sexes et différence des générations," *op. cit.*

10. Évelyne Sullerot, *Quels pères? Quels fils?, op. cit.*

11. *Ibid.*

12. Christiane Olivier, *Les Fils d'Oreste ou la question du père, op. cit.*

13. Évelyne Sullerot, *Quels pères? Quels fils?, op. cit.*

14. Geneviève Delaisi de Parseval, *La Part du père*, Seuil, 1981.

15. Donald Woods Winnicot, *L'Enfant et sa famille*, French trans., Payot, 1991, quoted by Christiane Olivier, *Les Fils d'Oreste ou la question du père, op. cit.*

16. Consider Bernard This, *Le Père, acte de naissance*, Seuil, 1980, and Aldo Naouri, *Le Couple et l'Enfant*, Odile Jacob, 1995.

17. Évelyne Sullerot, *Quels pères? Quels fils?, op. cit.*

18. Christiane Olivier, *Les Fils d'Oreste ou la question du père, op. cit.*

19. René Zazzo, *L'Attachement*, Delachaux and Niestlé, 1991; Boris Cyrulnik, *Sous le signe du lien: une histoire naturelle de l'attachement*, Hachette-Pluriel, 1992; Hubert Montagner, *L'Attachement et les débuts de la tendresse*, Odile Jacob, 1988.

20. Christiane Olivier, *Les Fils d'Oreste ou la question du père, op. cit.*

21. *Ibid.* Christiane Olivier also considers the case where the child is a girl. Mothers who want their little girls "just for themselves," she writes, "thus lock the child into a relationship where she becomes obliged to conform to the Other's wishes under penalty of losing her love. And that remains the universal feminine fear: of not matching up to the Other's demands, to fashion. The entire woman resides in this fear and our magazines talk of nothing but ways to adapt and be pleasing."

22. *Ibid.*

23. Irène Théry, "Différence des sexes et différence des générations," *op. cit.*

24. Évelyne Sullerot, *Quels pères? Quels fils?, op. cit.*

25. Louis Roussel, *La Famille incertaine, op. cit.*

26. Irène Théry, "Différence des sexes et différence des générations," *op. cit.*

27. *Ibid.*

28. Louis Roussel, *La Famille incertaine, op. cit.*

29. Jean-Claude Kaufmann, La Trame conjugale: analyse du couple par son linge, Pocket-Agora, 1988.

30. Alain Ehrenberg, *Esprit*, November 1993.

31. Catherine Labrusse-Riou and Mireille Delmas-Marty, Le Mariage et le Divorce, PUF, 1988.

32. Catherine Labrusse-Riou, "La filiation en mal d'institution," *Esprit*, décembre 1996.

33. Caroline Éliacheff, Vies privées. De l'enfant roi à l'enfant victime, Odile Jacob, 1997.

34. Irène Théry, "Nouveaux droits de l'enfant, la potion magique?," *Esprit*, March-April 1992.

35. Yves Lernout, président de l'Association des magistrats de la jeunesse, Droit de l'enfance et de la famille, No. 29, 1990.

Chapter 15

1. References borrowed from Henri Guillemin, *Regards sur Nietzsche, op. cit.*

2. See above, Chapter 7.

3. Arnaud de Vaujuas, "Tenir parole dans une société de séduction," *Christus, op. cit.*

4. Étienne Perrot, s.j., "Trois fidélités idolâtriques," *Christus*, January 1996.

5. Michel Foucault, Histoire de la sexualité, t. II, *L'Usage des plaisirs, op. cit.*

6. Roland Barthes, *Fragments d'un discours amoureux, op. cit.*

7. Pascal Bruckner and Alain Finkielkraut, *Le Nouveau Désordre amoureux*, Seuil, 1979.

8. *Le Monde*, 22 April 1997.

9. Maurice Merleau-Ponty, *Phénoménologie de la perception*, Gallimard, 1976.

10. This fundamental revolution in the conception of the company (a revolution that has been too little described and insufficiently analyzed) corresponds to what has been called corporate governance or governement by shareholders. This began in the United States in 1989, but only really took hold after the publication, in London in 1992, of the famous report written by the former president of Cadbury-Schweppes, Sir Adrian Cadbury.

11. Robert Castel, *Métamorphose de la question sociale: une chronique du salariat*, Fayard, 1995.

12. Irène Théry, "Différence des sexes et différence des générations. L'enjeu

de l'institution," *op. cit.*

13. Philippe Engelhard, *L'Homme mondial*, *op. cit.*

14. See Chapter 6.

15. Louis Roussel, *La Famille incertaine*, *op. cit.*

16. Michel Albert, *Capitalisme contre capitalisme*, Seuil, 1991.

17. Jean-Paul Fitoussi, *Le Débat interdit*, Arléa, 1995.

18. Mircea Eliade, *Le Mythe de l'éternel retour*, Gallimard, 1969.

19. Étienne Barilier, *Contre le nouvel obscurantisme. Éloge du progrès*, Éditions Zoe, Genève, 1995.

Also from Algora Publishing:

CLAUDIU A. SECARA
THE NEW COMMONWEALTH —
From Bureaucratic Corporatism to Socialist Capitalism

The notion of an elite-driven worldwide perestroika has gained some credibility lately. The book examines in a historical perspective the most intriguing dialectic in the Soviet Union's "collapse" — from socialism to capitalism and back to socialist capitalism — and speculates on the global implications.

IGNACIO RAMONET
THE GEOPOLITICS OF CHAOS

The author, Director of *Le Monde Diplomatique*, presents an original, discriminating and lucid political matrix for understanding what he calls the "current disorder of the world" in terms of Internationalization, Cyberculture and Political Chaos.

TZVETAN TODOROV
A PASSION FOR DEMOCRACY —
Benjamin Constant

The French Revolution rang the death knell not only for a form of society, but also for a way of feeling and of living; and it is still not clear as yet what did we gain from the changes.

MICHEL PINÇON & MONIQUE PINÇON-CHARLOT
GRAND FORTUNES —
Dynasties of Wealth in France

Going back for generations, the fortunes of great families consist of far more than money — they also symbols of culture and social interaction. In a nation known for democracy and meritocracy, piercing the secrets of the grand fortunes verges on a crime of lèse-majesté . . . *Grand Fortunes* succeeds at that.

CLAUDIU A. SECARA
TIME & EGO —
Judeo-Christian Egotheism and the Anglo-Saxon Industrial Revolution

The first question of abstract reflection that arouses controversy is the problem of Becoming. Being persists, beings constantly change; they are born and they pass away. How can Being change and yet be eternal? The quest for the logical and experimental answer has just taken off.

JEAN-MARIE ABGRALL
SOUL SNATCHERS: THE MECHANICS OF CULTS

Jean-Marie Abgrall, psychiatrist, criminologist, expert witness to the French Court of Appeals, and member of the Inter-Ministry Committee on Cults, is one of the experts most frequently consulted by the European judicial and legislative processes. The fruit of fifteen years of research, his book delivers the first methodical analysis of the sectarian phenomenon, decoding the mental manipulation on behalf of mystified observers as well as victims.

JEAN-CLAUDE GUILLEBAUD
THE TYRANNY OF PLEASURE

The ambition of the book is to pose clearly and without subterfuge the question of sexual morals -- that is, the place of the forbidden -- in a modern society. For almost a whole generation, we have lived in the illusion that this question had ceased to exist. Today the illusion is faded, but a strange and tumultuous distress replaces it. No longer knowing very clearly where we stand, our societies painfully seek answers between unacceptable alternatives: bold-faced permissiveness or nostalgic moralism.

SOPHIE COIGNARD AND MARIE-THÉRÈSE GUICHARD
FRENCH CONNECTIONS—
The Secret History of Networks of Influence

They were born in the same region, went to the same schools, fought the same fights and made the same mistakes in youth. They share the same morals, the same fantasies of success and the same taste for money. They act behind the scenes to help each other, boosting careers, monopolizing business and information, making money, conspiring and, why not, becoming Presidents!

VLADIMIR PLOUGIN
INTELLIGENCE HAS ALWAYS EXISTED

This collection contains the latest works by historians, investigating the most mysterious episodes from Russia's past. All essays are based on thorough studies of preserved documents. The book discusses the establishment of secret services in Kievan Rus, and describes heroes and systems of intelligence and counterintelligence in the 16th-17th centuries. Semen Maltsev, a diplomat of Ivan the Terrible's times is presented as well as the much publicised story of the abduction of "Princess Tarakanova".

JEAN-JACQUES ROSA
EURO ERROR

The European Superstate makes Jean-Jacques Rosa mad, for two reasons. First, actions taken to relieve unemployment have created inflation, but have not reduced unemployment. His second argument is even more intriguing: the 21st century will see the fragmentation of the U. S., not the unification of Europe.

ANDRÉ GAURON
EUROPEAN MISUNDERSTANDING

Few of the books decrying the European Monetary Union raise the level of the discussion to a higher plane. European Misunderstanding is one of these. Gauron gets it right, observing that the real problem facing Europe is its political future, not its economic future.